P9-DUK-526

The RANDOM HOUSE Guide to Writing

THIRD EDITION

Sandra Schor
Judith Summerfield

both of Queens College
The City University of New York

First published under the title
The Random House Guide to Basic Writing

 RANDOM HOUSE • NEW YORK

To J. M. S.

Third Edition
987654321
Copyright © 1986, 1981, 1978 by Sandra Schor and Judith Summerfield

Library of Congress Cataloging in Publication Data

Schor, Sandra.
    The Random House guide to writing.

    Includes index.
    1. English language—Rhetoric. 2. English
language—Grammar—1950–   . 3. College readers.
I. Summerfield, Judith, 1941–   . II. Title.
III. Title: Guide to writing.
PE1408.S316   1986   808′.042   85-19290
ISBN 0-394-33796-4

Manufactured in the United States of America

Designed by John Lennard
Cover Design: Lawrence R. Didona

Acknowledgments

Pages 17–18—"On Keeping a Diary" by William Safire. © 1974 by The New York Times Company. Reprinted by permission.

Pages 33, 34, 36—Excerpt from "Writing American Fiction" by Philip Roth. Reprinted with the permission of Farrar, Straus & Giroux, Inc., from *Reading Myself and Others* by Philip Roth, Copyright © 1961, 1975, by Philip Roth.

Pages 44, 66–67—Excerpts from *A Distant Mirror* by Barbara Tuchman. Copyright © 1978 by Barbara Tuchman. Reprinted by permission of Random House, Inc.

Pages 47–48—Selection from *The Autobiography of Bertrand Russell: 1872–1914* by Bertrand Russell. Copyright © 1969 by George Allen and Unwin. Reprinted by permission of Simon & Schuster, a Division of Gulf & Western Corporation.

Page 57—Excerpt from "The Rhetorical Stance" by Wayne C. Booth. Reprinted by permission of National Council of Teachers of English.

Page 58—Excerpt from pages 83–84 of *Lyndon Johnson and the American Dream* by Doris Kearns. Reprinted from "Who Was Lyndon Baines Johnson?", Part 1: "The Man Who Would Be Loved," by Doris Kearns, which originally appeared in *The Atlantic*. Copyright © 1976 by Doris Kearns. Reprinted by permission of Harper & Row, Publishers, Inc.

Page 59—Excerpt from "Baseball Stories—The Lure of the Bullpen" by George Plimpton. Copyright © 1976 by Harper's Magazine. All rights reserved. Reprinted from the May 1976 issue by special permission.

Page 60—From "The Case Against Regular Physicals" by Richard Spark from *The New York Times Magazine*, July 25, 1976, p. 10. © 1976 by The New York Times Company. Reprinted by permission.

Pages 61–62—Excerpt from "Life After Death?" in *Newsweek*, July 12, 1976, p. 41. Copyright 1976, by Newsweek, Inc. All Rights Reserved. Reprinted by Permission.

Page 62—Excerpt from "The Road Less Traveled" by Michael Parfit from *The New York Times Magazine*, July 25, 1976, p. 12. © 1976 by The New York Times Company. Reprinted by permission.

Pages 62–63—Excerpt from "Soliloquy on James Dean's Forty-Fifth Birthday" by Derek Marlowe. Reprinted by permission of John Cushman Associates, Inc. Copyright © 1976 by Derek Marlowe.

Page 67—From *The Complete Book of Running*, by James F. Fixx. Copyright © 1977 by Random House, Inc. Reprinted by permission.

Page 67—From *Capra Chapbook Anthology*. Copyright 1979 by William Nolan. Reprinted by permission of Capra Press, Santa Barbara.

Page 68—Copyright © 1979 by Howard Ruff. Reprinted by permission of Times Books, a division of Random House, Inc.

Page 69—Cartoon drawing by Lorenz; © 1979 The New Yorker Magazine, Inc.

Page 75—"Skid Road Stroganoff," from *The I Hate to Cook Book* © 1960 by Peg Bracken. Reprinted by permission of Harcourt Brace Jovanovich, Inc.

Page 80—Reprinted from *Penn's Woods West* by permission of the University of Pittsburgh Press. © 1958 by the University of Pittsburgh Press.

Pages 90–91—"Why I Want a Wife" by Judy Syfers. From *Ms.*, December 1971. Copyright © 1971 by Judy Syfers. Reprinted by permission of the author.

Page 95—Letter to the Editor entitled "For Women Only" by Thaddeus A. Budner, *The New York Times*, January 28, 1980. © 1980 by The New York Times Company. Reprinted by permission.

Pages 101–104—"The Great American Tease: Sport as a Way Out of the Ghetto" by Bob Oates, from *Los Angeles Times*, May 15, 1979. Copyright 1979. Los Angeles Times. Reprinted by permission.

Pages 105–106—From "Five Ways to Reform the

Olympics,'' by Bill Bradley, *The New York Times,* July 21, 1976. © 1976 by The New York Times Company. Reprinted by permission.

Pages 114–116—"Air Bags Are a Proven 'Vaccine'" by Jeffrey Cressy. From *Newsweek,* July 23, 1984. Copyright 1984 by Newsweek, Inc. All rights reserved. Reprinted by permission.

Page 128—Excerpt from ''I Dreamed I Stopped the Show'' by Nora Ephron. Reprinted and adapted by permission of International Creative Management as agents for Nora Ephron. First published in *Esquire,* Dec. 1974.

Page 145—Excerpt from ''Behold the Crazy Hours of the Hard-Loving Wife'' reprinted by permission of William Morrow & Co., Inc. from *In the Flesh*. First published in *Esquire.*

Page 158—From *Agee On Film* by James Agee. Copyright © 1958 by The James Agee Trust. Used by permission of Grosset & Dunlap, Inc.

Page 168—Excerpt from article by Mary Murphy, *TV Guide,* January 5–11, 1985. Reprinted by permission.

Page 173—From *The New York Times,* April 3, 1977, p. 19. © 1977 by The New York Times Company. Reprinted by permission.

Pages 175–176—From Robert Lipsyte, ''A Short Trip,'' *The New York Times,* November 23, 1967. © 1967 by The New York Times Company. Reprinted by permission.

Pages 200–202—''A Young Son Makes a Father's Day'' by Herbert Hadad. From *The New York Times,* June 19, 1983. Copyright © 1983 by The New York Times Company. Reprinted by permission.

Pages 202–204—''Stranger's Stare: Baleful or Beckoning?'' by Glenn Collins. From *The New York Times,* April 11, 1983. Copyright © 1983 by The New York Times Company. Reprinted by permission.

Pages 204–206—''Living with my VCR'' by Nora Ephron. From *The New York Times Magazine,* December 23, 1984. Copyright © 1984 by Nora Ephron. Reprinted by permission of the New York Times Company and International Creative Management.

Pages 206–208—From *Growing Up* by Russell Baker. Copyright © 1982 by Russell Baker. Reprinted by permission of Congdon & Weed, Inc.

Page 213—Excerpt from *Guinness Book of World Records* © 1976 by Sterling Publishing Co., Inc., New York. Reprinted by permission.

Page 217—Excerpt from ''Big Two-Hearted River'' reprinted from *In Our Time* by Ernest Hemingway by permission of Charles Scribner's Sons. Copyright 1925 Charles Scribner's Sons.

Page 226—Reprinted from the June 18, 1984, issue of *People Weekly* Magazine by special permission; © 1984, Time, Inc. All rights reserved.

Page 227—Advertisement reprinted by permission of the copywriter, Ron Finkelstein, CBS Records.

Page 228—Portion of advertisement reprinted by permission of R. T. French Company.

Page 239—Advertisement reprinted by permission of Hofstra University.

Page 242—Excerpt from *Nigger: An Autobiography* by Dick Gregory with Robert Lipsyte. Copyright © 1964 by Dick Gregory Enterprises, Inc. Reprinted by permission of the publishers, E. P. Dutton.

Pages 242–243—Excerpts from ''Heather Lamb, telephone operator,'' from *Working: People Talk About What They Do All Day and How They Feel About What They Do* by Studs Terkel. Copyright © 1972, 1974, by Studs Terkel. Reprinted by permission of Pantheon Books, a division of Random House, Inc.

Page 244—Portion of advertisement reprinted by permission of Howmet Aluminum Corporation.

Page 247—From National Geographic *World* © National Geographic Society 1976.

Page 248—Excerpt from ''I Remember'' by Joyce Maynard. Reprinted by permission of Curtis Brown, Ltd. Copyright © 1974 by Triangle Publications, Inc.

Page 250—Portion of advertisement reprinted with permission of The IBM Office Products Division.

Page 251—Portion of advertisement reprinted by permission of American Motors Corporation.

Page 252—Portion of advertisement reprinted by permission of *Cosmopolitan.*

Page 252—Portion of advertisement reprinted by permission of The Mennen Company. Photo used with permission of The Mennen Company.

Page 254—Portion of advertisement reprinted by permission of Triangle Publications, Inc.

Page 271—Adapted from ''Sharks'' by Elizabeth Keiffer, *New York Times Magazine,* May 4, 1975. © 1975 by The New York Times Company. Reprinted by permission.

Page 277—From *The New York Times,* January 31, 1980. © 1980 by The New York Times Company.

Page 284—Advertisement reprinted by permission of Killington Ski Resort.

Page 289—Portion of advertisement reprinted by permission of Longines-Wittnauer Watch Co., Inc.

Page 290—Portion of advertisement reprinted by permission of College Entrance Examination Board.

Page 299—Advertisement reprinted by permission of Christian Children's Fund, Inc.

Page 301—Advertisement reprinted by permission of Primauté Advertising, Inc.

Pages 305–306—From Marie Winn, ''The Pleasures and Perils of Being a Child Prodigy,'' *The New York*

Times Magazine, December 23, 1979. © 1979 by The New York Times Company. Reprinted by permission.

Pages 307–308—From Janet Maslin, "Film: Eastwood Stars in and Directs 'Bronco Billy,'" *The New York Times,* June 11, 1980. © 1980 by The New York Times Company. Reprinted by permission.

Page 322—Advertisement reprinted by permission of Sony Corporation of America.

Page 324—Advertisement reprinted by permission of Ralston Purina Co.

Page 326—Advertisement reprinted by permission of the California Almond Growers Exchange.

Page 332—Advertisement reprinted by permission of Hunt-Wesson Foods, Inc.

Page 333—Advertisement reprinted by permission of Western Electric Co., Inc.

Page 339—Advertisement reprinted courtesy of Keye, Donna, Pearlstern, Inc., for Realty Hotels, Inc.

Page 339—Advertisement reprinted by permission of The Stride Rite Corporation.

Page 361—Advertisement reprinted by permission of Colgate-Palmolive Co.

Page 366—Advertisement reprinted by permission of Shulton, Inc.

Page 367—Advertisement and cartoon reprinted with permission of *The Wall Street Journal* © 1977 Dow Jones and Company. All rights reserved.

Page 368—Headline reprinted by permission of The Reader's Digest.

Page 370—Advertisement reprinted by permission of BMW of North America, Inc.

Pages 374 and 378–379—From "Remarkable American Women," p. 114. Life Special Report © 1976 Time Inc. Reprinted with permission.

Page 377—Advertisement for Novara brand Oil of Youth Moisturizer reprinted by permission of Schmid Laboratories, Inc.

Page 382—Excerpt from Ben Patrusky, "Drowning in Drink," reproduced courtesy of *Signature* magazine. © 1975, Diners Club, Inc. From Reader's Digest, July 1975.

Pages 394–395—List adapted from "Homonyms," *The Lincoln Library of Essential Information,* by permission of The Frontier Press Co.

Page 414—Excerpt from *Reader's Guide to Periodical Literature* reproduced by permission of The H. W. Wilson Company, publisher. *Reader's Guide to Periodical Literature* © 1984.

Page 447—From "Air Force Tries 'Superglue'" by John Noble Wilford, *The New York Times,* January 29, 1980.© 1980 by The New York Times Company.

Pages 448–450—From "Do People Really Eat People?" *Time,* October 22, 1979, p. 106. Reprinted by permission from *Time,* The Weekly Newsmagazine; Copyright Time Inc. 1979.

Preface

Every book needs a reader. We are fortunate in having had many—both instructors and students—who have read *The Random House Guide to Writing,* used it in their classes across the country, and sent us their suggestions and comments, which we willingly take up in this Third Edition. We have done the work any writer would be eager to do—revise a manuscript in response to suggestions from receptive readers. The *Guide's* friends will note that the book remains a comprehensive guide to writing; it continues to engage student writers in the repeatable acts of writing—finding ideas, writing and rewriting drafts, getting useful reactions from readers—by which they become more skillful and more confident writers. Instructors and students alike have found that this workshop atmosphere brings writing to life in the classroom. So we have not tampered with our basic approach to the teaching of writing nor with our conviction that writers, through continued practice and support from instructor and peers, discover that they have ideas worth writing about. The lively tone of the *Guide,* valued by instructors and students, remains untouched.

But we have introduced several changes that should make the *Guide* a more efficient daily resource for instructors to use in the classroom and for students to use on their own.

—Most important, the Third Edition pays closer attention to revision and to reading, both of students' own texts and of the selections in the *Guide* (especially those collected in Chapter 9).

—In a new section, Part 2, "A Guide to Revision," we have tried to bridge the gap that inexperienced writers face between doing exercises in a textbook and writing their own essays. We offer new *exercises for revision.* At the ends of Chapters 6, 7, and 8, students are invited to do a variety of exercises both on the selections in Chapter 9 and on their own writing, and then to study the significant changes that result when they try a new beginning or a new ending, a shift in voice, person, or tense, a shift in tone that results from addressing the reader or from choosing another narrator's stance.

—In Chapter 9 we bring together a collection of student and professional writings to encourage the more energetic reading that a writer does. We are convinced that as students are learning to write, they are stimulated by reading the work of other writers, classmates no less than professionals, and ideas for their own writing take on form and value. We encourage use of the journal to keep track of ideas, events, memories, associations, and questions that arise as students read.

—In addition to these new readings in Chapter 9, we offer new sample essays throughout the *Guide*. And in Chapter 6 we trace the way two writers go about composing their drafts, from first idea to finished essay.

—Additional exercises on sentence combining, finding the right word, subject–verb agreement, and many other topics are offered where appropriate.

—A new sample research essay and the new MLA documentation guidelines (as well as the traditional MLA documentation style) are presented in Part 5, "A Guide to Research."

John Clifford of the University of North Carolina at Wilmington has recorded his own experience with *The Random House Guide to Writing* in a new edition of his highly successful Instructor's Manual. He discusses such practical composition strategies as freewriting, teaching grammar and writing together, classroom atmosphere in a writing community, grading, and using small groups effectively; and he presents a complete semester's syllabus of rhetorical and grammatical lessons, including suggestions for assignments. He also provides an up-to-date bibliography useful to any teacher of writing or administrator of a writing program.

We appreciate the industry and encouragement of all our reviewers, including those of the First and Second Editons. Reviewers of the Thrid Edition are: Mindy Altman, Queens College of the City University of New York; Colleen Anderson, Jefferson Community College; Robert Banfelder, Queensborough Community College; Patrick Bizzaro, East Carolina University; Robert Connors, Louisiana State University; Joy DeSalvo, Youngstown State University; John Fleming, West Valley College; Mary Frosch, The Spence School; Karen Greenberg, Hunter College; Francis Hubbard, University of Wisconsin, Milwaukee; Ralph Jenkins, Temple University; Mary Makofske, Ramapo College; Mary Ann McKeever, Oakton Community College; Betty Messenger, Ohio State University; Kathryn Osterholm, Clarion University; Ronald Shook, Utah State University; Joceyln Siler, University of Montana; Ronald Smith, University of North Alabama; Nancy Sorkin, Philadelphia College of Textiles and Science; Katherine Stone, Georgia State University; Monika Sutherland, Edgecombe Technical College; Karen Thomas, Boise State University; Richard VanDeWighe, University of Colorado at Denver; Maria Elena Yepes-Sauceda, East Los Angeles College; and Tilly Warnock, University of Wyoming.

We are again indebted to colleagues at Queens College, who in working with the *Guide* during the last eight years have both enlarged our view of its range and sharpened our understanding of its usefulness. Special thanks go to Mitchell Levenberg of Queens College and Mark Goldblatt of Queensborough Community College for their help with this edition, and to Joyce Kinkead of Utah State University and Ariel Slothower of De Anza College for allowing us a writer's exchange with their students in freshman English.

Again, we appreciate the support and guidance of the Random House team: our editor, Steven Pensinger, and Cecilia Gardner, Cynthia Ward, Ed Maluf, June Smith, and Seibert Adams.

Sandra Schor

Judith Summerfield

Contents

PART 2 A Guide to Revision   107

PART 4 Punctuation, Capitalization, and Spelling   359

16 Punctuation and Capitalization   360

To the Student

A student in one of our basic writing classes wrote about himself as a writer in this way:

> When I start to write, it presents a lot of problems. For example, I am self conscious of what I am writing and I am always fearful of using incorrect grammar. Another problem I have is staying on the main topic. When I write, it's like having mini-explosions going off in my mind. Thousands of words, sentences, and ideas keep flashing in and out of my head. It is a nuclear war between my hand and my brain. The actual results usually amaze me. In my mind it is clear and concise—on paper it becomes a jumble.

To many of you, this battle is nothing new. Most college students would like to write well but arrive at college shaken by previous skirmishes or with little or no real writing experience. A few believe they are already good writers only to find that the first paper they hand over to their college English instructor carries back disappointing news. Have they been misled? Or does the news from up front mean that here is yet another English teacher to be "psyched out" with another personal set of requirements they must learn to satisfy?

You may be one of these people, in one group or another, victimized by the mysterious demands of a mysterious skill. It is our belief that at least some elements of writing can be demystified, and this book has grown out of that conviction. Certainly we don't promise you a set of formulas that guarantee you will write effortlessly. Nor do we say that writing well will automatically land you a good job one day. But writing well has never *hurt* anyone's chances for a job and has *helped* a lot of people get their thinking in order. We know that in any art the magic of excellence eludes recipes. But we also know from our own writing and from our years teaching in the classroom and working individually with students in the writing lab that there are methods writers use and habits they cultivate to make writing less of an ordeal and, perhaps, an occasion for quiet pleasure. We hope the *Random House Guide to Writing* will serve you in and out of class as a reliable guide to writing and as a flexible reference handbook to grammar and usage. It puts together writing and grammar, laying out the basic principles of writing essays and strong English sentences before it offers advice about problems in usage that cause most of the errors writers make.

We hope you will take advantage of the scope of the *Random House Guide*. Both publisher and authors feel that students in basic courses deserve, in a single book, a comprehensive guide to writing. But the book, remember, will never be a substitute for your own writing. When you are learning to write, your own writing is the primary text. Many whole essays are nonetheless included (especially in Chapter 9), some written by professional writers, others by students like yourself. Though you may feel you write better or worse than these students, we can assure you that your serious observations about the essays of your classmates are indispensable to strengthening your own writing ability in a classroom/workshop atmosphere. Since your writing deserves the reactions of a range of readers, not only those of your instructor, all of what you write need not be read by your instructor at all. Writing is a lifelong skill that should be tested in more places than on the English teacher's desk. Not until other people report to us how our words move them do we know exactly what the words on our page have managed to say. Now we invite all of you—students and teachers alike—to respond to this book in that same spirit, offering observations on what we have written and suggestions for change.

part 1 | As You Write

chapter 1 | Writing Immediately

1.a GAINING CONFIDENCE

In your mind, the notion of writing may be uncomfortably linked to writing an "assignment," a chore you desperately undertake to satisfy a deadline for a teacher or a boss. If you have this dread of writing, it may be because you never write anything unless you have to. A lot of people, but certainly not all, share your dismay. On the contrary, many people write often and willingly, people who would confess to you that writing has a private value of its own.

This book invites you to think of writing as a personally valuable skill—not as a single act, but as a number of acts that you repeat with increasing confidence every time you write. Independent of assignments and deadlines, teachers and jobs, writing can help you find out what you think. And knowing what you think can be a secret weapon in your life, a continuing source of personal confidence and pleasure. As you work on a piece of writing, intermittently writing and thinking and writing again, you are gathering strength as a writer. Here at the outset, we want to emphasize that you improve as a writer not because your writing shows somebody else what you know, but—more importantly— because it *exercises and widens your ability to think*. Since every time you write you'll need, among other things, to get started, to discover what interests you, to put down a first draft, and to express your thoughts in sentences, you'll be practicing and improving the same skills every time you write.

Like many inexperienced writers, you may wonder how you can get at all the ideas you have. Whether you're writing a letter to a friend or composing a business memo, the first thing to do is to write, for you can discover ideas *as you write*. When you write, just as when you think you're moving forward and back—rushing forward with a thought, and then slowing down to reflect on it, to rethink and to question. Writers know that writing moves quickly *and* slowly, forward and back. But beginning writers often slow themselves down in another way—by looking back over the sentences they write to cross out words, change spelling, or fuss over the placement of a comma. They're worried that they'll get "it" wrong and often don't give their writing a chance to gather momentum. Stopping and starting to keep things correct, they interfere with their own progress through the dreaded writing assignment.

But writing is *recursive,* involving much back-and-forth movement. Like the most seasoned writers, you will often look back into the sentences you've already written, not to edit prematurely, but to discover the ideas still locked in the words you've already written. Regular writing practice makes it easier for you to bring out your ideas, and once your ideas are in writing—even in the crudest form—it's easier to see connections among them. Nor should it be a surprise that connections among thoughts are almost inevitable: one thing you do relates to another and another and another, and the thoughts jammed into your mind begin to assume a shape, an arrangement that makes writing and rewriting more orderly. But writing is not entirely a private matter. The reactions of other people to what you write may later send you back for more ideas, plainer connections, a better way to arrange your sentences on the page, before you're satisfied that you have landed on what you want to say—and said it.

Unfortunately, understanding that writing is recursive may not save you time at first. The only immediate shortcut lies in the flexibility of your behavior. Instead of feeling trapped in a rigid start-to-finish sweepstakes or becoming stalled midway in your writing by not knowing what else you can say, you are able to recognize precisely which actions you need to perform to get your piece of writing moving again. "I need to do some freewriting." "I need to produce more details." "I need to discover what the details in the third paragraph mean." "I need to rewrite my opening because at last I know what I'm saying." The amount of time saved has a way of showing up later, since the experience you gain from working on one piece of writing increases your confidence and control as you begin to take charge of your next piece of writing.

1.b FREEWRITING

To get your writing moving forward right away, we suggest that you try an exercise: *freewriting*. Take out a pen and a pad of paper, sit quietly for a moment, and relax. Think about whatever you want: nothing, or where you are, where you've been, or what you want. Set a timer for ten minutes. Put your pen to your paper and begin.

Remember only *not to stop*. Keep writing for ten minutes. You may babble, you may yammer, you may feel silly and embarrassed, but don't stop. And don't go back to correct spelling, to change a word, or to cross out. Keep writing. There is no such thing as a writer's block when you do freewriting.

If you can't think of what to write next, just repeat your last word or phrase until a new word rises, rises, rises, rises, rises. . . . Or write, "I'm stuck, I'm stuck, I'm stuck. . . ." When you get tired of "I'm stuck," another word will come to you. At the end of ten minutes, *stop*.

For now, let's not ask why. Begin.

Samples of freewriting Here are some freewriting exercises by students in college writing classes. The first three are by people just starting out. The last two are by people who've been at it for a while.

1. What to write what to write next, will I have a lot of stuff to do at work today. I'm never going to be able to do this for ten min. What did I put down so far will the bookstore be crowded, will they have the book I have to get how did he write a whole page so far. I hope we don't have to do this often. I don't want to have to read this in front of everyone. I better write down something because this isn't enough.

2. Right now I got a tooth ache and a headache. I want to go home. I want to go home, and lay down. Go to McDonald's and get something to eat, but my tooth is hurting too much. "hum" "hum" What am I going to write about? I don't know what to write about. This is one of the problems I always had. I want to go swimming or play ball. Should of stayed in bed. Wish that I had money. My tooth is killing me but I am going to fight the pain. Everyone else is writing a lot of things and I don't know what to write. I want to go home. One more class to go, I do not think I can stand very much more of this tooth ache. I can't write any more because I have nothing to say. OK yesterday I went to the park.

3. I think that I have adjusted a little better to college now that this is my third day here. I have found that there is a lot of different things in college than in high school. Perhaps more difficult, but the idea that one has to adjust to these new ways of learning. Right now I am uncertain about what to write thinking, thinking, thinking, something has just come up in my mind. It's about my art teacher. He looks mean and, and, and, and, and, old fashion. He speaks much too fast for me to take notes. The course is not what I expected. To me it's kind of boring to stay for 2 hours in this class and listen to this stranger. I am undecided if I should drop this course, I think I won't because this girl I know goes to this class, maybe it's foolish just to go to a class you don't like because there's a nice girl you know in the class. But I think that with a little bearing down I can adjust to this teacher's way of teaching. I want to go home and eat, and talk to all my friends, and go and play basketball.

4. I'm smoking. Why? My chest feels so heavy it's as if someone had been sitting on it all night. Yet I love to smoke, especially when I'm nervous like now. The fly in the room is bothering the hell out of me. It keeps buzzing around in my head and near my writing hand which holds my pen. My pen. My pen which is grey in color. I remember the pen I took with me cross-country and how I screwed it up

when I dropped it in this guy Ron's fire and how I couldn't write letters home because I needed to buy a pen but in Alaska if you don't have a car it's hard to get around to the store to buy a pen. My pen, my pen my pen my pen my pen my pen my pen my pen I wonder how long the days are in Alaska now? Is it a period of only 2 hrs. of darkness or 4 or 6? Someone told me that in the winter the sun only comes up at noon and then it goes down at 12:15. That sounds like lunch time. I'm hungry. I didn't bring my lunch today, so I'll have to spend some money. I can't afford to buy a greasy lunch here in the caf. The caf. Loud music, pinball machines, rattling of plates, smells of food, vending machines, garbage on the floor, people smoking pot, girls in halter tops, tops, tops and short shorts and I want to get off this track so tell Judy there's 6 minutes left right and how I didn't really want to move to Canada and how lucky I am.

5. What is it like to write? I remember when I would look at the paper and it would stare blankly back at me. It hardly happens now, maybe because too much is happening. The more that happens the more I have to write to clear and sort. Writing is clearing, writing is sorting. I can't get over the flow when I remember my first freewriting experience. I want to say a lot but a piece is always held back so what usually ends up on paper is only a surface reflection of the deeper depth. What is it like to write. What is it like to live? I can't separate the two, I need one to do the other & wouldn't think of doing one without the other. My head always wins the race & my pen & cramped hand slowly come in a poor second. If I could write what I think, put the thoughts down. Not so much the thoughts that I can verbalize, but the ones that just hang, waiting to be formed into thoughts by a mind too weak to gather them all together. Writing is wondering if you can write & writing what you wonder.

You may be asking what practice like this can do to help you. A careful look at the samples may justify "writing immediately" as a way of plunging into writing ice cold.

1c. YOU CAN WRITE IMMEDIATELY— YOU HAVE THE GRAMMAR

For one thing, you can write immediately in English because you know that language. You have the grammar. You don't have to take a course in identifying subjects and verbs before you begin writing. You can see in the freewriting exercises that although not everything written there is a sentence, every writer knows how to compose sentences:

I hope we don't have to do this often.
My tooth is killing me but I am going to fight the pain.
The fly in the room is bothering the hell out of me.

What am I going to write about?
What is it like to write?
What is it like to live?

In ten minutes of nonstop writing, these writers, and you too, rely on the habit of English grammar to write sentences without thinking about grammar at all. Although you may not realize it, you have been seeing grammar wherever you turn—in books, in advertisements, in newspaper headlines, even in the yellow pages of your phone book. When you speak or read, you don't have to think about grammar because you use it and respond to it automatically. For example, you can understand the following advertisement because you understand English grammar.

Why do you smoke?

Without a second thought, you know you are being asked a question, and you know it long before you reach the give-away question mark at the end. You don't need to study this book to understand that "Yes" is not an acceptable answer to the question "Why do you smoke?" "It's a habit"; "Because I'm nervous"; "To keep my hands out of the Hydrox cookies"—all these are acceptable answers because they meet the demands of the question "Why?"

Although you may feel that there are trouble spots in your use of grammar, these shouldn't prevent you from writing immediately. We hope to take some of the guesswork out of your decisions by giving you a step-by-step understanding of how sentences work. You don't need to understand sentences perfectly *before* you write because you will learn *as* your writing gets under way. This book does not postpone writing until after you master fifteen weeks of grammar drills. The truth is that you can write *immediately*. We assume you'll leave behind your dread of grammar once your freewriting shows that you know more about grammar than you think you do. You can consult the grammar and usage sections of this book as you need them to understand sentences, and you can use them as a handy reference guide when you need answers to specific questions.

You will be working on sentences all the while you are writing whole essays, learning that you can proofread for "correctness" after you have tried out your ideas in writing. Every day that you write, you progress as a writer, building confidence, making use of the skills you already have, and extending them through regular, nonpressured writing practice, a kind of writing practice you may never have had.

1.d YOU CAN WRITE IMMEDIATELY— YOU HAVE THE IDEAS

Another glance at the freewriting samples may persuade you that you already have in your head not only enough grammatical structures, but also enough memories, experiences, doubts, ideas, and dreams about your own unfolding life to allow you to begin writing right now. Asked to freewrite about anything, is it any wonder that writers begin by writing about writing? That is their immediate concern—ten minutes of writing. But see how they move from writing into all kinds of ideas and feelings:

Fear: I don't want to have to read this in front of everyone.
Desire: I wish that I had money.
Observation: My pen is grey.
Memory: Yesterday I went to the park.
Speculation: I think . . . I can adjust to this teacher's way of teaching.

All these are glimmers of thought released at a given instant from people's heads. Your own freewriting is no different. It is an exercise that puts you in touch with your own thinking.

Invention, or discovering something to write about, is the writer's first concern, and freewriting, as we have seen, is the first swing in that direction. *Writing itself produces ideas and brings them forward so that you can see them.* Your page of freewriting may be messy and disconnected; it may defy everything you have ever learned about editing your work and being careful; it may simply turn inside out the disordered thoughts in your head; but *after ten minutes, you will have a page of written thoughts* that you can get at for further consideration if you wish or that you can simply get out of your way. This kind of writing can be free and exploratory. It is like freethinking or daydreaming on paper. Your pen follows from the present moment to a word or a phrase or a memory that pops into your head by means of some private association. You eventually may come upon a subject that preoccupies you (getting a job, going to Mexico) or that holds out some special appeal or fear (moving into your own apartment). Freewriting loosens you up, limbers your muscles, strengthens your hand and mind. Writing is no longer an exercise that tires you quickly or an act that you distrust because it has embarrassed you. Rather, it gets you into shape for the athletics to come.

Daily freewriting is your first method of invention because it makes immediately available to you some of the ideas that are in your mind. That is why we begin with it here. Your daily freewriting exercises bring your thoughts out to where you can reach them. Just how ideas come to us as we write, we don't know. But, for whatever reasons, putting words on paper leads us to think of more words and the patterns to hold them. Although freewriting can begin by focusing on a subject (Chapter 2), for now we will concentrate on the freest writing. First, however, we need to add a few words about personal experience as the raw material for that writing.

A professor we know tells a story about the most fluent, the most articulate person he ever met. Another professor? Not at all. He is a truck driver whose truck has been rammed by a convertible speeding into a left turn from a right lane. The truck driver is full of clear ideas and lively language. He is fluent because he is telling about an event that matters to him, an event that he knows the truth about and feels powerfully about. Having his trailer smashed by a maniac who was driving on the wrong side of the road makes him eloquent. He never swerves off the subject. He is convinced, and he convinces everybody listening, that he is the only one on earth who can tell this story.

Each day some of us are truck drivers rammed by convertibles. We want to yell our heads off about something we have experienced. We want to make somebody understand the truth of what happened to us and how we feel. Sometimes the convertible is a teacher, a landlord, or an unexpected idea about marriage. But it rams us in the side when we least expect it.

As a writer, you are now entering a new relationship with such experiences because the one agreement you must keep with yourself is to write about things that matter to you. Which of the day's experiences keep your mind's motor running long after your car's motor is shut off? What ideas won't be put to bed when your body is ready for sleep? To enjoy writing is to explore ideas that steal your attention, to write about them and allow them to explain the unprecedented demands they place on your thinking.

But perhaps you consider yourself a person who doesn't feel passionate about events. You are a take-it-or-leave-it person. Things don't faze you much, you say.

We doubt that. Take-it-or-leave-it symptoms are often the result of unsureness, and there *are* events that we all experience that leave us unsure. We don't know exactly how we feel. We can't yell our heads off even when we think we should because we haven't made sense out of what we've been through. Writing can be a way of working through these experiences because the demands of writing teach us to observe our experiences more intelligently.

Suppose that you were riding home from work on a crowded bus. There you were, sitting in the first row, behind the driver. The bus crept through rush-hour traffic. At the Maple Avenue stop, a dozen people filed into the bus, tossing coins into the hopper. The last one was an elderly woman. She came up close to the driver and whispered that she had left her purse at home, that she had no money. The driver answered, ''Sorry, Ma'am. This bus doesn't give free rides.'' The woman pleaded. The driver refused. The passengers began to murmur, but the woman stood fixed. The bus driver said, ''I'm not moving until you leave this bus.'' The woman didn't budge. A man in the back row offered the woman the fare. She refused, saying, ''I don't take handouts.'' The bus driver stared out the window. The woman finally left the bus.

These observations leave you with dozens of judgments, questions, and speculations: The bus driver was stubborn. The bus driver was following orders. The woman was a spy from the bus company, testing the driver. The driver had given free rides in the past and had been reported. He was guarding his job. The woman had a lot of pride. She tried to get a free ride, but she wouldn't accept the fare. That's a strange kind of pride. Was it pride, or was it something else? If the bus hadn't been so crowded, maybe the bus driver would have agreed. The bus driver had had a bad day. The woman had done this before. The bus driver had her number. The woman was a wealthy eccentric who got her kicks out of doing strange things. She had a roll of $100 bills in her pocket.

We all have experiences, and we all wonder about what we observe during those experiences. Writers turn their experiences and their wonderings into writing.

As you sit on the bus every day, you *see*. As you work at your job in the supermarket or in the library or in the liquor store, you *see*. You have experiences with customers. You overhear conversations. You think about your boss. You wonder where she goes after work and what her love life is like. You wonder about dreams—about your own and others'. You wonder about ''where you are'' in life and ''where you're going.'' You think about college and why you're here.

You wonder whether the woman next to you in your English class will look at you. You wonder whether the man across the room in your French class will smile back if you smile first. Should you take the chance? You wonder. You sit in your class, and your mind wanders. You remember your first date. You remember your first funeral. You remember the first time you won something after a struggle with your parents.

And still the most common complaint of beginning writers is, ''I have nothing to write about.'' But when beginning writers tap their experiences and call on their memories, make observations, and think about their lives, they often find that they have too much to write about and not enough time.

Exercise 1 This exercise is designed to tap your own resources. As you work through the parts that interest you, keep in mind that you are opening yourself to what may be new experiences and new ways of thinking about your experiences. Concentrate on what you see rather than on how you feel. Try these exercises over the next two weeks.

1. Stand for at least fifteen minutes in a corner of the college union or the college ''hangout'' and record what you see and hear. Take in all you can. Notice the man in a rush. Notice the woman wearing sandals in the snow.
2. As you go home from work or school, observe. If you're walking, look at the houses, stores, empty lots, trees, or whatever you're accustomed to passing without noticing. If you drive, slow down—take in what you can. If you take public transportation, watch people, record what they're saying verbatim.
3. Describe a vivid dream as you remember it.
4. Watch a young child. What do you see? Write down exactly what the child does.
5. Recall a ''first'' experience—write down what you remember of the first day of school, a first date, the first job, the first time you were refused something important. Concentrate on what happened, who did what, who said what.

The observations you just made were recorded without comments. For example, ''Recall a 'first' experience . . . . Concentrate on what happened, who did what, who said what.'' You tried to eliminate your feelings and restrict yourself to an accurate record of observable events. You left out how you were affected, whether you thought an event was terrible or terrific. The result is like a photograph.

But listing a series of events, no matter how accurately, can grow boring:

I got up out of bed at 5:00. I studied my chem notes until 8:00. Then I grabbed a piece of toast and a cup of coffee. I picked up Jeannette on the way to class and talked about the atomic number of a few elements. Later I told her about my date with Karen the night before. We got to the lecture hall at 9:28. My hands were pretty sweaty. Jeannette appeared calm.

As a writer, you need to recognize that all the events you experience are raw material. And your very first freewriting encourages you to explore the events of your daily life for vivid personal details. Eventually, your writing takes more shape. You become more aware of a reader who wants to find out what the details mean to you, the writer. To find out, ask yourself questions about the events you observe:

1. Why did I get out of bed at 5:00 in the morning?
2. Why did I have to study my chem notes? Do I usually cram for tests? Didn't I study before? If not, why not?
3. Who are the characters in this little drama? Does each one matter?
4. Does Karen have anything to do with my chemistry test?
5. And what about Jeannette, what do I really think of her? How does she affect me? Does she make me feel nervous? jealous? stupid? How do these events relate to the way I usually take tests? to what I *must* do in school? to what I want to do for the rest of my life?

Now your mind is working on the material. You have gone back to ask questions that lead to more ideas for your writing. Here is another stage of the same piece of writing, incorporating some of the answers to the questions:

I got out of bed at 5:00 because the test wouldn't let me sleep. With only the test on my mind, I studied my chem notes because I hadn't gotten to them last night. Oh, that was a great night with Jeannette's friend Karen, though badly timed, badly timed. Timing, in fact, is a big problem for me. I do reckless things at the last minute, perhaps to give myself an excuse for not doing well on my tests. Then I try to cram, and my guilt feelings increase as time slips by. I managed to eat some toast and coffee and stopped for Jeannette on my way, hoping to pick her brain about the atomic number of uranium, but she wanted to talk about Karen and what I thought of her, since Jeannette, after all, had spent the evening at home, studying like crazy. Sometimes she makes me feel stupid, or at least regretful that I am such a coward and can't face up to trying my best without excuses. I wished my feet would take off in a direction away from Lecture Hall 301, but there they were, keeping step with Jeannette's, all the way into the room. I sat down like a robot. I am a very poor test taker, while Jeannette is all cool. She sat there chatting amiably with some guy she wanted to make time with later. When the tests arrived, I wondered why I subject myself to these horrifying ordeals, and I wondered if I would ever get to engineering school. I was in a panic. Jeannette, however, was calmly placing an extra Bic pen and her pocket calculator next to her paper as she began.

Usually you can count on the details you select to attract readers because answering questions that matter to you uncovers why *your* subject is different from other subjects—what single feature of it is unforgettable to *you*. People are interested in what is important to other people, interested in how they perceive differences among similar habits, similar people, similar tests. You secretly want to compare the way you study with the way Jeannette does, your methods of surviving in the world with hers.

And since you are the world's expert on you, you are ready right now to begin your research—into your mind and memory—as your first writing acts.

Later discussions in this book will attempt to give you insight into *form*— into ways of arranging your ideas so as to emphasize the one idea that matters most. You will begin perhaps by telling a story from your own experiences. Telling a story is a form. You will then be urged to look for a "point" in the story. Arranging your story as an illustration of that "point" is another form.

But arrangement of raw material comes later. Perhaps today you try a ten-minute freewriting exercise. Suppose that here and there in it you mention the beach. Your research has already begun. The beach is on your mind, and you are the only living expert on your own beach-going activities. You reread your freewriting to locate a special idea about the beach; you look for sentences that reveal your attitude about why you go to the beach. You think about the beach and remember your feelings the last time you went. You may identify a conflict, a tension that pulls you in two directions at once—for example, "I remember going to the beach every Saturday in July and August even though I despised it." That is an idea that arouses your curiosity. What didn't you like? What drove you there? Had you merely stated your activity—"I spent every Saturday and Sunday in July and August at Oak Neck Beach on Long Island Sound"—the sentence might have led to nothing more than a shrug and a "so what?"

Take your time. Read your freewriting carefully, but don't be too hard on yourself. And don't expect consistency. You may have produced a fantastic page of freewriting on Tuesday, only to find that on Thursday, your page is dull and embarrassing. Remember how you felt on Tuesday, how much you unearthed in your writing, and keep writing.

Chapter 2 discusses other ways to get started, methods other than freewriting that help you notice your experiences and find ideas in them. For now, in ten-minute turns, you can rely on all the living you have done until now, the raw material of your life. You have been through a childhood; twelve years of schools and teachers; assorted relatives—siblings, parents, aunts, and cousins; friends. You have lived in one or more places; visited around the corner or across the world. You have worked for money, had a boss and a job to do. You have been exposed to religion or ethical teachings. You have been aware of your own sexuality and the sexuality of others. You dress a certain way. You eat certain foods. You go to the movies and look at a newspaper. You may have had to master a skill: driving a car or programming a computer. You dream. In short, you may not be an expert on most things, but you are a specialist about yourself. And inexperienced writers learn fastest when they include themselves in their subject. You are your own most specific subject, and you can interest your reader.

Keep your pen and paper ready because you can untangle what is happening to you in your life through your writing. As you coax your surface ideas onto paper, you may soon find the roots of what bothers and burdens you. Writing and thinking and rewriting will help you think more clearly and with more complexity. As the writer of the third freewriting sample said, ''Maybe it's foolish just to go to a class you don't like because there's a nice girl you know in the class.'' Is that a problem worth poking at? Maybe, although it will take the writer's personal time and effort to find out.

As you begin to write, your optimism may suddenly dip. That is to be expected. Writing is not, after all, an instantaneous act. No immediate ''high'' lies in store for you as you unload your first word. But you will improve with regular practice, and a few months from now, it will be interesting to reread what you have written today. Writing requires your time, your patience, and your effort. We think you'll find you're worth all the time and effort that it takes.

Exercise 2 Freewrite for ten minutes every night for two weeks. When you have fourteen entries, reread your freewriting. Then do the following:

1. Select two passages from your freewriting to read aloud in class. Since freewriting is often personal, feel free to omit whatever you would rather not make public. Be prepared to say briefly why you chose these passages.

2. Underline two or three brief passages that particularly interest you. In the back of your notebook, enter the ones that you may wish to explore in more extended writing later in the semester.

3. Underline any phrasings that you feel most accurately and eloquently say what you mean.

4. Find four or five passages that contain highly specific details.
   Example:

descriptive features of people, places, weather conditions, times of day	concrete quantities, dimensions, weight
	names, dates, place-names
actual verbatim conversation	facial expressions or gestures

5. Find three passages that, by contrast, are vague and lack concreteness. Imagine that you have submitted these passages to the editor of a magazine who is interested in your subject. Write five highly specific questions that the editor might raise about each passage, such as

   When did this event occur?
   Who else was present?
   Was there any background noise or smell?
   What occurred just before this event?

6. Find and recopy four or five whole sentences. How do you know they are whole sentences?

chapter

2 | Getting Started

When Brooklyn College opened its writing center to all students who wanted to improve their writing, the staff surveyed the reasons that students gave for walking in and asking for help. ''Getting started'' was the reason most frequently given:

> I have to write a paper on some aspect of the 1960s, and I can't seem to get going with it. I've known about it for two weeks, and now it's due tomorrow, but I still can't get started. It's such a big subject that I don't know where to begin.

Or:

> My teacher assigned us a topic to write about. We have to select an event that changed our lives in some way. So I have to come up with an important event in my life and say how it changed me. I told him nothing important has ever happened to me. I sit down to get started, and, as usual in my life, nothing whatever happens. It's due Friday. Maybe if I don't turn it in, something important will happen? *Help!*

Chapter 1 has already suggested freewriting as a way to get started. But after you practice freewriting, there are other workshop methods you can use to move further blocks out of your way. College students who come to writing workshops learn how to rely on these methods to get started and to keep going.

2.a FOCUSED FREEWRITING

One way to begin freewriting is to focus your thoughts on a subject at the moment of writing. This *focused* freewriting may take any form whatever. If your subject is the movies, you may tell how envious you are of the actor who stars in the movie you saw last weekend; you may write about late-night reruns on TV and how your family always hollers when you stay up to watch them; you may write a page or two on movies about the Vietnam War or on science-fiction films; you may ramble on about Jane Fonda or the old Marx Brothers movies; you may describe the vague expectations you feel each time you take a seat in the dark. More likely, your focused freewriting may contain all, some, or none of these thoughts, in a freeflowing stream of ideas spilling into one another. Here's what to do.

1. Focus your thoughts on your general subject (for example, going to see a movie).
2. Freewrite for ten minutes.
3. Don't stop. Keep writing for ten minutes.
4. If your thoughts wander, let them.

This is the focused freewriting of a student in a freshman writing class. It begins with the Beatles and the 1960s. Where does it end?

THE BEATLES AND THE 1960s

The Beatles the 1960s what a great time to be around. Long hair and psyche-delic music, torn jeans and flowers in your hair and happenings and Love-Ins and a belief that the world could be changed for the better. All you needed was Love, like the Beatles said. The Beatles. They said it all. Come Together and everyone did. Boy, I wish I could have been old enough to enjoy it all. I remember the first time I saw John Lennon's picture on the *Sergeant Pepper* album, I ran out to buy Granny glasses even though I could see perfectly Ok and my earliest memory is still running around the house screaming "Yeah! Yeah! Yeah!" probably because my brother was playing Beatle records all day and my parents kept yelling at him to turn them off and it all seemed like something exciting and new was happening like some kind of revolution in my own house. Then I remember my brother talking about the Beatles breaking up and how it was the end of the 1960s and that things would never be the same again and that some kind of hope was gone. He really felt sorry for me because he knew I'd never know how great it really was and that listening to their records wasn't the same as waiting for new ones to come out and everyone running out to buy them and talk about them and kind of bask in the moment like they were part of a great historical moment. But I still feel affected by it all and I think I am what I am today because of the Beatles and all that happened in the 1960s and I don't think there's any one around today who hasn't been influenced by them somehow whether in the way they dress or act or think or listen to music or wear their hair. But it sure would have been great to be there and know they were still out there writing music. Maybe my brother's right and I did really miss out on a great thing, to be able to listen to them when everyone else was listening to them for the first time. Because I think being part of any great thing as it's happening is something that affects you for the rest of your life.

The writer begins with the 1960s, moves on to the Beatles and their influence on that decade's generation, and concludes with their influence on himself and his own generation. This focused freewriting has moved him toward the realization that even though the Beatles have had a great influence on his life, he still regrets not having been old enough to enjoy that influence as it was taking place. This freewriting about the Beatles has allowed the writer to understand how a cultural phenomenon, lived through by one generation, can have a direct influence on another, yet how much more exciting it is to experience the event as it is taking place.

Exercise 1   1. Find two unrelated ideas in a passage of your focused freewriting, and state each one in a sentence. How did your mind bridge the two ideas? How did you get from one to the other? Describe your thinking as best you can.

2. In each of three passages of focused freewriting, find the one idea that you would like to write more about. Keep track of *ideas to write about* in the back of your notebook.

3. In a classmate's focused freewriting, underline the two or three most provocative passages, and return the freewriting to the author. On a separate sheet of paper, write down as many details as you remember about one of the passages; then write five questions about the passage that you would like the author to answer concretely.

Narrowing the subject   The student whose focused freewriting we have just seen is now ready to approach the paper he wants to write with questions that have become more complex. What might his topic be? It might be his regret at not having shared his brother's memories. But he planned to write about the 1960s. Has he discovered in his freewriting a link between the Beatles and his own life?

The writer tests his ideas by writing several statements, any of which might become a controlling idea for an essay. In each case, as you see below, he thinks first about the Beatles in particular and then about the 1960s in general; finally, he attempts to write a sentence that summarizes the content of the proposed essay.

The Beatles in particular: *I believe that the Beatles have had a direct influence on me and my generation.

The 1960s in general: *I believe that the life styles of the 1960s can be compared with the life styles of the 1980s.

Content of my paper: I could show the impact of the Beatles on 1960s culture and discuss how they have influenced me and my generation.

The Beatles: *Writing about the Beatles makes me sorry that I wasn't old enough to enjoy them in the 1960s.

The 1960s: *Writing about interesting people or events of the 1960s makes me wish I had been there.

Content of my paper: I could discuss why other interesting people or events of the 1960s (Woodstock, Bob Dylan, hippies, peace demonstrations, astronauts on the moon, Twiggy, the Mets) would have been important to see or experience at the time.

Whichever topic the writer decides on, his paper will be more than a summary of what happened in the 1960s. The opening sentence for his paper might be any of the sentences marked with an asterisk, depending on which idea means most to him and how narrow he wants to keep his topic. Every one of the ideas uncovered in his freewriting ensures that the writer will interweave his personal feelings and observations with the large subject area of his paper, the 1960s. Since his problem was to confront a subject too large to write about, his focused freewriting has been a way of narrowing down the subject. Focused freewriting allows you to search freely through your mind, funneling a large and often vague subject into a narrower topic for writing that touches one of the centers of your own life.

2.b CONSULT YOUR JOURNAL

Another instrument of research and source of ideas for writing is a journal you might keep to help you remember, collect, and explore your thoughts and experiences.

Buy a hardbound notebook, and keep it exclusively as a journal. Write something in it almost every day. Enter the date. Chiefly, a journal is not a diary of everything you do in a day, but an account of ''what got to you that day.'' Oddly enough, what makes a writer's journal special is that it is about ordinary events—events involving friends and jobs and passers-by—that bring out reactions worth noting.

Do not record everything you do. Selection is the key to a good journal. Record only what grabs you: intimate ideas about the events of the day that you consider personally outstanding. Since many writers keep journals, you may want to look at some of the entries they make, usually in longhand, at the end of the day. Here are three student journal entries:

1. My fingers are so fat! I couldn't believe what happened at the bowling alley today. My fingers got caught in the ball. I felt like a fool. I had to wash the ball off. I was so embarrassed. I felt like everyone knew what was going on.

2. Well, bravo for women's lib! seems that in McDonald's there is an unwritten law that the grill person must be a guy, but today I challenged this so-called rule. One of the reasons it was thought that girls should not work this station was because they weren't fast enough. But contrary to this opinionated fact, girls can be just as fast as the guys, as we proved to the manager today. I think he left me *alone* at the grill on purpose to see if I would break under the pressure. But I didn't, and surprisingly enough the manager admitted that I was just as capable as any of the guys.

3. DEDICATED TO STANLEY DIAZ, MY OLD MAN

Sittin' on my bed, feeling very mellow as I listen to Charlie Parker knock out "My Old Flame." Bird had the first solo, Miles takes up where he left off, Max Roach is on drums, J. J. Johnson is on trombone. Tommy Potter's on bass and Duke Jordan is at the piano. Yeah, they's why I feel mellow. Charlie Parker will make you feel cool and relaxed. Charlie Bird Parker eases your mind. He's like a therapist, up and down the scales, breathing easily, speaking calmly, rationally, exploding every now and then just to show you the way. But even his explosions, which occur in descending and ascending flurries of countless notes, are controlled and planned to the very last note that you were momentarily afraid would not fit in between a certain number of restricting beats and measures. Yeah, Bird had it planned to the last note, and I suppose that's what you have to do if you're going to do something right.

And I'm thankful that he did play that way. Thankful because, just from listening to him play "Embraceable You," "Dewey Square," "Scrabble from the Apple" and "My Old Flame," four cuts on a record, four small spaces of time each measuring about three and a half minutes, four Jazz pieces, just from hearing those songs, I have my entire head and mood changed around. I can literally go from sad to happy or at least from sad to mellow.

Music is real important to me. I need it to survive.

Every few days, reread your journal entries and underline passages that strike you as interesting, thoughts that you want to give more time to. The following essay by William Safire talks about the importance of taking charge of your own diary and keeping your thoughts accessible.

ON KEEPING A DIARY

Diaries are no longer dear; as the invention of the telephone began the decline of letter-writing, the invention of the tape recorder has led to the atrophy of the personal diary. Many of us record our words but few of us record our thoughts.

Why is a diary stereotyped today as the gushing of a schoolgirl or the muttering of a discontented politician, unworthy of the efforts of a busy person? Perhaps because we are out of the habit of writing, or have fallen into the habit of considering our lives humdrum, or have become fearful of committing our thoughts to paper. . . .

Diaries remind us of details that would otherwise fade from memory and make less vivid our recollection. Navy Secretary Gideon Welles, whose private journal is an invaluable source for Civil War historians, watched Abraham Lincoln die in a room across the street from Ford's Theater and later jotted down a detail that puts the reader in the room: "The giant sufferer lay extended diagonally across the bed, which was not long enough for him. . . . "

Diaries can be written in psychic desperation, intended to be burned, as a hold on sanity: "I won't give up the diary again," wrote novelist Franz Kafka; "I must hold on here, it is the only place I can." Or written in physical desperation, intended to be read, as in the last entry in Arctic explorer Robert Scott's diary: "For God's sake look after our people."

But what of people who are neither on trial nor freezing to death, neither witnesses to great events nor participants in momentous undertakings? To most of us, a diary presents a terrible challenge: "Write down in me something worth remembering," the neatly dated page says; "prove that this day was not a waste of time."

For people intimidated by their own diaries, here are a handful of rules:

1. *You own the diary, the diary doesn't own you.* There are many days in all our lives about which the less written the better. If you are the sort of person who can only keep a diary on a regular schedule, filling up two pages just before you go to bed, become another sort of person.

2. *Write for yourself.* The central idea of a diary is that you are not writing for critics or for posterity but are writing a private letter to your future self. If you are petty, or wrongheaded, or hopelessly emotional, relax—if there is anybody who will understand and forgive, it is your future self.

3. *Put down what cannot be reconstructed.* You are not a newspaper of record, obligated to record every first time that man walks on the moon. Instead, remind yourself of the poignant personal moment, the remark you wish you had made, your predictions about the outcome of your own tribulations.

4. *Write legibly.* This sounds obvious, but I have pages of scribblings by a younger me who was infuriatingly illiterate. Worse, to protect the innocent, I had encoded certain names and then misplaced my Rosetta Stone; now I will never know who "JW" was in my freshman year at college, and she is a memory it might be nice to have.

Four rules are enough rules. Above all, *write about what got to you that day* . . . .

2.c ASK QUESTIONS

Another way to launch a topic is to ask yourself questions that will lead you into an exploration of the topic. But what kinds of questions, you wonder. Sometimes you have the good luck to meet an expert on an important subject—nuclear energy, the American theater, or government legislation. You experience a good deal of frustration when you suddenly don't know what questions to ask. You feel like a dummy. You don't know how to use the kernel of information you have—about the raising of the drinking age, or *A Streetcar Named Desire,* the play you saw last night—to get at more questions. You can't do what good journalists know how to do—parlay a scrap of information into a full-blown interview. Here are a few lead questions that can train you to penetrate most topics. If you use them often and freely, they'll work for you.

1. Ask, "What is it?"

You approach your topic by defining it or analyzing it into its components: What is this? What are its parts? What elements make it whole?

In the case of raising the drinking age, the questions might be: What exactly is at issue here? What is the argument for raising the drinking age? What is the drinking age in most states? To what age would it be raised? What would such a law state? How is such a law passed? Who would be responsible for enforcing it?

In the case of *A Streetcar Named Desire,* the questions might be: What kind of play is it? a love story? a tragedy? Is it a story about life in the South? Are the characters believable? What makes them different from or similar to other characters you've seen or read about? Are they typical of a particular region or time in history? Are they typical Americans? Do men and women have different responses to this play? What might a feminist think of Blanche? of Stella? of Stanley?

2. Ask, "What is it most like? What is it not like?"

Try to fit your topic into a wider range of similar topics, events, and occasions. Ask broad questions at first, for example: Is there an analogy between lowering the drinking age and lowering the voting age to eighteen? Why do different states have different drinking laws? Why do some states want to raise the drinking age and others, to lower it? What are drinking laws like in other countries? What is the rate of alcoholism among teen-agers in various states or countries? What is the historical background of our own drinking laws? What has caused changes in the laws over the years? What consequences have such laws had for society? for the economy? Is there an inconsistency in being old enough to serve in the military, but not old enough to be served? These questions of comparison may help answer your first set of questions, What is it?

Questions about the play might include: What other plays, movies, or even books does *A Streetcar Named Desire* remind you of? Compare any film version of the play with any stage version. How do they differ? What happens when a play or a novel is made into a film? How would this play be affected? Can a particular acting performance change one's view of a character? How would you compare Ann-Margret's performance as Blanche in the 1983 TV version with Vivien Leigh's performance in the film thirty-five years earlier? How is this play similar to other plays by Tennessee Williams? to other plays with similar settings, the South in the 1940s and 1950s? Has there ever been such a contrast of characters in anything else you've seen or read? It's up to you to tap the inexhaustible possibilities for questions of comparison and contrast.

As you think of elements of comparison, do not neglect time, especially past and future: Why would there be more demand to raise the drinking age now than there was ten years ago? Is the age requirement likely to change again ten years from now?

Would a relationship such as the one between Stella and Stanley be likely to exist today? Are such marriages still written about or shown in plays or movies? Why is this play still read and performed today? What accounts for its appeal?

3. Ask, "What is my point of view?"

You might ask yourself questions like these: Do I agree with any law that raises the drinking age? How would this affect me? How would it affect my friends or my relationships with my friends? Would my point of view vary depending on whether I drank? whether I drove? whether I lived in one state rather than another?

More questions about *A Streetcar Named Desire* might include: Would coming from a working-class family change my reactions to the play? a rich urban family? a poor rural one? Do I wholly sympathize with Blanche? Am I impatient with her? Have I ever been disappointed in love? Have I ever had a dream and lost all hope of retrieving it? How do my own relationships compare with these? Can I see Stanley's point of view? Does this play affect my opinions on marriage? on love? on going bowling or playing poker? on loyalty? on hope? on life in general?

These three searching questions—What is it? What is it most like? What is my point of view?—will give you more questions and, finally, more material to write about.

Exercise 2 **1.** Apply the three questions to a movie you have recently seen:
   Ask: What kind of movie is it? What happens in this movie?
   Ask: What is it like? another movie? a play? a TV show? a book?
   Ask: What is my point of view? What are my specialized connections to it?
2. Apply the three questions to an issue in the news:
   Ask: What is the event at issue? What has happened?
   Ask: What other event does this one remind me of? Are the two events alike or different?
   Ask: What is my point of view? Am I a participant? a bystander? What are my specialized connections to the event?

2.d TALK TO A FRIEND OR A TEACHER

When a problem arises, writers—like doctors or architects who have professional problems—consult their colleagues without embarrassment or loss of face. One of the best ways to mobilize a topic before you write is to air the ideas you have been gathering with a fellow writer, a tutor, your teacher, or just a sincere and interested friend. Begin by telling your friend what you have been thinking of saying. Encourage your friend to ask you a number of questions that relate to your topic. Since you have been asking yourself questions, you will be ready to turn your thinking to someone else's questions. Describe as precisely as you can how you feel about your topic, what worries you about it, what still seems unclear to you. Try to see your topic from your friend's point of view. Let her ask you questions about what is unclear to her, and be as precise as possible in your replies. Supply her with details. Answer questions like "Who?" "When?" "Where?" "What kind?" "Then what did you say?" In particular, answer the question "Why?" Tell what you consider to be the single most important idea you have on this topic, and tell *why* it is important. Does she agree? State your attitude toward the topic in a single sentence. Ask one basic question about your idea, and then answer it. If your friend seems confused, can you understand why? Can you eliminate that confusion? Do you see why your friend is skeptical? Have you found the heart of your interest in the subject?

If you're one of those students who say, "I can tell you my ideas. It's just when I get to writing them down, I freeze up," then tell your ideas to a cassette. Talk in a relaxed conversational manner about what's on your mind. Then play your cassette back, and take notes as you listen. Jot down the important ideas and phrases.

At this point, you will be ready for class discussion. Even if you are by habit a nonparticipant, make yourself take part in these discussions because you stand to gain some first-rate advice on your paper. Begin by saying, "I have a lot of stories about times I went with my friends to see a movie, but I am not sure what my main point is. Am I talking about the movies we saw or about the way I imagined myself to be Stanley Kowalski?" Trust yourself. Describe your doubts. Every writer, professional and beginner, has doubts. And because your teacher and classmates have had similar doubts, they often can help you resolve your own. So when the occasion presents itself to talk about your writing, use it. If a teacher invites you to his office to talk about the assignment, go. If a friend asks what you think of her idea, tell her—and don't stop there. Ask her what she thinks of yours. But don't believe an answer without being given good reasons for that answer. Ask, "*Why* do you think so?" Then measure the answer you get against what you feel is true.

In short, corner someone you respect—a fellow writer, a wife, a husband, a good friend. Test your ideas on that person, and offer precise responses that tell *why*. Try to enunciate in one clear statement why you are personally interested in your topic and what it is you want to find out about it.

2.e DO SOME RESEARCH

Even in your earliest papers, which depend for ideas on memory and personal observation, a very preliminary kind of research can often stimulate your writing. Writing always has dealt with the same concern: getting hold of a reasonably good topic that can go somewhere as you find out more about it. The questions that you have been raising may send you to the *Reader's Guide to Periodical*

Literature or to the card catalog at your library (Chapter 18). Read one or two articles to gain an overview of the topic before you begin writing. Simply keep track of the name of the article and its author, and give credit when you incorporate anyone else's ideas among your own (see the sections in Chapter 18 on documentation). Every paper requires some kind of research: remembering, observing, reading, talking with others, listening. Papers of personal experience rely on memory and observation; other types of papers often call for more extensive research, generally in a library. Your freewriting may constitute enough research for a start, but a library may yield a one-page magazine article central to your idea that can get your writing moving. To write anything, you have to know what you are writing about. A writer who "throws the bull" is doomed. So is someone who is lazy. If you need to read or watch a TV documentary or talk to an expert to stimulate your thinking, do it.

Research is an important activity for writers. Chapter 18 discusses another, more elaborate activity that takes the form of more formal library research. For now, it is important to know that the research you are doing for your early papers will differ only in degree from that described in Chapter 18. Its purposes are the same: (1) to identify a subject you know something about or can easily research further; (2) to limit your subject to one that is neither too small to be productive nor too large to handle; (3) to discover an idea and your attitude toward it; and (4) to find out what you want to say about your subject so that you can present enough information to persuade your reader. Be on the alert for opportunities to do research easily. It need not be a tedious, dusty job. Talking to someone who knows about your topic, visiting a place you plan to write about, reading a short article or two on your topic need not take place in the stacks of your library. Research for your early papers can provide you with a quick burst of ideas that reassure you that you have a promising subject and are on the scent of a worthwhile topic.

2.f BRAINSTORMING

Brainstorming may be the most efficient way to get your writing started, particularly when ideas speed through your mind. Write a list of all the ideas that pop into your head about your subject. The list may consist of single words or phrases that describe feelings, observations, incidents, facts, or attitudes relating to your subject. As in freewriting, your purpose is to put your ideas on paper as quickly as possible. Everything you write is valuable. Don't hold anything back.

Underline the items on your list that mean something important to you. In the following list, notice the words that the writer chose to underline because they seemed most important to him as he thought about the paper he would write.

influence	my brother	excitement
generations	Beatles breaking up	historical moment
Love-ins	my house	memories
flowers in your hair	my parents	Sergeant Pepper

<u>1960s culture</u>	Yeah! Yeah! Yeah!	<u>my own life</u>
society	<u>revolution</u>	dress
John Lennon	records	long hair
Granny glasses	Come Together	<u>sharing</u>
torn jeans	<u>regret</u>	<u>not old enough</u>
psychedelic music	screaming	<u>hope for change</u>

Separate general from specific ideas

Although general and specific ideas will be discussed more fully in Chapter 3, for now remember that you need both kinds of ideas to organize your thinking. Some of the items in the list above about the 1960s and the Beatles are general ideas, and some are specific details or examples. For example, "influence" and "regret" are two of the broadest terms; "1960s culture" is less broad; and "John Lennon," "Granny glasses," "psychedelic music," "Love-ins," "torn jeans" are more specific details that illustrate 1960s culture.

You should understand that no idea is absolutely general or absolutely specific. You can decide only what is more general or less general, more specific or less specific. Try to group your ideas by including certain specifics under larger, more general headings. For practice, look at a diagram of the example in the exercise that follows:

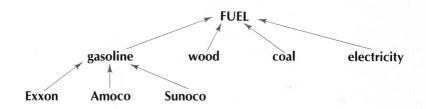

The word *fuel* includes *gasoline* as one of many kinds of fuel. The word *gasoline* includes *Exxon* as one of many brands of gasoline.

most general		fuel		least specific
less general		gasoline		less specific
least general	▼	Exxon	▲	most specific

In the exercises that follow, you will have a chance to test your ability to identify general and specific ideas.

Exercise 3 In each of the following groups, number the words to indicate the movement from general to specific. Use "1" for the most general, "3" for the most specific, and "2" for the item in the middle.

   Example: Exxon __3__ fuel __1__ gasoline __2__

1. dessert _____ food _____ ice cream _____

2. writer _____ poet _____ profession _____

3. first baseman _____ athlete _____ ballplayer _____
4. human being _____ Roberta _____ woman _____
5. walk _____ move _____ limp _____
6. soar _____ fly _____ move _____
7. temperature _____ 32° _____ information _____
8. bitter _____ painful _____ distasteful _____
9. artistic _____ talented _____ musical _____
10. assassinate _____ kill _____ murder _____

Exercise 4 Change the following general statements to specific ones.

> Example: On holidays, I love to do special things.
> On the Fourth of July, I love to go tuna fishing.

1. The piece of furniture makes a funny noise.
2. Let somebody hold your book.
3. The food my aunt served was not very good.
4. Weapons are important to certain groups of people.
5. That woman killed somebody.
6. I can see the stars tonight.
7. The government took action against the criminal.
8. Put these papers together, please.
9. Doctor, something is hurting me.
10. Exercise can cause pain.

Exercise 5 Write a concrete equivalent for each of the following abstract statements.

> Example: Boredom is a good teacher.
> On my eight-hour shifts as a night watchman, I learned to
> observe the skies and predict rain.

1. Wisdom comes with experience, not with age.
2. The greatest beauty may be mistaken for ugliness.
3. The smaller we are, the freer we are.
4. Continuity may require interruptions.
5. Bravery is often accidental.

Working toward an outline Once you've identified items as being general or specific, group together the items that relate to one another. Begin each grouping with the most general (*g*) word that includes other *g* words and specific (*s*) words beneath it. Omit words or phrases that do not relate easily to the most general words:

g	influence	*g*	regret
s	John Lennon	*s*	my brother
s	Sergeant Pepper	*s*	Beatles breaking up
s	dress	*g*	historical moment
s	long hair	*g*	not old enough
s	records	*g*	sharing
g	1960s culture	*g*	excitement
g	my own life	*g*	memories
g	generations	*g*	hope for change
g	revolution		

Not all your items will lend themselves to grouping. Remember, your *g* and *s* labels are relative at best. But if you study your groupings, you often can detect a relationship between the groups, as between "influence" and "regret" in the example above. The first grouping indicates the influence that the writer feels the Beatles and the 1960s have had on his own life as well as on his generation. At the same time, the second grouping indicates the underlying regret about not having shared the excitement of that particular historical moment. In working a freely associated list toward an outline, what you are actually doing is moving from a wide subject to a narrow topic and finally to the controlling idea of your paper.

Narrow down your subject.

Subject (stage 1):   The 1960s (This decade is the large *subject* area.)

Topic (stage 2):   The Beatles: their music and life style (Those particular aspects of the Beatles' music and life style that influenced the writer's generation is the *topic*.)

Controlling idea (stage 3):   I believe that even though I did not experience the Beatles firsthand, they have had a great influence on me and my generation. (The idea that includes the writer's attitude toward the idea itself is his *controlling idea*.)

At this point, you are ready to expand your controlling idea, in stage 3, by writing more specific statements that support your idea. These statements provide the skeleton of an outline.

Subheading: In music, dress, politics, and hair style, there is hardly an element in the life of the 1980s generation that hasn't been directly or indirectly influenced by the Beatles and the 1960s culture, which they helped to create.

Subheading: Despite our capacity to enjoy the Beatles even now, in the 1980s, it would have been more exciting to experience them, as well as other 1960s phenomena, while these events were taking place.

Spread your outline across a large sheet of paper, and fill in the space below each subheading with details and specific supportive items from your list that will make your statements convincing: "torn jeans," "long hair." "Sergeant

Pepper," "John Lennon," "Granny glasses," "psychedelic music," other events or people of the 1960s that have influenced you, a comparison of your brother now and then. Since this is a paper of personal experience, your memory is your chief research instrument. You will use it to dive into your mind frequently and poke around in the depths for usable material.

2.g A SPECIAL WORD TO DIEHARDS

Perhaps you are thinking that all this talk about getting started is not for you. Maybe you are a skeptic. Maybe freewriting, asking questions, and keeping a journal seem gimmicky to you. You embarrass easily, or you are too self-conscious to undertake something as revealing as freewriting. You want to be very much on top of your writing. Sitting down to write the paper itself may be the only way you can comfortably get started. Well, even if you are convinced that it won't work, we suggest that every now and then, you take another crack at freewriting. When you least expect it, you may find your freewriting pulling out the raw data stuck way back in your mind.

But when you won't or can't freewrite, try to begin by thinking a bit and then attempting to write an essay in one burst. Call it a "crash-through" draft, and crash on until it's finished. Then underline the best parts of what you've written, and distinguish the general ideas from the specific details. See if you can write a loose outline from your draft and a sentence describing how you feel about your topic. If starting on a rough draft seems too much of an undirected risk, put your crash-through into letter form. Write to someone real: "Dear Professor Brewer," "Dear Uncle Bert," "Dear Joan Benoit." With such an immediate audience, you can often write with greater conviction. However you attempt your crash-through, it may only in its final sentence produce the idea you have been struggling to dislodge. Although most of the crash-through is thereby doomed to the wastebasket, writing it may produce some valuable specific details that you thought you had forgotten. Pay dirt sometimes lies at the end of a dig. A true first draft can then begin with a general idea that has evolved from the specifics in your crash-through. You are now ready to think seriously about general and specific ideas and to undertake the whole essay.

chapter 3

Reach for the Whole Essay: The Narrative Essay

3.a TELLING AN EXPERIENCE

From the start, it is important to reach for the whole essay. Then you can work on paragraphs, sentences, and words to make your whole piece of writing more clear and more effective. In Chapters 1 and 2, all our strategies for getting started took us finally in the direction of grouping specific details under more general ideas because that relationship—between the general and the specific—provides the basic arrangement for the whole essay.

Although we can shape experiences and ideas into many forms, the most ancient way in which human beings have shaped their experiences is by telling a story about them. As beginning writers, most of you can feel confident of your own storytelling ability because all your lives you've heard family anecdotes, read stories, and told jokes. Very likely you will remember, virtually word for word, certain specific details of stories that were repeated all through your childhood by a parent or grandparent. Besides having heard stories, you have gone to the movies and watched TV. You've listened attentively as your friends recounted their experiences blow by blow, and you've cornered your friends as you told of your experiences in detail, often blow by painful blow. Narrating a story is the first form your writing will take because it is the form you naturally know most about.

Remember that the experiences you write about need not be earthshaking. Beginning writers usually overlook everyday events as being uninteresting and unworthy. But a good place to begin is with common, ordinary experiences, especially those that for some unaccountable reason won't fade from memory, but persist in your mind.

Exercise 1 In ten minutes of writing, tell the story of one memorable experience you had as a child. Here are a few ideas that might prompt you to recall one specific incident to tell about:

1. Waiting
2. Getting lost
3. Performing in a school play or concert
4. Falling in love
5. Learning to swim
6. Seeing something you shouldn't have seen

Now read the following essay, which begins to grapple with a common but unforgettable experience a student had while taking a road test:

ROAD TEST NUMBER ONE

Most of us have experiences in our lives when we feel like fools. We even know, as the event is happening to us, how silly we look. We soon learn that not only can't we reverse our embarrassment, but anything we try to do to help ourselves makes us look more foolish. When I took my first road test, I was able in only five minutes to convince a driving inspector that I wasn't even qualified to drive a bumper-car in an amusement park.

It was a clear, beautiful day in early May. There was not one drop of rain, snow, or sleet on the ground, which would have provided a good excuse. Although my driving instructor appeared nervous as he sat in the car with me, waiting for the inspector, I didn't feel a bit anxious. I had to remind him, when he washed the window for the third time, to calm down.

"Remember to adjust the mirrors when he gets in," he said as he gave the final touch to the front mirror.

"Yeah, I know, and signal, I know."

About five minutes later a stationwagon pulled up in front of the line. Five men in blue uniforms stepped out, each carrying a list of names and a black binder. One of them approached the car, and suddenly all the calmness I had instilled in myself vanished. I felt my tension rise. I began shaking.

"Katherine Lee, that you?" he asked.

"Yes," I nervously replied although at the moment I had a tremendous urge to say, "No, that's not me!" But common sense and the fifteen dollar bet I had courageously made with my brother kept me from saying it.

"All right, get in and start the engine," he said as he sat down in the front seat. "Let's just pull out and turn around the corner."

At that point I felt my throat go dry as pictures of my fifteen dollars going down the drain flashed through my head. I couldn't utter a word, except, "Yes." As I was pulling out of the lane, I already had realized I had forgotten to signal. "Oh well, maybe he won't notice," I prayed to myself. The turn at the corner was a very sharp one. I had driven too far out before starting to turn, so I was left with no choice but to make a very quick turn. This time he couldn't have avoided noticing; he, literally, fell off his seat.

"Slow down a bit," he cautioned. "Now drive down the street and park behind that blue car."

Pulling alongside the blue car, I cautiously checked in the front and rear mirrors, being careful to avoid trees, bushes, people, cars, and all the other things my instructor had warned me against. I backed up into the space and managed to maneuver the car into the right position, but the car was a foot away from the curb. "Not bad," I thought, "at least I parked." I put the car in neutral and stopped.

"All right, you can go now," he said, scribbling away on his report. At this point I got out of the car, thinking he meant I could *go,* like in *leave.* The thought didn't occur to me that we were about two miles from the test area. I thought he meant I could go, so I got out of the car! "No, no, get back in here. I meant *in* the car, in the car," he said with a look on his face that read, "Oh no, I got one of the *dumb* ones!"

Getting back in the car, I felt like a fool, so you can imagine how ridiculous I felt when, as we were driving down a two-lane, one-way street, I asked him, "Which way should I go?"

To which he replied in the same sarcastic tone of voice, "There's only one way to go."

"Oh," I said, trying not to appear more dumb than I had already proven. Driving back I managed to pass two intersections without even looking. He took note. Then for the *pièce de résistance,* the street the test area was on was a two-lane, two-way street with no markers; I drove down the *left* side. I thought the cars were just parked wrong. The agony of my defeat was confirmed when he got out and said, "Have a good day," like I really needed one. Well, I failed; wonder why? That was just number one; I went on to take road test number two and number three and managed to fail with equal success. I always advise anyone planning to take a road test in the near future, to take it from a fool who knows: "Use your head and think first about what you are being asked to do, and don't, don't get out of the car when you are asked to go."

—Katherine Lee

Another student wrote an account of a robbery that proved to have some surprising aftereffects. Read this essay and see if it bears any resemblance to the essay about the road test.

ROBBERY

Very often, a bad experience causes you to reevaluate yourself and those around you, and sometimes your new insights are far more significant than the bad time itself.

When my house was robbed last month, I learned that the things in life we value most are often not those with the highest price tags.

I sensed something was wrong the day I saw several neighbors gathered around, talking on the corner. As soon as I got out of my car and called my greetings over to them, their muffled hellos and strange glances tipped me off. Then Rosie, my nine-year-old sister, came bolting over, yelling, "Katie, we got robbed!" I stopped, looked over at the small crowd, and then headed toward the house, with Rosie tailing behind me. I flew up the stairs until I got to the foyer. At last I stopped and looked in.

I guess I had expected to see an empty house, but instead what I saw was room after room of open closets and empty drawers. Sifting through the mess was my mother. She seemed unusually calm. I asked only, "What's gone?"

"I'm not sure," was her response. "It looks as if they were just looking for money."

I noticed the untouched crystal and china in the dining room. All the appliances, the stereo, and the new television my parents had just bought were still there. I asked, "Did you call the police?"

"Yes," she said, "they've already dusted for fingerprints."

Then Rosie started yelling, "It was that Martha! I know it! I told the cops that!" As she ran her little fingers over the dusted furniture, she added, "I bet she wore gloves, too."

"Did they hurt the cats?" I asked my mother.

"I don't think so. They're behind the sofa." The two cats were sitting motionless and wide-eyed in the corner, but they seemed unharmed. My mother continued, "When the police came, I went upstairs for the first time and found my room a mess. They took my coin collection and the gold chain you gave me for Mother's Day."

Later on, we also found that about seventy dollars from the china cabinet and some pieces of silver had also been taken. Ironically, the money was from my sister Rita's paper route. Every week, my mother would write her a check to pay her bill, and Rita would give my mother the money for food shopping. For the first time, Rita had put aside some extra cash, and that was the money that was taken.

Next I asked my mother, "What about your rings?" I have always admired her birthstone and engagement rings. Even though she rarely wore them, I knew they meant a lot to her as well.

"No, I had them hidden behind the drawer in my jewelry box."

All I could say was, "Thank God."

Next, we went upstairs. My mother's room was the hardest hit. Her bureaus were emptied all over the room. Her wedding gown had been pulled out of its box, as had the gown we children had all been christened in. I was shocked. How nasty, I thought to myself. Two drawers, which had been filled with pictures, cards, and old school projects, were emptied, the contents dumped haphazardly around. This was where they had found the coin collection. I remember thinking to myself that the things that were taken, except for the money, were all irreplaceable items, the result of thirty years of collecting. I felt really sorry for my mother.

My brother's and sisters' rooms had been lightly combed over, but the one I share with my sister Mary was untouched. I assume they opened the attic door, saw stairs, and didn't bother to go any farther. Annette, my brother's girlfriend, offered another theory: ''They probably got to your room, Kate, saw the condition it was in, and said, 'I think someone beat us to this room!' '' As it happened, Mary and I were lucky. She had left 160 dollars on the dresser, and, because I'd heard of a mugging in my school, some of my best jewelry lay right beside it.

We decided to leave the mess downstairs for a while and go have a cup of tea. There's a lot to be said for the healing powers of a good cup of tea. It was then that we talked about the possible suspect. Early in November, a neighbor, Martha, had been caught robbing houses on the block. Since then, several people on the block, including us, had been getting prank phone calls. As soon as you'd answer, you'd hear the click of someone hanging up. My sister Rita, who is thirteen and ''feeling her oats,'' as my father puts it, after hearing the click would always say, ''Sorry, we're home!'' I guess today no one picked up the phone, and so the joke was on us. Maybe we should have taken these warnings more seriously, but I guess we all thought it would never happen to us. Of course, we have no proof it was Martha, and though the police questioned her, nothing was ever recovered.

Dinner that night was rather somber. No one wanted to talk. My father broke the silence by telling about the braces he was going to order for the basement windows. He said, ''I thought to do it before last Thanksgiving but put it off. That's okay, though; we'll get everything locked up around here. They got us once, but not again.''

The worst part, in retrospect, was that things of great sentimental value were taken. There is no insurance to cover that kind of loss.

—Kathleen Devine

3.b STORIES AND NARRATIVE ESSAYS

Why do we call the accounts these two students wrote ''essays''? Why not simply call them ''stories''? What's in an essay that is not in a story?

Perhaps a closer look at stories will show us what is special about them. For one thing, the writer has *one* experience to relate, one string of events to put before the reader. Unrelated events and other experiences are omitted. The narrative essay, like the story, is also single-minded because it is full of a single story. Certainly, it makes use of the techniques of fiction: it has characters (you, among others) and a setting (the route of your road test, your house); it has snatches of what real people say to one another (''Katie, we got robbed!''); and, most important, it usually has a chronological order. It unfolds events as they happen in a period of time. What happened first is generally told first; what happened next is told next. Telling a story means relating a sequence of events that happened on a particular occasion to particular people. Events that occur day in and day out are, in themselves, never a story:

> A person needs to start the day in solitude and privacy. I ride a bus to school daily. I have to stand all the way, since the stop before mine attracts a small mob changing from the intercity bus. I am jostled, though I always manage to study a minimal amount. I usually reach school frustrated and a little shopworn.

A story happens only once. Notice in the previous examples the naturalness of the *once*: "Road Test Number One"—"a clear, beautiful day in early May"; "Robbery"—"the day I saw several neighbors gathered around talking on the corner." The paragraph above has no *once*. By contrast, the following sentences are a story because they are about one person on a specific bus *at a definite time*. This paragraph depends for its narrative force on stating when the events happened: "Last Tuesday."

> A person needs to start the day in solitude and privacy. Last Tuesday, I boarded the Q72 bus, searched hopelessly for a seat, and, as usual, established myself midway up the aisle, clinging to an overhead strap. A man sitting nearby observed every move I made. I confess I felt awkward as I opened my Italian text. When he saw my book, he tapped my arm. "*Scusi,*" he said, "*per piacere,*" and he rose, offering his seat. I would have grabbed it, but the woman standing next to me rushed forward, muttering something in a brisk Italian that instantly went beyond my Italian I, and plunged into the seat, shopping bag and all. By the time we reached the college, my new friend was talking, in English to be sure, about a local bar, and although I headed quickly for the door, he was holding one of my books. I turned to take it, annoyed at this daily kind of nuisance, annoyed that I couldn't have the space and time I needed to prepare myself for the day ahead.

But, as we will see, there is more to writing an essay than telling a story.

An essay is *more* than a story, although it may include a story. Nor is it, at the other extreme, a report bulging with facts and figures that can be checked out in a library, although essays may include some of that. Above all, an essay states an *idea* you have in your head about a real experience, a real problem, or a real person or place. In an essay, you express your attitude about a specific experience or problem in a personal and interesting way. Even your earliest stories will hold an idea scrambling to get out. In fact, every story, written or told, makes a point; it's an essential feature of narrative that the teller or writer anticipates an audience that asks, "So what?" "What's the point?" "Why are you telling me this story?" In the narrative essay, you bring the point of your story up front. Notice how both "Road Test Number One" and "Robbery" state an idea and an attitude in the very first paragraph. One writer wants us to know what she learned from her embarrassing road test: in an embarrassing situation, "anything we try to do to help ourselves makes us look more foolish." The other writer wants us to know what she learned when her house was robbed: "When my house was robbed last month, I learned that the things in life we value most are often not those with the highest price tags." Your controlling idea is often stated in a sentence or two in the first paragraph of your essay. It is like having the address of your idea. You know where to find it.

3.c THE CONTROLLING IDEA

The point you wish to make in telling a story controls the way you organize and represent an event. And the general truth of your idea will depend on how convincingly you illustrate it, defend it, or prove it in the remainder of your essay so that other people can say, "Yes. That statement is true. I have been in situations where it would also apply to me." A clearly stated idea that you understand helps you to *control* the rest of your essay because you can choose to include only those details that strengthen it. In the same way, your controlling idea helps you to screen out details that have nothing to do with the point that it expresses. The simple experience and the controlling idea are the two essentials of a narrative essay.

How does a writer formulate a controlling idea for an essay? *How do ideas take shape?* Consider the following passage about the murder of two teenage girls in Chicago in 1960, which opened a longer essay by Philip Roth.

Several winters back, while I was living in Chicago, the city was shocked and mystified by the death of two teenage girls. So far as I know, the populace is mystified still; as for the shock, Chicago is Chicago, and one week's dismemberment fades into the next's. The victims this particular year were sisters. They went off one December night to see an Elvis Presley movie, for the sixth or seventh time we are told, and never came home. Ten days passed, and fifteen and twenty, and then the whole bleak city, every street and alley, was being searched for the missing Grimes girls, Pattie and Babs. A girl friend had seen them at the movie, a group of boys had caught a glimpse of them afterward getting into a black Buick, another group said a green Chevy, and so on and so forth, until one day the snow melted and the unclothed bodies of the two girls were discovered in a roadside ditch in a forest preserve west of Chicago. The coroner said he didn't know the cause of death, and then the newspapers took over. One paper ran a drawing of the girls on the back page, in bobby socks and Levis and babushkas: Pattie and Babs a foot tall, and in four colors, like Dixie Dugan on Sundays. The mother of the two girls wept herself right into the arms of a local newspaper lady, who apparently set up her typewriter on the Grimeses' front porch and turned out a column a day, telling us that these had been good girls, hard-working girls, average girls, churchgoing girls, et cetera. Late in the evening one could watch television interviews featuring schoolmates and friends of the Grimes sisters: the teenage girls look around, dying to giggle; the boys stiffen in their leather jackets. "Yeah, I knew Babs, yeah, she was all right, yeah, she was popular . . . " On and on, until at last comes a confession. A skid-row bum of thirty-five or so, a dishwasher, a prowler, a no-good named Benny Bedwell, admits to killing both girls, after he and a pal cohabited with them for several weeks in various flea-bitten hotels. Hearing the news, the weeping mother tells the newspaper lady that the man is a liar—her girls, she insists now, were murdered the night they went off to the movie. The coroner continues to maintain (with rumblings from the press) that the girls show no signs of having had sexual intercourse. Meanwhile, everybody in Chicago is buying four papers a day, and Benny Bedwell, having supplied the police with an hour-by-hour chronicle of his adventures, is tossed in jail. Two nuns, teachers of the girls at the school they attended, are sought out by the newspapermen. They are surrounded and questioned, and finally one of the sisters explains all. "They were not exceptional girls," the sister says, "they had no hobbies."

About this time, some good-natured soul digs up Mrs. Bedwell, Benny's mother, and a meeting is arranged between this old woman and the mother of the slain teenagers. Their picture is taken together, two overweight, overworked American ladies, quite befuddled but sitting up straight for the photographers. Mrs. Bedwell apologizes for her Benny. She says, "I never thought any boy of mine would do a thing like that." Two weeks later, maybe three, her boy is out on bail, sporting several lawyers and a new one-button-roll suit. He is driven in a pink Cadillac to an out-of-town motel where he holds a press conference. Yes, he is the victim of police brutality. No, he is not a murderer; a degenerate maybe, but even that is changing. He is going to become a carpenter (a carpenter!) for the Salvation Army, his lawyers say. Immediately, Benny is asked to sing (he plays the guitar) in a Chicago night spot for two thousand dollars a week, or is it ten thousand? I forget. What I remember is that suddenly, into the mind of the onlooker, or newspaper reader, comes The Question: is this all public relations? But of course not—two girls are dead. Still, a song begins to catch on in Chicago, "The Benny Bedwell Blues." Another newspaper launches a weekly contest: "How Do You Think the Grimes Girls Were Murdered?" and a prize is given for the best answer (in the opinion of the judges). And now the money begins to flow; donations, hundreds of them, start pouring in to Mrs. Grimes from all over the city and the state. For what? From whom? Most contributions are anonymous. Just the dollars, thousands and thousands of them— the *Sun-Times* keeps us informed of the grand total. Ten thousand, twelve thousand, fifteen thousand. Mrs. Grimes sets about refurnishing and redecorating her house. A stranger steps forward, by the name of Shultz or Schwartz—I don't really remember—but he is in the appliance business and he presents Mrs. Grimes with a whole new kitchen. Mrs. Grimes, beside herself with appreciation and joy, turns to her surviving daughter and says, "Imagine me in that kitchen!" Finally, the poor woman goes out and buys two parakeets (or maybe another Mr. Shultz presents them as a gift); one parakeet she calls Babs, the other Pattie. At just about this point, Benny Bedwell, doubtless having barely learned to hammer a nail in straight, is extradited to Florida on the charge of having raped a twelve-year-old girl there. Shortly thereafter I left Chicago myself, and so far as I know, though Mrs. Grimes hasn't her two girls, she has a brand-new dishwasher and two small birds.

This is a disturbing and ugly listing of details—from parakeets to appliances—in a hideously strange case. And you may well be uneasy about it. What is the point, after all?

If you had one comment to make about this whole passage, what would you say? Begin your comment with "I think" or "I learned." Remember that there is no right or wrong answer. In 1960, millions of people read in the newspapers about the Grimes girls. Each reader's comment about the events would have been different according to his or her experience. Remember that people have different reactions to the same events. What you will be formulating is your own attitude toward these details about the Grimes girls.

I think ————————————— .
I learned ————————————— .

Consider your own comment along with the following comments made by other students:

1. I think that living in the city is more dangerous than ever.
2. I learned that people's sorrows can be alleviated by luxurious gifts.
3. I think that what this piece says is that Americans react in strange ways to violence.
4. I learned that it is dangerous to see Elvis Presley movies at night.
5. I learned that a lot of people gave Mrs. Grimes money.
6. I think that Americans make heroes out of criminals.
7. I learned that a tragic crime can be turned into a farce by the mass media seeking public attention.
8. I think that Benny Bedwell was a bum.
9. I think that every American should own a parakeet.
10. I think that any girl who gets into trouble is out there looking for it.
11. I learned that all men are potential rapists.

Now drop the words *I think* or *I learned* and any other words that don't relate to the events themselves.

1. I think that   living in the city is more dangerous than ever.
            Living in the city is more dangerous than ever.
2. I learned that   people's sorrows can be alleviated by luxurious gifts.
            People's sorrows can be alleviated by luxurious gifts.
3. I think that what this piece says is that   Americans react in strange ways to violence.
            Americans react in strange ways to violence.
4. It is dangerous to see Elvis Presley movies at night.
5. A lot of people gave Mrs. Grimes money.
6. Americans make heroes out of criminals.
7. A tragic crime can be turned into a farce by the mass media seeking public attention.
8. Benny Bedwell was a bum.
9. Every American should own a parakeet.
10. Any girl who gets into trouble is out there looking for it.
11. All men are potential rapists.

Notice that two of the comments merely restate the facts of the piece:

> A lot of people gave Mrs. Grimes money.

> Benny Bedwell was a bum.

Five of the comments express opinions that deal with only a small portion of the facts presented in the passage:

> People's sorrows can be alleviated by luxurious gifts.

> It is dangerous to see Elvis Presley movies at night.

> Every American should own a parakeet.

> Any girl who gets into trouble is out there looking for it.

> All men are potential rapists.

Two more sentences express opinions that deal with most, but not all, of the facts in the passage:

> Living in the city is more dangerous then ever. (This statement omits the reactions of the public to the crime and to the mother.)

> Americans make heroes out of criminals. (This statement omits the fact that the mother, who is not a criminal, is made into a heroine and receives gifts of appliances and parakeets.)

Each of the remaining two sentences contains a personal idea that fits the whole passage. This idea controls the whole essay. It is an umbrella statement that covers the details of your subject as well as your attitude toward those details. The controlling idea must state the point of your essay. It must get to the one important thing that's on your mind—the idea that everything else spins out of. Either of the following sentences uses all the details in the ''story'' about the Grimes girls. Either one might express Philip Roth's attitude toward the details.

> Americans react in strange ways to violence.

> A tragic crime can be turned into a farce by the mass media seeking public attention.

But does it? What *was* on Philip Roth's mind? Why has he produced such a meticulous, relentless account? If you suspect a motive behind his work, if you suspect that he is working with great diligence to convince us of something, if you believe that he is trying to make a point about American life or American crime or American cities, if you are left wanting the reason for Roth's writing the story about the Grimes girls, you've picked up Roth's strategy. In the next paragraph of Roth's essay, he asks:

> And what is the moral of the story? Simply this: that the American writer in the middle of the twentieth century has his hands full in trying to understand, describe, and then make credible much of American reality. It stupefies, it sickens, it infuriates, and finally it is even a kind of embarrassment to one's own meager imagination. The actuality is continually outdoing our talents, and the culture tosses up figures almost daily that are the envy of any novelist.

Roth, who is a major American writer, has presented the stupefying, sickening, infuriating details of the Grimes case in order to show what is on *his* mind as a writer: how impossible it is for an American writer to make up anything as bizarre as real-life events. In fact, this is only the beginning of Roth's essay ''Writing American Fiction,'' which for several more pages goes on about American writers. His real interest is not the Grimes case, but what the case demonstrates about the infuriating ways Americans behave. He cites examples of several public events that occurred in 1960 (the year the essay was written) whose actors are ''the envy of any novelist.'' How many relatively recent events can you name that would prove that Roth's point is still valid? The American hostages held in Iran? The Russian boycott of the 1984 Olympics? The attempted assassination of the Pope? Wouldn't you say, in fact, that Roth's general point might be valid at any time and that specific examples of a freshly stupefying, sickening, infuriating event might be supplied for any year?

You usually reach an understanding of an experience long after it has occurred. The memory of an event buzzes around in your mind—failing a road test, discovering a robbery, working in a restaurant, gaining a new insight into your parents as people. From the details of these experiences, you come to some general truths about them. The statement of your controlling idea is often a *generalization* because it states an idea that the writer believes not only is true about his or her own experience, but also can be generalized to the experiences of others. In the following essay, a writer relates an incident in which he came to an understanding. Read the whole essay, and see what the writer generalizes from this event that could apply to all of us.

CHANGES

One moment is sometimes all it takes to change the course of a relationship. I think I can pinpoint the exact time the relationship between my father and me changed from one of hostility to one of friendship.

We were never very close. He grew up in a large, Depression-era farm family— eleven children—and his own father was distant and autocratic. When I was young, my father treated me much as his father, I suppose, had treated him. He, too, was rather distant and autocratic. Certainly, he was the ultimate authority in all things, and to challenge that authority openly was unthinkable.

Something had to give. As I came of age in the late 1960s, the times were motivation enough, I suppose, for something so stern and unbending as my father's will not to continue unchallenged. Two scenes come to mind. The first, which took place in the summer of my freshman year in college, was sharp but settled nothing. It was a wedge driven into the already widening gap of our relationship. It served to drive us apart. The event that instantly seemed to close that division took place one year later.

The first experience took place one night when I arrived home at about 3:00 A.M. after a night of driving and probably drinking with friends. He had always been restrictive about hours and behavior, but in the year I had spent away at school, I had grown used to settling things for myself—or in reality not settling things like that at all—and living as I pleased. He met me at the stairs and said that I was not on my own, that he'd had enough of my lack of discipline. Real autocratic father talk. Usually, when he started like this, I was submissive and looked away, and took it. This time, however, I just stared back, defiantly. He told me not to stare, but I continued, and he pulled back his fist to hit me. And in that instant, as I waited for the blow, he and I both suddenly knew that I would hit him back; he did not swing.

That moment separated us. The next experience brought us together.

The following summer, my last one at home, we were with some friends at the lake. My father, who hadn't water-skiied in years, decided to show us all that he still could. The lake was rough, but he was not to be discouraged once his mind was made up. I was the driver of the boat. He stood up in good shape and was doing fine until we hit the big water just outside the bay. There he fell very hard, amidst the violent two-foot swells. I turned the boat around and circled back; I could see only his back as he rose and sank with the water. Waves broke over his head. His wind was gone, and he was hurt. As I closed in, I saw suddenly a look of real terror in his eyes. I saw real terror in my father's eyes for the first time. He saw that I saw, and in that moment, all our barriers broke down. There was no confrontation, no tears, no violence, no heart-to-heart talks, just one look. He thought he was about to die, and he was afraid. That was all. That was everything. There was nothing more to hit out at, nothing more to rebel against, and nothing more that needed to be said. Then or now.

—Tim Ervin

Exercise 2 Answer the following questions about "Changes."

1. Why does Ervin make a general statement about all relationships before he talks about his relationship with his father?
2. What do you believe caused Ervin to write this essay?
3. Which words tell you when Ervin begins to tell a story about a specific event? Give examples.
4. Which techniques in this narration might lead you to think you are reading fiction? Be specific.
5. Before he describes the second of his two incidents, Ervin "gives away" the outcome by saying, "The next experience brought us together." Why?

Experiences like Ervin's may become a part of you long before something flashes and you realize that there is a general point to be made about them. You sense that an event stands out in your mind, and you want to know why. Any experience that stands out from the crowds of others deserves your attention.

You might want to try this:

1. Think hard about one experience. Freewrite about it.
2. Try to recall details you may have temporarily forgotten.
3. If possible, talk to someone who was there with you.
4. Write down what you remember as you remember it.
5. Try to determine what the experience taught you. Write it down. Say, "From this experience, I learned that _____."

Then, when you write your essay, your controlling idea and your experience will constantly reinforce each other. In your first pieces of writing, you should state your controlling idea first, although this in no way suggests that the general idea came before the experience. We carry our experiences and observations around with us indefinitely, seeing them somewhat veiled, until an illuminating idea flashes and we *understand* their significance.

Less often, writers allow the evidence to come first, as we saw in the Roth piece, because the evidence is so powerful or their writing so artful that writers trust their readers to independently formulate their idea as they read. Then readers feel gratified when their own interpretation is reinforced by the writer's statement of the controlling idea at the end.

Either way, in a narrative essay—the kind of essay you are beginning with—the arrangement is so visible as to *introduce* you to the basic rhythm of the essay. A narrative essay has two parts: you have one specific episode to tell, and that episode leads you to make a point—your controlling idea—from which the rest of your essay follows.

3.d THE NARRATIVE ESSAY

One specific: your episode	Road-test experience	Robbery experience	Water-skiing experience
One generalization: your point	One foolish action leads to another.	Robberies teach us that the things in life we value most are often not the ones with the highest price tags.	One moment is sometimes all it takes to change the course of a relationship.

Or, as the arrangement usually appears in an essay, the reverse:

Arrangement

Part I	One generalization: your point	One foolish action leads to another.	Robberies teach us that the things in life we value most are often not the ones with the highest price tags.	One moment is sometimes all it takes to change the course of a relationship.
Part II	One specific: your episode	Road-test experience	Robbery experience	Water-skiing experience

The hardest task— writing the first draft Writing the first draft may be your hardest task. Within five minutes, your mood varies from despair to sudden optimism and then to despair again. You had a clever way to begin; but now that you have it on paper, it fizzles. Everyone you've spoken with says your idea is workable; yet here you are, and nothing works.

Chapter 6, "Revising the Whole Essay," presents two drafts of two student essays and goes into detail about how you move from a rough draft to a more finished one. Meanwhile, remember to keep your progress legible. If your first draft gradually comes to look like a maze of insertions, arrows, crossings out, hysterical underlinings, and exclamation points, copy it over, preferably typing it, so that you can see your progress clearly. An already illegible paper inhibits you from making changes. Who wants to work with a mess like that? Remember that a revision of a first draft does not mean correcting only spelling and punctuation. It is a *re-vision*, a *seeing again* of your ideas. If you work on a word

---

TIPS FOR WRITERS—WRITING THE NARRATIVE ESSAY

1. Find out through freewriting, thinking, conversing, or reading which experiences interest you.

2. Invention. Engage in one or more techniques for getting started. Your writing begins as you locate ideas through close observation. Record whatever you can remember about an event, a person, or an object. Recall an experience that interests you. Do a focused freewriting on that event, write an associative list, talk about it with a friend, do some brief research (talk to a person who shared the experience with you), or, if you have a tentative idea in mind, do a crash-through of an essay, perhaps in letter form.

3. Separate general from specific. Mark your more general ideas *g* and the more specific details *s*. It is a good idea to write out the general ideas in full sentences. Keep your details in words or phrases. Group specific details under a related general idea. Look for connections among the groups.

4. Choose the groups that interest you.

5. Write a trial statement of the controlling idea suggested by this experience. Begin by stating your attitude toward your subject and what you learned from it. Write, "I think _____" or "I learned _____."

6. Tell the personal experience. Be honest. Be vivid. Include the details that surfaced in your invention strategies.

7. Turn your attention back and forth to the writing acts you need to repeat as you work out your idea and your illustrative experience. At the end, mention again why your experience proves your point. Adjust your beginning.

8. Get a reaction to what you have written from your class or from a friend.

9. Revise your essay.

BASIC ARRANGEMENT FOR A NARRATIVE ESSAY:

Part I: Generalization—your controlling idea
Part II: Your specific experience

processor, you always will have a copy that you can freely edit, one to which you can add sentences easily or on which you can move paragraphs about. If you do not have access to a word processor, you may want a pair of scissors handy so that you can cut up your paper and reorganize it. For this practical reason, write on only one side of the paper.

In all, a paper may need to be written out three times:

1. A first draft like the ones in Chapter 6 (pp. 110–111 and 116–117). You make changes on this draft.
2. A legible working version of the first draft, with some changes worked into it and with your controlling idea up front. You can read it aloud or have copies made for readers to comment on.
3. A revised and proofread draft, incorporating changes suggested by readers, to be neatly typed, doubled-spaced, on one side of the page, finished, and submitted (Chapter 6, pp. 120–122).

Exercise 3 In class, do any of the following exercises that interest you. Do *not* tell the "point" of your story.

1. Tell a joke.
2. Tell about something that happened to you in the last week.
3. Relate an anecdote you heard on a TV talk show.
4. Relate an anecdote about your mother, wife, sister, or girl friend.
5. Relate an anecdote about your father, husband, brother, or boy friend.
6. Relate an experience you had when you were a child.

Exercise 4 In class, do any of the following exercises that interest you. After you tell your story, tell the "point" of your experience. If you become interested in one of these exercises, write a brief account of the experience. Then write the point of your story or say what it taught you.

1. Tell of an experience you had while getting your driver's license. What is the point of your story? Say it in a sentence.
2. Tell of an experience you had with extrasensory perception. What is the point of your story? Say it in a sentence.
3. Tell of an experience you had with a computer. In a sentence, tell what that experience taught you.
4. Tell of a *last* experience you had (the last time you saw someone dear to you, the last day of a job, the last time you visited a place). In a sentence, tell what the experience taught you.

Exercise 5 Here are two brief personal anecdotes. Write a controlling idea for each one.

1. One day in May, my mother served us a big bowl of beautiful strawberries. I put a few on the edge of my plate to save while I ate my corn, pot roast, and string beans. Suddenly my brother Jack yelled, ''Look out! There's a spider over you.'' I glanced up, and when I looked back down, two of my strawberries were gone. I reached my left arm up around my plate and continued eating my pot roast. My brother Bert suddenly rolled his corn cob in my direction, and, without thinking, I brushed it back with my arm. Bert swiped the rest of my strawberries, and I had string beans for dessert.

2. One summer, my older sister and I traveled alone to Italy to meet our grandfather for the first time. Before we left, my father sat us down and told us to stay alert at all times. We had to guard our luggage and our money, keep our passports in our special pockets, and above all we were never to talk to strangers. When we reached Milan's airport, we claimed our bags, checked through customs, put our passports safely back in our special pockets, when a big man came over to me and reached for my suitcase. He kept saying something in Italian about our suitcases and about money. I threw my sister a quick glance and ran for it. She ran, too. We ran and ran, our bags banging painfully against our legs. Every time my sister slowed down, I yelled, ''Don't stop. Keep running.'' We were both getting tired. Finally, I could make out what sounded like my name and then my sister's name and then my father's name. We both stopped running and let ourselves be hugged.

Exercise 6 Write a narrative essay suggested by one of the following topics. Your essay will contain a statement of your generalization and a detailed account of your experience.

1. Happiness does not depend on money.
2. How I discovered family pride (or ethnic pride).
3. Children often suffer injustice at the hands of adults.
4. How I discovered my modesty.
5. On being responsible for an incompetent person.
6. A lesson about bosses.
7. How I discovered that my mother (or father) is not perfect.

chapter
4 The Essay and Its Paragraphs: Arranging the Support for Your Idea

In college, much of your writing will need to explain and inform rather than tell stories about events that you experienced. Clear, exact writing is an indispensable skill to everybody, including college students. If you think that "writing for college" must have an "intellectual" ring to it, if you think that you must use four-syllable words in complicated sentences, forget it. Your job is to show as plainly as you can how much of a subject you understand.

We hope you have spent many weeks turning events of your own life into narratives, each of which had a point, both for you and your reader(s). In representing events, you were able to rely on the powerful support of chronology, the way events happen in time. In "explanatory" writing, sometimes called "expository" writing, you will no longer rely on chronology alone. While it is true that some ideas and details are organized around time, others demand different principles, another kind of system that you, the *writer*, must consciously decide on. When you aren't telling stories, how can you organize your thinking? Are there a few other natural shapes for essays that will hold your thinking in an orderly way?

4.a A CONTROLLING IDEA AND ITS SUPPORTING PARAGRAPHS

The narrative essays you have been writing have followed a two-part arrangement:

Part I: Your controlling idea

Part II: Your specific episode

In other kinds of writing, an even greater interplay exists between general and specific. As you read the following sentences from Chapter 1 of *A Distant Mirror,* Barbara Tuchman's history of the "calamitous" fourteenth century, you will notice that instead of citing one specific episode to explain one general statement, Tuchman offers several specific examples to support one general statement. Follow her arrangement:

When the 14th century opened, France was supreme. . . .

"The fame of French knights . . . dominates the world."
As a result of Norman conquests and the crusades, French was spoken as a second mother tongue by the noble estate in England, Flanders, and the Kingdom of Naples and Sicily. . . .

The architecture of Gothic cathedrals was called the "French style"; a French architect was invited to design London Bridge; Venice imported dolls from France dressed in the latest mode in order to keep up with French fashions; exquisitely carved French ivories, easily transportable, penetrated to the limits of the Christian world.

Above all, the University of Paris elevated the name of the French capital, surpassing all others in the fame of its masters and the prestige of its studies in theology and philosophy. . . .

Paragraph 1:   Controlling idea (France was supreme.)

Paragraph 2:   Supporting idea (topic sentence about the dominance of French knights) plus specifics

Paragraph 3:   Another supporting idea (topic sentence about the dominance of the French language) plus specifics (French was spoken in England, Flanders, Naples, and Sicily.)

Paragraph 4:   Still another supporting idea plus specifics (about the prevailing French style of architecture)

Paragraph 5:   And a fourth supporting idea plus specifics (about the dominance of the University of Paris)

In Tuchman's book, specific details bring each of the supporting ideas to life. Each idea and its own bundle of increasingly specific details form a paragraph to support the author's claim that France was supreme. Each supporting idea is a little more specific than the controlling idea but less specific than the details that accompany it.

1. A controlling idea is an umbrella statement for an essay.
2. A topic sentence is an umbrella statement for a paragraph or a group of paragraphs.
3. A topic sentence is more specific than the statement of a controlling idea, but it is more general than the details that follow.

4.b WHAT DOES A PARAGRAPH LOOK LIKE?

As a reader, you recognize a paragraph because its first line is indented from the left margin and begins a solid section of print with space around it. Paragraphing helps you read because it permits you to absorb writing in manageable doses and to pause before the next dose, although the length of these unbroken doses is by no means uniform. A paragraph can be a skinny line or two or can go on without relief for fat pages of unbroken text. In newspapers, for example, because of the narrowness of the columns and the nature of the news, paragraphs often are a single sentence in length. Such very brief paragraphs have a purpose—they enable you to speed through the day's news. In books and essays, paragraphs have undergone many changes over the years. A hundred years ago it was fashionable to write paragraphs three times longer than those we write now, and long before that there were no paragraphs at all. Today five to eight sentences generally stand together to form a paragraph averaging between 150 and 200 words. This modern paragraphing offers a reader another important advantage: besides helping your eyes, paragraphing divides a writer's work into effective sections that support the controlling idea.

How do you know when to signal for a paragraph?

Paragraphs generally follow *shifts* in thought, changes from one part of a topic to another, or changes from the general idea to the specific case. These are natural movements in thinking that you signal, often intuitively, when you begin a new paragraph.

The following paragraphs are from a student essay entitled "Risks." One reason the writer of this essay begins new paragraphs is to show that he is getting down to specific cases. A new paragraph shows the change from a general observation to a specific event or time.

Risks are unavoidable. I've never met a person in my life who hasn't taken a risk. If you don't risk anything you will never be able to gain anything. For all practical purposes, you would be living in limbo. Everything in life involves some kind of risk, and love affairs are no exception. Love affairs always involve the risk of getting hurt, but sometimes for reasons beyond love itself.

Change to a specific case:

Two years ago I had an affair with a beautiful girl. We were about the same age, and we shared the same interests, which enhanced our relationship. We were crazy about each other, and we always hated to part company. I remember that I never had any difficulties with her or her parents, but I found out soon enough about the complications that would pop up. In the meanwhile, though, we continued to share a beautiful relationship. We were never closer. I think our relationship reached its peak because everything after was all down hill.

Change to a more specific time:

One Sunday I called for her at home. It was the same procedure. Her parents greeted me. Then they asked me to sit down and have something to eat or drink. . . .

In narrative writing, you use certain introductory words or phrases to help signal a new place or a new time, and you indent to begin a new paragraph:

In the morning, – – – – – –
– – – – – – – – – – – –.

One Sunday, – – – – – – – –
– – – – – – – – – – – –.

By the next spring, – – – – –
– – – – – – – – – – – –.

On the other side of town, – –
– – – – – – – – – – – –.

Outside my window, – – – –
– – – – – – – – – – – – –.

In St. Louis, – – – – – – – –
– – – – – – – – – – – –.

In writing that is not storytelling, other purposes press you to indent for a new paragraph. Again, certain introductory words or phrases will signal the new paragraph. One such purpose is a change from one specific reason to another:

First, – – – – – – – – – – –
– – – – – – – –.

Second, – – – – – – – – – –
– – – – – – – –.

Finally, – – – – – – – – – –
– – – – – – – –.

A change from one example to another also calls for a new paragraph:

For example, – – – – – – – –
– – – – – – – –.

Another example is – – – – –
– – – – – – – –.

Indent to show the progress of a comparison or contrast:

X, as we know, is – – – – –
– – – – – – – –.

In the same way, Y is also – –
– – – – – – – –.

> X has always struck me as − −
> − − − − − − −.
>
> Unlike X, Y strikes me as − −
> − − − − − − −.

Other pairs of words work together to begin new paragraphs. Here are a few examples:

> A few writers − − − − − − −
> − − − − − − −.
>
> Most writers, however, − − −
> − − − − − − −.
>
> On the one hand, − − − − − −
> − − − − − − −.
>
> On the other hand, − − − − −
> − − − − − − −.
>
> In this climate, − − − − − −
> − − − − − − −.
>
> In hotter climates, − − − − −
> − − − − − − −.
>
> The earliest records show − −
> − − − − − − −.
>
> Later records show − − − − −
> − − − − − − −.

Exercise 1 Indicate where in the following passage you would begin a new paragraph. Identify the word or phrase that signals a paragraph shift.

Three passions, simple but overwhelmingly strong, have governed my life: the longing for love, the search for knowledge, and unbearable pity for the suffering of mankind. These passions, like great winds, have blown me hither and thither, in a wayward course, over a deep ocean of anguish, reaching to the very verge of despair. I have sought love, first, because it brings ecstasy—ecstasy so great that I would often have sacrificed all the rest of life for a few hours of this joy. I have sought it, next, because it relieves loneliness—that terrible loneliness in which one shivering consciousness looks over the rim of the world into the cold unfathomable lifeless abyss. I have sought it, finally, because in the union of love I have seen, in a mystic miniature, the prefiguring visions of the heaven that saints and poets have imagined. This is what I sought, and though it might seem too good for human life, this is what—at last—I found. With equal passion I have sought knowledge. I have wished to understand the hearts of men. I have wished to know why the stars shine. And I have tried to apprehend the Pythagorean power by which number holds sway above the flux. A little of this, but not much, I have achieved. Love and knowledge, so far as they were possible, led upward toward the heavens. But always pity brought me back to earth. Echoes of cries of pain reverberate in my heart. Children in famine, victims tortured by oppressors, helpless old people a hated burden to their sons, and the whole world of loneliness, poverty, and pain make a mockery of what human life should be. I long to alleviate the evil, but I cannot; and I too suffer. This has been my life. I have found it worth living, and would gladly live it again if the chance were offered me.

—Bertrand Russell,
The Autobiography of Bertrand Russell: 1872–1914

4.c CHIEF SKILLS IN PARAGRAPHING

Paragraphing is an important technique to master because, through paragraphs, you control the design of your whole essay. As you write, you move back and forth between general ideas and specifics, taking pains to support your general idea with interesting specifics or rephrasing a general idea to show the limits of the details you include. Paragraphs show these moves. Each of the specific details or experiences you think of to support, prove, or illustrate the controlling idea of your essay will have a paragraph of its own and sometimes more. These paragraphs give you the space to fulfill the promise of your ideas and display their importance to your essay. You can improve your ability to write convincing paragraphs by sharpening the following skills:

Find the subdivisions of your essay Draw on your focused freewriting to crash out a rough draft of an essay or make an outline or do both. In this draft or outline, find what you consider the sentences that deliver your chief idea—the ones that hold general statements rather than specific or concrete details. Underline these important sentences with a straight line. Draw a wavy ~~~~ line under the most general ones. These sentences with wavy lines under them locate the subdivisions of your essay. Then on another sheet of paper, make note of the details that best illustrate or explain each of the generalizations. One of these sentences, or one you will write later, will introduce your essay and become the statement of your controlling idea. Later, as you rearrange and rewrite your essay, you will probably find yourself adding or changing the subdivisions, which, with their bundles of details, become the paragraphs that finally support your controlling idea.

Provide specific support Now that you are noticing how a generalization attracts details to it to form a paragraph, you may need more examples, more illustrations or explanations, or you may need to make the ones you have much more convincing. At first, paragraphs can be disappointingly sparse and skeletal. Here are some techniques for converting a frail start into solid support—strong, muscular writing on the bones of your general ideas.

1. Write out a brief account of an experience that demonstrates your idea.
2. Compare your idea with another idea or with a similar idea that occurred to you at another time or place or that occurred to other people.

3. Tell how your idea came about and what it might lead to.

4. Try to restate your idea to make it clearer, but be careful not to repeat what you have already said.

5. Comment on the statement of your idea. Tell how you feel and what you think about it.

6. Examine the statement of your controlling idea. Tell what you learned from your supportive data that would be generally useful to other people reading your essay.

TIPS FOR WRITERS—WRITING PARAGRAPHS

1. Write in full paragraphs.
2. Develop your ideas to show their implications.
3. Don't worry about writing too much. Most writers cut later.

Understand levels of generality

Our introduction to the concepts of "general" and "specific" in Chapter 2 stressed that these terms are relative. Look at page 23 to see how the word *fuel* includes *gasoline* and how the word *gasoline* includes *Exxon*.

Now let us consider sentences instead of words, since your paragraphs generalize and substantiate by means of the sentences you write. Is the following sentence general or specific?

The cost of goods is inflated today.

It would be impossible for anyone to answer that question without comparing that sentence with other sentences. Consider whether each sentence in the next paragraph about inflation is less or more specific than the sentence you've just read, and consider whether each of the following sentences is less or more specific than the sentence that follows it.

1. Mrs. Peggy Burdowski paid $1.69 for a can of tuna fish on November 9, 1985, at the A&P on School Street. Canned fish has tripled in cost in the United States in the past five years. The price of gold has risen to unprecedented heights on the European market. The cost of everything is inflated today. The United States has a 13 percent inflation rate. The United Kingdom has a 23 percent inflation rate. Real estate in Washington, D.C., has skyrocketed in cost. The house that former President Ford bought for $34,000 in 1957 was sold in 1977 for $137,000 and might sell for $300,000 today.

The levels of generality for these statements look like this:

1 The cost of everything is inflated today.
2 The United States has a 13 percent inflation rate.
2 The United Kingdom has a 23 percent inflation rate.
3 Real estate in Washington, D.C., has skyrocketed in cost.

3   Canned fish has tripled in cost in the United States in the past five years.
3   The price of gold has risen to unprecedented heights on the European market.
4   The house that former President Ford bought for $34,000 in 1957 was sold in 1977 for $137,000 and might sell for $300,000 today.
4   Mrs. Peggy Burdowski paid $1.69 for a can of tuna fish on November 9, 1985, at the A&P on School Street.

A paragraph about inflation may use these facts in the following order, starting with the most generalized observation:

2. The cost of goods is inflated today in most countries of the world. The United States has a 13 percent inflation rate, while the United Kingdom has a 23 percent inflation rate. The inflation rate in the United States is evident in everything from real estate to tuna fish. The house that former President Ford bought for $34,000 in 1957, for example, was sold in 1977 for $137,000 and might sell for $300,000 on today's market. And consumer reports in the local newspaper document that Mrs. Peggy Burdowski paid $1.69 for a can of tuna fish on November 9, 1985, at the A&P on School Street, as against 39 cents for a similar can seven years ago.

Diagram A   **most general**   **The cost of goods is inflated today.**

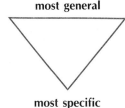

most specific   **Mrs. Peggy Burdowski paid $1.69 for a can of tuna fish on November 9, 1985, at the A&P on School Street. . . .**

Notice that the paragraph builds from a number 1 sentence, which contains the most general statement, to the number 2 sentences, whose information makes inflation a little more specific by telling where in the world it occurs and at what rate. The paragraph next offers information in number 3 sentences, by naming a few groups of commodities that have increased in cost and telling where the increases have occurred. The paragraph concludes with some force at the number 4 level, the most specific level, by naming real people and telling what they must pay for specific items at specific times.

But suppose the paragraph were in reverse order:

3. Mrs. Peggy Burdowski paid $1.69 for a can of tuna fish on November 9, 1985, at the A&P on School Street, as against 39 cents for a similar can seven years ago. The house that former President Ford bought for $34,000 in 1957 was sold in 1977 for $137,000 and may bring $300,000 on today's market. But the United States isn't alone in buffeting a skyrocketing inflation rate. Japan has a 96 percent inflation rate, and Britons are reeling under a 23 percent inflation rate. The evidence is all around us that the cost of goods is inflated today in most countries of the world.

Diagram B   most specific

Mrs. Peggy Burdowski paid $1.69 for a can of tuna fish on November 9, 1985, at the A&P on School Street. . . .

most general   The cost of goods is inflated today.

Whether we work deductively (as in paragraph 2, which starts with the generalization) or inductively (as in paragraph 3, which starts with the specific examples and leads to the generalization), the order moves clearly and purposefully through the levels of generality. (See more on deductive and inductive reasoning in Chapter 5, pp. 97–99.)

Write a sentence that tells the general topic of your paragraph

In expository writing, topic sentences would become an outline of your essay if you were to read them one after the other. They present the major subdivisions of your controlling idea and guide you in writing paragraphs full of details that suit your purpose and plan. Since a topic sentence expresses the generalized idea of your paragraph, it helps you decide which details to include as support. A topic sentence also helps you to screen out details that do not support the generalization and to eliminate them. Think for a moment that your paragraph is a miniature essay. Then your topic sentence is as much a key to the paragraph as the controlling idea is a key to the essay. Learning to arrange generalizations and specifics in a paragraph is part of the business of arranging ideas in the whole essay.

The topic sentence in each of the following paragraphs is italicized:

> *I may have been the best fighter, but I was also the poorest.* I owned one T-shirt, two pairs of pants, several pairs of shoes with holes in them. My jackets were torn and patched, and hardly a day went by when my pants didn't split somewhere. And although I had won nearly all my fights, and was on the verge of turning professional, I had never been able to afford a first-class mouthpiece to protect my teeth. I had to wait until the other fighters finished so I could borrow their headgear, or their trunks or bandages. I wanted my own training gloves, my own gear.
>
> —Muhammad Ali, *The Greatest*

In this paragraph, Muhammad Ali proves the generalized statement that, despite his ability as a fighter, he was very poor. He supplies details about his success along with specific examples of his limited wardrobe and the kind of equipment that he couldn't afford to own.

> *Remarkable as it may seem, Wednesday night, while the whole city crashed and roared into ruin, was a quiet night.* There were no crowds. There was no shouting and yelling. There was no hysteria, no disorder. I passed Wednesday night in the path of the advancing flames, and in all those terrible hours I saw not one woman who wept, not one man who was excited, not one person who was in the slightest degree panic-stricken.
>
> —Jack London, ''The Story of an Eyewitness''

Every sentence in London's paragraph supports the generalization expressed by the topic sentence—that, remarkably, the Wednesday night of the 1906 San Francisco earthquake was "a quiet night."

But as you develop flexibility and control, you may find that starting every paragraph with a topic sentence is too mechanical. You may want to give more than one paragraph to an idea and its development. The same topic sentence can govern two or three paragraphs to come.

Exercise 2 In the following paragraphs, practice moving between general statements and specific details.

1. The following sentences describe Harry Truman in 1940, when he ran for reelection to the Senate. What's missing is an opening general statement describing Truman's condition at that time. Read the details and provide a suitable general statement to fill in the blank.

_____ . His mother was eighty-eight years old, and they were threatening to foreclose the mortgage on her farm, which later, as you'll see, did happen. But Harry couldn't give her any financial help. Hell, at the beginning of the campaign he couldn't even afford stamps to write to people, old friends, asking for money. Later, he did manage to borrow $1,000 from a St. Louis contractor, which was repaid after the Democratic primary.

—Merle Miller, *Plain Speaking*

2. The next two paragraphs about the Sun Myung Moon sect offer opposing points of view. Supply an opening general statement for each paragraph.

_____ . Some parents have hired professional "deprogrammers" to kidnap their children and free them from Moon's spell. Some have sued the Church for holding the youths against their will, a charge difficult and humiliating to prove when the kids swear they prefer Moon's Family to their own.

_____ . Some feel it may be better than drugs or drifting aimlessly around the country. Others look with favor upon it as a Christian youth movement, without understanding exactly what the members do or believe.

—*Psychology Today,* January 1976, p. 36

3. Charles Darwin describes in detail an unforgettable event that he experienced during his South American expedition. Write a general statement that explains the entire passage.

_____ . I happened to be on shore, and was lying down in the wood to rest myself. It came on suddenly, and lasted two minutes, but the time appeared much longer. The rocking of the ground was very sensible. The undulations appeared to my companion and myself to come from due east, whilst others thought they proceeded from southwest: this shows how difficult it sometimes is to perceive the direction of the vibrations. There was no difficulty in standing upright, but the motion made me almost giddy: it was something like the movement of a vessel in a little cross-ripple, or still more like that felt by a person skating over thin ice, which bends under the weight of his body.

—Charles Darwin, *Voyage of H.M.S. Beagle*

Exercise 3 Supply a paragraph of specifics for the following general statements.

1. Much is said about the pain of growing up in poverty, but not much about the pain of growing up rich.
   This is the opening statement of an impassioned letter to the editor of *Ms.* magazine. Even if you have never been ''rich,'' write five sentences, each one giving a specific reason why growing up rich involves pain.

2. From a very early age, perhaps the age of five or six, I knew that when I grew up I should be a writer.
   This sentence was written by George Orwell, a writer known for his astute social views of the 1930s and 1940s. Other famous people have also sensed the course of their lives from earliest childhood. Write a few sentences that concretely demonstrate how you know you are going to be a writer—or a dancer or a mechanic or a musician. Substitute any profession you choose for ''writer.''

3. My parents for as long as I have known them have been the most ideal couple I've ever seen.
   This sentence was written by Robert W. White. Write five sentences, each one giving a reason why you call your parents—or any other couple you know—an ''ideal'' couple.

4.d KNOW WHAT EACH PARAGRAPH DOES FOR THE WHOLE ESSAY

Paragraphs in short essays perform many functions. They can open your essay, close your essay, line up support for your controlling idea, develop ideas, provide transitions between ideas, and single out an important sentence or two for special emphasis.

In the middle: paragraphs of support What do paragraphs in the middle section of your essay do? They achieve the enormously important work of supporting your controlling idea by treating the rest of your ideas fully and reflectively. As you formulate your thinking about your topic and let your ideas roll forward, you'll discover ideas in your essay that you'd like to expand—by adding examples, reasons, causes, consequences—the life signs that your writing is authoritative and solid. Remember that readers want to find out something new, something they don't already know. The information your readers must have is generated in the paragraphs of support. And since the effectiveness of this central information finally determines whether or not your essay will persuade your readers, you may need to arrange each paragraph as rigorously as if it were a small, whole essay. Then each paragraph will satisfy the readers with its own valuable contribution to the larger essay. Strong paragraphs of support are critical: they make your essay unique; they increase your readers' interest and challenge any resistance they might have to your subject.

KINDS OF SUPPORT   Although an essay may develop along a single line of thinking (for example, you may devote an entire essay to comparing two things), more likely you will have a complex idea to develop. You can follow the complexity of your idea best—and control it best—by shifting from one line of thinking to another as the material requires. These different ways of thinking show up in the flow of your paragraphs. Your subject naturally sweeps you into the kinds of development that are most appropriate to it as you deepen your thinking—telling an anecdote, explaining or analyzing a process, formulating a definition, or whatever. In a first draft, no writer can be expected to think consciously about the kind of paragraph he or she is writing; but all writers sooner or later become aware of their method, especially as they reread their work and check each paragraph they've written against their plan for the whole essay, testing to see if the details they've arranged in paragraphs really support their controlling idea. So write your first draft freely. Let your intuition help you decide what to write next; later, shape up your paragraphs consciously and deliberately.

Here are some sample paragraphs that support generalizations in recognizable patterns. Notice that an expository paragraph grows out of the writer's need to support generalizations:

1. General statements followed by examples

> Soap operas are a consolation to the lonely and the frustrated. Their audience consists mainly of women, women of all ages who are at home pursuing the eternal routine of household chores, or those who do not have much to occupy them and sit there alone. As a matter of fact, the soap-opera addicts are mostly people who are alone, either for the day, until the husband and children come home, or forever. They turn on the television and are turned on themselves because here are the well-known voices that speak to them, not of cleaning the refrigerator or doing the ironing, although these will also be dealt with in well-spaced advertisements, but of the infinite situations, exciting adventures, romantic entanglements of TV fiction. The soap opera takes the viewer out of the drab, predictable, everyday world into a life of possibility.

All the examples in this paragraph support the generalization of the topic sentence, the first sentence in the paragraph. The need to support the generalization drives the writer to form a paragraph. The details explain who the lonely and frustrated are and how soap operas console them.

In the next paragraph, the general statement appears after a few sentences of introduction. It serves as the topic sentence of the paragraph and is followed by examples. The topic sentence is italicized.

> Most people have the popular misconception that all the bait you need for fishing is a rusty can of worms. They think that the lowly worm will lure anything from a one-pound flounder to a hundred-pound shark. This, however, is not the case. *There are many fish in the ocean that wouldn't give a worm a second glance.* The mighty cod, for example, will reject anything but large chunks of clam belly. Fluke prefer a thin strip of squid that's tapered at the end. Weakfish seem to gorge themselves on grass shrimps, and striped bass rarely reject live eels. Remember this the next time you go fishing so that you won't waste your day drowning worms.

The examples of "many fish . . . that wouldn't give a worm a second glance" are cod, fluke, weakfish, and striped bass. The details included in the examples testify to the writer's experience as a fisherman and his ability to prove his generalization.

2. Telling the story before you make the point

Why tell the story first? A vivid anecdote leading to a generalization attempts to persuade the reader subtly. This paragraph, from George Orwell's *Homage to Catalonia,* is such an episode from his description of the grim and ironic conditions during the Spanish Civil War. The topic sentence is italicized.

> Towards the end of March I got a poisoned hand that had to be lanced and put in a sling. I had to go into the hospital, but it was not worth sending me to Sietamo for such a petty injury, so I stayed in the so-called hospital at Monflorite, which was merely a casualty clearing station. I was there ten days, part of the time in bed. The *practicantes* (hospital assistants) stole practically every valuable object I possessed, including my camera and all my photographs. *At the front everyone stole, it was the inevitable effect of shortage, but the hospital people were always the worst.* Later, in the hospital at Barcelona, an American who had come to join the International Column on a ship that was torpedoed by an Italian submarine, told me how he was carried ashore wounded, and how, even as they lifted him into the ambulance, the stretcher-bearers pinched his wrist-watch.

Notice Orwell's final "chaser." The closing example of the wristwatch being stolen is a rather sophisticated maneuver. We suppose that most beginners would either start with the topic sentence or lead up to it and end with it. Orwell, who is one of the most effective prose writers in English, amuses us by giving us this detail as a sensational encore in support of the generalization that "at the front everyone stole . . . "

3. Details leading to a general statement

As you read the following paragraph of student writing, notice that the writer waits until the last sentence to reveal what the details in the paragraph mean.

> Every table and chair in the library was occupied with someone intently studying or frantically poring over books and articles. A feeling of concentration and tension came from every corner. Crowds clustered at the card catalogue, and the two Xerox machines were so overworked they were literally heating the space around them. It was exam time at the college.

4. Cause and effect

In the following paragraph, by William H. Whyte, the opening statement generalizes that a lack of interest among business executives in hiring liberal-arts majors leads to certain consequences.

> It is among undergraduates that the business bias against the liberal arts sets up the most far-reaching chain of consequences. When the upperclassman finds at first hand that the recruiters prefer [people] with the technical specialties, the word gets around the campus very quickly indeed. To the freshmen and sophomores who are pondering a choice of major, this is the real world talking. Why, then, the liberal arts? Sales work, they hear, is about the only slot they would qualify for if they took English or history or politics or such, and they have the strong feeling, not entirely erroneous, that the offer is made only because the recruiters can't interest the preferred ones in sales. So they listen politely when an occasional alumnus or speaker at a career-counseling meeting speaks glowingly of the liberal arts and the full man, the need for culture, and so on. Then they go sign up for something practical.

The consequence, or effect, stated in the final sentence is that students avoid majoring in the liberal arts and enroll instead in "practical" courses.

5. Exploring a condition for reasons why it exists

In this paragraph, from Sir Thomas More's *Utopia* (published in 1516), the visitor to Utopia gives reasons why men and women should examine each other naked before they marry. Note that More's most convincing reason is presented in the form of a comparison.

> In choosing their wives they use a method that would appear to us very absurd and ridiculous, but it is constantly observed among them, and is accounted perfectly consistent with wisdom. Before marriage some grave matron presents the bride naked, whether she is a virgin or a widow, to the bridegroom; and after that some grave man presents the bridegroom naked to the bride. We indeed both laughed at this, and condemned it as very indecent. But they, on the other hand, wondered at the folly of the men of any other nations, who, if they were

to buy a horse of a small value, are so cautious that they will see every part of him, and take off his saddle and all his other tackle, that there may be no secret ulcer hid under any of them; and that yet in the choice of a wife, on which depends the happiness or unhappiness of the rest of his life, a man should venture upon trust, and only see about a hand's breadth of the face, all the rest of the body being covered, under which there may lie hid what may be contagious, as well as loathsome. All men are not so wise as to choose a woman only for her good qualities; and even wise men consider the body as that which adds not a little to the mind: and it is certain there may be some such deformity covered with the clothes as may totally alienate a man from his wife when it is too late to part with her. If such a thing is discovered after marriage, a man has no remedy but patience. They therefore think it is reasonable that there should be good provision made against such mischievous frauds.

6. Defining

A paragraph of definition presents *your own* clear definition of a term as it suits the purpose of *your* essay. Don't simply quote a dictionary, though you may work a dictionary definition into a more personal form. Wayne Booth, in the following paragraph from "The Rhetorical Stance," defines the word *rhetoric* classically as "persuasion" and then brightens the definition by restating it in the colloquial language of a student.

> I suppose that the question of the role of rhetoric in the English course is meaningless if we think of rhetoric in either its broadest or its narrowest meaning. . . . But if we settle on the following, traditional, definition, some real questions are raised: "Rhetoric is the art of finding and employing the most effective means of persuasion on any subject, considered independently of intellectual mastery of that subject." As the students say, "Prof. X knows his stuff but he doesn't know how to put it across." If rhetoric is thought of as the art of "putting it across," considered as quite distinct from mastering an "it" in the first place, we are immediately landed in a bramble bush of controversy. Is there such an art? If so, what does it consist of? Does it have a content of its own? Can it be taught? Should it be taught? If it should, how do we go about it, head on or obliquely?

7. Likenesses and differences (comparison and contrast)

You often can explain something by showing, in a paragraph, how it is like or unlike something else. Both items usually have some element in common: remedies for illness, in the paragraph below about acupuncture; women in the life of Lyndon Johnson, in the paragraph about Lady Bird Johnson.

In comparing the mysteries of acupuncture with the mysteries of aspirin, Felix Mann hopes to justify the use of acupuncture, since the success of both is based on clinical observation rather than on medical theory. Notice that the generalization in the first sentence applies to both elements of the comparison.

Some doctors or patients may indeed wonder how one can practise a form of medicine where the theories on which that practise is based are possibly suspect. Just as a doctor will prescribe aspirin because he knows what are its effects in the body of a patient, so an acupuncturist will needle a certain acupuncture point because he knows what the consequent reaction of the body will be. It is of secondary importance to the doctor to know just why it is that aspirin has its specific effects, no matter how intellectually interesting such knowledge might be. At the time of writing little is understood of why the known effects of aspirin take place, yet aspirin, with its simple chemical formula, is the most commonly used drug in the world.

—Felix Mann, *Acupuncture: The Ancient Chinese Art of Healing*

The following contrast between Lady Bird Johnson and her mother-in-law begins in a methodical, point-by-point fashion, moving back and forth from Lady Bird to Rebekah, from Rebekah to Lady Bird on every point discussed. But midway, we understand that the point of the paragraph is to convey the character of Lady Bird. Lady Bird is the center, and the contrast with her mother-in-law serves to enhance her portrait.

To both mother and wife Lyndon Johnson would always ascribe a scarcely credible perfection. But it is evident that they were crucially different women. The mother's inordinate passion for her son had been employed to spur achievements which she herself had determined. The wife endeavored to sustain and better organize the energy which Rebekah had been instrumental in setting loose. Where Rebekah withdrew into a stony anger over her husband's spontaneity, Lady Bird gracefully hosted unexpected throngs, welcoming the political friends Lyndon perpetually invited to their house. Where the mother confided her severest disappointments to her son, Lady Bird complained to no one. Amid the most complicated intrigues and struggles of her husband's career she remained outwardly composed and reasonable. If his incessant demands and orders (he instructed her to avoid full skirts and low shoes; often picked out her clothes; depended on her not only to manage the house but to lay out his clothes in the morning, fill his pens and his lighter, put the correct pocket items in place, pay his bills—in short, to manage him) or his occasional abuse in front of company became too much for her to bear, she possessed, or soon developed, a strange ability to take psychic leave. "Bird," Johnson would call out at such moments, "are you with me?" And straight off, her accustomed alertness and competence reappeared. Without such devotion and forbearance, without a love steadily given and never withdrawn, the course of Lyndon Johnson's continuing ascent in the world of politics becomes inconceivable.

—Doris Kearns, *Lyndon Johnson and the American Dream*

You can develop a great range of subjects, both personal and public, by contrasting a situation with a corresponding one at an earlier point in history or by speculating on what changes might evolve by a future date. Here is a paragraph that contrasts the arrival of a relief pitcher on the baseball field today to such an arrival years ago. Notice that this contrast is not made point by point.

Instead, a description of the relief pitcher as he used to arrive is rendered in its entirety, and then a complete description of the modern relief pitcher arriving in a golf cart follows.

> When the bullpen gates open, just about everyone in the ball park peers across to watch the relief pitcher step out of the enclosure. He used to come to the pitcher's mound by foot, his warm-up jacket hung loosely off his pitching shoulder, walking with the slow stride of a man with a lot on his mind, and sometimes he had a word to say as he passed one of his outfielders, and you could see him look back up at the scoreboard to check what the situation was; he had a long way to go, and there was plenty of time to sit there and relish the awful responsibility facing this man. Nowadays, the pitcher travels from the bullpen in a mechanical conveyance (back in 1960 all the parks were supplied with electric golf carts shaped like baseball caps), and some of his dignity—the sense of being the lone warrior sent to patch things up—is obviously diminished by being driven to the mound in this monstrous toylike gadget, sitting next to the driver with his glove in his lap like a rather embarrassed guest being delivered up to a fancy-dress party.
>
> —George Plimpton, "Baseball Stories—The Lure of the Bullpen"

8. Classification

See Chapter 5 (pp. 86–87) for a full discussion of classification.

9. Analogy

The subject of your essay can be spotlighted unexpectedly by the use of analogy, a vivid comparison that springs from the writer's imagination. When you write an analogy, you draw an extended and specific comparison between what you wish to explain and something else that your reader is likely to consider a rather unexpected object of comparison. Analogy often carries the pleasure of luminous surprise, even shock, because your reader might never have hit on the one connection that has sprung from your imagination. (See Chapter 5, pp. 84–86, for more discussion of analogy.) Here, Peter Elbow, in *Writing without Teachers,* draws an analogy between writing without getting feedback from readers and being blind and deaf. Notice that the specifics of the analogy lead the readers finally to the generalized point at the end.

> Imagine you are blind and deaf. You want to speak better. But you are in perpetual darkness and silence. You send out words as best you can but no words come back. You get a few clues about your speaking: perhaps you asked for something and didn't get it; or you got the wrong thing. You know you did something wrong. What you aren't getting is the main thing that helps people speak better: direct feedback to your speech—a directly perceived sense of how different people react to the sounds you make. This is an image of what it is like when you try to improve your writing all by yourself. You simply don't know what your words make happen in readers. . . .

Another writer, James Thurber, in *The Years with Ross,* uses an analogy to show an odd similarity that struck him: that his editor went to work on a manuscript the way a skilled mechanic goes to work on a car. It is the emphasis on supportive detail that shapes this paragraph of vivid writing.

Having a manuscript under Ross's scrutiny was like putting your car in the hands of a skilled mechanic, not an automotive engineer with a bachelor of science degree, but a guy who knows what makes a motor go, and sputter, and wheeze, and sometimes come to a dead stop; a man with an ear for the faintest body squeak as well as the loudest engine rattle. When you first gazed, appalled, upon an uncorrected proof of one of your stories or articles, each margin had a thicket of queries and complaints—one writer got a hundred and forty-four on one profile. It was as though you beheld the works of your car spread all over the garage floor, and the job of getting the thing together again and making it work seemed impossible. Then you realized that Ross was trying to make your Model T or old Stutz Bearcat into a Cadillac or Rolls-Royce. He was at work with the tools of his unflagging perfectionism, and, after an exchange of growls or snarls, you set to work to join him in his enterprise.

Opening and closing paragraphs

An effective opening paragraph works in two ways at once: it attracts the attention of your reader, and it launches the main ideas of your essay without delay. But most important of all, it sets up expectations in the reader's mind. The closing paragraph then satisfies your reader's expectations, confirming that you have made the point your opening paragraph promised. Your essay is clearly finished, and your reader is not left hanging or abandoned.

A closing paragraph should keep the whole essay visibly before the reader. Perhaps some of the sets of paragraphs that follow will illustrate the merits of keeping the whole essay in mind as you write and rewrite the opening and closing. By adjusting your beginning and ending to each other and to what you have accomplished in between, your essay becomes more and more coherent and unified. Experienced writers return to reevaluate their openings and endings after they have written the body of their essay.

Opening: Health maintenance has become our national obsession. Logic suggests that in order to maintain health, we must prevent disease, and that this is best accomplished by eating balanced meals, exercising regularly—and seeing the doctor once a year for a check-up. This latter ritual, the annual physical, has been extensively promoted by physicians and enthusiastically accepted by patients as an effective means of maintaining health. But is it?

Closing: Perhaps future developments will allow us to be more optimistic. For the present, it must be concluded that the annual physical examination has proved to be little more than an elaborate and expensive ritual that has not fulfilled its promise.

—Richard Spark, M.D.,
"The Case Against Regular Physicals"

Opening: Being a black ''conservative'' is perhaps not considered as bizarre a being a transvestite, but it is certainly considered more strange than being a vegetarian or a bird watcher. Recently a network television program contacted me because they had an episode coming up that included a black conservative as one of the characters, and they wanted me to come down to the studio so that their writers and actors could observe such an exotic being in the flesh.

Closing: So being a black ''conservative'' is not quite as distinctive as it might seem.
                —Thomas Sowell, ''A Black Conservative's Dissent''

Opening: Every year at least half a million Americans marry someone who is a parent already. When people go into a second or subsequent marriage, they are full of great hopes of improving on the past. Unfortunately, these do not always turn out to be realistic—especially when children are involved.

Closing: While there are special tensions in stepfamilies, there are many advantages. Stepfamilies are often less claustrophobic than ordinary families. They offer more diverse ties to people outside the immediate family circle, which can be a great help to children as they make the transition to independent adulthood. Stepfamilies can be just as happy as other families, even happier. It just takes more work, and an acceptance of a hard fact of life—that while spouses are replaceable, parents are not.
                —Brenda Maddox, ''Neither Witch Nor Good Fairy''

TIPS FOR WRITERS—OPENINGS AND CLOSINGS

OPENINGS

Attracting Your Readers

The opening paragraph must catch your readers' attention and hold it for those first important moments while they're deciding whether to give your essay a chance or turn it down cold.
Here are a few ideas for opening paragraphs that demonstrate the range of possibilities:

1. Question a universally accepted truth. (Imagine anyone saying we don't need a physical examination once a year—see p. 60.)
2. Startle your reader with bizarre or alarming information. (Who isn't morbidly interested in the remembrances of someone pronounced dead who unexpectedly recovers?)

Life After Death?

The experience is a familiar one to many emergency-room medics. A patient who has been pronounced dead and unexpectedly re-

covers later describes what happened to him
during those moments—sometimes hours—
when his body exhibited no signs of life. According to one repeated account, the patient
feels himself rushing through a long, dark tun-
nel while noise rings in his ears. Suddenly, he
finds himself outside his own body, looking
down with curious detachment at a medical
team's efforts to resuscitate him. He hears
what is said, notes what is happening but cannot communicate with anyone. Soon, his attention is drawn to other presences in the
room—spirits of dead relatives or friends—
who communicate with him nonverbally.
Gradually, he is drawn to a vague "being of
light." This being invites him to evaluate his
life and shows him highlights of his past in
panoramic vision. The patient longs to stay
with the being of light but is reluctantly drawn
back into his physical body and recovers.

—*Newsweek,* July 12, 1976, p. 41

3. Use a strikingly fresh analogy in your opening sentence. (See the discussion
of analogy in Chapter 5, pp. 84–86.)

Discovering backpacking is a bit like leaving home for the
first time. There's a mixture of pain and new freedom, and
your family is not sure it approves. The comparison is im-
perfect, of course; the pain of the hike is only physical, and
from backpacking you always return. But there's a root
similarity. In wilderness, as in that first apartment, you find
independence that you didn't know was there.

—Michael Parfit,
"The Road Less Traveled"

4. Open with an anecdote or a brief narrative. In a few sentences, make it
vivid.

Twenty-one years ago, on September 30,
1955, a young American was killed while
driving a car. His name was Pablo Efran
Pizarrow of 218 East 95th Street, New
York City. He and three friends were on
their way home from a movie when a stranger ran to the car window, shouted "Are
you Demons or Dragons?" and then shot
Pizarrow through the head. The film that
the dead boy had just seen was *East of
Eden.* On the same day, at the very same
hour (5:45 P.M. Pacific time), at the intersection of Routes 466 and 41 near Paso
Robles, California, the driver of another
car, a silver Porsche Spyder, ended his
own life at 86 miles an hour in a crash that
almost severed his head from his body. The

driver was the star of *East of Eden*. His
name, James Dean.

—Derek Marlowe,
"Soliloquy on James Dean's Forty-Fifth Birthday"

5. Use a striking quotation (preferably by an authority) that points directly to your main idea. Here is a quotation from C. G. Jung that might well open an essay that attacks massive rock concerts:

Great conglomerations of people are always the breeding grounds of psychic epidemics.

—*Collected Works*

6. Refer to a common condition. (Almost everybody knows somebody who is in a second marriage and living with stepchildren.)

Keep the language of your opening paragraph direct and simple. Avoid a lot of words that don't move fast. If you have to write effectively anywhere in your essay, you have to do it right here, up front, where the life of your essay depends on it.

Launching Your Essay

In addition to attracting your readers' attention, your opening paragraph must launch your topic and send your essay specifically and immediately on its way.

1. Don't start too far back from your controlling idea. If it is "Boy Scout camps are a waste of time," say so. Don't go back to the founding of the Boy Scout movement in 1908 by Lord Baden-Powell, who was chief scout of the world.

2. In a short essay, don't write a general, abstract opening paragraph that fails to mention your specific subject area. If your subject is flying and you think your controlling idea will be "If you really want to, you can overcome your fear of flying," then don't open with a paragraph like the following one. No one could possibly tell what your subject is from this much too general opener:

Almost everybody has some deep and secret fear. Sometimes a fear so handicaps people that they spend a large share of their energy trying to go on with their lives normally in spite of that fear. It is not unusual to find people living lives of mounting personal and business difficulties because they never squarely and honestly try to locate the source of their fear and fight back.

3. Avoid a dull opening paragraph that repeats itself and says nothing new. The following paragraph, for example, contains three sentences, but all three say the same old thing:

People spend a lot of money on clothes because styles change every year. If designers didn't dress their models differently every season, you and I would save a pile. We are the losers, while the designers and manufacturers laugh all the way to the bank.

4. Avoid "old-reliable" beginnings like the dictionary definition ("Webster defines *fear* as . . .") and the familiar quotation. One beginning writer, for example, whose topic was fear of flying, turned President Franklin Roosevelt's much-quoted statement into an opening cliché:

> Franklin Roosevelt once said, "The only thing we have to fear is fear itself."

5. If writing openers is difficult for you, write them last or try a few and scrap most of them.

CLOSINGS

1. Write a final paragraph that logically fulfills the expectation set up in the opening paragraph.
2. Echo the tone and language of the opening paragraph in the closing paragraph. If you used a metaphor, go back to it. Pick up the thread of an analogy, or recapture in different words the tone of the assertion you made in your opener. See that the final paragraph relates in spirit to the opening paragraph.
3. Speculate freely about what your opening generalization implies for the future, or end with your own general evaluation of the points you have made.
4. Close with a convincing quotation, a clever anecdote, a twist of irony, or a humorous remark that directly illuminates your discussion.

In writing the closing paragraph of your essay there are certain things to avoid:

1. Avoid summarizing your main points in "1,2,3" fashion. Why bore a reader who has just been through the essay and needs no reminder of the outstanding points?
2. Avoid introducing something new in the closing. It would be pointless to conclude the essay on physical examinations (see p. 60) by suddenly stating your outrage about increased rates for Blue Cross/Blue Shield.
3. Avoid a sudden irrelevancy. In an essay on sanitation workers, don't conclude with a remark about the good work done by your local police department.
4. Avoid a sudden reversal.

> While all these facts warn us that annual physical examinations are unnecessary and may be dangerous, I advise you to keep going down to your doctor annually because there are always new and baffling diseases around.

5. Avoid a final apology.

> I know this argument is not too convincing, but it's the best an amateur like me can do.

6. Avoid a final complaint.

> This was a tough assignment and there wasn't much information to be found on it, nor do I know personally any sanitation workers who would let me interview them.
>
> **7.** Avoid a final, rash promise or impossible claim.
>
> In conclusion, I can swear that private garbage trucks will soon be rolling down the avenues in your neighborhood.

Exercise 4 Justify the paragraphing in your most recent essay. Why did you indent when you did? Would you change any of your decisions to indent? Why?

Exercise 5 Write paragraphs that develop the word *student* in the following ways.

1. Define *student*.
2. Compare a student with a nonstudent (or a poor student with a ''grind'').
3. Classify types of students.
4. Tell what conditions support a good student.
5. Tell what the special consequences of being a good student are.

Exercise 6 Write a paragraph of the kind indicated for each of the following topic sentences.

1. Dominant impression—general statement and details (see p. 77):
   As soon as she stepped into the room, you knew she had plenty of money to spend.
   Anyone could tell she had just come from the hairdresser's.
   Anyone could see he had just broken up with his girl friend.
2. Cause and effect:
   Several reasons were offered for changing the October camping rules.
   Several things happened after I switched my major from _____ to _____ .
   Several changes led Professor _____ to give up teaching.
3. Classification:
   In my Utopia, there would be three kinds of work.
   In my Utopia, citizens would move from place to place in two ways.
   Marriages in my Utopia would be preceded by several kinds of trial arrangements.
4. Definition:
   Before I go any further, I should offer my definition of *writer*.
   Let me first establish what I mean by *retirement*.
   I should say what I have in mind by the term *hard work*.

Exercise 7 Develop two paragraphs for each of the following topic sentences. Do not use the same method of development for both paragraphs. For example, one paragraph may show causes or results and the second, a comparison. One may build on details and the second, on reasons. One may offer a single illustrative anecdote and the second, many smaller details.

1. Sitting in outdoor cafés is an entertaining pastime.

2. Some comedians tell you the truth about yourself.

3. What constitutes ''pornography'' is always open to disagreement.

4. My favorite spot in the whole world is _____ .

5. Children's after-supper games have a distinctive quality.

6. He did not fit the stereotype of someone with a falcon tattooed on his arm.

7. She was certainly not a typical dental hygienist.

Exercise 8 Choose five of the following sentences. Use each sentence as the opening sentence of a paragraph. Write the next four or five sentences to support what you decide to be the primary idea contained in the opening sentence.

1. It was a marriage that was headed for the rocks.

2. I left school because I needed time to think.

3. I went to the woods because I wished to live deliberately.

4. Although I have forgotten most of what I learned about playing the piano, I do remember how to play ''Autumn Leaves.''

5. Whenever I visit my Aunt Sara, she piles me up with her old costume jewelry.

6. Whenever I see Jim, I think of the good times we used to have at the beach.

7. Ever since I was a child, I've been terrified of escalators.

8. Although my father suffered through wars and revolutions, through the loss of family and friends, he has a zest for life.

9. It was a face that only a mother could love.

10. Joan married Jim because he was faithful.

Exercise 9 Describe the organization of the following paragraphs. Locate the topic sentence, and comment on the kinds of support in each paragraph.

1. Marriages were the fabric of international as well as internoble relations, the primary source of territory, sovereignty, and alliance, and the major business of medieval diplomacy. The relations of countries and rulers depended not at all on common borders of natural interest but on dynastic connections and fantastic cousinships which could make a prince of Hungary heir to the throne of Naples and an English prince claimant to Castile. At every point of the loom sovereigns were thrusting in their shuttles, carrying the strand of a son or a daughter, and these, whizzing back and forth, wove the artificial fabric that created as many

conflicting claims and hostilities as it did bonds. Valois of France, Plantagenets of England, Luxemburgs of Bohemia, Wittelsbachs of Bavaria, Hapsburgs of Austria, Visconti of Milan, the house of Navarre, Castile, and Aragon, Dukes of Brittany, Counts of Flanders, Hainault, and Savoy were all entwined in a criss-crossing network, in the making of which two things were never considered: the sentiments of the parties to the marriage, and the interest of the populations involved.

—Barbara W. Tuchman, *A Distant Mirror*

2. The inner spirit of running is also different from that of most other sports. It can be as competitive or noncompetitive as you choose to make it. In touch football, there's no convenient way not to try hard. In tennis, you've got to try to put the ball out of your opponent's reach. Golfers become so immersed in the game that they tie themselves into tense, tangled knots even during a friendly round. Runners, on the other hand, can run as gently or as hard as they want to. With a stopwatch you can try to run a course faster than you've ever done it before. You can attempt to run your friends into the ground, or you can treat a run as if it were nothing more than a romp through the countryside, bouncing along only hard enough to set the juices to bubbling gently. Even in a race there's no need to run at full throttle if you don't want to. You'll get a good workout even if you run at less-than-maximum speed.

—James F. Fixx, *The Complete Book of Running*

3. When I first started running I considered hills my enemy. They were hard to run on, made me slow down and shorten my stride, and left me winded. But it finally occurred to me that if hills were hard to run on, they might be doing me some good. And so they were. Running uphill strengthens the quadriceps, increases cardiorespiratory capacity and makes it easier to run uphill next time. You can't, of course, run uphill as fast as you can downhill; that's simply one of the things runners learn to accept.

—James F. Fixx, *The Complete Book of Running*

4. From the beginning, he took nicknames. In Oak Park, Illinois, only his parents called him Ernest; he hated the name. He never wanted to be just himself; he could have fun with a nickname, use it for cover, wear it like a mask. Real names limit you, freeze you; he wanted to keep moving. As a boy, on Walloon Lake in the forests of Michigan, his favorite sister called him "oinbones." When he was a young writer, prowling the Left Bank in Paris, his first wife called him "Tatie." To the fishermen who knew him in Key West during the Thirties, he was "Hem." In the Second World War, when he ranged the bloody Hurtgen Forest, the GIs dubbed him "The Kraut Hunter." And in the last decades of his career, as the father of a lean, gutsy prose style which had shaped a generation, he was "Papa." No other American author ever approached his worldwide popularity. Public adulation built him, nurtured him and eventually helped to destroy him.

—William F. Nolan, *Last Days of the Lion*

5. Because of the impossible complexity of our society, price, wage and rent controls cannot be universally, fairly and intelligently administered. As a result, rising commodity prices, taxes, and the cost of government regulation will squeeze some manufacturers to the point where they will stop making many mass-market products. The inevitable result of price controls is shortages. Milton Friedman has said, "Economists may not know how to stop inflation, but they know how to cause shortages. Simply impose price controls." This will lead to black markets and further breakdown in the respect for law and order on the part of middle class Americans. Today we don't have the patriotic fervor of World War II to ensure our voluntary compliance with the laws against illegal "Black Markets," as this is a period of great cynicism and deteriorating respect for law.
—Howard J. Ruff, *How to Prosper During the Coming Bad Years*

5 | Reach for the Whole Essay: Exposition and Argument

"Just tell the press the Ambassador feels it would be inappropriate to comment until he's had time to study the complete text."

Reaching for a whole essay eventually involves arranging its parts. After you have crashed through a whole essay, you will become involved in the careful examination of paragraphs because you need space and form in which to develop your ideas. In Chapter 4, we emphasize that writers develop paragraphs to accommodate the need to support their generalizations. The paragraphs of an essay supply the structure for that support. Freewriting frees you from a concern with structure; you don't need to think about paragraphs—examples, anecdotes, details, and explanations may run alongside your generalizations in no particular order. You put your thoughts down as they occur to you. In freewriting, the important impulse is to keep writing. In an essay, you have a new need: to be orderly, to plan. You build paragraphs to verify your assertions. Every paragraph becomes a showcase of support.

Sometimes writers start with the generalization and then write out the support they have been storing up to justify it. On other occasions, a writer begins by parceling out the details of support, planning for the reader to be gradually, even unthinkingly, led to the generalization, which the writer withholds until the end. This spirit of thought, this moving from support to generalization or from generalization to support, underlies all writing. But writing that explains a complex idea or argues a difficult position—such as the writing you are required to do in college—justifies its assertions with the utmost care and exactness.

We've seen that one way to organize our thinking is to tell our experiences as stories. But our thoughts do not always have to follow the orderly progression of events as they occur in time. There are other ways, ways that depend more heavily on selection. We can observe our experiences and then infer something that is generally true about these experiences. We must then select only the most vivid and telling of them to persuade our readers that our generalized inference is justified. Writers treat their readers as a lawyer treats a jury. The jury must agree that, yes, these experiences, these data, necessarily lead to these conclusions.

5.a EXPOSITION

Not all writing hammers out a tough argument, but most writing attempts to convince. All writers want to make their point convincing to the reader, even gently, or why bother to write at all? Writing that states its controlling idea and calmly tries to convince the reader with clear support or explanation is called *expository* writing, or *exposition*.

Description can be an aid in expository writing. It may have a hidden agenda, since a writer's goal might well be ''I want my reader to see this the way I have seen it, and I therefore choose the details that will restrict the reader's vision to my view. I want the reader to understand clearly what I am trying to say.''

Describing   One of the reasons people delight in coming together is to share experiences. Yet we don't all possess the same ability to tell another person precisely what we've been through. Some people can describe a place so that it springs to life as they speak—what it looked like, what the weather was, how the light struck, how the air smelled, who was there, what they did, what the mood of the place was—while others simply say, "It was beautiful" or "I had a great time" and leave it at that.

Describing is a skill that engages us in the rigorous use of details. It requires that we observe what we see closely and intelligently. When we look at a small area of beach, for example, we make a number of separate observations about the sand and what we see there:

rough sand	a container for suntan lotion
pebbles	clumps of feathers
dried seaweed	the rusted hook of a can opener
smooth pieces of glass	a Kodak film wrapper
pale, smooth driftwood	shells

But the longer we look, the less satisfied we are with general observations. We soon discover that we need appropriate words to express the distinctions we begin to notice. Not all dried seaweed looks the same. We may learn the name of the particular vegetation we are looking at by hearing other people refer to it by name. We may ask someone, or we may consult a book that shows the difference between sea lettuce and sea moss. If we observe shells with enough interest and perception, we may see the rolling curves of a channeled whelk, the fan of a bay scallop, and the tiny mottled form of a periwinkle before we know the names of these shells.

The part of an essay or a paragraph that is richest in details is usually description. Writers may undertake whole essays of description to make a point, although more likely a descriptive passage is part of a narrative or an explanation.

In the essay that follows, the writer engages the reader in her experiences of being the first-born as she remembers them. To her, all the experiences of her early years, all the events of her childhood, centered on the order of birth.

Notice that the technique she employs to present her information—her exposition—reinforces the movement between generalized statements and, in this case, the exuberant recounting of specific events. The authenticity of these very personal details gives the essay richness and accuracy. We *trust* writers who use details well because details verify that they know what they are talking about. The writers have been through the experience and remember the fine points. They are authorities. They draw sensible inferences from the details they have observed. Read the essay, and then read the statement of the controlling idea that follows.

LAMENTS OF A FIRST–BORN

Lucky! That is what some people say when they hear I am the eldest of four children in my family. "How wonderful it must be to get all the privileges and not be hassled by older brothers and sisters!" If only they knew how willing I would be to slip down a notch or two in my family's birth order. Being the eldest offers only token benefits;

the truth is that the eldest's early life is often far more restricted than the comparable teen-age years of the younger siblings. Anyone who believes otherwise is one of many duped by a widespread myth.

The flip side of that myth is my feeling that I'm missing something by not having an older brother or sister to guide me. I always believed that the first-born should be patient and level headed; I never understood why I, of all people, was chosen to fill the first slot, impatient, quick-tempered person that I am. Also, I have never felt that I had the ability to be a good role model for my sister and brothers to follow. Birth order, of course, is unalterable, but sometimes contending with my fate wears me thin.

Since my mother is the second-born of three children, she does not know what it is like to be the eldest. My mother's older brother did what many first-born Italian sons did—he got away with murder! He treated my mother as though she were a lower form of life. He let her do all the household chores without lending a hand and tormented her with his constant teasing. My mother, then, did not grow up very sympathetic to the plight of the first-born. Her brother was not unhappy: he lived like a king! So I didn't exactly start out with full support from Mom.

Then my sister, Janine, came along, and that was the beginning of my experiences as the big sister, the first-born, the guinea pig. That is what I felt like: an experimental subject used to test how well old-fashioned discipline, standards, and expectations work on a child of the seventies. But in this case, the guinea pig was not a passive subject. During my teen-age years, I had, in effect, to break in my mother. I love her, but often she was unaware that I was *me*, living in the world of *today*. The realities of her adolescence had little to do with the realities of mine, and there were many tense moments between us because she would not realize this. Of course I created some of our problems, but I believe that I also gained some ''rights'' by standing firm. Car privileges, later curfews, even the company I kept—these were all bitter standoffs fought over the course of my teen-age years.

By the time Janine was growing up, the groundwork had already been laid; the same restrictions were not in effect for her or for my brothers. I had dug the trenches. I spilled the blood in battle. Now they smile and wave to each other in the victory parade. This is not to say that the younger children are allowed to do as they please. But they have more space than I did at their ages. My brothers, Raymond, fifteen, and Michael, thirteen, were riding their bicycles all over the neighborhood at an age when I was not allowed to ride to the schoolyard on the next block. My brothers seem to visit their friends' homes more often than I ever did, and they are allowed to pop over to see friends my mother has never met without a barrage of questions: they have escaped the hot interrogation light that nearly evaporated my last ounce of patience.

My sister and brothers were also allowed to stay outside later than I was and watch TV at hours unknown to me at their ages. I remember well those Sunday nights during my early-grammar-school years when Mom would rush me upstairs to get my pajamas on before the Walt Disney hour at 7:30. That was my *late* night! When Janine, Ray, and Mike were going through those same years, they were allowed to stay up until 9:00 or 10:00 on weeknights for ''something special.'' (Less special than Disney!) And now they stay up even later.

Of course I realize that because we live in a male-dominated society, part of the reason my *brothers* had more freedom sooner than I did is because they are of the "stronger, smarter sex." It is amazing that these superior creatures have tried to take advantage of their privileges many times, have come home from their games bruised and crying, have had their shiny bicycles stolen from under their noses, and have squandered their money on toys and record albums used incessantly for a week and then discarded. Nevertheless, society still favors the males, and my brothers benefit from the prevailing sexism.

However, my sister, Janine, who is nineteen now, has also been living in a more open teen-age world than I knew. Like my brothers, she is not questioned as much as I was. The later curfews I managed to wrench out of my mother are assigned to her automatically. Even the "pleasure" of going to a bar under-age, which I never knew, was once granted to my sister. Mom was not thrilled about it, I will admit, and she told Janine that she would probably not be allowed in, but she let her go. I was very gracious about it; I gave her a few of my ID's and wished her luck. But she did not get in. And in a brief flash of vengeful satisfaction, I was glad she had failed. I had to wait. So would she. She did not deserve special treatment. But the point is that our reasons for not getting into a bar under-age were different: I was stopped by my mother; she was stopped by a bouncer.

While my sister may not *look* older than she is, her intelligence and common sense place her far beyond her years. She has always excelled in school and is talented in sports and music. I remember reading in my psychology textbook that research indicated first-born children are more intelligent and capable than their younger siblings. I find this highly amusing. Janine has always been brighter than me; I cannot help but think that somehow all the brains in the family trickled down to my sister and that I missed out on yet another "first-born advantage."

Getting responsibility and blame is what I do not miss out on. When my mother is out, I'm in charge of my two brothers, who have never considered me their superior in any way. Though well aware that my mother is following the natural course by putting me in charge, I am sure that they have never accepted me as any kind of authority figure. Bedtime deadlines become a joke once Mom is gone, and even when the boys finally do go upstairs, the routine of getting ready for bed becomes a mini-Olympics of pillow fights, wrestling matches, and trampoline competitions on the mattresses. Inevitably, Michael gets hurt in these sporting events. My mother and I have always warned him of this consequence. Many times in the past, after the decisive blow has been struck, Michael has come crying to me, *me* the "dumb ugly sister" who told him not to knock around with his *macho* older brother in the first place.

All of this would not have bothered me so much had the little darlings received just punishment from my parents. But the worst they ever got was a lecture, nothing that ever prompted them to change their ways in the least. . . . Later on, *I* would be blamed for my brothers' poor behavior.

But the main reason I never appreciated being the eldest was that *I* wanted an older brother or sister to turn to in moments of confusion, anger, or ignorance—someone to learn from, to tell me what I could expect in my near future, to entertain me with stories of teen-age adventures. I wanted someone older to fill in the gap between my parents and myself, to give me the insight into today's world that my parents could never give me. I am twenty-one now and more aware than I had been of how to deal with people, how to form relationships; but I am still learning. And I remember those lonely times of years gone by, and I do my best to be there for my sister when she needs to talk about friends, school, romance, and other important parts of her life. We have always been close, Janine and I, and while we do not always agree, we completely trust each other. I try to be a friend to my brothers as well, but because we are so far apart in age, there's not much I can say or do to reach them. But if they ever need someone in the future, I hope they will turn to me.

Though I am not pleased to be the eldest, I can complain only so much. Even though my brothers usually don't listen to me, there are those rare golden moments when they not only listen but are considerate and thankful, letting me know that they do in fact love me and are proud of me. I think that all three appreciate my sacrifices, at least to some small extent; but meanwhile, the boys' bedroom antics bubble on, and my sister still gallivants about town . . . while I am still home "raising" Mom. Just when I think I've got it all figured out, my youngest brother, Michael, announces he would rather be the oldest than the youngest. But birth order, he explains, is an unalterable thing, and so he is trying to make the best of it.

—Denise Di Stephan

Statement of controlling idea: Being the eldest offers only token benefits; the truth is that the eldest's early life is often far more restricted than the comparable teen-age years of the younger siblings.

Notice how new paragraphs in the essay you have just read shift from one example that supports the main point to another such example. Each of the laments on the writer's agenda of complaints has its own collection of specific details and requires a new paragraph:

Since my mother is the second-born of three children, she does not know what it is like to be the eldest.

Then my sister, Janine, came along, and that was the beginning of my experiences as the big sister, the first-born, the guinea pig.

By the time Janine was growing up, the groundwork had already been laid; the same restrictions were not in effect for her or for my brothers.

Getting responsibility and blame is what I do not miss out on.

All of this would not have bothered me so much had the little darlings received just punishment from my parents.

But the main reason I never appreciated being the eldest was that *I* wanted an older brother or sister to turn to in moments of confusion, anger, or ignorance. . . .

Her mother's childhood; her sister, Janine; her brothers, Ray and Michael—each discussed in a separate paragraph—get the full and unhurried attention of the writer.

HOW TO ORDER EXAMPLES Choosing good examples is only half the skill involved in writing rich, detailed paragraphs and essays. You must then deliver them, not haphazardly, but in an order that smoothly links the purpose of the paper to the effect you want the reader to experience. In your expository essays, three principles can help you arrange your details in an effective order. They are order of time, order of space, and order leading to a climax.

1. Order of time

Narrations, descriptions of events, explanations of how to do something, and any other writing that is dependent on time are organized by time words and phrases like these:

First, . . .	Since my mother . . .
Second, . . .	Then my sister, Janine, came along . . .
After that, . . .	. . . Janine, who is nineteen now, . . .
Now, . . .	I am twenty-one now . . .
Next, . . .	
Later, . . .	
Then, . . .	
Finally, . . .	
The next evening, . . .	
The following day, . . .	

Use such time words to help you make transitions from one occurrence to the next. When you explain a process, it is essential to explain the steps in sequence. Notice how the time words in the following recipe organize the steps in the preparation procedure.

SKID ROAD STROGANOFF

4 servings

8 ounces uncooked noodles	2 teaspoons salt
1 beef bouillon cube	½ teaspoon paprika
1 garlic clove, minced	2 3-ounce cans mushrooms
⅓ cup onion, chopped	1 can condensed cream of
2 tablespoons cooking oil	chicken soup, undiluted
1 pound ground beef	1 cup commercial sour cream
2 tablespoons flour	chopped parsley

Start cooking those noodles, first dropping a bouillon cube into the noodle water. Brown the garlic, onion, and crumbled beef in the oil. Add the flour, salt, paprika, and mushrooms, stir, and let it cook five minutes while you light a cigarette and stare sullenly at the sink. Then add the soup and simmer it—in other words, cook on low flame under boiling point—ten minutes. Now stir in the sour cream—keeping the heat low, so it won't curdle—and let it all heat through. To serve it, pile the noodles on a platter, pile the Stroganoff mix on top of the noodles, and sprinkle chopped parsley around with a lavish hand.

—Peg Bracken, *The I Hate to Cook Book*

2. Order of space

When you write a description of a person, an object, or a scene, space can be your organizer: you describe a person from hair to sneakers, a museum building from front steps to rear parking lot, your bedroom from doorknob to the pile of books dumped under the window. You describe something as you see it from a particular vantage point. You capture the view from your classroom window by detailing first what is nearest and gradually extending your observations to the horizon or by beginning with what is on the horizon (mountains?) and moving inward toward the man selling pretzels on the steps of the Humanities Building. *You* determine the order because you must decide what you want your readers to "see" first. They can't read all your words at once, so they will follow the only possible order: the order of your sentences and the order of the details you choose.

Organize your descriptions with words like these:

Under . . .
Above . . .
To the left . . .
On the right . . .
Behind . . .
In front of . . .

In the following paragraph, the student, who writes fondly about getting dressed while standing on the heater in his dining room, uses space signals to mark off the little area that was warmed by the heater ("to the right," "behind," "on the left"):

> On winter mornings, the heater in our dining room gave a cold kid a warm welcome. It was an old-fashioned kind that was just a grate in the floor, topping off a tube coming from the furnace. You didn't have to fool with gadgets, knobs, and thermostats; you just stood on it and felt great. The kitchen door was *to the right* of the grate, and the light from that room let you see just enough to get your shoes on the right feet and shirt buttons in order. *Behind,* the warmed wall with its tiny dried drops of paint supported the dresser. *On the left* stood a small walnut desk and chair. By pulling the chair out in front of you, you would have a perfect three-sided dressing room. I think that just this feeling of being boxed in made you feel warmer. Today modern heating systems might be cleaner or safer or have some other glorious advantage. But for me they'll never replace that feeling as my cold toes stepped onto the warm squares of the heater back in our dining room.

3. Order leading to a climax

In any kind of writing, you sort out the data available to you and seize on details and explanations that best suit your purpose. Rarely are whole essays written to describe every aspect of a person or an object in its entirety. Such completeness may be useful in a travel brochure, which makes available to tourists complete information about every part of a country they may be touring. You might also expect, and rightfully, a complete description of an item you wish to buy from a mail-order catalog. But in essays, such ''molecular'' descriptions offer excessive and unnecessary detail. Too much irrelevant information distracts a reader, often permanently. If you are describing a place, for example, study your reaction to it. Zero in on a single dominant impression you are left with. State that impression in your controlling idea. Then present your details in order of increasing importance, saving as the final crowning detail the one that will clinch it for the reader. For example:

Dominant impression: Darkness
Controlling idea: My aunt's lonely life is reflected in her dark and gloomy living room.

Details in order of increasing importance:
  chairs and sofa are upholstered in dark gray
  walls are papered with maroon trellises and maroon roses
  ceiling needs paint—is spidery gray
  heavy maroon draperies are always drawn
  aunt rarely puts on lamp at night
  when she watches TV, she sits alone in the gloom

Climax: The relationship of the aunt's emotional life to her dark living room reaches a climax with the final detail that shows her sitting alone in the gloomy living room watching TV.

Or let us say you want to describe your uncle. Your purpose is to prove that he is the grouchiest member of your family. The details you choose must therefore work toward that purpose. You exclude those that don't. You leave out the generous birthday presents he gives and the nifty clothes he wears. But you include as examples of his grouchiness the times he fails to smile at family jokes, the way he expects your aunt to clean up after him, the irritation in his voice when he speaks to his eight-year-old son. You include the evening your father had his heart attack and your uncle complained about trivia all night. You clearly plan for the last example to be your clincher. Here's the brief essay:

Uncle David is the grouchiest member of our family. Although we have some pretty comical relatives, Dave never cracks his face, not even at Thanksgiving dinner when the rest of us are laughing so hard that it's difficult to eat. Not Dave. He never loses the rhythm of putting sweet potatoes and turkey into his sour face.

His son, Andrew, who is only eight, is often the target of his father's growling. Uncle David, who I suspect loves Andrew although all evidence points to the contrary, never lifts a finger to help the child or show him any affection. ''Get it your-self'' is the you-better-move-your-ass-without-bothering-your-old-man reply. Usually my Aunt Ada runs in to rescue Andrew, on the way wiping up around David if something has spilled and cleaning and serving without ever being thanked. My mother and father and I watch in perpetual disappointment.

I still find it hard to believe the stories my mother tells about Uncle David the night my father had his coronary. David raced over to take my mother to the hospital, and then whined all the way there about his broken air conditioner and how expensive it would be to have it repaired. Then he spent the night out in the corridor with my mother, grumbling constantly about the nurses drinking Coca-Cola in the intensive care unit while his brother was lying there dying. David means well, and I know we'd probably miss him if he forgot to show up at one of our family get-togethers. Fortunately, he is the only grouch we have.

Exercise 1 In the description exercises that follow, be vivid. Use color, shape, motion, smell, heat, cold, texture, mood. Use organizing words—*first, second, above, below,* and the like—wherever they can help clarify your description.

1. Describe a place that is dominated by one of the following impressions. Include the physical details of the place, but show clearly that your sense of the place is dominated by one impression. Save the best details for last.

   steamy   full of gadgets
   noisy   glassy
   full of books   crowded with trucks

2. Describe the contents of your closet, from left to right, then from top to bottom.

3. Go to your college cafeteria. Pick a person you see there and describe him or her from shoes up.

4. Describe a person who affects you in a particular way. Consider the following characteristics as possible themes to unify your description, or decide on your own. Save the best details for last.

   saintly   philosophical   paranoid
   sickly   cheap   "out-to-lunch"
   generous

5. Explain a process you know well: how to play a game (tennis, poker, hockey, and so on), how to make a favorite dish (lasagne, egg salad, onion soup), or how to do something (build a fire, develop film, record a TV show).

Defining An additional skill that relies on accurate use of details is *defining*. In expository writing, you may have to start by telling your reader what your terms mean. If you are explaining financial aid at your college, for example, you must tell your reader what you mean by financial aid: "Financial aid at my school is monetary assistance granted to a student. It may come as a scholarship or as income that the student earns by working at campus jobs." The essay may then take up any number of questions: Who is entitled to financial aid? How many credits must a student be carrying to qualify? What is the role of the federal government? How can middle-income parents be helped to educate their children? Where do students work? Is this program typical? But the meaning of financial aid must be clear if the reader is to understand your discussion in the way that you intend it.

It is useful to see definition as an outgrowth of description. When you describe, you are singling out one individual object from the class of objects to which it belongs. *A description is specific,* in the same way that narratives are specific. Suppose you are asked to describe a chair. Your response might be, "Okay, which chair? I have to choose a specific chair and describe it." A description provides specific details that tell about a particular item at a particular time in a particular place (for example, the dark red armchair near your bed; the old brown leather chair your dentist had before he replaced it with a cool green plastic one). Your description of a chair distinguishes it unmistakably from every other chair because you emphasize the details that set it apart from other chairs.

A definition is general. A definition of a chair has to include all the details shared by every object we can call *chair.* How can you write a clear definition? You will discover what an interesting and demanding assignment this is if you try to take a simple term and define it without looking in a dictionary. Is it enough to say, "A chair is something a person can sit on"? What about a bed? Can't a person sit on a bed? What about a stool? Doesn't a person sit on a stool?

A definition serves two functions: (1) it places the object in a class of objects that are like it, and (2) it tells how the object is different from other members of the same class. For example, when you look for the word *chair* in your dictionary, you may find, "a seat, especially for one person, usually having four legs for support and a rest for the back and often having rests for the arms" (*American College Dictionary,* p. 244). As definitions go, these details can't be rivaled for usefulness because they concisely separate *chairs* from all other *seats:* from *stools* (which have no back), *benches* (which are seats for more than one person), and *couches* (which are comfortable enough for reclining). How could a dictionary possibly offer *descriptions* of specific objects (for example, the dark red armchair near your bed)? Such a description would be useful only for the red chair near your bed and for no other chair. An artist usually renders a specific object in a painting or drawing. Writers, however, must be prepared to do either—define or describe—depending on their purpose.

Exercise 2 Define and describe each of the following words. Remember, your definitions must include details that apply to all garbage, all food, and so on. Your description must include details that apply to specific garbage (or specific food, or whatever) in a specific place at a specific time.

1. Define *garbage*.   Describe garbage.
2. Define *food*.   Describe food.
3. Define *soldier*.   Describe a soldier.
4. Define *police officer*.   Describe a police officer.
5. Define *bed*.   Describe your bed.

Exercise 3 Comment on this description of Pennsylvania:

> Pennsylvania means many things to different people. To one it means the glow of steel mills along the Monongahela at night or strip mines in Venango County or the milky water of the Clarion at Johnsonburg. To another it means the trout streams of Centre County, duck hunting at Pymatuning, a cabin on the upper Allegheny, maple trees at Myersdale in autumn, the long beach bordered by cottonwoods at Presque Isle, or the ski slopes at Ligonier when the snow lies deep upon the mountains. Or it means an eagle seen from Mt. Davis fighting its way through a thunderstorm, a deer starved and winter-killed in Elk County, acres of trillium along Thorn Creek, or the pink mountains of Bedford County when the wild azaleas bloom. For each of us there is a favorite picture or recollection. Mine takes me back a good many years.
>
> I was in Miss Murphy's class in the sixth grade when I first learned the etymological meaning of the word Pennsylvania. . . .
>
> —Edwin L. Peterson, *Penn's Woods West*

Comparing and contrasting

Showing likenesses and differences is second nature to us. It is the route our minds take to explain the choices we make. In conversation, we run through comparisons very casually. Who hasn't compared summer with winter, husbands with wives, dormitories with apartments, Republicans with Democrats? But exactly how does a writer go about the acts required to compare items in order to make a point in an essay?

CHOOSE COMPARABLE ITEMS

First, your choice of subjects must have enough in common to make a comparison possible. Comparing grapefruits with fur coats will drive you bananas. Contrasting the duties of the Supreme Court with the rules for playing hockey is far-fetched. You may, however, need to compare two things to help you decide issues that are important to you. Usually, these two things have a common base. For example, should you live at home or on your own? Should you take a three-week trip to Europe or live there for a year?

Look at the following list, which compares living at home with living on your own.

A **living at home**	*B* **living on your own**
don't have to pay bills, cook, clean, or do laundry	grow in responsibility and self-reliance
have a lot of free time	privacy
have a family to console, advise, and take care of you when sick	be able to use or abuse whatever luxuries you have
have certain luxuries like furniture, food, stereos, phone, cars, air conditioning, and heating	pay your own phone bills
	little time for social activities
limited use of electricity and phone	live in dirt
	eat an unhealthy diet

have to keep things clean   little or no furniture, stereo, cars, air
become too dependent   conditioning, or heating
little or nothing belongs to you

The writer concludes that living on your own is a lot less comfortable than living at home, yet it creates more responsibility and develops self-sufficiency. Notice that the controlling idea in the following essay of comparison states the writer's preference, although not every comparison will lead to a preference. Essays of comparison can merely record differences, to support a generalization about the most significant differences. An essay of comparison can proceed along one of two strategies:

SEE THE STRUCTURE OF YOUR COMPARISON

1. Compare A and B point by point.
2. Tell all about A; then tell all about B.

COMPARE A AND B POINT BY POINT

Living at home begins with the special advantage of having few responsibilities and much free time. If you are the first to watch the mailman drop the letters through the slot every morning, you are also the first to joyously toss all those electric, phone, or insurance bills onto the kitchen table like so much junk mail and be free to rummage through your latest video-cassette catalogs or the newest issue of *Soap Opera Digest*.

Living on your own, though, means opening all those bills and paying for them before the lights and phone are turned off, all of which makes getting a job a necessity, meaning less free time and maybe even fewer of your favorite magazine subscriptions.

Living at home also means having those home-cooked meals prepared for you after a long day of hanging out with friends or catching the latest *Star Trek* movie after classes.

Living on your own means cooking, or even burning, your own meals or perhaps eating out on a restricted budget, meaning alternate evenings at McDonald's and Burger King.

At home, you are often amazed how quickly things get done, like your clothes being washed and dried and folded before you even knew they were dirty.

Living on your own means waiting for the last possible moment to do anything, waiting until you are down to your last pair of underwear, then dragging a month's supply of clothes to the nearest laundromat, no less than ten blocks away, using too much bleach and too little detergent, running out of quarters, losing at least one sock, and at last dragging it all back home, only to be folded and rolled into various geometric shapes.

Living at home also means being able to find things where they're supposed to be found, always having the right size stereo and TV set, cars, chairs, air conditioners for the summer and heating for the winter, and a food supply that just always seems to be there. It also means that things are always dusted and germ free and that exterminators are invited only as a precaution.

Living on your own means finding large dust pockets in every corner and having few chairs, the softest being somewhat ripped. Living on your own means a small fan in summer and little or no heat in winter, a transistor radio, a childhood record player you once played Donald Duck songs on, a black-and-white TV set that gets only one channel, and a can of bug spray standing on top of the refrigerator.

Even at home, with all those luxuries surrounding you, you are still apt to get yelled at for various forms of abuse or overuse, such as spilling things on the carpeting or furniture, playing the stereo too loud or too long, leaving all the lights on when you leave the house or when you go from one room to the next, wrecking the car, making too many phone calls, having your friends over in the middle of the night, or eating too much or too little food. Abusing anything too much or too long brings a quick reminder that you wouldn't if you had to pay for anything.

On the other hand, if nothing else, living on your own means the freedom to spill or break, the freedom to leave on all the lights, to play your stereo all night, to be on the phone days at a time, to invite all the friends you want whenever you want.

Although living at home means someone always being there when you're in trouble or consoling you when you're down or taking care of you when you're sick or giving advice when you are confused, it also means someone always being there when you're not in trouble or sick or confused; there is always someone there whether you want them there or not. And again, if nothing else, living on one's own means having the privacy you never had, the privacy to study, to watch your favorite TV show, to talk to friends without your mother yelling at you to wash the dishes or your sister or brother playing the stereo too loud in the next, or maybe even the same, room.

Living at home also brings the danger of becoming too emotionally and financially dependent on others. You don't face up to certain responsibilities, such as paying rent, having to work to live, cleaning and cooking, or just becoming an active and self-reliant member of society.

Living on your own—when you are old enough to do so, of course—becomes an essential step both physically and emotionally toward accepting responsibility and learning how to function in the real world. So you must realize that living on your own is always an inevitable step you must be prepared to make. Certainly, you can start by learning a few skills and accepting a few responsibilities while still at home. You could get a part-time job and even share in paying some of the bills, or you can learn how to cook certain essential meals or do the laundry even when you are not down to that last pair of underwear. This would ease you into the disadvantages of living on your own and so make the task of cutting those "apron strings" a lot less difficult and a lot more satisfying.

TELL ALL ABOUT A; THEN TELL ALL ABOUT B

Living at home may mean few responsibilities and much free time, but it can never adequately prepare you for the responsibility and self-reliance needed to live on one's own and thus to function effectively in society.

Living at home can mean the exhilaration of waiting for the morning mail, knowing that anything like bills can be easily tossed aside while you search for the latest issues of *Car Stereo* or *Soap Opera Digest*.

More than not having to pay bills, living at home means the freedom to avoid other responsibilities, like cooking or buying food or having to wash, dry, fold, and even put away your own clothes. This not only means a lot more time to stay socially active, to be able to hang out with friends after classes or catch the latest *Star Trek* film, but it also means a better chance of staying healthy, of having just the right amount of nutrients in your food, of having dishes clean, tables dusted, rooms disinfected, and dogs and cats properly inoculated.

Living at home can also mean air-conditioned summers and heated winters and hot and cold running water. It may also mean the comfort of soft beds or couches, of having the latest TV or stereo systems.

Living at home means having someone to take care of you when you are ill, to console you when you are in trouble, or to give advice when you are confused. Think of the advantages of a live-in nurse, such as a mother, to read to you or take phone messages, or a live-in companion such as a brother or a sister, to remind you about your favorite rock show, which you may be missing because of homework, while your father goes out in the middle of the night to buy everyone ice cream.

On the other hand, living on your own means taking on all those responsibilities you avoid at home. It means dreading the morning mail because of all those bills and usually having to get a job to pay for them. This certainly means less free time, fewer magazine subscriptions, and a backlog of *Star Trek* films. But it also means the freedom to use or abuse all the things you pay for, such as the phone or the electricity or whatever furniture there might be, and not getting yelled at for it.

Living on your own means eating what you want when you want and not having to do your laundry until you are down to your last pair of underwear, although it may also mean having to drag a month's supply of clothes several blocks to the nearest laundromat, using too much bleach and too little detergent, running out of quarters, and then dragging it all back home again where you fold it all into various geometric shapes.

Living on your own also means doing your own cleaning or not doing it—the choice is yours. However, you may sometimes find yourself clawing your way out of huge dust pockets looking for the old broom your parents gave you as a going-away present. Living on your own also means a lot less furniture, the one soft chair in the house being somewhat ripped, one small fan in the summer, no or little heat in the winter, a childhood record player you once played Donald Duck songs on, a small black-and-white TV with one good channel, and that can of bug spray always on top of the refrigerator.

Living on your own—when you are old enough to do so, of course—becomes an essential step both physically and emotionally toward accepting responsibility and learning how to function in the real world. So you must realize that living on your own is always an inevitable step you must be prepared to make. Certainly, you can start by learning a few skills and accepting a few responsibilities while still at home. You could get a part-time job and even share in paying some of the bills, or you can learn how to cook certain essential meals or do the laundry even when you are not down to that last pair of underwear. This would ease you into the disadvantages of living on your own and so make the task of cutting those ''apron strings'' a lot less difficult and a lot more satisfying.

Exercise 4 Choose one of the following pairs of topics, and write two brief essays comparing them. Organize the first essay by telling all about topic A and then telling all about topic B. Organize the second essay by comparing A with B point for point. Begin both essays with the same controlling idea. In it, state your preference for one topic in the comparison and give a general reason why you hold that preference. Which essay do you consider more effective? Why?

A	B
1. Marriage	Living together
2. Strenuous exercise	Moderate exercise
3. The sciences	Liberal arts
4. My first impressions of _____	What I think of _____ now
5. My ambition five years ago	My ambition today
6. My belief in God when I was a child	My belief in God today
7. My relationship to my father as it used to be	My relationship to my father as it is now

WRITING AN ANALOGY Another interesting form of comparison is *analogy*. An analogy is an extended and unusual comparison between two items. It explains one thing by showing in vivid and unexpected detail how similar that thing is to another. The following paragraph presents an analogy between the reading tastes and the food tastes of children:

> . . . A group of professors of education . . . recently proposed that the list of "required reading" in schools should be based upon a study which they have just sponsored on the tastes of school children. . . . Would any pediatrician base the diet which he prescribed for the young submitted to his care simply on an effort to determine what eatables they remembered with greatest pleasure? If he knew that the vote would run heavily in favor of chocolate sodas, orange pop, hot dogs and bubble gum, would he conclude that these should obviously constitute the fundamental elements in a "modern" child's menu?
>
> —Joseph Wood Krutch

Krutch goes on from this analogy to argue *against* letting children's tastes determine what they read, just as anyone with common sense would argue against letting children's tastes for junk food determine what they eat.

Analogies are often exciting to read because the unexpected and imaginative comparison of two things we had not thought similar gives us a surprising insight. Below is an exercise in analogy in which a student writer compares Thanksgiving dinner at home to a free-for-all.

THANKSGIVING DINNER IS LIKE A FREE-FOR-ALL

On Thursday night, all my relatives gathered at my house for our annual rhubarb known as Thanksgiving. The rumble was over a cooked bird and all of its usual companions. The action began when my uncle plunged his fork into the midsection of the sweet potatoes. After that, everyone was going at it. A quick right and my little cousin started gnawing away at the drumstick. I decided to get in the action and threw a wild left. It connected against the lip of a glass from which a bloodlike substance emerged and bathed the tablecloth. My mother nursed the injury with a sponge. A few flurries were thrown, but more than not it was just talk. I was proclaimed champion when all the gladiators defaulted because of injuries, the most common ones being nausea and upset stomach. When cleanup time came, a few cousins engaged in their own donnybrook. They put their grasping hands all over each other's plates and silverware. The outburst was quickly resolved by allowing each opponent to place two items in the dishwasher. When it was time to depart, the combatants scurried away as if someone had screamed ''Fire!'' in the arena.

The success of the paragraph lies with the appropriateness of the comparison because there are so many elements of Thanksgiving dinner that are like a free-for-all:

Getting at the food requires fighting skills.

The excitement and energy of the struggle to eat cause minor injuries and spills among the participants.

Cleaning up causes fresh outbursts and flare-ups.

But the success of the paragraph also comes from the vigor of the language. The specific words the writer chooses ring of the fight and tighten the analogy:

rhubarb	nursed the injury
rumble	champion
midsection	donnybrook
a quick right	outburst
a wild left	combatants
connected against the lip	arena

Before you write an analogy, think back to the invention stage, and outline in writing the similarities between your two items. Emphasize the similarities and omit differences. Be plain and systematic as you cite the similarities. Strengthen your language with the kinds of words pertinent to your comparison.

If any analogy forms your entire essay, you will offer a statement that says ''X is very much like Y—Thanksgiving dinner is like a free-for-all''; but you can use analogy as an element in a longer piece of expository writing when you want to argue vividly for or against an issue and also when you want to explain effectively or entertain. Many writers use an analogy to begin their essays because it is a fresh, unexpected attention getter that attracts readers. Consider the following opening paragraph:

> Sneakers get walked all over and never complain. They get tied too tight, or they don't get tied at all. Sometimes they're knotted together, while at others they're strewn carelessly about, denied any acknowledgment that they are a pair. To make matters worse, sneakers are disposable—whenever you've gotten to the point where you can't stand the sight of them any longer, you can buy new ones. It's as simple as that. They can be broken in so that every inch of your foot rests comfortably, but then it's never the same as when they were fresh and new and gripped you with a sturdy assurance. They are to be used until they are no longer considered useful; no amount of attachment will prevent you from buying that brand new pair of vanilla-ice-cream-white sneakers. But then again, when one tires of something these days, chances are you will leave it behind without stopping to appreciate what you've got and look for something—or more importantly, someone—to replace it.

Notice that the writer reaches the subject of his essay—the dangers of a relationship that is taken for granted—as he springs open the analogy in the last line, with the phrase "or more importantly, someone."

CLASSIFYING   Another offshoot of comparing is *classifying*. You can classify persons, things, or experiences according to principles of division you establish. When you write an essay of classification, you can feel the comparing process at work underneath all your decisions. Suppose that for a study of the media, you wanted to classify TV shows. What principles of division might you try? One principle might be the *type* of show. You ask, "What kinds of shows are on TV?" On this principle, you propose five types: talk shows, situation comedies, adventure series, sporting events, and specials.

Your controlling idea might say:

> TV shows can be classified according to the kinds of entertainment they offer.

Another principle might be *audience*. You ask, "Who watches the shows?" On this principle, you propose three types of shows: shows for children, shows for general audiences, and shows of special interest for adults.

Your controlling idea might say:

> TV shows can be grouped according to the kinds of audience they attract.

Classification is neat and orderly. It can be used to develop an entire essay, with each division a paragraph, or it can simply help you with your thinking. As you classify, be careful of two things:

1. Keep your principles of division logical.

   For example, if you divide TV into daytime, prime-time, and situation comedies, your classification will not be logical because the subgroups overlap. There are situation comedies during the day and during prime time.

2. Do not omit an important subgroup.

   If you divide TV into daytime and prime time, your classification will be incomplete. A reader would immediately say, ''What about late-night TV?''

Exercise 5 Practice classifying by completing the following exercises.

1. Choose five of the headings from the list below and classify each one into as many subgroups as you want, according to at least two principles of division.

Example:	**phone calls: duration**	**phone calls: callers**
	quick calls	nuisance callers
	conversational calls	occasional callers
	interminable calls	regular callers

2. Write a whole essay of classification. Break down one of the items from the list below into as many subgroups as you need. Begin your essay with a statement of your controlling idea that states your classification. Use as many paragraphs as your classification scheme requires.

   Example: Friends

   Controlling idea: When you live at the beach, you have all-year-round friends and fair-weather friends, who begin to show up around Memorial Day.

   Supporting paragraph 1:   All-year-round friends

   Supporting paragraph 2:   Fair-weather friends

   Conclusion: State your attitude toward the two types of friends, or the way you deal with the problem, or your reasons for putting up with it.

   List:

college teachers	disc jockeys	weddings
college students	musical groups	relationships
newspapers	hijackings	hostages
relatives		terrorists

Causes, reasons, and effects   Showing causes, reasons, and effects is another natural way of thinking. It is the way our minds function when we dig behind an event or a statement and ask, ''What were the causes of such and such? Why did such and such happen?'' And it is the route we take when we ask, ''What are the consequences of such and such? Something happened, and what were the effects?''

TIPS FOR EXAM TAKERS

Classification is a convenient way to frame answers to essay tests. A typical question in a history exam might be:

Describe the reasons for the rise of Cuban nationalism.

Your answer:

We can classify the reasons for Cuba's nationalism into three groups: geographic, economic, and political. Let us examine each one in turn.

TOPIC SENTENCES:

¶1   Cuba's geographic position so close to the United States strengthens the island's nationalism.

¶2   Cuba's struggle for economic self-sufficiency enhances a grass-roots nationalism.

¶3   Fidel Castro's intense political leadership exploits nationalist pride.

You continue developing each paragraph with geographic, economic, and political details to support each classification.

(See Chapter 20, pp. 450–456.)

Suppose you get an A in a biology course. If you dig to find out why, you get to the causes or reasons:

because you studied hard
because you studied the right materials
because your instructor liked you
because you benefited from studying with Jim
because you were a brilliant lab researcher
because your mother is a biologist

If you consider the consequences of getting an A in your biology course, you find the effects:

Your cumulative index will reach 3.0.
You'll become a biology major.
You'll get a summer job at the state biochemistry lab.
You'll make your mother happy.

If you were writing an essay on the causes or effects of your getting an A in biology, your controlling idea might look like one of these:

I got an A in biology because _____ .

My getting an A in biology had the following results: _____ .

There are several reasons why I got an A in biology this semester.

My getting an A in biology this semester had several consequences, some of them trivial, some of them important.

SAMPLE ESSAY SHOWING CAUSES AND EFFECTS The following essay combines a narrative technique with an explanation of cause and effect. It was written by a student to show how getting married involved more than he had imagined. By going through the details of his first few months of married life, the writer supplies the specific causes of his "reeducation."

MARRIED

The minister stood before us, speaking the same sober words he had in the rehearsal, and we heard none of them. Who had time for serious reflections? There was still the reception ahead of us, and then the honeymoon in Mexico, and of course there was also settling in at the new apartment when we returned. So now the words sailed by: Amy did; and then I did. We were wife and husband. Little did we suspect that we were also *married*.

Our first real inklings of the idea of "marriage" came about four months later. Amy had kept her job, and I had kept mine as well; we reasoned that since each one of us had been supporting ourselves, if we simply combined our incomes—*married* them, so to speak—we would still get by. We reasoned wrong. Somehow the arithmetic didn't work, and our April rent check bounced. We looked over our records—where had the money gone? Here, there, and everywhere it seemed—and nowhere, too. A lot of the money had gone nowhere, frittered away on little nothings, monogrammed towels, monogrammed potholders, monogrammed stationery . . . if nothing else, we knew our initials. So we sat down with pencils and paper and organized an exact budget. But a month later, the arithmetic still didn't work, and our May rent check bounced as well. Amy asked her boss for a raise, and she got one—in exchange for substantial overtime. I asked for a raise too, and was laughed out of my boss's office; it was the kind of treatment I'd have quit over in the past. But of course that was out of the question now.

We made June's rent, barely. But Amy's overtime was causing new and unanticipated problems. I now had to cook our dinners (eating out was, again, out of the question), which meant we ate mostly hot dogs and Pop Tarts. This sharing of chores led eventually to a more profound sharing: food poisoning. I defrosted, refroze, and then re-defrosted a pound of ground beef, and we both wound up in the hospital. Her insurance covered both of us but did not cover our particular ailment; my insurance covered our particular ailment but did not cover her. By the end of the summer, we were a thousand dollars in debt.

To pay off our debt, we turned to our parents. We borrowed half the money from her parents, half from mine. At the time, it seemed the most diplomatic course to take. What we didn't foresee was the question of which parents to pay back first. We based our decision, finally, strictly on economic factors; we determined that her parents were slightly better off than mine, so we decided to repay mine first. In effect, we only offended mine first: did we think that they were paupers? or just cheap? or was it that we simply felt closer to her parents? My mother cried; my father gestured and stalked about. And then, of course, we offended her parents: we had taken *them* for granted. Her father cried; her mother gestured and stalked about. In the end, we took out a loan from the bank and repaid both sets of parents on the same day.

Things have settled down a lot since then. We've climbed out of debt, and I've learned to cook. More importantly, Amy and I have learned that a marriage is a practical as well as a romantic partnership.

SAMPLE ESSAY SHOWING REASONS   When we talk about causes, we can often point to something *specific* as a cause of something else: "The lights in the house blew out *because* lightning struck the power station." Sometimes causes are not so obvious or definite, especially when we talk about feelings. When we discuss our feelings, we usually talk about *reasons* for those feelings: "There are three reasons why Dr. Becker prefers to practice medicine in a small town."

In the following essay, Judy Syfers discusses the reasons *why* a wife is desirable, even to a wife. Notice that her title, "Why I Want a Wife," and the question in the second paragraph, "Why do I want a wife?," set us up for the reasons that follow.

WHY I WANT A WIFE

I belong to that classification of people known as wives. I am A Wife. And, not altogether incidentally, I am a mother.

Not too long ago a male friend of mine appeared on the scene fresh from a divorce. He had one child, who is, of course, with his ex-wife. He is looking for another wife. As I thought about him while I was ironing one evening, it suddenly occurred to me that I, too, would like to have a wife. Why do I want a wife?

I would like to go back to school so that I can become economically independent, support myself, and, if need be, support those dependent upon me. I want a wife who will work and send me to school. And while I am going to school I want a wife to take care of my children. I want a wife to keep track of the children's doctor and dentist appointments. And to keep track of mine, too. I want a wife to make sure my children eat properly and are kept clean. I want a wife who will wash the children's clothes and keep them mended. I want a wife who is a good nurturant attendant to my children, who arranges for their schooling, makes sure that they have an adequate social life with their peers, takes them to the park, the zoo, etc. I want a wife who takes care of the children when they are sick, a wife who arranges to be around when the children need special care, because, of course, I cannot miss classes at school. My wife must arrange to lose time at work and not lose the job. It may mean a small cut in my wife's income from time to time, but I guess I can tolerate that. Needless to say, my wife will arrange and pay for the care of the children while my wife is working.

I want a wife who will take care of *my* physical needs. I want a wife who will keep my house clean. A wife who will pick up after me. I want a wife who will keep my clothes clean, ironed, mended, replaced when need be, and who will see to it that my personal things are kept in their proper place so that I can find what I need the minute I need it. I want a wife who cooks the meals, a wife who is a *good* cook. I want a wife who will plan the menus, do the necessary grocery shopping, prepare the meals, serve them pleasantly, and then do the cleaning up while I do my studying. I want a wife who will care for me when I am sick and sympathize with my pain and loss of time from school. I want a wife to go along when our family takes a vacation so that someone can continue to care for me and my children when I need a rest and change of scene.

I want a wife who will not bother me with rambling complaints about a wife's duties. But I want a wife who will listen to me when I feel the need to explain a rather difficult point I have come across in my course of studies. And I want a wife who will type my papers for me when I have written them.

I want a wife who will take care of the details of my social life. When my wife and I are invited out by my friends, I want a wife who will take care of the babysitting arrangements. When I meet people at school that I like and want to entertain, I want a wife who will have the house clean, will prepare a special meal, serve it to me and my friends, and not interrupt when I talk about the things that interest me and my friends. I want a wife who will have arranged that the children do not bother us. I want a wife who takes care of the needs of my guests so that they feel comfortable, who makes sure that they have an ashtray, that they are passed the hors d'oeuvres, that they are offered a second helping of the food, that their wine glasses are replenished when necessary, that their coffee is served to them as they like it. And I want a wife who knows that sometimes I need a night out by myself.

I want a wife who is sensitive to my sexual needs, a wife who makes love passionately and eagerly when I feel like it, a wife who makes sure that I am satisfied. And, of course, I want a wife who will not demand sexual attention when I am not in the mood for it. I want a wife who assumes the complete responsibility for birth control, because I do not want more children. I want a wife who will remain sexually faithful to me so that I do not have to clutter up my intellectual life with jealousies. And I want a wife who understands that *my* sexual needs may entail more than strict adherence to monogamy. I must, after all, be able to relate to people as fully as possible.

If, by chance, I find another person more suitable as a wife than the wife I already have, I want the liberty to replace my present wife with another one. Naturally, I will expect a fresh, new life; my wife will take the children and be solely responsible for them so that I am left free.

When I am through with school and have a job, I want my wife to quit working and remain at home so that my wife can more fully and completely take care of a wife's duties.

My God, who *wouldn't* want a wife?

As Judy Syfers gives detailed, personal, knowing reasons why she would like to have a wife, she is also, quite intentionally, expressing her own feelings about a wife's role. Her controlling idea is ''There are so many reasons why a wife is desirable that even I want one.'' Is there an unstated idea?

''Why I Want a Wife'' suggests that a great deal of pleasure for the reader is in a flood of rich detail; but much of the pleasure depends on the orderly way the details are grouped into paragraphs. Each of Judy Syfers' reasons has its own bundle of details:

I want a wife who will work and send me to school.

. . . I want a wife to take care of my children.

I want a wife who will take care of *my* physical needs.

I want a wife who will not bother me with rambling complaints about a wife's duties.

I want a wife who will take care of the details of my social life.

I want a wife who is sensitive to my sexual needs . . .

I want the liberty to replace my present wife with another one.

And so on.

TIPS FOR WRITERS—EXPLAINING AND INFORMING

1. Identify a large subject area. Find out what interests you through freewriting, thinking, conversing, reading, and/or getting suggestions from a teacher.

2. Invent or locate ideas. Engage in one or more invention techniques. Your work begins by locating ideas through closely observing, focused freewriting on your subject area, brainstorming, talking with a friend, doing some brief research (in a book or magazine article or by interview), or writing a crash-through draft, perhaps in letter form. Underline ideas that matter to you.

3. Separate general ideas from specific details. Mark general ideas g and specific details s. Write out the general ideas in full sentences. Group related details under the general idea that seems to include them.

4. Study the groups. Get a sense of organization that is appropriate to these ideas. Will your controlling idea be supported by details or by examples? Are you comparing two things? Are you explaining why? Are you showing effects?

5. Write a temporary generalization that summarizes your thinking and includes the details you have. Write "I think _____." State your attitude toward your subject, and concisely tell *why* you feel that way. For a comparison you may want to write:

   I think X is like (or different from) Y because _____.
   I think X is more (or less) _____ than Y. I prefer X (or Y) because _____.

   For a cause and effect essay, you may want to write:

   I think X was caused by _____ for these three reasons: _____.
   I think the consequences of X are _____.

6. Set up an outline with your controlling idea at the top. Under it, write the main headings that are somewhat more specific than the idea. Jot down details under each heading. Adjust your controlling idea as you add or subtract details.

7. Write a first draft. Move back and forth between your general statements and specifics. Understand your principle of organization. Is it based on

chronology? geography? a climactic order of importance? Keep the best details for last. Keep writing. You can make changes later.

8. Reread your draft and make the immediate changes that *you* feel are necessary.

9. Recopy your draft if you need to. Get a reaction from a friend or fellow writer.

10. For your revision, go back for more ideas, a clearer outline, a better statement of your controlling idea. Cut irrelevancies. Expand the most important sections. Think. Make details as vivid as you can.

11. Rewrite.

THE IMPORTANCE OF ASKING WHY   In writing that explains, remember that *why* is the most important wedge into conditions that seem impenetrable. When things happen to you that you don't immediately understand, take them apart and ask yourself questions about them: ''Why?'' ''What are the reasons?'' ''How do I know?'' ''What are the results?''

TIPS FOR EXAM TAKERS

Essay exam questions are often written as cause or effect questions:

Discuss the causes of the American Revolution.
Discuss the effects of the American Revolution.

As you respond to the exam question, you think about the big question: *Why?* ''Why did the Revolutionary War occur?'' ''What caused it?'' Gather all the specifics you can, and then think about putting the specifics into some order. These are the specific causes, and you end with the one you consider most important:

Great Britain exploited the colonies' natural resources.
Great Britain discouraged the economic development of the colonies.
Aristocratic Britons wanted the colonists to remain inferior.
The Stamp Act stirred protests and boycotts.

The causes or the results can be *classified* according to several principles:

We can classify the *causes* of the Revolutionary War into the pressing economic, political, and ideological issues of the time.

or

We can classify the *results* of the American Revolution into the effects it had on the political, economic, and psychological framework of the new American community.

or

We can classify immediate and far-reaching effects of the Revolution.

or

We can classify the effects of the war on the young nation or on Great Britain.

Exercise 6 Choose two of the following occurrences. For each one, write three or four sentences that state possible causes. Then, for each one, write three or four sentences that state possible consequences.

1. The price of gasoline reaches $2.50 a gallon
2. Your car skids
3. The incumbent president is not reelected
4. Someone you know leaves college

5.b ARGUMENT

Since an expository essay requires that you move consciously back and forth between your point and your support, it is a particularly useful form for persuading. Arguing is persuading, but with exceptional care to logic and strategy and with careful consideration of your audience. It is an extreme form of persuasion, a very carefully arranged exercise in reasoning that appeals to your audience's logic. Arguing in this sense does not mean yelling and quarreling; it means giving reasons for or against an idea, bringing in a weight of evidence to convince your reader.

Explore your subject through writing You don't have to begin your first draft with a solid argument to end up with one. Arguing is a form of writing that requires you to think through a subject to its central issues and take a position for or against an idea about it. Explore your subject through freewriting, focused freewriting, or writing a list—the same brainstorming strategies you would apply to any other writing assignment. It may be that through writing—particularly as you freewrite about both sides of an issue—you will find your position. Many beginners at argument worry because they see both sides of an issue and don't know which side to take. Use your writing to find out. It is to your advantage to see both sides; keep writing about both, making lists pro and con. And then decide.

It may be that you have vague ideas but need to do research. If a controversy is a public one, you often have a sense of the issues involved—you may even be leaning to one position or another—but you don't have the solid, specific knowledge to explain why you've chosen your position. That is to be expected. Without study, how many of us can rattle off convincing arguments about an issue—any issue: Should the draft include women? Should classrooms be built without windows? Should rock concerts that are held in large coliseums be outlawed?

Remember that, as in any other essay, you are working toward a statement that expresses your idea about a subject and your attitude toward it (Chapter 2). As you freewrite, crash through a first draft, and then rewrite, keep in mind that you are leading toward a position: ''I think women should be treated equally in all areas of public life, including the draft.'' ''I think that windowless classrooms allow for better learning.'' Remember as well that you must build support for your position, mustering all the evidence you can to convince your reader that you *do* know what you're talking about.

Consider your audience   When you argue an issue with a friend, you can be fairly casual in your approach. You can argue on a personal level; you can be emotional; each of you may tolerate a little ranting and raving—if you want. Suppose that you are discussing the subject of women being included in the draft: since you do not have many facts at your fingertips (information about nations that already draft women; ancient societies that used women warriors), you focus on your *feelings*. You feel that men and women should be treated equally in all public matters; you think that women are as strong as men, that women function well under stress. But you have no data. Instead you cite anecdotes about strong women and weak men you know. You say you *think* there were psychological tests performed somewhere that proved women were durable.

For Women Only

To the Editor:

As a 16-year-old male, I am very concerned about reinstatement of the draft. I have also been thinking about whether or not women should be drafted.

It seems to me that *only* women should be drafted—to compensate them for all the wars they missed out on. This way it will be a model affirmative-action draft.

THADDEUS A. BUNDER
New York, Jan. 28, 1980

When you *write* an argumentative essay, you leave the safe environment of friends. You go public with your argument. Ranting and raving, being vague about facts, relying on personal experience and feelings as support for your position will not convince your readers that you have studied the issues. Who are your readers? You must assume that your readers first of all are familiar with the issue. They have thought about it or are now engaged by the questions you raise; they can be expected to raise other questions that you have overlooked. Picture your readers. Get inside their minds. Assume that they are question askers, that they make you face hard questions about both sides of your argument. Readers don't let you off easily. ''What do you mean,'' they ask, ''when you say that women should be treated equally?'' ''What does *equal* mean?'' ''Equal before the law?'' ''If so, what obligations should the law impose?'' ''What about the E.R.A.?'' ''If the pool of young men and women is larger than the military need, what determines selection: training, sex, marital status, experience?'' ''What about combat duty?''

You can assume as well that all your readers not only are alert, intelligent, and knowledgeable about your subject, but also will pay careful attention to logic and strategy. But groups of readers will respond differently to selections of facts and figures, even to styles of writing. For example, writing an argument *for* the draft to young women ages seventeen to twenty will appeal to their patriotism and to their independence and achievements in the women's movement. An argument directed at the mothers of these young women might need to recognize the changing world and the broadening benefits of the military for women.

Readers detect fallacies—common errors that writers make when they attempt a logical argument. They are suspicious if you drop a ''statistic'': ''Nine out of ten women are as strong as men.'' ''Who says so?'' your readers challenge: ''Strong in what ways?'' ''Is that an opinion or an established fact?'' ''Is it from an authoritative source?'' ''Who is your authority?'' Remember that your sentences lead your reader to find questions just under the surface of what you have said. You'll have to keep on your toes in the preparation and in the explicit writing of your argument.

Take a stand

Your essay should present your position as solidly as possible. When you take a stand for or against an issue, prepare to back your position with the best information you can find and with your best powers of reasoning. For example: Classroom buildings should be built without windows. For or against?

An essay of argument requires that you commit yourself to one side or the other—your argument should never be half hearted. Remember, even when you are not 100 percent certain, taking a stand for the sake of your essay can bring you to your true position with more confidence because you have forced yourself into a thorough investigation of the sides. If you're *for* windowless classrooms, you're going to marshal the best argument you can to convince your reader that a cement structure without glass leads to better lectures, livelier discussion, greater concentration, and clearer vision and hearing—in short, learning that is more effective than that in a conventional school building with rows of windows.

Dispose of the opposition

But is commitment enough? Not if you have readers who oppose your point of view by claiming to feel intense claustrophobia in the confines of four windowless walls, whose flesh begins to sweat and whose concentration is undermined by thoughts of wanting to get out into sunlight and fresh air. The writer must take the opposition into account. Again, you must get inside the readers' minds. You imagine their counterarguments, their reasons. You acknowledge their position and then knock it down, reason by reason. If a reader thinks he will feel claustrophobic by spending hour after hour in a windowless classroom, then you respond by saying, ''That may be true, but students rarely spend more than an hour and a half in a class without a break for air, refreshment, or exercise.''

The opposition might add, ''But an absence of daylight and sky inhibits learning. There are no vistas, nowhere for the imagination to reach beyond the immediate lesson.''

Then you say, "I understand students' needs to extend their horizons, but most students are merely distracted by the passing campus scene. Their effort at concentration dissolves into daydream. The truly imaginative mind must first focus hard on new information—without distraction. After the new information sinks in, a really new idea emerges."

After you recognize the opposition, answer it bluntly and effectively. Then take up your own positive points and, in careful succession, often leaving the best point for last, drive home your argument.

Plan logically

Your argument should appeal to your readers fairly and logically. They don't want to be harassed. Using rash, questionable "facts" and sweeping statements to make a point can be just as aggressive as pushing and shoving to get on a bus. As an essayist, you are not a rabble-rouser. You use moderation, effective language, and, above all, reason. You move carefully and with a plan. Also, you assume that your readers are intelligent and will recognize a compelling argument. And because your readers are intelligent, they are as much on their guard in reading as in any other transaction. They do not want to be swindled. They can smell a phony. Lacking another defense, they apply skepticism and a "show-me" attitude. You can best show your reader by following one of two basic movements in argument.

INDUCTIVE REASONING

One of the movements in argument is the method not only of science, but also of everyday living. This method is called *inductive reasoning*. You deal first with the data, then lead the reader from the data to an intelligent observation. In fact, most of what we know is an educated guess based on data, and partial data at that. We get a hunch and go after more data that will lead us to a reasonable conclusion. We say, for example, that the ocean is salty. Yet we ourselves have tasted water samples only at Long Island and Carmel. But people who have tasted ocean water off the coasts of India and Chile support our claim since they also say it's salty. Oceanographers have measured the saline content of great quantities of ocean water. Yet no one has tested (or tasted) the entire ocean. We draw a conclusion about all ocean water from a partial sample. Scientists call such an assumption—that ocean water is salty—a hypothesis. A *hypothesis* is an unproved theory. After scientists have collected a reasonable amount of data—water from the ocean, for example—they conclude that the data support the hypothesis. Good arguers, in the same way, try to provide adequate evidence and a broad enough sample to make the reader see the reasonableness of the conclusions.

How does this principle of arguing inductively guide us in writing? For an essay arguing for windowless classrooms, you might start writing by observing as many occasions as you reasonably can when students in such a classroom work without being distracted. Are these students letting the daily basketball practice outside their classroom interfere with the day's lesson on the gold standard? Students in a windowless classroom don't know that basketball exists. And again, are students distracted by the unusual 93° May heat? In the air-conditioned windowless classroom, it's a neat 72°. Or are students watching the pileup of January snow outside that is being plowed into mountainous heaps by snow-clearing equipment while the teacher shouts above the noise to explain the patterns of justice in aboriginal Australian societies? And does the constant traffic of jet planes to and from the nearby airport cause the teacher to interrupt her sentences five times?

On the basis of these specific observations, we generalize that students are not distracted by outside events when they learn in windowless classrooms. This becomes our hypothesis. We may look for more evidence. There is a group of students taught by an English teacher who has vision difficulties. In the windowless classroom, the teacher cannot be distracted by glaring daylight because the artificial light in the room is glareless and evenly distributed.

On the basis of the evidence we have compiled, we lead our reader to the concluding generalization, that a windowless classroom conserves the best energies and the attention of teacher and students. In short, *windowless classrooms allow for efficient learning.*

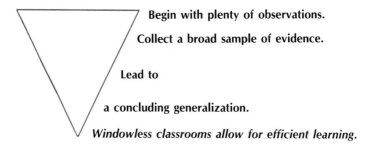

Begin with plenty of observations.

Collect a broad sample of evidence.

Lead to

a concluding generalization.

Windowless classrooms allow for efficient learning.

In a sense, the inductive approach keeps the verdict under wraps until the readers themselves can examine the available evidence. The verdict that is presented to the reader comes in last.

DEDUCTIVE REASONING Deductive reasoning is the more conventional approach of essay writers. In *deductive reasoning,* the movement is the opposite of that in inductive reasoning. Examining the available evidence is part of the writer's preliminary research. But when you write your essay, you assert your conclusion in the opening paragraph, in the position your controlling idea normally occupies: *Windowless classrooms allow for efficient learning.* Then you exhibit the argument that demonstrates the truth of this conclusion. You accomplish this in subsequent paragraphs by showing the data you have collected. In an essay organized on principles of deductive reasoning, *your reader knows exactly where your argument is heading.* What you do is set up an argument called a *syllogism.* Here is the most famous classical model of a syllogism. Notice the three elements:

All men are mortal. (Major premise)

Socrates is a man. (Minor premise)

Socrates is mortal. (Conclusion)

In the case of windowless classrooms, your argument might be stated in bare bones as the following syllogism:

Minimizing distractions allows for efficient learning. (Major premise)

Windowless classrooms minimize distractions. (Minor premise)

Windowless classrooms allow for efficient learning. (Conclusion)

The major premise of a syllogism is a generally accepted hypothesis: no one would argue with the statement that all men are mortal or that minimizing distractions allows for efficient learning. The work of your essay, then, is to demonstrate the truth of the minor premise: to discuss those distractions that windowless classrooms minimize. But the essay organized deductively states the conclusion first.

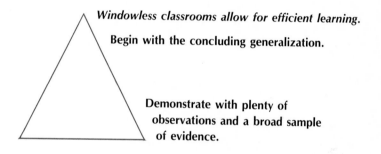

Windowless classrooms allow for efficient learning.

Begin with the concluding generalization.

Demonstrate with plenty of observations and a broad sample of evidence.

From there, the writer moves into the details of the argument.

Fallacies of argument   Fallacies are common errors in logic and are sometimes made by speakers and writers in presenting their arguments. Be careful of these:

1. Do not mistake opinion for fact.

    Opinion: Women are as strong as men.

    Fact: Under a microscope, female muscle tissue is indistinguishable from male muscle tissue.

2. Don't overuse facts and figures, but check the ones you do use, and document them.

    NO: Nine out of ten women show few signs of stress. (Who says so?)

    YES: A study at the University of California, Berkeley, showed that women under stress of fatigue carried out their daily responsibilities as efficiently as men under the same conditions.

3. Do not use the word *all* when you mean *some* or *most*. Do not use the word *none* when you mean *few*. Be careful not to assert something about every member of a group when it would be impossible to prove your assertion.

NO: There are no hospital patients who want to listen to the TV blaring all day long.

YES: Most hospital patients prefer quiet afternoons to the endless blaring of "The Odd Couple" and "All in the Family" reruns.

4. Do not reduce a complex argument to two options.

NO: Either the American brewers take the nitrosamines out of beer or the next generation will be genetically damaged.

Ask yourself if there are other possibilities.

YES: Can people learn not to drink beer? Can the United States import Danish beer, which is low in nitrosamines? Can we expand production of Coors beer, which contains no nitrosamines?

5. Do not assume that since A came before B, A therefore caused B. Don't claim too much on the basis of a temporal sequence.

NO: The patient's improved attitude brought about a remission of the disease.

YES: The patient's improved attitude may have been one of many changes that led to remission of the disease.

As you see, argument is a decent and respectable way to develop ideas; what's more, it can be personal and can move people to action. When you argue an idea, you must put forward convincing and specific reasons, not only logically, but also dramatically. The best oral arguers use all the skills at their disposal to convince you. They cite facts and figures and speak as logically as they can, but they do not stop there. You have heard the arguments of senators

---

TIPS FOR ARGUERS

To write a good argument:

1. Explore your subject through writing. Make lists pro and con.
2. Come to a clear position. Take a stand.
3. Understand your opponent's argument, and try to refute it, point by point.
4. Refine the logic of your argument through several drafts.
5. Arrange your evidence in a convincing and dramatic order. Often you can save the best reason to the end and clinch your argument.

REMEMBER: You don't have to start with a solid argument to end up with one.

and presidents. You have heard members of the clergy sermonize, and you have listened to politicians campaigning for office. They raise their voices, they smile, they gesture, they suddenly interrupt with an appealing story to illustrate their point; and before you know it, you are nodding and agreeing with them. In the same way, the best writers of argument will advise you to make use of the most effective writing skills at your command in order to win your readers to your position. Your words and sentences must work for you on the page, where your voice, your smile, and your gesture cannot operate.

Exercise 7   Arguments move a reader to action. Read the following essay by journalist Bob Oates. Then answer these questions:

1. Which of the opposition's arguments does Oates dispose of? How?
2. What are the points he argues to prove that most black athletes are "throwing away their future"?
3. Does Oates argue deductively or inductively? How do you know?
4. What would Oates expect the citizens who read this article to do? Who is Oates's audience?

THE GREAT AMERICAN TEASE:
SPORT AS A WAY OUT OF THE GHETTO

Starting in junior high and continuing through college, most black athletes are wasting their time in sports and "throwing away their future."

It's a "cruel myth" that sports are good for the black community. They do more harm than good.

Those are the opinions of an increasing number of black sociologists, administrators and athletes who are telling young blacks this:

—There's more chance of becoming a surgeon or architect than an all-star outfielder.
—For every O.J. Simpson, Julius Erving or Reggie Jackson, hundreds of thousands of young American athletes try and fail.
—The myth that a sports career is an escalator from poverty to the good life damages every black community in the nation. Actually it's a "treadmill"—not an escalator—"a treadmill to nowhere" for virtually every high school kid who tries to get aboard.

"You can work out the odds with a pencil and paper," says Harry Edwards, a sociology professor at Berkeley. "Less than 900 black athletes are earning a living in sports—and not more than 1,500 overall including coaches and trainers. By comparison, there are perhaps 3 million black youths between [the ages of] 13 and 22 who dream of a career as an athlete. The odds are 20,000 to 1 or worse. Statistically, you have a better chance of getting hit by a meteorite in the next 10 years than getting work as an athlete."

A 6-foot-8 former college basketball captain who also set the school discus record at San Jose State, Edwards says the tragedy is that, in dedicating their boyhood to games, "most guys lose the best chance they'll ever have" to prepare themselves for rewarding jobs.

Speaking as one of the nation's leading sports sociologists, he puts it this way: "They try to be an O. J. or a Reggie J. or a Dr. J. and wind up a No J—no job at all."

. . .

A former athlete himself, Edwards says: "I think it's treasonous for black athletes who have made it to tell young blacks that if you work hard, you can do it, too. Ninety-nine percent are going to fail."

Arthur Ashe, a former Forest Hills and Wimbledon tennis champion, strongly advises against inviting the lucky few ("Walt Frazier or O. J. or Abdul-Jabbar") to appear before schoolboys.

"Invite a benchwarmer or a guy who didn't make it," Ashe suggests. "Ask him if he sleeps every night. Ask him whether he was graduated. Ask him what he would do if he became disabled tomorrow. Ask him where his old high school athletic buddies are."

. . .

. . . Henry P. Organ, a black Stanford Ph.D., has gone so far as to advocate that blacks get out of major league sports entirely and stay out.

"The soundest option for the black community appears to be a massive exodus from varsity and professional athletics," Organ says. "This should be done for several generations. Organized sports have been a trap for black youth, from which few recover. The black community is more in need of teachers, not coaches; more in need of proper nutrition, not drugs; more in need of health scientists than center fielders; more in need of economists than pivot men."

As a first step, Organ thinks Stanford should stop giving athletic scholarships to black students and stop recruiting blacks for varsity athletics.

. . .

Another myth, experts say, is that blacks are better athletes than whites, thus accounting for their large number in the pro leagues.

According to Roscoe C. Brown Jr. of New York University, they're there because of "the disproportionate amount of energy spent in the ghetto developing" sports skills.

"What we need is balance," Brown says. "We need more education. Black youngsters pour too much time and energy into sports. They're deluded and seduced by the athletic flesh-peddlers, used for public amusement—and discarded."

With more emphasis on education in the black community, Brown says, "we'll still have top black athletes, but we'll also have more black doctors, educators and political scientists."

The solution to the problem, many believe, starts with counseling in junior and senior high school. In Denver, Jerome Biffle, a former Olympic gold medal winner in the broad jump who is now a high school counselor, says: "I tell the student athlete: 'Never plan your life around a pro sports career. Even if you make it in the pros, there is no guarantee you will be a pro very long. There are just too many great young athletes and too few jobs.'"

The evidence is, however, persuasive that most schoolboys don't listen to counselors. Their role models are the black athletes who have made it big—the lucky few—and the kids want some of that.

Told that the sports world is a gigantic lottery in which almost nobody can win, they pursue it anyway, feeling they'll be in the fraction of the 1 percent beating the system.

Can this destructive pattern be headed off?

Edwards thinks a concerted effort in three directions might have an effect. He believes the attack should proceed simultaneously in the colleges and communities and on the individual level.

"Individually," Edwards says, "I think every youngster with some athletic talent should give it a shot. But he should do it intelligently, and this is what I mean by that: If by your senior year you're not a High School All-American—and if after one season of college sports you're not an All-American of some kind, second team, third team or honorable mention—you should forget a professional sports career. You're never going to make it no matter how hard you try. The great athletes all show class early."

This is one of the good things about sports, Edwards says, explaining: "You can find out early on if you've got it. And if you haven't, there's no point in wasting the rest of your teens and 20s struggling for something that will never be. You have time to concentrate on books and a different kind of life that will be more rewarding anyway."

Second most important, Edwards thinks, the presidents and chancellors of America's great universities—and any colleges that play varsity football—should personally take the responsibility for overseeing the education of varsity athletes.

. . .

The very least that any college president should do, Edwards insists, is to make sure that every student on an athletic scholarship is making "normal progress" to a degree every year.

But at most schools this would result in declarations of ineligibility for many athletes.

"The average [black] individual in college sports has no idea even of what a college is," Edwards says. "In most instances he's a first-generation college individual who thinks that just being on campus is going to college."

Accordingly, later on, when he fails in a professional sports bid, he has nothing to fall back on because he learned nothing in college.

"The surveys all show about the same thing and the Southwest Conference is typical," Edwards says. "In that conference in 1978, 67 percent of the black athletes majored in physical education and two-thirds never graduated. Only 25 percent of the whites majored in phys ed and 75 percent graduated."

. . .

This makes physical education the wrong major for most blacks; at the same time it's perceived as just right for black athletes by many athletic departments, which feel they can control eligibility patterns easier in physical education than in, say, literature or history.

All this, in Edwards' opinion, reinforces the status of sports as a "treadmill to nowhere" for most athletes. They not only miss out on a pro sports career after years of helping their alma mater, they aren't even equipped by their college experience to do anything else.

"One of our goals should be more education for blacks . . . " Edwards says. "It's extremely disappointing to me that the only individuals who can assure this—the college presidents and chancellors—don't."

As his third recommendation, Edwards calls on the black community "to press the legitimacy of academics over athletics." Every time it honors or encourages a black athlete, this community is reinforcing the wrong role model, he says, recommending that it put more effort into creating and establishing more realistic role models.

. . .

"Of the 4,800 instructors at UC Berkeley, 19 are black," he says. "For the youngster with an aptitude for both athletics and academics, there are more black sports models than academic models even here."

The tragedy of the black athlete is always an individual tragedy—except for the handful who get to the top and stay awhile—but in the long run it's even worse for the black community, Edwards says.

"Virtually every boy who tries to be an athlete comes back disillusioned," he says. "He comes back as a non-contributor, an under-contributor or a mal-contributor—and the community suffers. With the same effort he could have come back a teacher or doctor."

And that, Edwards says, even goes for Dr. J. With the effort he put into basketball, Dr. J. could have been a brain surgeon.

Exercise 8 Read the following essay by Bill Bradley. As you read it, remember that he wrote it in 1976, long before the Soviet invasion of Afghanistan in 1980 and long before the Soviet boycott of the 1984 Olympics in Los Angeles. Consider whether or not Bradley's arguments are relevant today, and then do one of the following exercises.

1. Write a rebuttal to Bradley, disposing of his key points and arguing your own support for the current format of the Olympic Games.

2. Write an argument in favor of reforming another major institution. Follow Bradley's five-pronged approach. Here are a few suggested topics:

The Oscar awards
The Nobel Peace Prize
Choosing a high-school or college valedictorian
Electing a member of the local school board
Airport check-ins

FIVE WAYS TO REFORM THE OLYMPICS

The Olympic Games are scheduled for Moscow. It is 1980. The political disputes of previous years—the North Korean pull-out in 1964, the racial protests of 1968, the terrorist attack of 1972, and the China-Taiwan dispute of 1976—are part of the Olympic legacy as much as the spirit of sportsmanship of Pierre de Coubertin, founder of the modern Olympic Games. The Russians have spent $2 billion on the stadiums, dormitories and various other monuments. ABC has contributed $100 million for United States television rights. The Soviet commissars of sport expect their athletes to win all the medals except five, which will go to East Germany. Although the United States team, amateurs (high school students largely), has trained hard, it is no match for the Soviet Army professionals. The Kremlin's propaganda machine prepares story after story about the prospect of nationalistic triumphs and how they will represent the superiority of the Soviet system.

Suddenly, two weeks before the opening ceremony, the President summons the head of the United States Olympic Committee to the White House. Two days later, the highest United States Olympic official, by profession a car dealer, announces our withdrawal from the Olympics, fulfilling a threat made four years earlier in the heat of the China-Taiwan dispute. The head of the United States Olympic Committee and the President justify the action on grounds of national security, and the Soviet committee exiles 40 commissars of sport. A few aristocrats on the International Olympic Committee issue statements about the value of fair play. But the Olympic Games as we knew them in the post-World War II era are dead.

Maybe the Olympics won't end exactly that way, but many people have called for their abolition on the grounds that they have been too expensive and too political. I believe the United States should discontinue its participation in the Games unless the promotion of mutual understanding among nations becomes a more central focus of the quadrennial festival.

First, the Olympics should be open to everyone. An athlete's skill should be the only requirement for eligibility. Amateurism is impossible to interpret or to enforce with uniformity in a world with disparate political and economic values. In 1964 I played on the United States Olympic basketball team in Tokyo. We beat the Soviet Union for a gold medal. Two years later I was playing for the team of an Italian meat-packing firm in the European Cup championship. We met (and defeated) the Soviet team in the semifinal. Man for man they were the same as the Soviet national team in Tokyo, except now they were called the Soviet Army Club Team. They were professionals paid for playing basketball, yet by international standards they were amateurs.

Second, team sports should be eliminated from the Olympics. They too easily simulate war games. One has only to consider the Soviet-Hungarian water polo game in 1956, the Soviet-Czechoslovak ice hockey match in 1968, or any time the Indians and Pakistanis meet in the field hockey final, in order to see that the "friendly combat" of the playing field whips up national passions. Even participants in team sports frequently feel they represent their countries more than themselves and compete for national prestige rather than for the joy of collective fulfillment that a team's quest for excellence can uniquely provide. If the public demands world champions, each sport can sponsor a separate world tournament, but not in the Olympics.

Third, everyone in the Olympics should get a participant's medal. Silver and bronze medals should be eliminated and the gold medal should go only to someone who breaks an Olympic record. Then an athlete would compete against a standard, not against another athlete or another country.

Fourth, the Olympics should be situated permanently in Greece, the country of their origin. All nations who compete in the Games should help underwrite the expense of a permanent facility that ultimately might become self-sustaining. Every four years, the world's youth would return to Mount Olympus in a spirit of friendship to compete in the finest athletic installation in the world.

The present system of financing the Olympics promotes the incursion of the festival into the politics of the host nation. Furthermore, the quadrennial expenditure of vast sums of money ($600 million in Mexico City, $800 million in Munich, $1.5 billion in Montreal) for capital projects that are little used after the Games is incredibly wasteful.

If the appeal of a purified Olympics could be parlayed into a sharing of the financial risks and rewards by all nations, each Olympiad could be made a time to focus on the oneness of the world instead of a time to champion the nationalistic grandeur of increasingly expensive physical facilities.

Fifth, the Olympics should be more participant-oriented. The athlete has gotten lost amid the site competitions, the multi-million-dollar construction projects, the TV cameras and the hordes of tourists. I would like to see the Games become more of a festival.

Everything should be aimed toward providing the participant with a unique experience. By lengthening the Games to two months, events could take place at a less feverish pace. Athletes could spend more time in the Olympic Village getting to know each other. The normal diversions of the village might be expanded to include cultural and artistic expressions from various parts of the world. Though the emphasis would still be athletic, the presence of other disciplines would recognize the value of the whole person. In such an environment the stress would lie not on the rewards to be taken home but the experience of living for two months in a microcosm of the world. Such an Olympics might even contribute to mutual understanding among nations.

part 2 A Guide to Revision

chapter

6 Revising the Whole Essay

You begin to reread what you have written while you and your essay are still honeymooning. The first rosy glow of success persists. You wrote it. It's yours. And you know you're going to cherish it, despite any doubts that are already seeping in at the edges of your confidence. Your stubborn impulse is to resist those doubts. After all, you planned on being finished by now. And you know that you can't change just *one* word. One word leads to another . . . and another . . . and another.

When you think of writing as a series of repeatable acts, revision is in your plans from the start. By the second or third essay you write, the barrier you have always felt between writing and revising weakens. Writing, you discover, *is* revising. Instead of condemning yourself to a first draft forever, you know that you can keep writing, keep clarifying, keep adding details, keep deleting what doesn't belong, keep finding out what you mean. You make more lists, reread your freewriting, weigh your general statements against the specific details that support them. And you try to write your way out of strained, cramped sentences into a simple clarity.

Your outline may help you. Keep it nearby, checking what you've written against your plan. If you have no outline, a good time to formulate one is after you've written your first draft. At least, try to extract your controlling idea and your main subheadings of thought. Then examine the structure of your logic as you see it, perhaps more distinctly, in outline form.

After carefully studying the logic of your main ideas, do a quick proofreading—supply missing words, repair faulty sentences, and be on the lookout for misspelled words. Then recopy your draft so that you can ask friends to read what you have written without handicapping them with the messy insertions and corrections of your first version.

6.a GIVING AND GETTING REACTIONS

When you hand over a piece of writing to friends for a reaction, you should request in return the most constructive, concrete reaction they can give you. Similarly, when *you* give a reaction to someone else's writing, be precise enough to help the writer put his or her finger on the very sentences and words that need rewriting. A teacher need not see everything you write. Writers can learn from each other. Your friend may hand your work back saying, "I think this is terrific. One or two weak spots but, on the whole, terrific." Your heart is lighter. Sometimes, however, you sense something fishy. Your friend avoids your eye. "I guess you're not through working on it yet," he says. You snatch it back, muttering. In either instance, your friend's responsibilities as a reader have collapsed because his comments are too indefinite. They leave you stranded. But if you secretly arm yourself with the right questions, you can convert your helpless friend (or yourself) into a useful critic. First of all, no matter how vague his first reaction, don't let him get away. *You* can help him be more precise. It won't matter whether you've written an essay, a letter to the chairman of the board of the Subaru Company, a paragraph about a poem, or a recommendation to your boss about locking up late at night. You can use some or all of the following questions to guide a reader in revealing what you've actually said. Is your reader saying, "It's not here on the page. I don't see it"? You may have *intended* to say a lot of things, but you may have missed. Try out these questions:

1. What's in this piece of writing? Which parts absolutely have to remain? Why?
2. Do the essential parts get enough attention?
3. Can any part be eliminated? Why?
4. Is there anything you want to hear more about? Why?
5. What do you remember as being outstanding? Why is it outstanding?
6. Is the outstanding feature important to the whole piece of writing? In what way?
7. Does any part jar you? Does the paper change course?
8. Can the best part go last?
9. Do you feel any part can be shortened? Which part, and why?
10. Can any dialogue or quotations be added? Does the included dialogue or quotations enhance the writing?
11. Do any parts seem unclear to you? Which ones?

12. Is the beginning effective? Does it attract you to read what follows?

13. Does the essay satisfy you? Does the ending, in particular, satisfy you? Does it relate sensibly to the beginning?

14. Without looking back at the piece of writing, can you state its controlling idea?

6.b FIRST SAMPLE ESSAY

The first draft Here is the first draft of the essay about the road test. Many of the changes have been written right on the page itself. Since some of the changes affect more than a word or a line, the facing pages show whole passages that were rewritten. Notice that all revisions are numbered and that reasons for each change are given. Read the revisions and reasons carefully, and compare the new version to the original underlayer. Then turn back to page 28 and read the revised whole draft.

Road Test Number One

1 ~~A Beautiful Day in May~~

2 *Insert* It was a *clear* beautiful day in early May. ~~The weather was perfect.~~ *There was not one drop of rain,*

3 *snow, or sleet on the ground, which have* ~~A little rain or sleet~~ would ~~of~~ provided a good excuse. ~~but no such~~

~~luck.~~ *Although* My driving instructor ~~was a tall man who reminded me of a~~

4 ~~biology teacher I once had. He~~ appeared nervous as he sat in the

car with me, waiting for the inspector, ~~But~~ I didn't feel a bit

5 anxious, I had to remind him to calm down. *when he washed the window for the third time,*

"Remember to adjust the mirrors when he gets in," he said as

he gave the final touch to the front mirror.

6 "Yeah, I know, and signal, I know."

About five minutes later ~~an Olds~~ *a* stationwagon pulled up in

7 front of the line. ~~In front of me were a Comaro, a Datsun,~~ and a

Cadillac.

~~I was fourth. I thought I had a lot of time but~~ *F*ive men stepped out, *in blue uniforms*

each carrying a *one* list of names and a *long* black binder. ~~Suddenly all the~~ *One of them approached the car, and*

8 ~~calmness I had instilled in myself~~ vanished. ~~At that point I felt my~~ *I felt my tension rise. I*

9 ~~throat go dry~~ *began shaking.* ~~as I realized the fifteen dollars I had bet my~~

~~brother might go down the drain~~

10 ~~He asked if I was Katherine Lee.~~ *"Katherine Lee, that you?" he asked.*

"Yes," I replied, ~~I said I was~~ although at the moment I had a tremendous urge to

11 say ~~I'm not~~ *"No, that's not me!" But common sense and the fifteen-dollar bet*

I had courageously made with my brother, kept me from saying it.

12   "All right, get in and start the engine," he said. ~~He got in~~ *as he sat down*
in the front seat. "Let's just ~~and told me to~~ pull out and ~~go~~ *turn* around the corner.

13   *Insert* As I was pulling out of the lane, I realized I had forgotten
to signal. Maybe he ~~didn't~~ notice. *"Oh, well, won't* ~~I thought. Then I know I had~~ *prayed to myself*
~~really failed, no question about it. The truth is I failed two more~~

14   ~~tests but what happened next on road test number one made me feel an~~
~~utter fool. You can't imagine how sharp~~ *any* *a very sharp one.* The turn at the corner was.

15   This time he literally fell off his seat. *he couldn't have avoided noticing; what happened I had driven too far out*
before starting to turn, so I was left there with no choice but to make a very quick turn.
"Slow down a bit," he ~~said.~~ "Now drive down the street ~~up~~
commanded *and*
~~you see that car?~~ Park behind ~~it."~~ *that blue car."*
Pulling
~~I pulled~~ alongside the *blue* car, ~~and~~ I cautiously checked in the front
and rear mirrors, being careful to avoid trees, bushes, people, cars,

16   and all the other things my instructor had warned me against. When
I backed up into the space and managed to maneuver the car into what

17   I parked, the car was ~~far~~ from the curb. Not bad, I thought, at
~~seemed to be the right position, but)~~ *a foot away*
least I parked. I put the car in neutral and stopped.

18   ~~What he said next really destroyed me.~~ "All right, you can
go now," he said, scribbling away on his report. At this point I
got out of the car, thinking he meant I could go, like in leave.

19   The thought didn't occur to me that we were ~~pretty far~~ *about two miles* from the test
area. I thought he meant I could go, so I got out of the car! "No,
no, get back in here. I meant in the car, in the car," he said with
a look on his face that read, "Oh, no, I got one of the dumb ones."

     I got back in the car. I felt like such a fool. So you can
imagine how ridiculous I felt when we were pulling out along a two-
lane, one-way street and I asked him, "Which way should I go?"
to which he replied in the same sarcastic *tone of voice, "There's only one way to go."*

20   ~~He said something sarcastic to me.~~
     Driving back, I managed to ~~go by~~ two ~~streets~~ *pass intersections* without even
He took note.

21   looking. Then, for the pièce de résistance, the street the test area

22   was on was a two-lane, two-way street with no markers, so I drove down
the left side. I thought the cars were just parked wrong. The
agony of my defeat was confirmed when he got out and said, "Have a
good day," like I really needed one.

23   *Insert*

Reasons for　　1. Make title more specific. Mention road test in title.
　　revisions　　2. Start with general statement of what I learned. Say what I learned. Bring 3 up to top. Introduce essay with idea of being the fool. Insert:

> *Most of us have experiences in our lives when we feel like fools. We even know, as the event is happening to us, how silly we look. We soon learn that not only can't we reverse our embarrassment, but anything we try to do to help ourselves makes us look more foolish. When I took my first road test, I was able in only five minutes to convince a driving inspector that I wasn't even qualified to drive a bumper-car in an amusement park.*

3. A clear, beautiful day *is* perfect weather. No need to repeat.
4. An irrelevant, and private, detail. Either explain what my biology instructor was like or eliminate.
5. *Show* how nervous the driving instructor was.
6. I like the dialogue. It brings the characters in the essay to life.
7. These names of cars are distracting. Get to the five men faster.
8. "All the calmness I had instilled in myself" is wordy.
9. Keep the narrative going. Do not interrupt with thoughts about the bet with my brother.
10. Try dialogue instead of indirect questions and statements. See point 6 above.
11. Try inserting thoughts about the bet with my brother here.
12. Give details. Let's have more real talk.
13. Give more details of how I felt. Insert:

> *At that point I felt my throat go dry as pictures of my fifteen dollars going down the drain flashed through my head. I couldn't utter a word except "yes."*

14. Do not interrupt narrative with a summary statement.
15. Give details. Here's the action.
16. Good details. Keep.
17. Rewrite for more concrete description of the parking act. *Be specific*. For example, Did I back in? How far from the curb was the car?
18. This sentence shows all my cards too soon. Eliminate.
19. How far?
20. Let's hear it!
21. Keep the inspector before the reader.
22. Comma splice.
23. Go back to idea of feeling like a fool. Has the fool learned anything? What happened to me as a driver? Did I take other tests? Insert:

> Well, I failed, wonder why? That was just number one; I went on to take road test number two and number three and managed to fail with equal success. I always advise anyone planning to take a road test in the near future to take it from a fool who knows: "Use your head and think first about what you are being asked to do, and don't, don't get out of the car when you are asked to go."

6.c SECOND SAMPLE ESSAY

The early work on an essay often x-rays a writer's mind at work. The following examples show the history of one piece of writing, "Fasten Your Seat Belt," from its earliest glimmers in ten minutes of freewriting to a fairly solid essay. It is entirely possible that you may rely on other methods to get your writing started, but whatever your method, your swing toward the writing of a strong essay with convincing paragraphs will be similar to what follows.

Remember that writing is *re*writing. You are always free to jot down notes, freewrite, brainstorm, or get more information. At any point, you can enter your composition and rearrange order, add sentences, delete whole sections, or change emphasis. The great excitement in writing is discovering what you *really* want to say.

Freewriting

It's great to be alive. Especially on Saturday nights. Steve. Steve. I really like Steve but he's got to stop going through red lights. Saturday night Steve picked me up at my house and it was funny the way Mom and Dad told us to drive carefully because there are crazy drivers out there and I hoped Steve would listen but he only faked it because after he drove out of the way he started speeding and went through two red lights not stopped even once and no seat belts me neither and I almost went through the windshield. Seat Belts. Seat Belts are real important. Except no one wears them. Not my friends ugh ugh ugh they're too restricting restricting. A lot of hot air air air bags they could help too even if no one else cares maybe the government could care. In some states seat belts are the law. Who cares? I care about Steve a lot and it's real scary like that commercial that shows all those kids turned into skeletons because they drink and don't wear seat belts and there's no air bag in the car Oh God no one listens unless something happens to them or someone they care about. And that's why when I found out about Steve last Saturday night after he dropped me off it hit me hard and I wish he would listen to those commercials or get caught a few times. Now I wouldn't go anywhere without a seat belt on. You should have seen us all buckled up last week when we went to visit Steve in the hospital hospital hospital. I hate hospitals. But when he comes out after his concussion maybe he'll start wearing them too, my Mom and Dad think so but they don't know the half of it.

After her freewriting, the author read the following article in *Newsweek* magazine. She used it to provide support, and quoted from it, in the final draft of her essay.

AIR BAGS ARE A PROVEN 'VACCINE'

The spinal cord is only about as big around as your little finger. Because it carries impulses between the brain and the rest of the body, bringing messages of movement and sensation, it's one of the most important structures in the body. If these impulses are interrupted, paralysis results.

I am no casual observer of spinal-cord injury. Eight years ago, my neck was broken and my spinal cord was damaged at the C-6 cervical level, leaving me with only limited use of my arms and hands. I have been a quadriplegic living in a wheelchair ever since. Were my neck broken about an inch higher, I would have been on a respirator for the rest of my life.

I was 18 years old and I had just finished my first year of college when a split-second, 25-mile-per-hour crash permanently changed my life. I remember sitting there waiting for the rescue crew, unable to remove my hands from the steering wheel. I hadn't had the luxury of an air bag, nor the common sense to buckle up. I wish I had had both.

In the past eight years not a day has passed that I haven't thought of my life before wheels. My ''new wheels'' constantly remind me of how inadequate the safety devices in our larger vehicles are.

Last year, more than 42,000 people died in auto accidents; 5,000 who survived were left with serious spinal-cord injuries. A spinal-cord injury—a permanent disabling condition—takes only a fraction of a second to happen. But in that same split second, an air bag would inflate. Since the first patent was applied for more than 30 years ago, the air bag has become a proven, relatively cheap device which works automatically.

Auto crashes are the leading killer and crippler of people like me, those who are under 35 years in age. The air bag is a proven "vaccine" for this most deadly and disabling "disease." But tragically, it has been withheld from the American public. After limited experiments, the automakers—with one exception—decided not to allow you and me to have this lifesaving device in our cars. And even last week, the federal government seemed reluctant to force the industry to provide it.

I recently testified before a Department of Transportation hearing in Los Angeles on auto safety, and while waiting my turn, I heard incredible things. People standing on two legs criticized the air bag because it *only* works in frontal crashes. More than half of the fatal car crashes are frontal crashes. Others maintained that the air bag is just another example of government regulation. Yet the issue here is not one of airline fares or gasoline prices but unnecessary injuries and deaths. I had the freedom not to wear my seat belt so now I'm confined to a wheelchair. What about my freedom to choose to use an air bag?

During the Los Angeles hearing, I also heard American auto manufacturers complain that the cost of installing an air bag is too high—that the extra cost would discourage potential buyers of new cars at a time of growing sales and renewed prosperity in their industry. A poll conducted for the Insurance Institute for Highway Safety has found that 9 out of 10 car buyers favor passive restraints as standard or optional equipment in new cars. And in a recent Gallup poll, Americans were increasingly concerned about auto safety. By a margin of 2 to 1, 60 percent to 31 percent, those surveyed said they favored a law that would require air bags in all new cars.

A few hundred dollars extra to install an air bag hardly compares to the catastrophic cost of caring for a person with a severe spinal-cord injury. Lifetime costs for one victim average $350,000. And there are about 10,000 new victims in the United States every year, 40 percent of them injured in auto accidents. That's $1.4 billion in health-care costs incurred each year because of car crashes, a tab for spinal-cord patients that is paid for in part by taxpayers through the Medicaid system. The hidden costs to society include higher health-, auto- and life-insurance premiums and an increased tax burden. The price tag on the psychological effects of a disabling injury are impossible to calculate. Air bags are a cost-effective measure for everyone.

At Rancho Los Amigos hospital where I work, we get about 170 new spinal-cord-injury patients every year. Half of them are under the age of 25, and 70 percent are on Medi-Cal, California's Medicaid system. The hospital is full of patients who were injured in car crashes: most were not wearing seat belts at the time of their accidents. And as you might expect, many are now air-bag supporters. Unfortunately, some cannot speak.

My crash was a very simple one. I was driving around a sharp turn on a country road when my back wheels went off the pavement. I ended up careening front-end first into a small ditch. A simple accident paralyzed me.

Last November a man in Texas was driving 50 miles per hour when his car left the road and flew 40 feet through the air, landing in a deep ravine. Bob LaRoche walked away from that accident—similar to mine yet a more powerful crash—because he was driving an air-bag-equipped Mercedes. His wife suffered a broken back and severe bruises and lacerations; the passenger side of the car was not air-bag equipped.

How many Americans can afford a $45,000 Mercedes-Benz? Should auto safety be reserved only for the wealthy? Seat belts work, I know, and I wish I had been wearing mine that summer night eight years ago. But now when I think of auto safety, I also think of a fire extinguisher. Hanging on the wall, it is useless in putting out a fire unless someone has the presence of mind to point it toward the flame. But a sprinkler system, mandatory in many places, is automatic.

That's the beauty of the air bag. It is truly the proverbial ounce of prevention that is worth a pound of cure. "Procrastination," someone once said, "is the thief of time." In the continuing case of air bags, procrastination is the thief of young lives. As a victim and as a provider of health care, I know that air bags would significantly reduce the incidence of spinal-cord injuries—and the waste of human lives.

—Jeffrey Cressy

The Outline
1. Wearing seat belts and having air bags in cars should be mandatory.
2. Traffic laws should be better enforced.
3. Some commercials for seat belts, drunk driving, and so on are very effective.
4. Accident victims swear that they might have avoided serious injury if they had been wearing seat belts or driving a car with air bags.
5. Either you or someone you care about has to be involved in an accident before you'll wear a seat belt.

The First Draft
1 Wearing seat belts and having air bags in cars should be mandatory. Also, all traffic rules should be obeyed and more strictly enforced.

Last Saturday night, my boy friend, Steve, dropped me off at home and then got into an accident by going through a red light. He also wasn't wearing his seat belt and so suffered a concussion.

Certain means must be applied to make sure that people not only drive carefully, but also will survive accidents. 2 One way of making sure that people drive safely is by strictly enforcing all traffic laws. Another method is to 3 continue to show commercials on TV about drunk driving, not wearing seat belts, and so on, which are often quite strong and effective.

To make sure that people survive accidents, the wearing of seat belts should be mandatory, as well as the installation of air bags in every car. 4 Many accident victims have sworn that if they had been wearing a seat belt as well as driving a car with air bags, they would have avoided serious injury.

5 Until any of these measures are applied or better enforced, it would seem that most people have to be personally involved or at least know someone who has been in an accident before they themselves will wear seat belts and obey all traffic rules. I know that since Steve's accident, my friends and I have started wearing seat belts, and we're even hopeful now that Steve will too.

Revising the Essay After completing her first draft, the writer turns it over to her friend Beverly for another point of view. Beverly then makes the following comments:

> What I'd like to know first is what happened to the skeletons? Here you give a really strong example of an effective, frightening commercial in your freewriting and then leave it out of your essay. Also, there's no question you've taken the "free" out of your writing. The essay is too rigid, too restricting, like the seat belts you talk about. You've got to open up, relax more like in the freewriting and at the same time make it a more fully developed essay. It's funny how just putting sentences together doesn't quite do that. What you need, I think, is a lot more detail, more examples, especially on the commercials. All you have to do is watch a lot of TV late at night and you'll get that. Also, what about telling us more about those accident victims. That seems to be really crucial. I want to know more. I'm not satisfied. You tell but don't show enough. That's the point. I want to know more. The part about Steve is great. I have a boy friend just like that. I think everyone knows someone just like that. What does Steve have to say about this? Maybe you should use dialogue. Why do you think Steve is going to wear seat belts now?

The first draft leaves Beverly dissatisfied because it doesn't flow the way a relaxed, fully developed piece of writing should. Its sentences are not fluent. They are abrupt and contain few details. No sooner do you meet an idea than it's behind you. On the whole, the rough first draft leaves you with a lot of unanswered questions.

The difference between an outline and a fully developed essay lies in the expansion of each subsection into a paragraph. In a paragraph, you play out your ideas. You grab hold of an idea and elaborate on it, inviting the reader to follow the steps in your thinking. In this rough first draft, the key sentences of the outline have merely been included in sentence form, without much further development. The essay remains essentially an outline. However promising the ideas in this outline, the rough first draft has taken them no further.

So the writer has to reenter the piece of writing. She has to work it through again in an effort to expand the ideas and show her readers plainly how she moves from one thought to the next.

Key sentence 1:   *Wearing seat belts and having air bags in cars should be mandatory.*

Key sentence 2:   *All traffic laws should be obeyed and strictly enforced.*

Ask questions: Why should these laws be made mandatory?
How can traffic laws be better enforced?

Examples: My boy friend, Steve, is always going through red lights and getting away with it. Stress this. People who survive serious accidents are always glad they wore seat belts. Find a quote someplace by someone to support this.

Comments: If people were made to wear seat belts, there would be a lot fewer deaths. The same goes for putting air bags in cars. People also should be stopped more often for violating any kind of traffic law, no matter how minor, and given larger fines and even jail sentences for things like drunk driving. Licenses could be revoked for longer periods of time than they are now.

Key sentence 3:   *Continue to show commercials on TV about drunk driving and seat belts.*

Examples: There's a commercial that shows a group of teen-agers about to go out for the night who are not wearing seat belts. Then all we see is darkness, and all we hear is the screeching of brakes and a sound of crashing. The next scene shows the same group of kids as skeletons. You also hear Michael Jackson's song ''Beat It'' playing in the background. Many of these commercials are put out by the National Safety Council or by MADD (Mothers Against Drunk Drivers), whose members' own children were killed in car crashes. Another commercial shows a father and his daughters about to go off for a ride. The daughters have all buckled up and then stare threateningly at their father until he does the same.

Comments: How do I feel about these commercials? They should be even stronger and more terrifying. The idea of skeletons is the right one, much stronger and more convincing than the father and daughters one. Putting in background music by Michael Jackson is a good idea to attract the attention of young people. The reason is that they tend to listen to their rock or sports idols.

Key sentence 4:   *Accident victims have sworn that if they had been wearing seat belts and driving a car with air bags, they could have avoided serious injury.*

Example:

Here I can use the *Newsweek* article on air bags. It mentions fatalities of those who don't wear seat belts also. Fortunately, once I had the topic, I began to pay careful attention to "everything" in magazines, newspapers, and so on, making sure to look at every ad and personal article, especially the ones in the front and back of magazines. What a find! But what to quote? Choose the quotes or passages that deal exclusively with air-bag and seat-belt safety. Choose striking language that's to the point.

Key sentence 5:

It would seem that most people have to be personally involved or at least know someone who has been in an accident before they themselves will wear seat belts or obey all traffic laws.

Ask questions:

Do I know anyone this has happened to?
Do I, my friends, wear seat belts now because of it, or did we always wear them?

Example:

Steve's accident. Will he start wearing a seat belt now that he's been in a serious accident? I could describe a conversation with him both before and after his accident:
Before his accident:

Me: Steve, how come you won't wear seat belts?
S: Too restricting.
Me: You just say that because everyone does.
S: Maybe everyone says it because it's true.
Me: What if you had an accident?
S: Time's up, it's up.
Me: Not necessarily. It could keep you from going out the windshield.
S: Eh, who's going out the windshield? Only people who can't drive get into accidents, not me.
Me: What about going through all those red lights?
S: So what. I'm careful, right? I know when I can get away with it. You have to know when you can get away with something. That's the sign of a careful driver.

Then the conversation in the hospital:

Me: How are you, Steve?
S: Lousy.
Me: I thought you said you couldn't get into an accident.
S: I was wrong.
Me: Did you go through a red light again?
S: I think it went through me.
Me: You weren't wearing a seat belt either, I guess.
S: What else is new?

Me: You know because of you, we all came over wearing our seat belts.

S: Good. Do it on the way home, too.

Me: That doesn't sound like you, Steve.

S: It isn't me. Me was a jerk.

Me: What made you change your mind?

S: A terrific headache.

Me: That would do it. You know I'm really glad you're alive.

S: Thanks. So am I.

Comments:	Can't quote the whole thing. Be selective. Emphasize his insistence that he's a careful driver (''I'm careful about it, right'') in the beginning and then contrast with his change of heart at the end.
Write controlling idea:	Wearing seat belts and having air bags in cars should be mandatory.
Rewrite controlling idea more fully:	Although we all know the dangers of car accidents, traffic laws should be better enforced and the wearing of seat belts and use of air bags in cars made mandatory because it seems that many of us have to be personally involved or know someone involved in a serious accident before we will buckle up and drive safely and carefully.
Conclusion:	Restate the controlling idea, along with Steve's final comments on accident. Bring the essay full circle. For final emphasis, remind reader what can happen if these rules are not implemented.
Think of title:	Everything starts untitled, but then what? ''Safe Driving''? ''Safe and Careful Driving''? Dull. Not an attention grabber. Find a pun, a song or book title. ''On the Road Again''? ''On and Off the Road Again''? Too humorous maybe. ''Fasten Your Seat Belt''? That's it. ''Fasten Your Seat Belt!'' Simple, to the point, and it sounds like the reader is going for an exciting ride.

The Submitted Draft

Fasten Your Seat Belt!

One Saturday night, my boy friend, Steve, picked me up at my parents' home and then proceeded to pass through every red light he came to. This was very common for Steve. All I could think of after his accident that night was his saying to me earlier, "I'm careful, right? I know when I can get away with it. You have to know when you can get away with something.

That's the sign of a careful driver." 1 There can be no doubt that traffic laws should be better enforced and the wearing of seat belts and the use of air bags in cars made mandatory because it seems that many of us have to be personally involved or know someone involved in an accident before we will buckle up and drive safely.

2 One way to ensure that people drive safely would be through the stricter enforcement of traffic rules. This could mean even higher fines or having one's license revoked for long periods of time or even extended jail sentences for dangerous actions like drunk driving. It is important, though, that the police stop offenders more quickly and more often no matter how minor the offense and that people are not sent away with just a warning. Too many people get away with traffic offenses too often and thus become habitual offenders, making life miserable for everyone on the road.

3 There are many organizations, as well as the federal government, that have sponsored various magazine and newspaper ads as well as TV commercials in order to convince people to drive more carefully. Such organizations include the National Safety Council, Americans for Air Bags, and Mothers Against Drunk Drivers (MADD), whose own children have died in car accidents. One TV commercial, which is shown rarely and usually late at night, shows a group of teen-agers about to go out for the night in a car but are not wearing their seat belts. Then all we see is darkness; all we hear is the screeching of brakes and the sound of a crash. The next scene shows us the same kids, except this time they all appear as skeletons. You can also hear Michael Jackson's song "Beat It" playing in the background. The song is used to attract the attention of young people, since young people tend to listen to their sports or rock idols.

Another TV commercial shows a father and his daughters about to go off for a ride. The daughters have all buckled up but then stare threateningly at their father until he does the same. It would seem the former commercial would be more effective because it is more frightening and more realistic.

One way to ensure fewer deaths and crippling injuries would be to install air bags in cars. 4 Actual victims have sworn that if they had been wearing seat belts or driving a car with air bags, they could have avoided serious injury. In one Newsweek article, a man describes an accident that left him paralyzed from the neck down: "I hadn't had the luxury of an air bag," he says, "nor the common sense to buckle up. I wish I had had both. . . . I had the freedom not to wear my seat belt so now I'm confined to a wheelchair. What about my freedom to choose to use an air bag?" Later he says, "The hospital is full of patients who were injured in car crashes: most were not wearing seat belts at the time of their accidents. And as you might expect, many are now air-bag supporters. Unfortunately, some cannot speak." (Cressy, 6)

5 One would hope that with the proper enforcement of traffic rules, with mandatory seat-belt use, with the installation of air bags in every car, and with repeated TV commercials and personal testimony, one would not have to wait to get involved in or to know someone involved in a serious accident before buckling up and driving safely. And so that reminds me of my last conversation with Steve at the hospital:

> Me: You know because of you, we all came over wearing our seat belts.
>
> S: Good. Do it on the way home, too.
>
> Me: That doesn't sound like you, Steve.
>
> S: It isn't me. Me was a jerk.
>
> Me: What made you change your mind?
>
> S: A terrific headache.

One can only hope that it won't take a hospital to bring each one of us to our senses.

6.d DISCOVERING IMPLICIT QUESTIONS

Until now this chapter has focused on the large ideas that control the development of your essay. But there may be occasions as you write when ideas run out and you find yourself stalled. You simply can't come up with enough ideas to keep on fueling your sentences. You've written only three or four sentences, and these seem to have exhausted your ready supply of ideas. An hour before, you would have sworn your head was full of ideas, but now that the writing is in progress, just a few ideas slip out, one by one. The clock ticks. You wait. Those ideas you have seem detached, abrupt, and threaten to give out entirely. Although you have in mind the basic scheme of what you want to say, your writing is skeletal and bare. You wonder how professional writers manage to have so much to say. How do they produce such richness and texture? Where do all those specifics come from?

For the answers to these questions, we must look to the act of composing sentences. You may be a writer who writes very minimally at first. You may have a clear notion of your point and a carefully thought-out controlling idea. You may be able to rattle off the essential features of an experience you plan to relate in your writing. But too often you express whatever you have available in your mind in a few sentences at most. What you may not do is make the most of these sentences. You haven't searched the sentences you've already written for hints of more ideas hidden there. Often, the sentences themselves suggest the details that they lack. Another way to say this is to say that *every sentence asks implicit questions,* or that you can enlarge your ideas by thinking of questions to ask about the key words in your sentences.

Consider this sentence:

My pockets were loaded.

To discover implicit questions in ''My pockets were loaded,'' decide which are the key words:

pockets
loaded

Here is one possible question this sentence might suggest. The question grows out of the key words:

1. *What* were my pockets loaded with?

One way you can answer this question is to supply details in the next sentence:

My pockets were loaded. I had shells and polished sea glass in them, as well as a few dimes, a Band-Aid, and a generous supply of sand that had spilled in to weigh me down.

Here is another possible question the sentence might suggest:

2. *Why* were my pockets loaded?

This question, too, can be answered by supplying details in the next sentence:

My pockets were loaded. Since my hands held tightly to the twins' rafts, I let them stuff all the treasures they found on the beach into my pants pockets.

Here is a third possible question the sentence might suggest:

3. *Where* were the pockets?

Here is the sentence sequence that answers this question:

My pockets were loaded. In the pocket of my new denim jacket, I had the keys to the Chevy and to Jake's car; in my blouse pocket, I had the slip of paper on which I'd scribbled the address of the party I planned to go to that night; in my pants pockets, I had Jake's old biology test, which he had brought along for me to look at; and in my rear pants pocket, I had my rain hat and a ten-dollar bill tucked way down.

Every sentence you write can be the source of more ideas. By raising questions about the key words of your sentences, you can refuel your writing.

Exercise 1 For each of the following sentences, decide on an implicit question that the sentence suggests. Then rewrite the sentence, and add a sentence that answers the question.

Example:	My files contain dozens of letters from people who used my diet.
Implicit question:	*What kind* of people were the letters from?
Sentence sequence:	My files contain dozens of letters from people who used my diet. They were from seriously overweight people who had lost seventy-five pounds or more.

1. He was often short with her.
2. The days were long and monotonous.
3. Most of the young people sat in the back of the bus.
4. The champion raised doubts about the fight.
5. In a dozen parts of the city, bombs went off.
6. I fell into his lap and covered him with kisses.
7. Sometimes a person has a grudge against his neighbor.
8. *The Graduate* made Dustin Hoffman a star.
9. She knocked me down, grabbed my pocketbook, and ducked around the corner out of sight.
10. Every evening after nine, the class gathered with Professor Loomis on the observatory roof to watch for the comet.

11. President Lincoln was shot at Ford's Theater.

12. It wasn't Scottie we saw with her, going into the Palm Room.

13. I do not mean by these comments to ridicule the zookeepers.

6.e COHERENCE IN THE TOTAL ESSAY

Link ideas between paragraphs As you revise, keep your paragraphs in touch with the controlling idea of your essay so that the whole essay holds together. Learn to provide connections from one paragraph to the next so that the main idea is visible from beginning to end.

Paragraphs have been said to "interpret" your thinking to your reader; that is, paragraphs help your reader understand what your writing means because every new paragraph makes another step of your thinking visible:

The first example is . . .
Another example is . . .
A final example is . . .

One reason for this is . . .
A second reason to consider is . . .
A third reason, and one no less important, is . . .

Let us now shift our attention to . . .
But what are the reasons for . . .
For a moment let us digress . . .

These steps should lead the reader to understand your idea in the way you want it understood. The connections between these steps, and thus the connections between paragraphs, should come from the logic of the controlling idea and the order of the parts that support it.

The surest way to achieve a flow from one part to the next is to present the parts in the best order possible: time, space, or climax (Chapter 5). Writing an essay is not like creating a shopping list, in which you write one item under another in any order that occurs to you:

eggs

strawberries

ginger ale

bread

The best connections between ideas are planned for in the writing of sentences. The idea of each sentence propels you to the next sentence, as in the following paragraph from *Self-Interviews* by James Dickey, the poet and novelist:

At any rate, in the Air Force I read a lot of poetry. I was not introduced to it by anybody in my family or any teacher or acquaintance. This has its disadvantages, but it also has one enormous advantage. If you get into poetry in this way, you come to look upon poetry as *your* possession, something that you discovered, that belongs to you in a way it could never have belonged to you if it had been forced on you.

Here, the sentence "This has its disadvantages, but it also has one enormous advantage" sets up in the heart of the original sentence an expectation for the next sentence.

But the connections can be made unmistakably clear when the text itself cannot prepare for the next idea. The writer resorts to emphasizing connections with useful phrases and techniques. *Key words* and *phrases* that appear at the end of one paragraph can be repeated for continuity at the beginning of the next:

End of paragraph: " . . . park behind that blue car."

Start of next paragraph: Pulling alongside the blue car, . . .

Pronouns that replace previously stated nouns (Chapter 15) can be used to highlight the connection between paragraphs:

Preceding paragraph: Five men in blue uniforms stepped out. . . . One of them approached the car . . .

Start of next paragraph: "Katherine Lee, that you?"*he* asked.

Using *synonyms* and *associated words,* rather than repeating exactly the same words, cements the connection between paragraphs:

End of paragraph:

. . . I am grateful to God that, through the influence of the Negro church, the *way of nonviolence* became an integral *part of our struggle.*

Start of next paragraph:

If *this philosophy* had not emerged, by now many streets of the South would, I am convinced, be flowing with blood.

—Martin Luther King, Jr.,
"Letter from Birmingham Jail"

To make connections explicit, to state connections plainly, writers have a bank of *set transitional phrases* to draw on. Some of the available phrases are grouped below according to purpose. These words often signal the need to begin a new paragraph:

Likeness: likewise; similarly

Difference: but; however; still; yet; nevertheless; on the other hand; on the contrary; in contrast; at the same time

Addition: moreover; and; in addition; equally important; next; first; second; third; in the first place; in the second place; again; also; too; besides; furthermore

Example: for example; for instance; to illustrate

Time:	soon; in the meantime; afterward; later; meanwhile; earlier; simultaneously; finally
Place:	here; there; over there; beyond; nearby; opposite; under; above; to the left; to the right
Purpose:	for this purpose; to this end
End:	in conclusion; to summarize; finally; on the whole
Restate-ment:	in short; in other words; in brief; to put it differently
Result:	therefore; then; as a result; consequently; accordingly; thus

Because these words provide obvious handles that a floundering reader can hang on to, cautious students are known to overindulge in these terms. Be on guard against using transitional phrases where your text would be clear without them. When you do use transitional phrases, be especially careful not to use them inaccurately—that is, where your material doesn't warrant the connection you choose. They are not ready-to-wear links to be used as desperate measures to fasten together reluctant ideas. Every link between sentences and paragraphs must make sense:

> Last year I couldn't hold down a job. *Similarly,* I took a plane to California for a rest.

Similar to what? Because there is no similarity stated, this is an unclear use of *similarly*.

> We both liked jazz and looked all over for a good spot. *Nevertheless,* we found one out in the suburbs, of all places.

Why use *nevertheless,* which suggests an opposition? The connection here is time, not opposition:

> We both liked jazz and looked all over for a good spot. *Finally,* we found one out in the suburbs, of all places.

Link sentences within a paragraph The same words and phrases that connect one paragraph to the next can be used to connect one sentence to the next within a single paragraph. Remember that sentences that flow into each other without the need for obvious links should be left on their own. Trust that most of your connections will be there naturally as your ideas sweep you forward. But if, as you reread your work, you sense that your reader may be looking for a clearer connection between two sentences, make the connection and get rid of the guesswork.

Keep your paragraphs unified Writers who write slowly and painfully are not the only ones working under stress. Writers who write freely and never stop to refuel are victims of another curse—the curse of plenty. Wandering from their subject, moving too far afield, offering too many examples that push the reader off the track, they find all details equally irresistible and have them down on the page before they realize it. If you have a tendency toward long-windedness, then proofread your writing for irrelevant sentences and unnecessary details that sabotage paragraph unity and dilute your effect.

Here is a lighthearted—and well-unified—paragraph of definition by Nora Ephron, taken from her magazine article "I Dreamed I Stopped the Show":

> There have been only a few times in my adult life when I have known for certain that I made a terrible decision in choosing to become a writer—and all of them have taken place at the theatre, at the musical theatre, when someone stopped the show. Anyone in the theatre can give you a nice, precise, obvious definition of what that means: a showstopper, they tell you, literally stops the show, to the point where the audience will not let the actors in the next scene get on with it. But that is not exactly what I am talking about. As far as I am concerned, a showstopper is someone who does something onstage so electrifying, so marvelous, so magical, and, most important, so seemingly within reach, that I want to go out and kill myself for not having stuck with my tap-dancing lessons at the Nick Castle School of Dance on La Cienega Boulevard in Los Angeles.

Here is a rerun of Nora Ephron's paragraph sabotaged by excessive details and irrelevant sentences:

> There have been only a few times in my adult life when I have known for certain that I made a terrible decision in choosing to become a writer—and all of them have taken place at the theatre, at the musical theatre, when someone stopped the show. *I saw Gwen Verdon do it in* Can-Can *and Ella Fitzgerald do it with Count Basie, and Barbara Luna stop* A Chorus Line *when she sang "Nothing."* Anyone in the theatre can give you a nice, precise, obvious definition of what that means: a showstopper, they tell you, literally stops the show, to the point where the audience will not let the actors in the next scene get on with it. *At the Kabuki theater in Tokyo, people in the audience shout out for a beloved star to strike a pose and hold it throughout their interminable applause. A Kabuki play usually takes most of the day to be performed.* But that is not exactly what I am talking about. As far as I am concerned, a showstopper is someone who does something onstage so electrifying, so marvelous, so magical, and, most important, so seemingly within reach, that I want to go out and kill myself for not having stuck with my tap-dancing lessons at the Nick Castle School of Dance on La Cienega Boulevard in Los Angeles.

The roll call of examples (Gwen Verdon, Ella Fitzgerald, and so forth) in the second sentence slows down the momentum of the paragraph and takes the reader away from the real point—Nora Ephron's personal and autobiographical definition of *showstopping*. The second assault on this paragraph's unity is the introduction of Kabuki theater, a subject totally removed from the writer's point and an even worse distraction.

Exercise 2 A perfectly good paragraph of student writing has had its unity sabotaged in similar ways. Find the offending sentences, and explain why they detract from the paragraph's unity.

> It was my first day of classes, and I began having difficulties as soon as I arrived at my first class. I had hoped to have economics first, but instead I had Spanish. I thought that I had gotten there in plenty of time, but there was no available space in that room. It looked as if the people in the room were staging a sit-in because they were sprawled out all over the floor. I remember reading a lot about sit-ins during the 1960s. The instructor for the course finally appeared. He called my name for attendance, and I replied from the hall. He smiled and said, ''I'm sorry, you will have to come a little early next time.'' Now, I have known a lot of great men who were always late. I don't know what he thought when I turned around and marched out of the building, but I know what I was thinking of.

6.f SUGGESTIONS FOR REVISING

Write as you think Remember that the second draft might never have been written if it were not for the mistakes of the first draft. Be willing to let your mistakes happen, but know when you are not satisfied. The route to a successful piece of writing is not *think,* then *write,* then *hand it in*. The route is a cycle of acts, any of which you can repeat whenever you need to. Remember that most of your thinking takes place *as* you write. Whether you are freewriting, writing a first draft, or adjusting a detail in a paragraph, you are working back and forth through your ideas, thinking, and writing, and rewriting. The route is a cycle:

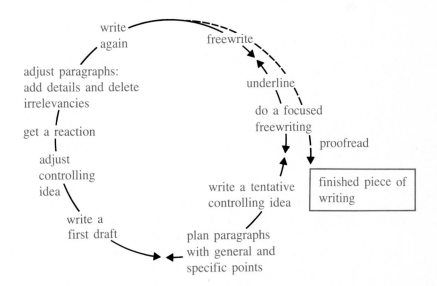

Allow enough time Give yourself time to return to your draft with fresh eyes—a week, if you can, an overnight, if you're really pressed. To revise is to *re-see,* to see things differently, and for that you need to put some distance between the acts of composing and of rereading.

Does the essay please you on rereading it? Does it surprise you in any way? What does it promise, and what does it deliver? Is there anything else you want to know? Does anything seem out of place? Is there something that doesn't belong except for the fact that you *like* it? Sometimes your most original idea doesn't belong in *this* essay no matter how much you want it there. Take it out. Or perhaps try moving it to another part of the essay. All parts are movable and removable.

Support your ideas Remember that no matter how good your ideas are, they always are vulnerable to attack. Support them. Details, illustrations, quotations—these are your weapons. With them standing behind you, behind everything you assert, you can't lose. Answer the "Why?" "How?" "When?" "Where?" and "What?" questions before the reader thinks of asking them.

Be selective But at the same time, don't overillustrate. Stick to whatever is absolutely essential to support your ideas. Do not distract your readers with irrelevancies or make them hunt for what's important.

Use your imagination There is no law that restricts the essay to a particular style or format. Expository writing can be creative. Don't hesitate to explore fictional and dramatic techniques, such as dialogue, metaphor, description, and anecdote. Bring your ideas to life.

Do some research Always do the "library" reading—books, magazines, newspapers, pamphlets— but don't ignore the personal research. There *is* life outside the library. Always think of your own experiences to illustrate a point, as well as the experiences of those around you. There is no personal experience that won't fit into a general context. Become part of your topic. The more you connect it to your own life, the more precisely you can write about it. Remember, your task is to convince your reader that only you could have written this essay.

Read the essay aloud How does it sound? Does it flow, or does it jam up in places, causing you to stop and start like a bad engine? The reader can be as disturbed by awkward writing as by unsupported ideas. Reading the essay aloud helps you to hear errors or awkward phrasings that may have passed by your eyes. If you can, read aloud to a friend.

Think of a title A title can be an important attention grabber, much like a first line or a first paragraph. A title—comic, serious, ironic, or technical—can set the tone for a piece of writing. A good title brings an essay into focus. It concisely suggests what the essay is all about.

Revising: adjacent exercises Many inexperienced writers grasp what it means to develop their ideas, not through rewriting, but through a kind of adjacent writing. Instead of working and reworking the whole essay, you might try the following alternatives:

1. Fastwrite the whole essay, getting down a hasty draft, organizing the parts as best you can, and not worrying about syntax and mechanics or even about putting in too many details here and too few there. The important thing is to get a draft onto paper.

2. Now choose one part of the essay for careful development and revision. For example, let us suppose that you are writing an essay about a commonly held misconception. You might begin by saying that many college students believe that owning a car is a luxury, but that you believe it is a burden. In your fast draft, you have sketched out both parts of your whole idea, although on rereading it, you find that you have not developed either idea. You scarcely deal with the luxury at all; you mention the high cost of gas and repairs but do not go much further.

3. Now write up only the first part—the explanation in full of why people believe that owning a car is a luxury. You might cite the convenience of traveling when you choose, the pleasure of not being herded onto crowded buses, the pride of ownership. By developing the first part, you have structured your thinking; supplying a detailed second part becomes a natural response to the first part. The expense of gas and repairs, for example, pretty soon lessens any pride of ownership, since you have little money left for food and clothing. The convenience of setting your own schedule is frequently interrupted by having to drive other family members about, and the privacy of travel, which you still crave, has simply become a snobby luxury you cannot afford.

4. Another possibility is to recast the discussion in the form of a dialogue between car owner and bus rider. Such a conversation will express the key points of the argument, since what often passes between two people as an exchange of questions and answers is, in fact, the central argument of an essay.

5. Another piece of adjacent writing that develops an idea is to do a page of description, setting the scene for either ride: a sardine's ride to school versus cruising to class. Although most of these descriptions would not appear in the final form of your essay, some of your best observations surely will find their way into your essay, enriching it with convincing sensory detail.

Other possibilities follow in the form of exercises.

Exercise 3   Rewrite half an essay that you have composed so that a first-person narrator governs the development of your ideas. Compare the first half with the second half. Is there a difference in tone? Is the argument more convincing or less convincing?

Exercise 4   Rewrite an essay that already presents a first-person narrator so that

1. the *I* is eliminated and replaced by *we,* and
2. the *I* is eliminated and replaced by a third-person subject.

Exercise 5   Rewrite the opening paragraph of an essay so that you address your reader as *you.*

Exercise 6   Divide the argument of an essay into two voices, one personified point of view arguing with a second, as in the discussion between a car owner and a bus rider suggested above.
Consider the following possibilities:

1. science/superstition
2. meat/vegetables
3. victory/defeat
4. exercise/sleep
5. father/son
6. mother/daughter
7. city/country
8. wife (husband)/lover
9. book/movie
10. speed/patience
11. plan/impulse
12. education/experience

Let each member of the pair speak in the first person.

Exercise 7   Skip the opening paragraph of an essay that you have written. Beginning with the second paragraph, read to the end. Now write a new opening paragraph without rereading the first one. Compare the two paragraphs, and comment on the differences between them.

Exercise 8   For an essay that you have composed, write an alternative opening paragraph, one that creates an analogy (p. 84) to explain your point. Then write a concluding paragraph that picks up resonances of the analogy.

Exercise 9 For an essay that you have composed, write an alternative final paragraph, one that speculates on a new but related direction your ideas might take.

Exercise 10 State the controlling idea for an expository essay that you plan to write. Try to fit the statement into the following pattern: Although X may be a problem, Y is so because of A, B, and C.

Exercise 11 State the controlling idea for an essay of comparison that you plan to write. Try to fit the statement into the following pattern: X is so, and Y is so; but I prefer X because of A, B, and C.

Exercise 12 State the controlling idea for a narrative essay that you plan to write. Try to fit the statement into the following pattern: X is generally true, and I have had the following experience that supports X.

6.g PROOFREADING

Once you have written your essay and revised it to your satisfaction, you will want to prepare a final copy to give to your reader. Sometimes your reader is your teacher, but by no means will you go through life preparing final drafts only for teachers in classes. Business letters, letters of complaint or request, reports for a supervisor on a job, or important personal letters that you want to be perfect all require that special and patient attention to the final draft that we call *proofreading*. Reading *proof* means checking copy for errors and making the needed corrections. In the same way, a photographer shows you proofs of photographs that can be touched up to correct the flaws and blemishes you notice. Your final draft, remember, represents *you* and deserves a special, intense final reading to make sure you are represented at your best.

Proofreading is hunting for mechanical errors that can be corrected ''locally'' and, usually, without further changes in the surrounding context. Proofreading means that you do for yourself what editors do before a manuscript by a professional writer is published. That is not to suggest that professional writers don't proofread their own work. They certainly do; but a publisher's job is to guarantee that no accidental errors exist to distress readers, and so the publisher provides expert backup people—editors and proofreaders—to check every letter and every mark of punctuation on every page. Spelling mistakes, common errors like *there* for *their, to* for *too, its* for *it's, -ie* for *-ei* become a nuisance to a reader. The repetition of a word, an omitted word, half of a set of quotation marks left out, a single mark of parenthesis, a misplaced comma or period, a typographical error, a wrongly used capital letter, or the absence of a capital letter distracts your reader's attention vrom the meaning of the sentence to the curious look of a word by itself *(vrom?)*. And you ought to remember that certain grammatical problems discussed in Part Three of this book—like the *-s* ending or the -*ed* ending—can sometimes be overlooked until you are ready to proofread, because matters of correctness can never be at the center of your mind as you put your ideas down on paper.

If careless errors in writing call the reader's attention to a word instead of to an idea, then perhaps the problem itself tells you how to solve it. Looking carefully at every word and at every letter of every word may be the best way to spot careless errors. The technique of proofreading requires you to change your usual way of seeing your work. Some people suggest reading out loud; others say you should read your writing from the end to the beginning, sentence by sentence. In any case, you've got to slow your reading speed to a crawl. Youve got to look at the makeup of word in a way that you have not occupy yoursef with in in the first heet of writint.

STOP. Did you notice any errors in the preceding sentence? Were you able to catch typographical or spelling errors in the normal pace of your reading? There were seven errors in all:

Youve	for	*You've*
word	for	*words*
occupy	for	*occupied*
yoursef	for	*yourself*
heet	for	*heat*
writint	for	*writing*

plus a repeated *in* at the beginning of a line.

If you caught all seven errors, you are already a skilled proofreader. But if you did not, you might profit from proofreading your work several times, each time on the hunt for one type of mistake. As you write more often, and as other people comment on your work, you will come to know the mistakes you most frequently make. If -*s* endings are your problem, you should proofread one time exclusively for them. If bad spelling is your affliction, you should proofread once through, word by word, with a vigilant eye for possible spelling devils (Chapter 17). If your typing is shaky, proofread once for typos and correct them carefully with a correction device or in ink. With practice, you will not need to proofread so many times, but you *must* proofread every page, whether handwritten or typed, before you consider it ready for a reader. And if you write your papers in longhand, be sure to form your letters clearly. Do not conceal your uncertainties about spelling or punctuation behind a smokescreen that will make even those words you are sure of unreadable.

Exercise 13 Proofread the following passages carefully. Correct all the errors you find, such as incorrect spellings, punctuation errors, omitted -*s* and -*ed* endings, and omitted words.

1. Many of the problem people have with other people can be trace to what they say to each other. I use to have serous problem in getting along with people because of the way I verbalized my thoughts. I would verbalize *all* of my thought, even the one "of the top of my head" that I hadnt thought much about at all, and I woul do it instantly. I now got along better with people because I hav vound a way to deal with my thoughts without hafing to verbalize all of then.

2. Learning lessons is a part of evry persons life. Im a very trustinb person, often geting mysef into scraps I later realize I could of avoided. After one of my scraps I learn that a favor may not be a favor at all.

3. Disasters are things that you can read about in the paper everyday. A funny thing about them is that their is nothing real about them I mean I realiz that they realy did happen but not to my little world. Disaster is something that only really bother me when its a disaster effecting my life. When I read in the news paper about a familly dyeing in a fire. I think about it for a minute but then quickily forget it. However if the fire, was on my block, or in my neihborhood, then it would be, a personel disaster. Personel disaster, make me think of God right away and pray for help. Tears usualy acompany my prayers along with steps to remeday the situation. However cruel it may seam I think disaster, ony really effects people when it hit home.

4. Although you have made an apointment with a tutor in the Writin Skills Workshop, you may not aware that you are particapating in a nation wide movement to improfe the writing skill of colege student by inivisual peer instruction. Like, the other srudents in writing workshops around the country, you have come either on your own or at the suggeshun of your instructor. In either case you, will probly agree their is no time to loose. You've decide to invest sometime out of a crowded week and you want you're investment to paid off. The tips that follow will help you make the most of this timely oportunity with a privat teacher. If, you have problems in scheduleing or in working with an assign tutor do not hesitate to see a supervisor and request a change, you are therefore encouraged to keep all your appointments regular.

6.h EXERCISES IN REWRITING

The following exercises in rewriting make use of the essays in Chapter 9 (pp. 189–208).

Exercise 14   The writers of essays 4 and 12 begin with a personal account and then move to a general observation.

1. For each essay, state the general observation first and move the personal account to a position after the general statement. What else would need to be changed?

2. Which paragraphs, if any, could be omitted?

3. Is there anything you would need to add?

4. For each essay, write a transition that would carry the reader from the general to the personal.

5. Does the language of each part reflect its purpose? Cite specific words or phrases to support your answer.

Exercise 15 Essay 8 is written inductively; that is, the experiences of the author are given before the author evaluates them and provides a controlling idea for the essay.

1. Recast the beginning so that the controlling idea is explicitly stated at the start of the essay.

2. How does this change affect the essay? Does this new organization seem more formal to you? less formal?

3. What is the difference to be expected in the response of a reader to an essay written deductively; that is, an essay that expresses its controlling idea conspicuously at the beginning (or near the beginning) of the essay? Why do you suppose the reader's response changes?

Exercise 16 Read essay 2 and answer the following questions.

1. What is the governing point of view of the essay? Change the point of view so that the narrator is writing about these events while they are occurring.

2. Rewrite the opening paragraph to suggest this change in perspective.

3. Which passages would need to be eliminated? Which would have to be rewritten to reflect the change?

4. What would you do to emphasize that the narrator is in the midst of this drama? Consider such grammatical features as governing pronoun, verb tense, and transitions.

Exercise 17 In essay 9, the author chooses to omit a discussion of his own appearance until he finally mentions his mustache and his nose.

1. Can you justify the omission?

2. Write a paragraph describing the author's face. Where might your paragraph be included? What effect would including it before paragraph 6 have on the reader?

3. Is the reader's understanding of the father's problem enriched by the proposed paragraph? Why or why not?

4. Which other essays in Chapter 9 omit major scenes or subjects? What is the effect of each?

Exercise 18 Essays 1 and 11 are written in a humorous tone.

1. Change the first three paragraphs in each essay to suggest a serious tone.

2. Locate other places in the essays where change is necessary to alter the tone. Are there many places or few? Why?

3. In each essay, which words convey humor?

4. How does adjusting the tone affect the ending?

Exercise 19 In essay 3, study the connections between paragraphs 1 and 2, 2 and 3, 3 and 4, and 4 and 5.

1. What is the logic behind these transitions?

2. Is the writer's contrast strengthened through these transitions? How?

3. Do the writer's definitions of independence govern his transitions? How?

4. Would you rewrite any of the transitions? Recast the one between paragraphs 1 and 2, making the connection less explicit. Do you like your transition better than the author's? Why or why not?

Exercise 20 Consider beginning essay 7 with paragraph 2.

1. How does the essay without paragraph 1 change its emphasis?

2. Does the writer's two-step definition of *courage* relate to his opening paragraph? In what way?

3. Account for the writer's shift from *I* in paragraphs 1 and 2 to *one* in paragraph 3. Is the shift justified?

Exercise 21 In essay 5, the writer imagines that he is entering the mind of another person in his story, so that we hear reactions from another (imagined) point of view. We hear what his father might be thinking; then we hear what his mother might be thinking.

1. What do these passages add to the essay?

2. Do you find them convincing? Why or why not?

3. In an essay that you are writing or have written, choose one or two of the people whom you have not allowed to speak, and then zero in on what they might be thinking or on what they might have actually said. What are the effects?

Exercise 22 In essay 6, notice how the writer represents an event in the present tense, so that we, as readers, have a sense of things happening right now, unfolding before our eyes.

1. How else does the writer accomplish this sense of immediacy?

2. If the essay had been written in the past tense ("The quiet landscape *lay*

peaceful and tranquil in the early morning dew. Five birds *swooped* by . . . '') what would have been lost? gained?

3. Experiment with one of your own essays, changing it from the past tense to the present. What do you accomplish? What other changes do you need to make?

4. In this essay, the writer represents one event. Or does he? Does he, rather, try to make this one event stand for many, for the way things generally are when he runs? Take one of your personal narratives, about something you do habitually, and make that one event stand for a general state or condition.

Exercise 23 Read essay 10 and do the following.

1. Write a précis of the essay (pp. 446–448).
2. Write an outline of the essay (pp. 24–26).
3. Stare at a fellow passenger in an elevator or on a bus. Using your experience, this essay, and any other information or intuition as source material, write about what you experience to be the ''boundaries'' of staring.
4. This article is written in a serious, often scholarly or scientific, tone. Would another tone be appropriate for this subject? Why or why not? If yes, rewrite the opening to convey the tone of your choice.

chapter 7 | Revising Sentences

7.a SENTENCES IN MOTION

Now you can begin to take *control* of your sentences, experiencing considerable pleasure as you tame them into saying precisely what you want. Now you can attend not only to writing essays, but also to rewriting *energetic* sentences that work well together, sentences that have a job to do: they must begin to reward your readers for their effort and move them unhesitatingly forward into the teeth of your ideas and into the complex development of your paragraphs. It is up to your sentences to safeguard the interest of your essay by holding your readers' attention to each sentence as it arises and by suggesting the promise in the sentences that follow. This chapter, then, will help you rewrite your sentences and get them moving. Remember that only *you* can unlock the energy in your sentences. Reorder the parts, and prune out the deadwood, the filler words that contribute nothing. Use strong verbs and clear connections. Your sentences should be plain and vigorous at all times. They must be in the best shape possible to do the work of showing your readers the clear, sure direction of *your* thinking.

7.b STRAINING FOR A "COLLEGE" STYLE

Many people with powerful things to say are embarrassed to show their writing to others because their sentences are not "elegant" or "complicated" enough.

They strain to produce sentences that sound "college" level. They say, "In the event a young person is prevaricating . . .," instead of "If a child is lying . . ." when they *know* the simple language is clearer. The truth is, the trend in good writing is always toward simplicity and clarity. Even some insurance companies, whose policies have always been impossible to read, have begun to revise the sentences they write so that anyone can read them. Note the difference in the following two sentences taken from Aetna Life and Casualty policies:

Old policy: Upon the happening of an occurrence reasonably likely to involve the Company hereunder, written notice shall be given as soon as practicable to the Company or any of its authorized agents.

Readable policy: If there's an accident or incident that may be covered by this policy, notify us in writing as soon as possible. You can give this notice to any of our authorized agents.

It is not always simple to write a sentence that *sounds* simple. Even experienced writers face uncertainties all along the way. The illustration on the next page shows you the muddled but indispensable rough draft of our own opening paragraph of the chapter you are now reading. Are you surprised at what an unruly beginning this chapter had? Maybe you imagine that all the sentences of professional writers stream flawlessly onto the page, whole. We hope our exhibit will confirm that, for most writers, writing sentences *means* revising them.

Revision may include changing a single word of a sentence as well as rewriting an entire essay. Notice our change from *writing interesting sentences* to *rewriting energetic sentences*. Any change you make, however trivial it may seem to you at the time, is an attempt to find out as precisely as you can what you are thinking. Any improvement you make in any part of a sentence puts you more and more securely in control of your idea because as you write it out in a sentence, as you force yourself to say it in a sentence, you are always working to refine your idea and make it clear.

Since sentences must be read in order and cannot be read upside down or backward or absorbed all in one glance, the very first sentence of your essay often sets the direction your reader will take. Every sentence that follows is linked into place because its idea in some way springs from the sentence before it and rolls toward the sentence after it and because the language in it refers to words or groups of words that appear in the surrounding sentences. Even the rhythms of your sentences are interconnected—suddenly yanking a sentence from the middle of your essay may be like gashing out a line in the middle of a song. Whenever you delete or change a sentence, you should adjust the stream of sentences before and after to close the gap in ideas, language, and rhythm. Adjusting only a single word or moving a phrase from the end of the sentence to the beginning, or from the beginning to the end, can often be enough to restore a seamless flow to your writing.

Experienced writers enjoy options as they compose their sentences, options that you, too, are entitled to enjoy, although the choices may cause you such indecision that you are more likely at first to suffer from them than enjoy them. It

~~Sentences in Paragraphs~~ — ~~Sentences in Essays~~ Sentences in Motion

~~This chapter is occasioned by your readiness to think about how you can control your writing.~~ *Now* You ~~will learn~~ *can begin* to *take* control your ~~expression so that it shows the clear promise~~ *of sentences, experiencing considerable pleasure as you tame them into saying* ~~of your essay in~~ precise *ly what you want to say.* ~~grammar.~~ Now you ~~will be~~ *can* attend~~-~~ ~~ing~~ not only to writing *essays,* ~~acceptable sentences without blunders~~ but also to *re*writing ~~interesting~~ *energetic* sentences that work well together, sentences that ~~work for you~~ *have a job to do*: they must *begin to reward your readers for their effort and* gather interest and move ~~your readers~~ *them unhesitatingly* forward into the *teeth of* ~~paragraphs that exhibit~~ your ideas and into the complex development of your paragraphs. ~~You must now write~~ *It is up to your* sen~~-~~ ~~tences that uncover what you mean and~~ *to safeguard the interest of your essay by* hold~~-on to~~ *ing* your readers' attention *to each sentence as it arises and by* ~~as they journey into the center of what~~ *suggesting the promise in the sentences that follow.* ~~you have to say.~~ This chapter, then, will help you rewrite

would be a lot easier, you think, were there only one way to express an idea; but you will soon find that without options, your sentences would be a lot less colorful and less accurate as well. So you ask yourself questions:

1. What is the best place in the sentence for this phrase? Where will it create the best link with the sentence before it or the sentence after it?
2. Can I say this in fewer words?
3. Does this idea belong in a new sentence? Will it overload the sentence?
4. Should I repeat my verb for emphasis? Or should I use a different verb to add another shade of meaning?
5. What can I say next? Where will my next sentence come from?
6. Should I turn to a new idea? Or does the idea in my last sentence need to be expanded or illustrated?
7. Will there *be* a next sentence?

Much of the discussion about the sources of ideas for your sentences has been included in Chapter 6.

7.c WHAT SLOWS YOUR SENTENCES DOWN?

A copy editor rewrites sentences to make them more concise and at the same time more vigorous and easier to understand. Learn to copy-edit your own sentences. Unnecessary words—deadwood—muddle your point and slow your readers' progress. A few tricks will help you to be more concise. Convert nouns and adjectives to verbs where possible. Reduce the number of prepositional phrases, especially prepositional phrases following *is* or *has* where a strong verb would locate the action where it ought to be—in the verb. For example:

> The East Wing of the National Gallery *has* Matisse's cut-outs *on regular exhibition*.

This becomes a sharper sentence by locating the action in the verb:

> The East Wing of the National Gallery *regularly exhibits* Matisse's cutouts.

''The East Wing *has*'' delays the meaning; ''The East Wing *exhibits*'' delivers the meaning faster.

Eliminate introductory elements such as *there is*, *there are*, and *it is* whenever the meaning will allow.

Study the editing in the following sentences:

NO: The new refrigerator ~~has a leak~~.
YES: The new refrigerator leaks.

NO: Our country ~~puts~~ *imprisons* a higher percentage of its population ~~into prison~~ than any other country ~~that is free~~.
YES: Our country imprisons a higher percentage of its population than any other free country.

NO: ~~Is~~ *Can* Anita ~~able to do the~~ studying tonight?
YES: Can Anita study tonight?

NO: ~~In~~ Our town, ~~there are~~ *has* a great many people who ~~do~~ care and want to help.
YES: Our town has a great many people who care and want to help.

NO: Give me ~~the exact~~ precise directions ~~that will take me~~ to your house.
YES: Give me precise directions to your house.

NO: ~~When I look back~~ *In* retrospect, I ~~am able to~~ see the error of my ways.
YES: In retrospect, I see the error of my ways.

NO: ~~There are acts with~~ *R*ock bands ~~that~~ sell out concert halls.
YES: Rock bands sell out concert halls.

NO: Parties like the one ~~I attended~~ yesterday ~~do~~ *are* not ~~tend to stay in my memory~~ *memorable*.
YES: Parties like the one yesterday are not memorable. OR: I usually forget parties like yesterday's.

NO: After work, I ~~proceed to~~ eat ~~my dinner~~ at a restaurant ~~that is located near me in my~~ neighborhood.
YES: After work, I eat at a neighborhood restaurant.

NO: ~~My failure on~~ *I failed* the final examination ~~was due to the fact that~~ *because* I had ~~an aching~~ *a* tooth*ache*.
YES: I failed the final examination because I had a toothache.

NO: The teen-ager is no longer a child ~~who is still~~ attached to the "umbilical
        cord." *During* Adolescence, ~~is the time when~~ teen-agers ~~are developing into~~ indi-
        viduals and ~~when they~~ cut ~~away from~~ "family ties." *become*

YES: The teen-ager is no longer a child attached to the "umbilical cord."
        During adolescence, teen-agers become individuals and cut "family
        ties." (Cut from thirty-three words to twenty-one words)

NO: Today's modern American citizen should be given a certain amount of
        responsibility so that he can grow to become an independent and produc-
        tive member of our contemporary society.

YES: The American government should give citizens enough responsibility to
        enable them to live independently and contribute to society. (Cut from
        thirty words to eighteen words) OR: Responsible American citizens have
        the ability to live independently and contribute to society.

Study the next paragraph and compare it with the revised version that follows. Notice the difference in conciseness:

Hockey is a very quick sport. ~~In order~~ *To* keep it ~~very~~ fast-moving, ~~hockey~~

~~is the only sport in which~~ substitutions are made while play is ~~actually~~ in

on ice skates
progress. Players whiz up and down the rink at speeds of 20 m.p.h. ,

ing
~~Wearing ice skates, they just~~ weave in and out of the opposition while

moving the puck. Their ~~main~~ objective is to score by firing a fast or

past
unexpected shot ~~that goes through~~ the opposing team's goalkeeper ~~and~~

D ing   *the goalkeeper*
~~into the goal. It is the goalkeeper's job to~~ dive in front of the goal, ~~when~~

blocks
shots that frequently go as fast as 100 m.p.h. ~~have to be blocked.~~

Revision:

Hockey is a very quick sport. To keep it fast-moving, substitutions are made
while play is in progress. Players on ice skates whiz up and down the rink at
speeds of 20 m.p.h., weaving in and out of the opposition while moving the
puck. Their objective is to score by firing a fast or unexpected shot past the
opposing team's goalkeeper. Diving in front of the goal, the goalkeeper blocks
shots that frequently go as fast as 100 m.p.h.

Eliminate all unnecessary *just*'s, *actually*'s, *very*'s. Combine sentences. Reduce
in order to to *to*. Eliminate obvious statements.

But a word of caution. Don't carry the effort to be concise to an extreme.
Good writing results from learning to express your ideas gracefully and fully.
Sudden shortcuts, omissions of words crucial to your exact meaning, missing
connections between ideas result in sentences that sound like telegrams and
wring the pleasure out of reading. For example, here again is the paragraph about
hockey; but this time, it is too concisely written. It no longer conveys the sense
of speed implicit in the fuller language of the previous paragraph:

Hockey is a quick sport. Substitutions are made while play is in progress. Players on ice skates going 20 m.p.h. score by firing a shot past the opposition's goalkeeper, who tries to block shots as fast as 100 m.p.h.

Exercise 1 The following sentences suffer from wordiness. Rewrite them as distinctly and as emphatically as possible.

1. In case you lose your way and drive around, call us on the telephone.
2. It was during the winter of 1976 that I learned to ski.
3. In New York, there are many theaters and restaurants.
4. Why weren't you happy with regard to the way your paper turned out?
5. Until the winter of 1976, I had never skied before.
6. There should be greater emphasis on friendliness in hospitals.
7. There is a woman in my French class who sits next to me and is always in need of conversation.
8. I can definitely see a number of improvements that could be made to make registration easier without a doubt.
9. We should never underestimate our opponents and think they are not as fast as we are.
10. Our success was due to the fact that our team had positive hopes and expectations.
11. I will never cease to be optimistic that good things can always come to pass, especially through hard work.
12. Up until the midterm, I had been receiving passable grades on my tests and papers, but nothing spectacular.
13. I was getting ready to go out of my mind due to the fact that I was so frustrated, when I came up with a beginning opening paragraph that chimed like a choir of church bells.
14. I don't think that a teacher should ever accuse a student without first having proof of what he is accusing the student of.
15. There are many times when a person begins to feel that she has been treated unjustly.

7.d HOW DO YOU MOVE YOUR READER FORWARD?

Write a variety of sentences There's nothing excellent about a long sentence simply because it's long or a short one because it's short. But too many long sentences or too many short sentences can be monotonous. If you want to intensify the power of your writing, reread what you've written—out loud if possible—with an ear cocked for too much sameness. Sentences that change patterns and lengths will keep your reader awake instead of *zzzzz,* lulled by the same old subject–verb–object rhythms that drone on and on.

Look at the variety of sentences in the next passage. Notice how much forward energy they gain by questions and answers, by the variety of sentence patterns, by short and long rhythms, and by repetitions and exclamations.

> Why am I so happy? It must be the triumph of the human spirit over genetics and environment. I know the same bad things Howard knows. I have my ups and downs, traumas, ecstasies. Maybe this happiness is only a dirty trick, another of life's big come-ons. I might end up the kind who can't ride on escalators or sit in chairs that don't have arms. Who knows?
>
> But in the meantime I sing as I whip up waffle batter, pour golden juice into golden glasses, while Howard sits in a chair dropping pages of The *Times* like leaves from a deciduous tree.
>
> I sing songs from the Forties, thinking there's nothing in this life like the comfort of your own nostalgia. I sing *Ferry-Boat Serenade,* I sing *Hut-Sut Rallson on the Riller-ah.* The waffles stick to the iron. "Don't sit under the apple tree with anyone else but me," I warn Howard, willing the waffle and coffee smells into the living room where he sits like an inmate in the wintry garden of a small sanatorium.
>
> —Hilma Wolitzer,
> "Behold the Crazy Hours of the Hard-Loving Wife"

Keep your verbs active   Read the following sentences, which are from college catalogs (the *Queens College Bulletin* and the *Yale College Programs of Study*):

> In the event of any increase in the fees or tuition charges, payments already made to the College will be treated as a partial payment and notification will be given of the additional amount due and the time and method for payment.

Made by whom?
Treated by whom?
Given by whom?

> Application Fee: All students are required to pay a non-refundable fee of $10.00 at the time of filing application for either matriculant or non-matriculant status in a master's degree program.

Required by whom?

> Transcripts are prepared upon written request and payment of a charge depending upon the number of copies requested at one time. Request forms are available in 11 sss.

Prepared by whom?
Requested by whom?

Members of the military are accustomed to reading announcements such as the following:

Platoon A has been reassigned to the automotive pool effective immediately.

All enlisted personnel will be issued class B passes for twenty-four hours except platoon A, whose passes have been revoked.

Who can overlook the air of mysterious authority in these statements? An unknown and depersonalized authority shields the college administrators and buffers the military brass from complaints and blame. All this mystery lies in the passive forms of the verbs ("has been reassigned," "will be issued," "have been revoked"). This is the language of the institution concealing the faces of the real people behind it. It is deliberately lifeless.

If you want your essays to come alive, you've got to show your face. You've got to invite people through your voice. Look at how these students' sentences spring to life when an active verb replaces a passive one and the performer is named:

NO: The willingness of a person to help in his community comes through when urban projects are participated in.

YES: The willingness of a person to help in his community comes through when *he participates* in urban projects.

NO: Children soon learn to put the alphabet together to form words. These words may later be recognized in the book.

YES: Children soon learn to put the alphabet together to form words. Later *they may recognize* these words in the book.

NO: The teen-age years are the most difficult times in a person's life. During this stage of life, many problems must be resolved. New adjustments toward life must be made. More responsibilities are imposed on teen-agers.

YES: The teen-age years are the most difficult times in a person's life. During this age, *adolescents encounter* many problems that *they must resolve*. *They must make* new adjustments toward life and *accept* more responsibilities.

Emphasize words or phrases by changing their position in the sentence

You can ensure your reader's attention by emphasizing the important elements of your sentences.

The usual order of words in English sentences is subject–verb–completer:

I love chocolate cake.

I've heard nothing about his wife, but I've heard a lot about Joe.

When you want to emphasize a part of your statement, you may have been doing it in ways that are terribly obvious:

I love chocolate cake!!!!!!!

I've heard nothing about his wife, but I've heard a lot about Joe.

Good writers avoid a parade of exclamation points or a smear of underlinings. They try to build emphasis into the grammatical construction of their sentences. A change in the usual order of sentence elements will pin the reader's attention to a word in an unexpected location:

> Chocolate cake I love.
>
> I've heard nothing about his wife, but about Joe I've heard a lot.

Remember that the positions in the sentence that draw the greatest natural emphasis are the beginning and the end. Suppose the positions of words in a sentence had the following price tags: $5, 39 cents, $10. With these prices in mind, you wouldn't throw $10 away on an unimportant word, as in the following sentences:

> $5   39¢
> Unemphatic: I went to the Montreal museum and found some interesting Es-
> $10
> kimo sculpture there.

Emphatic (emphasis on *Montreal museum* and *Eskimo sculpture*):

> $5   39¢ $10
> At the Montreal museum, I found some interesting Eskimo sculp-
>
> ture.
> $5   39¢
> Unemphatic: It makes people grow if they are responsible for someone or
> $10
> something.

Emphatic (emphasis on *responsible* and *grow*):

> $5   39¢ $10
> Being responsible for someone or something makes people grow.

Exercise 2   Rewrite the following sentences so that the least important element is tucked into the middle of the sentence.

> Example: I believe you are drenched.
>   You are, I believe, drenched.

1. He noted that the landscape was lovely.
2. However, improvements can be made.
3. It is safe to say that everyone is a little weary now.
4. We discovered that the weather was never neutral.
5. Much later in the year we found out that he had won a Nobel Prize.
6. After long months of study, you learn to rely on nobody but yourself.
7. We must remember that throwing something away is really throwing it back into the universe.
8. It occurred to me that the piano needed tuning.
9. They say that once they have their licenses, they'll drive me anywhere.
10. We discovered when we got to the airport that it was shut down because of fog.

Don't skip an essential link between two ideas in a sentence

Some sentences put forward one idea and present no problem. Other sentences attempt to deliver two or more ideas in a single container. If you jam two ideas into a sentence without showing the link between them, the continuity of your essay may suffer a break right there, in that sentence. Without a link, your readers may slow down and become stalled because they have no way to get across to the next idea. Consider the following sentence:

NO: Children should be taught to think of their bodies as enjoyable and knowable as no one's body can be considered perfect.

A link is missing in this sentence. The writer probably means that children can enjoy their own bodies even if they are not perfect or beautiful, but she has not expressed this connection. She has lined up the two ideas without relating them:

Children should be taught to enjoy their bodies.

No one's body is perfect.

Improved: Even when a child's proportions are not graceful and perfect, he can learn to enjoy his body through exercising, moving his muscles, and fulfilling his own needs independently.

Now consider another sentence:

NO: By reading a lot, you develop your mind and your vocabulary, and these two things are good in any walk of life.

This writer fails to explain the connections among reading, a good vocabulary, and an enhanced life. To make the connections clear, the writer decided to use more than one sentence:

Improved: Reading develops your mind because it trains you to grasp and express ideas through words. This ability to express yourself will improve your relationships with people no matter what you do in your life.

Don't overload a sentence with unconnectable elements

Sometimes you draft a sentence whose parts have no sensible connection. Rather than create a forced connection, break the sentence down into more than one sentence or explain the connection between the parts. (See the examples in the preceding section.)

Avoid writing sentences without internal connectors

Sometimes a sentence may be faulty and hard to understand because one part of the sentence does not make a logical connection with another part. It is particularly important to see that a subject makes a logical connection with its verb. (See the discussion of subordination and coordination in Chapter 11.)

NO: There are four more years here will have a great influence on my life.
YES: The next four *years* here *will have* a great influence on my life.

NO: You said you are a Taurus I feel you understand what I am talking about.
YES: *Since* you said you are a Taurus, I feel you understand what I am talking about.

NO: You want to be a policeman, there is good news and bad news.
YES: There is good news and bad news *if* you want to be a policeman.

NO: Dancing all weekend I am a good dancer.
YES: I go dancing all weekend *because* I am a good dancer.

or

YES: I am a good dancer, *and* I go dancing all weekend.

Avoid mixing sentence parts that don't make sense together

You have a right to expect words to tell you something, but these don't:

NO: Another unique function of reading is the media.

The subject and verb don't make sense together in this sentence. How can a function of reading *be* the media?

Let's backtrack and try to rearrange the idea in our minds. Does the following sentence explain the meaning?

Newspapers, magazines, pamphlets, periodicals, and other forms of the media depend uniquely on the public's ability to read.

Or does this sentence explain it?

We read to keep up with daily events and opinions that are recorded in the media.

Both meanings are possible. As a writer, try to take apart your idea and say it as precisely as you can. In particular, *test your subject's connection to its verb* to make sure that together the subject and verb carry out your intended idea.

Here is another example of a mixed construction:

NO: The word *laughter* can be one of the best things to do these days.

We cannot *do* the word *laughter*. The combination of words doesn't make sense. The writer may mean:

One of the best things to do these days is laugh.

or:

The word *laughter* suggests one of the best things to do these days.

Laughing is something to *do*. But a *word* cannot be done. It can only suggest or mean something to be done.

Avoid is when and is because

Constructions using *is when* and *is because* create sentence difficulties:

NO: A teen-ager is when you are neither an adult nor a child.
YES: A teen-ager is neither an adult nor a child.

or

A teen-ager is a person who is neither an adult nor a child.
(A teen-ager = a person)

NO: A wedding is when two families join histories.
YES: A wedding is an occasion when two families join histories.
(A wedding = an occasion)

NO: The reason I retired is because I wanted to enjoy my health.
YES: The reason I retired is that I wanted to enjoy my health.
(The reason is that . . .)

Don't disappoint expectations you create

not only . . . but also
both . . . and
either . . . or
neither . . . nor
so . . . that

As soon as one half of any of these constructions appears, the reader expects the other half to follow. If the other half fails to materialize, the reader has a sense of incompleteness, as though still listening for the "other shoe" to fall.

NO: He was not only a poor typist, and his voice was not clear on the telephone.

YES: He *not only* typed poorly *but also* spoke unclearly on the telephone.

NO: *Scenes from a Marriage* was so unusual, and it was the uncut version.

YES: *Scenes from a Marriage* was *so* unusual *that* Public Broadcasting System presented the uncut version.

In paired constructions, ask yourself which words are paired: two verbs? two adjectives? two clauses? Then use *not only . . . but also* or similar words directly before the words they apply to:

NO: They are *not only planning* to give the Seminoles lunch at the pool, *but also dinner* at the club.

YES: They are planning to give the Seminoles *not only lunch* at the pool, *but also dinner* at the club.

or

They are planning to give *not only the Seminoles but also the coaches and administrators* lunch at the pool.

NO: *Either the mugger* demands your money *or your life*.

YES: The mugger demands *either your money or your life*.

NO: You will *either ask for Ruth or Helen*.

YES: You will ask for *either Ruth or Helen*.

Don't make illogical comparisons

It is not logical to compare unlike things. Write a comparison fully enough to show the similarity between the things you are comparing:

NO: I like *the pitching on the Astros* better than *the Mets*.
      (*Pitching* is compared with a *team*.)

YES: I like *the pitching on the Astros* better than *the pitching on the Mets*.
      (*Pitching* is compared with *pitching*.)

NO: *Floating in the Mediterranean* is more serene than *the Atlantic*.
      (*Floating* is compared with an *ocean*.)

YES: *Floating in the Mediterranean* is more serene than *floating in the Atlantic*.
      (*Floating* is compared with *floating*.)

YES: *Floating in the Mediterranean* is more serene than *it is in the Atlantic*.
      (*Floating is compared with floating*.)

NO: *Mark's talent in mathematics* is as imaginative as *Ann in art*.
      (*Talent* is compared with a *person*.)

YES: *Mark's talent in mathematics* is as imaginative as *Ann's in art*.
      (*Talent* is compared with *talent*.)

WATCH OUT FOR *SO* AND *SUCH*

1. Do not use *so* or *such* for *very*.
   NO: Dr. Callahan is *so* strange.
   YES: Dr. Callahan is *very* strange.

   NO: It was *such* a waste of food.
   YES: It was a *very great* waste of food.

   NO: Leslie looked *so* beautiful.
   YES: Leslie looked *very* beautiful.

2. Do not use the superlative for *very*.
   NO: Dr. Callahan is the *strangest* person.
   YES: Dr. Callahan is a *very strange* person.

Exercise 3 Fill in the blanks in the following sentences with logical constructions.

1. I not only _____ after the guests left, but _____ as well.
2. Not only can you _____ , but you can also _____ .
3. We cooked not only _____ , but also _____ .
4. Ask for either _____ or _____ .
5. Either _____ the man or _____ him.
6. This country will either _____ or _____ in the next four years.
7. The chairperson explained, simplified, and _____ the new rules.
8. Bernice is educated, employed, and _____ .
9. We elected Raymond because he was compassionate, knowledgeable, and _____ .
10. Paris is so romantic that _____ .

WATCH OUT FOR *LIKE* AND *AS*

1. Use *like* with a *noun*.
   He stood there *like a blind man*.
2. Use *as* with a *clause*.
   He stood there *as a blind man does*.

Exercise 4 Rewrite the following sentences to correct illogical comparisons. If a sentence is correct, mark it with a *C*.

1. Running at the beach is more exhilarating than the yard.
2. I like jazz played on the clarinet better than the flute.

3. Going to school in Vermont is more fun than New York.

4. Annette's hair is shorter than Mark.

5. California's weather is more reliable than Florida's.

6. Mitchell likes spaghetti more than Eddie.

7. The left turn is sharper than the right.

8. The ride to Omaha is more interesting than Kansas City.

9. The wait for the bus was longer than the box office.

10. Skiing is more dangerous than football.

Fill in the blanks in the following sentences.

11. We like a picnic at the lake better than _____ .

12. The direction of *Guys and Dolls* pleased the audience more than

_____ .

13. Driving to the Grand Canyon is more expensive than _____ .

14. Cruising in a whaler is more exciting than _____ .

15. The president speaks before Congress more often than _____ .

16. O'Hare Airport is busier in summer than _____ .

17. His feet are larger than _____ .

18. The relationship between the president and his cabinet is stronger than

_____ .

19. Getting into the medical school in Seattle is harder than _____ .

20. Once in a while is better than _____ .

Don't use more than one negative One negative word *(no, not, nobody, none, no one, nothing)* is all that you need. Two negative words will not intensify your meaning. Using more than one negative is considered an error.

    NO: They were*n't* planning to do *nothing* tonight.

    YES: They were*n't* planning to do *anything* tonight.

Avoid using combinations such as *don't hardly, won't scarcely, can't barely*.

    NO: They *can't hardly* wait for the bell to ring.

    YES: They *can hardly* wait for the bell to ring.

7.e SUPPLYING DETAILS

Using modifiers When you return to a draft to revise it, one of your responsibilities as a writer is to supply your sentences with the necessary details to make your writing convincing and vivid. Aside from supplying specific names, dates, colors, smells, or feelings, you may find yourself describing events more fully and using *modifi-*

ers—words or parts of sentences that make other words more specific—to bring your writing to life.

What do modifiers do? They tell why, where, in what manner. They offer details of color and sound, of mood and attitude, of location and size. In fact, the more you write, the more you associate one idea with another, and the wider the range of specific details that you think of. If your problem is writing sentences that look like bare bones, then you must rethink the acts of mind that go into writing. One act is to observe carefully all that is around you. (You may want to follow the suggestions in Chapters 1 and 2 that deal with observation and memory.) A second act is to make the most of the sentences that you have already written. Remember, you can refuel your writing by asking questions about the key words in your sentences (pp. 123–124). The answers to these questions may fit into your sentences as modifiers.

Sentence combining   Modifiers, then, are parts of sentences—words, phrases, and clauses—that we slip into the basic sentence patterns to provide additional details. Ideas for modifiers are often hidden in the sentences you write. You simply have to discover them and expand your sentences to make room for them.

Sentence:	That woman is my grandmother.
Implicit question:	What does that woman look like?
Sentence sequence:	That woman is my grandmother. She is beautiful.
Sentence with modifier:	That beautiful woman is my grandmother.
Implicit question:	What is she doing?
Sentence sequence:	That woman is my grandmother. She is beautiful. She serving sandwiches.
Sentence with modifiers:	That beautiful woman who is serving sandwiches is my grandmother.

Sometimes the sentences you write already include modifiers as you compose them. The modifiers are there in your first draft. On other occasions, you compose skeletal sentences. You go back to ask questions and put the details you discover into separate sentences. The boundaries between what should be a separate sentence and what should be a modifier may seem to blur. Look again at your sentences. When you have several short sentences in a row, combine them, cutting out excess words and embedding the essential ideas from one sentence into another as modifiers:

beautiful ◄——————
That ⌃ woman is my grandmother.   ~~She is~~ (beautiful.)

Exercise 5   Ask an implicit question about each of the following sentences, and answer the question by including modifiers in the subject, verb, or completer slots of the original sentence.

Example:	The snowplow moved down the street.
Implicit question:	*How* did the snowplow move down the street?
Sentence with modifier:	The snowplow moved down the street clumsily.

1. I admired Greg's hair.

2. The explorer landed at the North Pole.

3. Larry's squash won first prize at the fair.

4. Driving can be fun.

5. The prime minister called an election.

6. The plane crashed.

7. My camp experience depressed me.

8. Iris and I wrote letters.

9. The lake froze.

10. Mr. Perdue roasted a chicken.

11. The singer fainted.

You can also go back to ask questions about the statement of your controlling idea. By underlining the key words in it, you can generate ideas for the topic sentences of your remaining paragraphs.

Learn to take all your sentences seriously; every one can be the source of new ideas.

Exercise 6   Here is a sabotaged passage from the novel *Great Expectations,* which was written by Charles Dickens in 1861. The passage has been broken down into kernel sentences—minimal sentences that contain the connection of one subject to one verb with perhaps one modifier. Using coordinators, subordinators, and modifiers, piece together the ideas contained in the sentences in a way that sounds pleasing to you. After you have completed the exercise, read the original version.

1. My sister was Mrs. Joe Gargery.

2. She was more than twenty years older than I.

3. She had established a reputation with herself and the neighbors.

4. Her reputation was great.

5. She had brought me up "by hand."

6. I had at that time to find out what that expression meant.

7. I had to find out for myself.

8. I knew her to have a hard hand.

9. I knew her to have a heavy hand.

10. I knew her to be much in the habit of laying her hand upon her husband.

11. I knew her to be much in the habit of laying her hand upon me.

12. I supposed that Joe Gargery and I were both brought up by hand.

Dickens's version:

My sister, Mrs. Joe Gargery, was more than twenty years older than I, and had established a great reputation with herself and the neighbors because she had brought me up "by hand." Having at that time to find out for myself what the expression meant, and knowing her to have a hard and heavy hand, and to be much in the habit of laying it upon her husband as well as upon me, I supposed that Joe Gargery and I were both brought up by hand.

Exercise 7 The following kernel sentences are taken from a passage in the novel *The Great Gatsby,* which was written by F. Scott Fitzgerald in 1925. Combine and arrange the sentences to form a pleasing paragraph, and then compare your version with the original.

1. My family have been prominent.
2. They have been well-to-do people.
3. They live in this Middle Western city.
4. They have lived there for three generations.
5. The Carraways are something of a clan.
6. We have a tradition.
7. The tradition is that we're descended from the Dukes of Buccleuch.
8. The actual founder of my line was my grandfather's brother.
9. He came here in fifty-one.
10. He sent a substitute to the Civil War.
11. He started the wholesale hardware business.
12. My father carries on the business today.

Fitzgerald's version:

> My family have been prominent, well-to-do people in this Middle Western city for three generations. The Carraways are something of a clan, and we have a tradition that we're descended from the Dukes of Buccleuch, but the actual founder of my line was my grandfather's brother, who came here in fifty-one, sent a substitute to the Civil War, and started the wholesale hardware business that my father carries on today.

Exercise 8 The following kernel sentences are taken from a passage in the novel *The Sun Also Rises,* which was written by Ernest Hemingway in 1926. Combine them, and then compare your version with the original.

1. That winter Robert Cohn went over to America.
2. He went with his novel.
3. His novel was accepted by a fairly good publisher.
4. His going made an awful row.
5. I heard this.
6. I think that was where Frances lost him.
7. Several women were nice to him in New York.

8. When he came back he was quite changed.

9. He was more enthusiastic about America then ever.

10. He was not so simple.

11. He was not so nice.

12. The publishers had praised his novel pretty highly.

13. It rather went to his head.

Hemingway's version:

> That winter Robert Cohn went over to America with his novel, and it was accepted by a fairly good publisher. His going made an awful row I heard, and I think that was where Frances lost him, because several women were nice to him in New York, and when he came back he was quite changed. He was more enthusiastic about America than ever, and he was not so simple, and he was not so nice. The publishers had praised his novel pretty highly and it rather went to his head.

Exercise 9 Combine the following kernel sentences into pleasing, flowing prose. Add or delete any words or punctuation if you need to.

1. The computer has taken over.

2. There is no doubt about it.

3. Store clerks no longer use adding machines.

4. Store clerks no longer use cash registers.

5. Computers are everywhere.

6. Even typewriters are becoming obsolete.

7. Manual typewriters are becoming collector's items.

8. Electric typewriters are soon to follow.

9. One day every student will be required to have a home computer.

10. Someday every desk in school will have a computer attached to it.

11. Someday teachers themselves will be replaced by computers.

12. There is no telling who may be replaced by computers.

13. Everyone will have to learn how to use them.

14. Those who do not learn will be left behind.

7.f SELECTING MODIFIERS

The opposite crisis that you may face when you are drafting sentences is not a lack of ideas, not a problem of scarcity, nor of invention; this one is a problem of plenty. You have too many ideas, all of them buzzing around in your mind, all of them demanding your attention at once. Experienced writers will admit that modifiers are at the heart of good writing, but they will hurry to raise a note of caution: however tempting a modifier may be, use it only if it helps you accomplish the purpose of your writing. Good writing contains a range of sentences—long ones streaming with modifiers as well as short, tight ones without a single modifier. Composing a sentence, therefore, may demand your sharpest powers of selection. It may test your skill in sifting through the many ideas that seem to arise in your head simultaneously. For in all this wealth of ideas, there is a risk. When your head swarms with details, you can easily become distracted from your point. The best way to keep your writing focused is to select for your sentences only those details that contribute to your main idea.

Modifiers and your purpose Here is an account of a news event from a Chicago newspaper. Think of a suitable headline for it, one that attracts readers and provides a clear sense of what the news story is about.

> A packed electric rapid-transit train crashed into the rear of another train parked in a station along the median strip of the Kennedy Expressway in northwest Chicago yesterday morning, injuring more than 400 of the 600 passengers. No deaths were reported.

Do not continue reading until you have written your headline. Compare the headline you wrote with these:

1. Rapid-Transit Trains Crash
2. Wreckage at Chicago Station
3. No Deaths in Yesterday's Train Crash

The actual headline read:

WRECKAGE AT RUSH HOUR

The chosen modifier, "at rush hour," attempts to involve the reader in the potential disaster of this accident. The writer is confident that readers will relive their own rush hours—the monotony of the daily routine, the jamming crowds, the mindlessness of a city's entire work force heading home after a day on the job, and, finally, the sudden and terrifying possibility of mass death.

Modifiers are words that are closely connected to the bones of your sentences—to the nouns and verbs. Rarely does an idea arrive without bringing with it a trail of associations: a person and his looks, a meal and its taste, a game and its action. Sometimes the sorting is instantaneous. You know immediately, even intuitively, what to let in and what to keep out. Other times, you write down more then you need. But there's no sense holding back ideas in the early stages—let them come. Later, once you've written a couple of pages and finally discovered what it was you meant to say all along, you may want to scratch out three-quarters of those modifying ideas that were part of the original gush because they now seem pointless and repetitive. Still, at other times, you may leave space in your writing for a detail that you know will fit your subject to a *T*, although you simply cannot come up with it. Consciously or unconsciously, the hunt is on. The detail may suddenly, miraculously materialize as you write, or that space may go unfilled or inadequately filled and nag at you for a long while.

So, this emphasis on modifiers does not mean that you should use a $20 adjective next to every noun or that you should trade short sentences for long, embroidered ones. The example below shows that the modifier is not just so much decoration. Modifiers are as important to the writer's purpose as are the subject and verb:

> *Meet Me in St. Louis*
> (MGM) is a musical that even the deaf should enjoy.
>
> They will miss some attractive tunes like the surefire ''Trolley Song,'' the grace-ful ''Have Yourself a Merry Little Christmas,'' the sentimental ''You and I'' and the naively gay title waltz. But they can watch one of the year's prettiest pic-tures.
>
> —James Agee,
> *Agee on Film*

In this paragraph, the modifiers hold the real surprise of this movie review. Agee's startling observation begins in the modifier—a dependent clause—''that even the deaf should enjoy'' this musical. Agee delivers this ironic insight at the outset: imagine a musical so graceful and handsome to look at that even people who can't hear the songs will find something in it to enjoy.

TIPS FOR WRITERS—CHOOSE MODIFIERS THAT WORK FOR YOU

It is pointless to say ''female women'' because all women are female. *Female* does not narrow the meaning of *women* and serves no purpose at all in your writing. Here are a few more examples of combinations that would contribute nothing to your work but dreary wordiness:

> *unimportant* trivia
> *sorrowful* grief
> to succeed *well*
> to assemble *together*
> a *good* benefit

The italicized modifier does nothing to advance your job. Instead, it repeats a quality you already know exists in the other word. It becomes deadwood.

Consider this example:
Wordy:

> Eating out was a *pleasurable* delight.

If you flinch and say, ''Show me a delight that isn't pleasurable,'' you understand why an effective writer often prefers no modifier at all to a repetitious one.

Preferred:

Eating out was a delight.

Still, this may be the place where you can flash the experience of eating out on one specific occasion, exactly as it struck you. Interesting possibilities of modifiers are:

Eating out was a *luxurious* delight.
Eating out was an *unexpected* delight.
Eating out was a *congenial* delight.

The decision about which details are crucial confronts painters and photographers as well as writers. What should you include? What can you leave out? Which details will best convey to your audience your message—the crucial thing you want them to know about an event or a scene or a person? In short, which details will unmistakably deliver your point? A well-composed sentence is like a well-composed photograph: it must include the essential details you need to keep your prose compact, vigorous, and purposeful.

Exercise 10 Rewrite each of the following news clippings, which suffer from overloaded sentences. You may need several sentences to include all the elements contained here in a single sentence.

1. While distressing to Coach Ed Kennedy and Panther fans at the time, Monticello High's opening-season setback on the soccer field may have been just what the doctor ordered as the rejuvenated Blue and White have thrown off their lethargy to win their last three starts and take over the lead in the Orange County League's big school division.

2. Frankly, it's an education for me to write this column. For example, due to letters I've received which are diametrically opposed to each other re the importance of Art; a topic I focused on for two weeks running because of timely associative events—namely: season's end art shows in the vicinity—I've been doing some reflective digging and in the process learned something about art.

3. MONTICELLO Police Chief Roger Bisland reports that the village is getting along very well so far without a sobering-up station for alcoholics by approaching the problem in different ways.

4.

> Very often the fluke and flounder are thought to be the same fish. Although in the same class, under the heading of flat fish, and in appearance very much similar, it will be found upon closer examination that there is considerable difference in many details of form and make-up.

5.

> George E. Bauer called attention to the predicament the firemen were up against last week when the large barn on the Gallagher property was burned. Mr. Bauer said the water pressure was so low on connecting that the service was absolutely useless. It was disgusting, he said, on connecting the fire hose, to find hardly enough water to fill a bucket, and with a big fire raging right under their noses and no means of fighting it except by forming a bucket line from a nearby cistern, which was soon exhausted.

6.

> In a presentation lasting nearly two hours, attorney John Coffey, with the help of planning, real estate and traffic experts, discussed why his client should be granted a change of zone on 16 acres of land on Jericho Tpke. in Woodbury to allow for construction of a shopping center. They contend such development would not be detrimental to the area.

7.g EXERCISES IN REWRITING SENTENCES

The following exercises on sentences make use of the essays in Chapter 9 (pp. 189–208).

Exercise 11 Sentence imitations. Read the sentences below, which are excerpts from the essays. Then consider the following four questions.

1. What do you notice in each sentence? In your own words, describe the sentence. Is it long? short? Does the sentence divide into distinct parts? Do the parts strike you as being joined or separated? Why? What is the order of the parts? On what principle did the writer determine the order (p. 146)?

2. Describe the punctuation. What can you infer about the writer's purpose from the punctuation?

3. Are any parts of the sentence repeated? Are any patterns repeated? How does

the sentence begin? How does it end? What can you infer about the writer's emphasis from your study of the beginning and ending?

4. For each sample sentence, write two sentences of your own, imitating the structure of the sample.

Sentences:

Essay 3:
1. Unlike my parents, I haven't *had* to get a job to support myself, and so I have had the time to do other things.
2. I have come to know how to get along with others, and I am free and liberated.
3. The boy, like my parents, has no problems in working, but because he is so naive and unsophisticated, he doesn't know when he is being swindled.

Essay 4:
1. Oh yes, Mommy's little baby, playful, mischievous, hard-headed, and ready for adventure.
2. I continued to scream, to cry, to squirm to escape from his rage.
3. All I could hear was the sound of things falling, echoing, breaking.

Essay 5:
1. Whatever warmth the sun still radiated was felt only skin deep.
2. The airport was filled with faces without identities: a beautiful stewardess sat behind the information desk, a little boy was crying for some candy.

Essay 6:
1. I stand on the edge of a field, pondering; the fields are soaked from last night's rain.
2. It is the condition of such an activity as cross-country that I entrust myself, stripped of my worldly goods, to nature.
3. Shoes and socks, a shirt, shorts and a watch: that is the extent of my wealth.
4. My blood is warmed, but my muscles are aching.
5. It is hard work as I slog, muttering a wise old saying I learned when I was a child.
6. Run! Runner, run!
7. For a reward, I will go riding today!

Essay 7:
1. Bloodletting and danger are as natural and as pleasurable to him as a game of poker is to me.
2. For a deed to be stamped "courageous," it must, I believe, fulfill two requirements: one, it must arouse a feeling of dread within the person involved, and, two, that person must face up to his anxiety and carry out what he believes to be his duty.
3. Talking among a group may not fit Hollywood's idea of fortitude, but I know the obstacles and pain I had to overcome; I know I was courageous.
4. One must realize that courage isn't engendered by one's actions, but it's spawned within oneself.

Essay 8:
1. The figure on the screen reminded me of Master Cho, my master and old family friend; I had had grand dreams when I started at sixteen: black belt and then the 1988 Olympics at Seoul.
2. If, for example, both knobs were directed forward, then a front kick was executed; if the right knob was held at rest while the left knob was pushed up, then a round kick was thrown.

3. During each round, as I faced my adversary, there appeared a pretty girl who stared at both of us.

4. Space Invaders, in 1978, and Asteroids, in 1979, started a trend toward increasing sophistication. Pac-Man, in 1980, marked the beginning of the big video craze.

5. (I lost interest when I found that the highest attainable bonus was a key.)

6. Video games don't deceive, but they can't make you laugh or kiss you when you're down.

7. I immortalize their names for you: . . .

8. Each successful score was followed by a joke, rather than by a curse.

9. Schoolwork, friends, be damned!

10. I can't quite decide whether this machine appeals to nationalism or nihilism; what is more obvious is what these machines replace: kisses, chats, hugs, friendship, and all the things we do when we reach out to another person.

Essay 9:   1. It's amazing, I mused, how one forgets the thousands upon thousands of compliments about looks that one has heard from early childhood until a few hours ago, yet remembers with painful clarity the insults.

2. I wondered if there had been some odious reference to my mustache or perhaps my—well, generous—nose.

3. He lay with his head to one side, his forehead highlighted in the dimness, his perfect little features serene.

Essay 11:   1. Now, though, I am against them for different reasons: Now I hate them out of knowledge rather than ignorance.

2. A child can operate a VCR, of course.

3. As I rewind the tape, I have no idea of what, if anything, will be on it; as I press the "play" button, I have not a clue as to what in particular has gone wrong.

4. I have knelt at the foot of my machine and methodically, carefully, painstakingly set it—and set it wrong.

Essay 12:   1. Sprawled on the sofa, I finally faced up to the grim task, took the list out of my notebook, and scanned it.

2. What's more, the entire class was listening.

3. Then somebody laughed, then the entire class was laughing, and not in contempt and ridicule, but with openhearted enjoyment.

Exercise 12   The following passages are sabotaged excerpts—in the form of kernel sentences— from the essays in Chapter 9.

1. For each passage, combine the kernel sentences to make natural-sounding, flowing prose. Change words, add or delete words, supply punctuation to give your version a writer's control over material and fluency of style.

2. Then compare your version with the original.

Kernel sentences:

Essay 3:   1. My life is different.

2. It differs from my parents'.

3. It is different in terms of independence.
4. Moreover, there is something else.
5. I feel it.
6. There are two types of independence.
7. One is characteristic of my parents.
8. The other is characteristic of myself.
9. The first is a type of independence.
10. It is mental.
11. It can be defined.
12. It is a mental attitude.
13. You want to be on your own.
14. You believe you can get along.
15. You can go without anyone's help.
16. This is usually attained after something.
17. You have gained a sort of sophistication.
18. Or you have gained a street-wise sense.
19. These come through social experiences.
20. These come through knowledge.

Essay 6:   1. The landscape is quiet.
2. The landscape lies peaceful.
3. It lies tranquil.
4. It lies in the dew.
5. The dew is in the early morning.
6. Birds swoop by.
7. There are five of them.
8. They are in search of something.
9. They are in search of breakfast.
10. There is a clock.
11. It chimes.
12. It is in the distance.
13. It is loud.
14. It is clear.
15. I stand on the edge.
16. The edge is of a field.
17. I am pondering.
18. The fields are soaked.
19. The soaking is from rain.
20. The rain happened last night.
21. I yawn.
22. Then I stretch.
23. I am moving in a circle.
24. The circle is wide.
25. I burst into exercises.
26. I do it quickly.
27. The exercises are a series.
28. They are to warm me up.
29. All seems well.
30. I set my timer.
31. I look in the distance.
32. I take in a breath.
33. The breath is deep.
34. Then I am off.

Essay 10: 1. They were strangers.
2. They were on a train.

3. They were two travelers.
4. They found themselves sitting.
5. They were sitting across from each other.
6. They were sitting in the car.
7. Something happened by chance.
8. Their eyes met.
9. But they did not look away.
10. They did not do it quickly.
11. They held their gaze.
12. The gaze was each other's.
13. The glance became fixed.
14. It became a fixed stare.
15. The stare was mutual.
16. The seconds ticked.
17. They ticked by.
18. What happened then?

Essay 11:
1. I tape now.
2. I tape for myself.
3. I tape all the time.
4. I tape when I am out.
5. I tape when I am at home.
6. I tape when I am doing other things.
7. I tape when I am asleep.
8. At this very moment I am typing.
9. I am also taping.
10. There is a bookshelf.
11. It is in a bedroom.
12. The bedroom is mine.
13. Its entire length is full.
14. It has been turned over to something.
15. That something is video cassettes.
16. The cassettes are mostly of movies.
17. They are numbered.
18. They are indexed.
19. They are stacked in order.
20. They are in a household.
21. Nothing else in the household is in order.

Essay 12:
1. My eye stopped on a topic.
2. The topic was "The Art of Eating Spaghetti."
3. This title produced images.
4. The images were mental.
5. They formed an extraordinary sequence.
6. A recollection came surging up.
7. It came up out of the depths of memory.
8. It was a memory of a night.
9. The night occurred in Belleville.
10. All of us were seated.
11. We were seated around the table.
12. It was supper time.
13. Uncle Allen, my mother, Uncle Charlie, Doris, and Uncle Hal were there.
14. Aunt Pat served supper.
15. She served spaghetti.
16. Spaghetti was a treat.

17. In those days it was exotic.
18. Doris had never eaten spaghetti.
19. I had never eaten spaghetti.
20. The adults were not good at it.
21. They didn't have enough experience.
22. We were in Uncle Allen's house.
23. All the good humor was there.
24. It reawoke in my mind.
25. I recalled the arguments we had.
26. They were laughing arguments.
27. They occurred that night.
28. They were about a method.
29. The method was a socially respectable one.
30. The method was for moving spaghetti.
31. The spaghetti moved from plate to mouth.

Exercise 13 Study paragraphs 4, 5, 6, and 7 of essay 8.

1. How does the writer achieve sentence flow—a seamless fluency of ideas and language—*within* these paragraphs? Consider his use of nouns, pronouns, verbs, phrases, and clauses. Consider, too, repetitions, transition words and phrases, and other devices of continuity (pp. 125–126).

2. How does the writer achieve continuity *between* these paragraphs? Could you improve the flow at any juncture? How?

Exercise 14 In essay 2, the writer uses both direct and indirect quotation. In doing this exercise, remember that direct quotation requires quotation marks around the exact words the speaker says (p. 373).

1. Rewrite as indirect quotation the passage in paragraph 2 that is directly quoted. What is the effect of the change on the reader?

2. Rewrite as direct quotation the passage in paragraph 3 that is indirectly quoted. What is the effect of the change on the reader?

3. In one of the essays that you recently have written, change an instance of indirect quotation (reported speech) to direct quotation. Discuss the effect of the change.

Exercise 15 Read essay 11, in which the writer frequently alternates long and short sentences. In particular, look closely at the lengths of sentences in paragraphs 1, 2, 8, and 10.

1. What is the effect of the first short sentence in paragraph 1: "I was against them"? What is the effect of the first short sentence in paragraph 2: "I rented one"? Do these sentences convey the author's tone? How?

2. In paragraph 8, the fourth and fifth sentences are interrupted by dashes. How do the dashes affect the reader? Imagine commas or parentheses in place of the dashes. Would they work? Why or why not? Describe the last four sentences in paragraph 8. In what ways are they similar to one another? What has the writer managed to do through that series of sentences?

3. Discuss the effects of long and short sentences in paragraph 10. Comment on the writer's choice of punctuation. What were her alternatives? Can you justify her choices?

4. Study the last essay that you have written. Find a long sentence that might gain emphasis by being followed by a short sentence. Write the two sentences.

chapter
8 Finding the Right Words

8.a ACCURACY

Use concrete words for vague words

There is no arguing with your math teacher, who urges, over and over again, that you check every number. "Be accurate," you are told. "There's a big difference between 84 and 48. The right answer is 1,568.87; 1,563.87 is wrong. 'Around' 1,500 is not exact enough. Be precise!"

What inexperienced writers often don't know is that preciseness can be just as crucial to good writing as to good mathematics. Suppose you saw the following paragraph in a weekly TV magazine:

> It is a fancy Hollywood party. Women are all dressed up, and men are trying to make deals; waiters serve fancy drinks. The talk is about many different things. Indeed, if you had not known better, you might have thought that you were watching a television show. Many stars are there. Suddenly, a less famous man walks in. He looks uncomfortable. He says nothing, not even to his wife, who is also all dressed up. He is Aaron Spelling.

You would suspect that the writer had in mind a party full of celebrities, perhaps in honor of Aaron Spelling, but you wouldn't know much more than that. Descriptions like "fancy," "all dressed up," "different things," and "many stars" don't make for informative—or exciting—reading. Every time you use a vague word, you sacrifice a chance to interest your reader with concrete, lively information.

Now read this version:

It is a Hollywood gala that rivals a scene from *Dynasty*. Beautiful women in
gowns that twinkle glide about the Empire Room at the Beverly Hilton Hotel;
powerful men queue up to court even more powerful men; and efficient waiters
pass out tall glasses of champagne. The talk, of course, always falls upon glam-
orous tales or some shrewdly maneuvered coup or fantastic scheme in the works.
Indeed, if a casual observer had not known better, he might have thought he
was in Denver watching the powerful Carrington clan operate. Joan Collins is
there. So are John Forsythe, Linda Evans, Diahann Carroll. Suddenly, a less
public face pauses at the entrance to the room. Slightly built, this man with sil-
very hair, trimmed in a way that gives him an impish look, merely stands still,
looking uncomfortable. He says nothing, not even to his beautiful golden-haired
wife, who is dressed in a shimmering black gown calculated to dazzle even the
actresses in the room. The sparkling diamonds on her fingers, around her throat
and at her ears suggest the power and wealth of her husband. Aaron Spelling
has arrived.

—Mary Murphy

Reading the second passage after the first is like seeing the white line again
after driving through fog. The second paragraph leaves you with precise understanding. You know what the beautiful women are wearing; you know the names
of the stars; and you can see the impish Aaron Spelling and his dazzling wife take
their places at the gala. Every word in the paragraph is working.

Look at this paragraph:

One of the worst factors about being a teen-ager is the situation of the age itself.
You're too old for the kinds of things a child does and too young for the things
an adult does. I want to discuss three aspects of the case of being in this bad
situation.

Vague words such as *factors, situation, kinds of things, aspect,* and *case* choke
the personal energy out of your writing. Not only is such writing dull, imper-
sonal, and lifeless, but it is imprecise. You can never be 100 percent sure of what
it means. Compare this revised version of the same paragraph:

What is most bewildering about being a teen-ager is the age itself. You're too
old to yell and cry for what you want and too young to argue with assurance
and experience. Three incidents from my own life show how I was hurt during
this period of transition.

The writer made the following substitutions:

Concrete	*Vague*
most bewildering	worst factors
age itself	situation [an unnecessary filler] of the age itself

yell and cry	the kinds of things a child does
argue with assurance and experience	the things an adult does
incidents from my own life	three aspects of the case
period of transition	bad situation

Exercise 1 Rewrite the following vague sentences to make them more precise. Change whichever words you have to, and invent any concrete details you need.

> Example: Recently, he was in the city doing some work.
>
> More precise: From 1983 to 1984, he worked as a claims inspector for an insurance company in Detroit.

1. Because of his sickness, the official gave up some of his work.
2. Something in the bathroom makes a funny noise.
3. The athlete had on nice clothes.
4. The woman in the bank looked at someone who had just come in.
5. The people who wrote the book received complaints from a lot of people.
6. It took them a long time to get furniture for their house.
7. The soldier thought about the holiday at home.
8. The appliance went on and off all night.
9. Because of what happened, the people came out of the building not dressed properly.
10. You can get rid of a president for certain reasons.

8.b ECONOMY

Guard against using unnecessary words. *More* words are not always better than *fewer* words. Learn to use one accurate word instead of two vague ones. Use one word instead of two that mean roughly the same thing:

> NO: At thirteen, I gave up my toys and *began to search* for a *replacement and substitution*.
> YES: At thirteen, I gave up my toys and *searched* for a *replacement*.
>
> NO: Parents usually won't *let you* be *alone or by yourself*.
> YES: Parents usually won't *give you privacy*.
>
> NO: Pressures from friends can lead to *distressing and disturbing* situations.
> YES: Pressures from friends can lead to *disturbing* situations.
>
> NO: The cat *maliciously and deliberately* attacked King.
> YES: The cat *maliciously* attacked King.
> *(Maliciously* implies *deliberately.)*

See also Chapter 7.

WATCH OUT FOR TOO MANY NOUNS IN A ROW

One of the pleasant characteristics of English is that it allows you to move a noun into the position of an adjective to do the work of an adjective without changing the ending of the noun (*kitchen* cabinet, the *Yale* game). This easy transfer adds color to your writing without adding unnecessary words. *Her IBM mind,* for example, consists of three snappy words. In some contexts, that can be a real economy compared with the eight words of *She has a mind like an IBM machine.*

But try not to put more than two nouns together. Phrases like the following suffocate meaning and force your readers to slow down as they sort out ideas. Remember that modifiers should clarify, not confuse.

CONFUSING:	CLEAR:
career educator workshops	workshops for career educators
railroad timetable improvement	improvement of the railroad timetable
high-school athletics-committee money problems	money problems of the high-school athletics committee

Note: In the *"confusing"* column, the noun being described (for example, workshops) comes last, after a string of modifiers. In the *"clear"* column, this noun comes first and is followed by phrases or clauses in explanation.

Readers frequently trip on sentences that contain too many nouns in a row. Bombarded with noun forms, they have no signals that say which of the nouns are modifiers:

High-school athletics committee money problems will be discussed at the next Board of Education meeting.

Readers stumble along, thinking that each of those first four nouns is about to tie to a verb, only to encounter still another noun along the way. The fifth noun, *problems,* finally ties to the verb, *will be discussed.*

Exercise 2   Read aloud the following phrases, which have been taken from textbooks, magazines, and newscasts. Notice what a mouthful each is. Rewrite each phrase for greater clarity, using no more than two nouns in succession.

Example: theater performance training
Rewritten: training for performance in the theater

1. state unemployment committee research
2. childhood personality growth graph
3. family vacation country
4. pocket camera film
5. television program options smorgasbord
6. sewage storage tank explosion

8.c DENOTATION AND CONNOTATION

The exact meaning of a word, the definition that you will find in a dictionary, is its *denotation*. We say that the word *weed* denotes an uncultivated plant. But the word *weed* may also have certain associations for you—weeds crowd out desirable flowers, they hurt the tomatoes and peppers you spent long hours cultivating, they run wild and take over your garden. These associations are the word's *connotations*. We say that the word *weed* connotes destruction and uncontrolled growth. We say that the word *weed* has *bad* connotations.

The word *wildflower,* on the contrary, also denotes an uncultivated plant, but this word carries with it pleasant overtones. Its "vibes" are good ones, of colorful roadside blossoms and delicate Queen Anne's lace that grow in pale profusion in country fields and meadows. We say that the word *wildflower* has *good* connotations.

Think of the word *house.* Its denotation is a building for human beings to live in. It is an uncharged word. Its connotations are neutral, neither bad nor good. The word *residence,* which is also a building for human beings to live in, has connotations of size and elegance. The word *dwelling* is slightly charged because it has poetic or legal connotations. *Dwelling* is the word that lawyers use in contracts and documents to describe a house. The word *hut* denotes a humble house and connotes crudeness and roughness. *Cottage,* which is also a humble house, connotes instead a cozier place. The *American College Dictionary* tells us that, along with *cabin* and *lodge, cottage* is often used by the "well-to-do" to refer to a second house where they go for recreation: for example, a summer cottage, a mountain cabin, a ski lodge.

Learn to use a reliable dictionary to determine the exact denotations of words. Many dictionaries list synonyms under the definitions. This list will show you the differences among words that mean almost the same thing and will make it easier for you to select the best word for your sentence.

8.d EUPHEMISMS

Another kind of strain in your writing may occur when you wish to avoid using "unpleasant" words. Although it is generally the best advice in writing to call even an unpleasant thing by its name, some expressions have become painkillers in our culture, and it is more important to recognize such substitutions for what they are than to expect to eliminate them entirely. Words that sugar-coat "impolite" or "unpleasant" ideas are called *euphemisms*.

For example, we use the words *men's room* or *powder room* instead of *toilet, mortician* instead of *undertaker.* We say *permanent* flowers rather than *artificial* flowers and *senior citizens* rather than *old people.* School systems refer to students with *poor reading and writing skills* as *underprepared.* They *excess* teachers instead of *firing* them. Soldiers in Vietnam were *wasted* instead of *killed.* Animals *killed* in laboratories are *sacrificed.* Students receive a *no credit* in a course rather than a *failure.* Appropriateness guides us in deciding when to use euphemisms to make life more bearable. While you may say, ''My uncle *passed on* last week,'' you would think twice before telling a new widow that her husband *kicked the bucket* while on the job that day. That would be insensitive. But you must understand the real meanings of words such as *passed on, wasted, excessed, no credit,* and *underprepared.*

See pages 181–185 for some tips on how to use a dictionary.

8.e LIVELINESS

In math, when you are accurate, you are correct: you solve your problem. In writing, when you are accurate, you are clear and precise: you deliver your message.

But in writing, accuracy has another virtue. It can pull your writing out of a slump. Once accuracy becomes a habit, you will be on a continuing word hunt. You will begin to notice words—not just words that you don't understand, but also words that yield nuances of meaning you had ignored in your own writing. As you read the newspaper or watch TV, you will become more sensitive to the exact meanings of the words you hear. Your own desire to come up with the ''right'' word will put you in touch with a great variety of words that are fresh, strong, and vivid. One relatively painless but effective way to improve your vocabulary is to hoard words, to save the words you like in a notebook. Make a list of the liveliest words you run into—not just the ones you don't understand— and try to use them in your writing whenever they are appropriate. Lively words make writing come alive. They enable your reader to live through your experience or think through your idea as *you* did. If you actually *sped* somewhere, why say you *walked?* If you mean *deserted,* why settle for *empty?* When you want to suggest a *towering* scaffold, why let it go at *tall* or *big* or *high?*

In addition to collecting words that you admire for their liveliness, keep a section of your notebook for words whose meanings you do not know. Write the word, the sentence in which you find it, and the best meaning that you find in your dictionary. Then, when your writing calls for it, you'll be ready to use the new word.

Use vigorous verbs Pay particular attention to your verbs. Because the verb is at the crossroad of your sentence's grammar (Chapter 10, pp. 214–218 and 223–225), it's also at the place where interest takes a turn for better or worse. We have already talked about the dangers of indefinite, all-purpose nouns, such as *thing, situation,* and *aspect.* Your readers now move to their most critical intersection. This is where *noun meets verb,* and a vigorous verb can turn your sentence from a limp string of ordinary words into magic.

Compare the following sentences with the livelier ones written by Joan Didion:

Flames were *coming* up behind her.
Lively: Flames were *shooting* up behind her.

A window *closed* once in Barbara's room.
Lively: A window *banged* once in Barbara's room.

The gas heater *goes* on and off.
Lively: The gas heater *sputters* on and off.

College girls *were* at the courthouse all night.
Lively: College girls *camped* at the courthouse all night.

I'd *go* seven hundred miles to Brownsville, Texas.
Lively: I'd *hitchhike* seven hundred miles to Brownsville, Texas.

Beyond the [old frame houses] *are* the shopping centers.
Lively: Beyond the [old frame houses] *spread* the shopping centers.

Examine your own sentences for repeated use of all-purpose verbs, such as *is, are, goes, has,* and *come.* Replace them with striking verbs that put some action into your sentences.

Exercise 3 List as many verbs as you can that make each of the verbs in the list below more specific.

Example: walk

wander	run	stroll
amble	race	stumble
stride	saunter	limp
lope	meander	trot

1. look **3.** frighten **5.** love **7.** talk

2. laugh **4.** hold **6.** tear

Avoid all-purpose adjectives Look again at your sentences to see if you rely on words like *nice, interesting, horrible,* or *incredible* to convey all the nuances of your meaning. Try the following exercises, replacing *nice* and *interesting* with more exact modifiers.

Exercise 4 A Lot of *Nice*

I met a really nice person yesterday. He was wearing a nice hat and nice shoes and a really nice coat, which looked like something a king would wear. What a nice day it was, so we both sat on the same bench, the nicest one in the park, and talked about our lives. I told him about the nice time I had had backpacking in Colorado, and he told me about the nice company he worked for, which he said provides him with a nice living with benefits so he could buy a nice house in a nice neighborhood. He also said he was married to a really nice woman and had two nice kids. I told him that it all sounded really nice and that I wish I could have a life as nice as that. He said I'd have to come over to his house one night, and his wife would make us all a nice dinner. I said that that would be very nice and that I would bring a nice bottle of wine. He said it would also be nice if I brought some pictures of my nice trip. What a nice idea, I thought. After he left, I thought to myself how nice it would be to meet a nice person like that every day.

Exercise 5   A Lot of *Interesting*

I saw a very interesting play last night. It was called *A Streetcar Named Desire,* which is such an interesting title that I had to see what it was all about. It was about an interesting woman named Blanche who goes to visit her sister, Stella, whose husband, Stanley, was probably the most interesting character of all. Don't get me wrong. They were all interesting. It's just that some were more interesting than others. What was really interesting was the relationship between Stella and Stanley. It was interesting the way they would fight all the time but always make up in the end. Also interesting was the fact that Blanche took baths all the time and talked about her past and the interesting life she had led back home. There was also an interesting character named Mitch, who was a lot less interesting than the others and who dated Blanche for a while until he found out about her interesting past. It was a bit too interesting for him. Indeed, the characters were all interesting, especially the interesting way they talked and the interesting things they said. Stanley was loud and vulgar; Blanche was soft and sensitive. This made for an interesting conflict. This, of course, all led to quite an interesting conclusion. The actors, too, were interesting but they lacked some of the more interesting qualities of actors like Marlon Brando, who was in the original movie. Overall, I was quite interested and had a very interesting evening and felt that I would want to see other interesting plays by Tennessee Williams, who is quite an interesting playwright.

8.f METAPHORS AND SIMILES

For suburban driving, Barbara Coats finds that her white BMW maneuvers beautifully. Driving her previous car, an American wagon, ''was like driving my living room behind me.''

Metaphors and *similes* are figures of speech. They use words imaginatively instead of literally. The woman mentioned above has never really driven with her living room behind her. But driving her big American station wagon felt that way to her.

Metaphors and similes show a comparison that exists between two unlike things in the imagination of the writer. Sometimes figures of speech are called *images* because they help us ''see.'' When you use figures of speech in your writing, you help your reader to see with sharp, fresh insight.

The following sentences are taken from an essay by Robert Lipsyte about a New York race track and the special subway that takes fans there.

Simile   A simile *expresses* a comparison. Look for the words *as* or *like,* which signal that a simile may be under way:

> The subway car is *as* free of talk *as* the reading room of a library . . .

(This sentence explicitly states that the subway car is as quiet as a library.)

> . . . the hot young jockey, finishes fourth in the first race, and the praying man collapses on the fence *like* a steer caught on barbed wire.

(This sentence explicitly states that a spectator falls on the fence like a steer caught on barbed wire.)

Metaphor   A metaphor *suggests* or *implies* a comparison. It does not use the words *like* or *as:*

> . . . the fans troop out to the subway station.

(The writer suggests that the fans move out in an orderly line like a body of soldiers. The verb *troop* implies the comparison.)

> A minute later they are straggling back, chanting the old litany, ''I woulda . . . coulda . . . shoulda . . . ''

(The writer suggests that the losers repeat their regrets as they would in a prayer. The words *chanting* and *litany* imply the comparison.)

Personification   *Personification* compares an inanimate object or a nonhuman thing to a person:

> . . . an old shuddering train lumbers in to carry them away.

(The train is compared to an old person moving clumsily and trembling as if from fatigue.)

Figures of speech let us see more clearly or in a suddenly new way. They suggest what a writer *feels* toward the subject, and they stir us to respond emotionally. They also delight our imagination with the writer's personal vision and language. For the full effect of these images, read Robert Lipsyte's complete essay, from which the above sentences are taken.

SHORT TRIP

The fare to the Aqueduct Race Track is 75 cents on the special subway train from Times Square. This includes a send-off: the narrow escalator down to the platform ends beneath the words Good Luck printed on the grimy-gold arch of a huge wooden horseshoe. The subway car is as free of talk as the reading room of a library, and, in fact, all the travelers are reading: The Morning Telegraph, The Daily News, the latest bulletin from Clocker Lawton. They are very ordinary-looking men and a few women, a bit older than most people these days.

It hardly seems 30 minutes before the train bursts out of the black hole and onto an elevated track that winds above the two-family houses and cemetery fields of Queens. It is nearing mid-day, in the butt-end of another year, and the travelers blink briefly in the flat, hard sunlight. They are standing long before the train skids to a stop. They run down the ramp toward the $2 grandstand entrances, then on to daily-double windows five minutes away from closing.

Before the race of the day, at any track, anywhere, there is a sense of happening, of a corner that might be turned, a door that might open. There is almost a merry ring to the parimutuel machines punching out fresh tickets to everywhere, and the players move out smartly, clapping down the wooden seats of chairs, briskly stepping onto the pebbled concrete areas that bear the remarkable signs, "No Chairs Permitted on Lawn." Seconds after noon, the first race starts. It lasts little more than a minute, just long enough to hold your breath, to scream, or fall to your knees against a metal fence and pray, "Angel, Angel, Angel."

But on this day, Angel Cordero, the hot young jockey, finishes fourth in the first race, and the praying man collapses on the fence like a steer caught on barbed wire. Another man smiles coldly as he tears up tickets, and says: "Dropping down so fast like that, you mean to tell me he couldn't stay in the money? Sure. Haw."

It is suddenly quiet again, and the day is no longer fresh and new, the day is tired and old and familiar. An old, hooded man from Allied Maintenance moves over the asphalt picking up torn tickets with a nail-tipped stick, tapping like a blind man among the empty wastebaskets. Men watch him to see if he is turning over the tickets looking for a winner thrown away by mistake. He is not.

The race track settles into a predictable rhythm. In the half hour or so between races, men study their charts, straddling green benches or bent over stew and stale coffee in the drab cafeteria or hunkered down beneath the hot-air ceiling vent in a cavernous men's room, the warmest spot at Aqueduct. As the minutes move toward post time, they gather beneath the approximate odds board. They interpret the flickering numbers—smart money moving, perhaps the making of a coup. At the last moment, they bet, then rush out on the stone lawn for the race. A minute later they are straggling back, chanting the old litany, "I woulda . . . coulda . . . shoulda . . ."

There are ebbs and flows throughout the day. People leave, others come, the machines jangle on. There is a great deal of shuffling in the grandstand area, and little loud talk. People move away from strangers. When men speak of horses, they use numbers, not names, and when they talk of jockeys, they frequently curse. It was, they whisper, an "election"; the jockeys decided last night who would win.

The day ends pale and chilly a few minutes before 4 P.M. and the fans troop out to the subway station. There is no special train returning: the city will get you out fast enough, but you can find your own way home.

Horseplayers are smart, and they all wait in the enclosed area near the change booths, ready to bolt through the turnstiles onto the outdoor platform when the train comes, and not a moment sooner. They stamp their feet, muttering, "Woulda . . . coulda . . . shoulda." The losers rail against crooked jocks, gutless horses, callous owners, the ugly track, the greedy state that takes 10 cents of each dollar bet.

Then they bolt through the turnstiles, quick and practiced, tokens in and spin out upon the platform. But there is no train yet, they all followed a fool, and now they curse him for five minutes in the cold until an old shuddering train lumbers in to carry them away.

Exercise 6 List all the figures of speech in the essay "Short Trip," and explain in detail why you think they are successful or unsuccessful. Tell how each figure of speech made you *feel* as you read it.

Mixed metaphor

A *mixed metaphor* troubles the reader by blurring two or more images rather than presenting one distinct image. In trying to create a bold comparison, an inexperienced or careless writer may begin a second image before completing the first one. The result is always confusing and often absurd:

> The spiritual heart of northern Italy, the great Cathedral of Milan, reaches hundreds of marble fingers to the sky.

(Can a heart have fingers, not to mention hundreds of marble fingers? The image is confusing to imagine.)

> She sailed into the room, her mane of hair thrown to the wind.

(Her motion is first likened to that of a sailboat in a breeze, but then the writer confuses the picture by likening her to a fast-moving horse.)

Often, a mixed metaphor is the preposterous product of mixed clichés:

> Sly as a fox, he was rotten to the core.

Exercise 7 Write a simile to convey each of the following impressions.

> Example: What it is like to drive your station wagon.
> Driving my station wagon is *like driving my living room behind me.*

1. What it is like to drive your car.
2. What it is like to take a final exam.
3. What it is like to vote for a candidate you're not 100 percent sure of.
4. What it is like to do some freewriting.
5. What it is like to live in your house (or room or apartment).
6. What it is like to be stopped by a police officer for speeding.

8.g CLICHÉS

The phrases displayed on the next page are *clichés*—expressions that were once interesting and imaginative but have become dull from overuse. All the zing is out of them. Beginners often reach for clichés to fill gaps in their writing because it is simpler to use a ready-made slogan than to think up a new phrase to capture an idea exactly. The effect is often zero. Your writing becomes tired and juiceless. Generally, avoid clichés and other trite, stereotyped expressions.

Occasionally, clichés (*"one in a million"*), slogans from advertising (*"Where's the beef?"*), famous quotations (*"Don't shoot until you see the whites of their eyes"*) can stimulate your writing because they can move easily

A golden opportunity

A Helping Hand

a warm heart

a warm welcome

False Starts

IT'S HIGH TIME

Living is easy

out of this world

The Secret of Our Success

into many different contexts and make sense. When that happens, include them in your first draft and don't worry about them. Keep writing. Then, in a later draft, get rid of all the phrases that have lost their sparkle.

Here is a little reading in clichés. See how many you can find:

Al, who followed in his father's footsteps, was one in a million. Besides, Lady Luck always smiled on him. One fine day that was as pretty as a picture, soon after he had moved into the little house he called his castle, Al received a phone call. You could have knocked him over with a feather, he was so surprised. The phone call offered a warm welcome from the local radio station WORN. It said they had a jackpot prize for him that was out of this world. All Al had to do was name the tune now playing on WORN.

"Stay tuned," they said.

But Al's radio was still packed up. He shrugged his shoulders. "At this point in time," he said, without beating around the bush, "my radio's buried six feet under. I guess it's just one of those things."

"The right answer!" cried the voice of WORN. "You win the WORN jackpot prize."

"Who, me?" said Al. "Well, truth *is* stranger than fiction," muttered Al, but then he secretly knew everyone in his family was smart as a whip.

Exercise 8 Write an essay that is filled with clichés. Use the story about Al as a model.

8.h INFLATED LANGUAGE

Words sometimes suffer from inflation. Words of importance are often worth less than you think.

A FABULOUS
BARGAIN WEEKEND   essential

**Great Get-away
weekend**   Great
                           Wine

incredible   indispensable

                           PERFECT

GREAT GOLF & TENNIS

Exercise 9 Make each of the following inflated ads more concrete by substituting as many specific words as you can for the word *great*.

1. Great Wine
2. Great Get-Away Weekend
3. Great Golf and Tennis

8.i WORDS REVEAL YOUR ATTITUDE

If you think about the clothes you are wearing right now, you see that they do more than cover your nakedness and keep you warm; they tell whether you are formal or informal, outgoing or shy, fashionable or practical, or they suggest something about the circumstances of the occasion. In the same way, words do more than convey your meaning; they may suggest whether you are pleased, angry, critical, or admiring.

See if you can detect in the following pairs of sentences how the writer's attitude changes from sentence to sentence:

Jerry *nagged at* me to walk the dog.
Jerry *reminded* me to walk the dog.

Dad always *snarled at* the neighborhood kids when they sat on his *jalopy.*
Dad always *chatted with* the neighborhood kids when they sat on his *trusty Chevy.*

Gloria was tall and *skinny.* As she left, she *hung* a fur jacket *on* her shoulders.
Gloria was tall and *slender.* As she left, she *draped* a fur jacket *around* her shoulders.

Marco *is short and fat.*
Marco *has a stocky build.*

Jerry thought Marco was a *loudmouth.*
Jerry thought Marco was *outspoken.*

Gloria was a biology major and a *dull grind.*
Gloria was a biology major and a *conscientious student.*

Marco wore *loud, synthetic* shirts and told *stupid* jokes.
Marco wore *bright, silky* shirts and told *original* jokes.

Grandmother said Dad was a *mama's boy* all his life.
Grandmother said Dad was a *devoted son* all his life.

8.j LEVELS OF USAGE—FORMAL, INFORMAL, SLANG

One of the difficulties in choosing your vocabulary is knowing when it is appropriate to use a certain word. You know intuitively that while you talk to your best friend one way ("I hear you!"), you talk to the personnel manager who is interviewing you for a job in quite another way ("Yes." "Yes, sir." "Yes, Miss Taylor."). You have a natural sense of audience that screens the words that come out of your mouth. Usually, you can trust your common sense to know what to say when.

In writing, as in talking, certain words are appropriate for certain readers. Professional writers always consider their audience before they begin writing. They consider the kind of magazine they are writing for and the type of person who reads that magazine. They write one kind of article about rifles for the *Ladies' Home Journal* and another for the *National Rifleman;* one essay about men's underwear for *Ms.* and another for *Playboy.*

If you are in a writing class, the other men and women in your class are your audience, and you can count on their interest. Readers in a writing class may differ sharply from one another in many respects, such as the morality under which they were brought up, how much money they or their parents make, how old they are, and above all, what interests they have. But in spite of these differences, their common attempts to write and to expand their understanding of themselves as they write provide a mutual bond. By now, you've probably noticed that the people in your class are willing to read anything you write as long as you make every sentence informational and lively.

But there are levels of language that you can choose for a particular audience or a special occasion. The level we use in this book, and the level you are probably using as you write, is an informal level. American writing—like American living rooms and American restaurants, like the clothes many of us wear to work, to teach, to study, even to attend weddings—tends to be informal rather than formal. You saw on page 140 the changes that insurance companies have introduced in the language of insurance policies. Some policies are now written on an informal level, and almost anybody can understand them. This is a level that is "safe" for most occasions.

Still, we know that not all language is safe on all occasions. Who hasn't suffered from using an inappropriate expression at one time or another? Older slang terms such as "cut it out" and "shake a leg" and newer ones such as "off the wall," "out to lunch," "bread" (money), and "split" (leave) may mark your academic or business writing as too informal, too much like casual conversation for those important transactions. For personal writing and for a special effect in other writing, of course, slang expressions may sometimes be precisely right.

Your choice of words, or *diction,* as word choice is called, ought to strike a balance between the simple, homey word and the pompous word with many syllables. Generally, it is a safe bet to choose a plain, everyday word wherever possible:

> NO: After a *double attempt to insert herself* through the *aperture,* she *con-ceded failure.*
> YES: After *two tries at climbing in* through the *window,* she *gave up.*

Occasionally, you can strike an interesting contrast by combining a small word (such as *liar, mad, sag*) with a word of many syllables:

immovable liar
mad computation
legendary sag

8.k USING YOUR DICTIONARY

Whatever the price of a good college dictionary, it is a bargain because in a single volume it provides a quick reference guide to an enormous amount of usable information. Kurt Vonnegut, the author of *Slaughterhouse Five* and many other books, confesses that:

> As a child, [I] would never have started going through unabridged dictionaries if I hadn't suspected that there were dirty words hidden in there, where only grownups were supposed to find them. I always ended the searches feeling hot and stuffy inside, and looking at the queer illustrations—at the trammel wheel, the arbalest, and the dugong.
>
> —*New York Times Book Review,*
> October 30, 1966

A reliable dictionary does more than list words. It spells words, shows you how to pronounce them, and gives you their meanings. It gives their histories and describes how they are used. Most recommended dictionaries also offer *synonyms* (words that have almost the same meaning) and *antonyms* (words that have almost the opposite meaning); they list forms with suffixes added, abbreviations, and foreign terms; and they provide facts of general interest, such as population figures, geographical names, names of famous people, names and locations of colleges and universities, tables of weights and measures, explanations of symbols, as well as pictures of machines and creatures, like a *pawl,* a *manatee,* or Vonnegut's *dugong.*

When Americans say "Let's look it up in *the* dictionary" as a way to settle arguments and keep the peace, they are mistakenly implying that every dictionary says the same things and carries the same unarguable authority. That is not true. Dictionaries are different. Each one represents the work of a separate committee of people who study the way words are used in the pages of contemporary writers. They keep rooms full of files noting new meanings for old words, new words, and special words, perhaps from the sciences or the arts, that appear in current newspapers and magazines. Then they write a dictionary based on their research. Usually, they have their own way of organizing entries. Some dictionaries, for example, list the oldest meaning first; others list the most important meaning first. Some dictionaries have separate alphabetically arranged sections at the back for names of people, places, and colleges and universities, while other dictionaries include these proper nouns among the words in the main part of the dictionary itself. Some dictionaries offer comments in the main entry on how a word is to be used. A college dictionary, which is a convenient size for most college students, contains about 100,000 words, whereas a full-sized, unabridged dictionary has about 450,000 words. In all dictionaries, regardless of their length, there is an explanation of how they are organized somewhere in the front. *Buy a good college dictionary, and learn how to make the most of it.*

Here is a list of some good college dictionaries:

The American College Dictionary (New York: Random House)

The American Heritage Dictionary of the English Language (Boston: Houghton Mifflin)

Funk & Wagnalls Standard College Dictionary (New York: Harcourt Brace Jovanovich)

The Random House College Dictionary (New York: Random House)

Webster's New Collegiate Dictionary (Springfield, Mass.: Merriam)

Webster's New World Dictionary of the American Language, college edition (Cleveland: Collins-World)

Get acquainted with your dictionary

1. Browse through the introductory material. Read the sections that explain how the book is organized.

2. Study the table of contents. Turn to each section listed and skim through the main headings.

3. Look at the pronunciation key (usually at the bottom of a page; sometimes on the inside cover). Try to say the sample words aloud. Notice the mark on the vowel as you say it. Then say the vowel sound alone.

   ăct   ă
   āble   ā

4. Read one or two entries for common words. Study the definitions. Pick out the one definition *you* think is most important. Notice whether it is listed first.

5. Study any special charts or tables—for example, an etymology key, which tells what other languages words come from; a key to foreign sounds; a list of abbreviations; and so on.

6. Browse through the dictionary, pausing to read whole entries of words here and there. (See the analysis of two typical entries below.)

7. Notice entries that start with a capital letter. These are chiefly names of people and places. Read whole entries to see what biographical and geographical information your dictionary gives you.

Now let's look at two entries from *The American College Dictionary:*

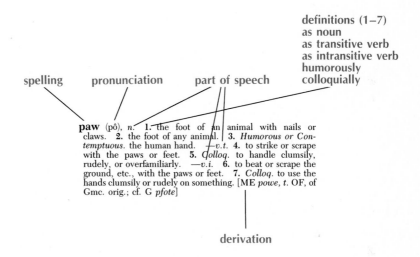

Some common dictionary terms and abbreviations

For a complete list of terms and abbreviations, see the prefatory pages of your dictionary.

	parts of speech	classification of words (nouns, pronouns, adjectives, adverbs, prepositions, verbs, and conjunctions)
n.	noun	
pron.	pronoun	
adj.	adjective	according to their meaning and usage in a
adv.	adverb	sentence; a word may be a noun in one
prep.	preposition	sentence and a verb in another—for example, *paw* as a noun:

The dog's *paw* was injured.

and *paw* as a verb:

The dog *pawed* the ground under the tree.

v.t.	transitive verb	an action verb, which is always accompanied by a direct object
v.i.	intransitive verb	a verb that never is accompanied by a direct object
conj.	conjunction	
colloq.	colloquial	refers to use in ordinary or familiar conversation
etym.	etymology	the study of the history of words in order to trace origin and change
der.	derivation	the origin or source of a word
O.E.	Old English	indicates that a word was derived from English as it was spoken before A.D. 1100
M.E.	Middle English	indicates that a word was derived from English as it was spoken between A.D. 1100 and 1500
obs.	obsolete	describes a word or a meaning no longer in use

Tips on using your dictionary

Suppose you are looking up the word *peaceful.*

1. Use the guide words at the top of the page. They will save you from hunting for your word up and down the columns of a dozen pages. *Peaceful* is between the guide words *paynim* and *Pearl Harbor.*

2. If you can't find *peaceful,* ask someone else how to spell it. If no one knows, write down several spelling possibilities:

peesful	pieceful	peesfull
peasful	piecefull	peaceful

Try them all.

3. Match the sounds of the word to the pronunciation key. Look for the bold accent. Notice the heavy dot that separates syllables. Say the word.

p ē s′ · fəl

Note: Most vowels that are in unaccented syllables are pronounced "uh." This sound is written as a schwa: ə.

4. Test the meaning of the word for the one that suits your sentence. In the case of *peaceful*, notice below its definitions the abbreviation *Syn.*, which means "synonyms." Words that have almost the same meaning as *peaceful* are listed there. Now, in one place, you find a choice of words for your sentence. Will it be *peaceful, placid, serene,* or *tranquil?*

> I can remember that my father was _____ even when his rug business was on the verge of bankruptcy.

The synonym section indicates that *serene* is used for people and suggests that a person who is serene also keeps his dignity. You choose *serene* to describe your father. And you found it by looking up *peaceful*.

> I can remember that my father was *serene* even when his rug business was on the verge of bankruptcy.

If you have any further interest in the word *serene,* you may be tempted to look it up next.

8.1 EXERCISES IN FINDING THE RIGHT WORDS

The following exercises in finding the right words make use of the essays in Chapter 9 (pp. 189–208).

Exercise 10 Compare essays 3 and 6 with each other and essays 10 and 12 with each other.

1. Comment on the range of vocabulary in each. The subject of which essay in each pair requires the more descriptive and vivid treatment? Does the writer's treatment satisfy you? Explain. How does the diction (use of words) contribute vividness to the essay? Use specific words as examples in your discussion. Would you change any passages so that the words are livelier? Which passages?

2. Which essay in each pair needs to be more analytical? Which words convey analysis and logical discrimination?

3. Based on your observations of all four essays, can you generalize about the importance of good diction in any essay?

Exercise 11 **1.** In essay 12, the writer uses an image to describe how reading the classics affected him when he was a schoolboy. (See p. 174 for a discussion of figurative language.)

   a. What is the image? Do you find it effective? What *is* the effect? Is there any place else in the essay where the language echoes the force of this image? Explain.

   b. Rewrite the passage without the image. State the idea literally. What is the net difference to the reader? Consider both the intellectual and the emotional difference.

2. In essay 4, paragraph 5, the writer says, ''The lightning bugs glittered in the night like stars broken into a million pieces.'' Discuss the effect of the image and its role in establishing the character of the narrator.

3. In essay 6, the writer frequently uses images to describe himself running and the landscape he runs through. Find and discuss as many of his metaphors and similes as you can.

4. In essay 7, the writer makes several vivid analogies (p. 84). How do they help him to define *courage?*

5. Rewrite a passage in an essay that you have written so that you express an intense experience by means of an image rather than literally. Do you like the effect? Why or why not?

Exercise 12 For each of the italicized words or phrases in the following passages, substitute a synonym of your own choosing. Evaluate the effect of the substitution. Use a dictionary to ascertain nuances of meaning. Which word strikes you as more successful? Why?

Essay 4: I was four, maybe five years old at the most, old enough to remember, yet too young to care. Oh yes, Mommy's little baby, *playful, mischievous, hard-headed,* and ready for *adventure.* It was the *heart* of summer, hot, exciting, and *unrestraining.* I sat at the kitchen table, *skillfully poking* holes in the top of a mayonnaise jar with the point of a pencil. It was almost night, and one could feel the *coolness* of the moon off in the distance. Once I was finished with the top, I screwed it carefully on the empty glass jar. *Suspiciously,* I *got* out of my seat and *headed* toward the door. ''And where do you think you are going, young man?'' with her arms folded, my mother *bellowed* from across the room.

Essay 7: A *popular* conception of courage is the image of a *rugged* individual *risking* life and limb in a *fierce* struggle, usually for some *revered* cause such as patriotism, chivalry, or self-honor. I find this definition to be wholly inaccurate on the grounds that it not only excludes *subtle* but nonetheless *legitimate* acts of courage, but falsely assumes that violent *brawls* require bravery on the part of those involved. The latter half of my disagreement, concerning violent disputes, brings to mind Philip, a boy I had known many years ago. Philip was absolutely *fearless*. He would think nothing of fighting *guys* twice his size, and, on occasion, throw rocks at a passing police car. I wouldn't consider this courage. Bloodletting and danger are as natural and as *pleasurable* to him as a game of poker is to me. Philip's *insanity* left no room for courage.

Essay 8:   The *mastery* of those *damned* controls proved both an *expensive* and a *time-consuming* process. The game seemed to have an ego booster built into it, which acted to keep my interest as I learned. During each round, as I faced my *adversary,* there appeared a *pretty* girl who stared at both of us. Her head would *bob* back and forth *indecisively;* the scene would then be *disturbed* by the master, who signaled for the match to "begin!" After a blow was scored, my *personification,* on the screen, would resume a starting position. This process *continued* until one side had scored 2 full points (blows being worth 1/2 or 1 point each).

Essay 11:   A child can *operate* a VCR, of course. Only a few *maneuvers* are required to tape something, and only a few more are required to tape something while you are out. You must *set* the timer to the correct time you wish the recording to begin and end. You must *punch* the channel selector. You must *insert* a videotape. And, on my set, you must *switch* the "on" button to "time record." Theoretically, you can then go out and have a *high old time,* knowing that even if you *waste* the evening, your video-cassette recorder will not.

Essay 12:   This title produced an *extraordinary* sequence of mental images. *Surging* up out of the depths of memory came a *vivid* recollection of a night in Belleville when all of us were seated around the *supper* table—Uncle Allen, my mother, Uncle Charlie, Doris, Uncle Hal—and Aunt Pat served spaghetti for supper. Spaghetti was an *exotic* treat in those days. Neither Doris nor I had ever eaten spaghetti, and none of the adults had enough experience to be good at it. All the good humor of Uncle Allen's house *reawoke* in my mind as I recalled the laughing arguments we had that night about the socially *respectable* method for *moving spaghetti from plate to mouth.*

Exercise 13   In an essay of your own, underline twenty key words. Then try to substitute a synonym for each of the words. Evaluate the effect. Which word of each set do you prefer? Be prepared to tell why.

Exercise 14   **1.** Here is a sentence from essay 1:

My mom frequently shouted, "Don't drive so fast; you're scaring me!" to my father, who gunned his Volkswagen as if it were a Ferrari.

What does the word *gunned* mean? that is, what is its denotation? What are the word's connotations? How do the word's connotations aid the writer in making his point? (See p. 171 for a discussion of denotation and connotation.)

2. Answer the same questions about the italicized words in the following sentences.

Essay 2:   He was furious; he shouted at me, "You're not going to fare any better than an uneducated *housemaid*."

Essay 4:   The dog glared at me as though his *tolerance* was beginning to fade.

Essay 5:   Mother sat, *lecturing* to me about dos and don'ts of my departure.

Mother *pecks* me on the cheek.

Essay 7:   *Bloodletting* and danger are as natural and as pleasurable to him as a game of poker is to me.

Essay 8:   My *playmates* were sufficient, and when I tired of one, there was always a *replacement* waiting in the wings.

Exercise 15   Read essays 4, 5, 6, 8, 9, 11, and 12; in each essay, locate five strong verbs— vivid verbs that you might enjoy using in your own writing on an appropriate occasion. (See p. 172 for a discussion of the power of strong verbs.) Be prepared to discuss the precise effect of each verb. Write a list of alternative verbs and tell the difference in meaning between the verbs in each pair. Which ones have almost identical meanings?

chapter 9

Reading Writing: Sample Student and Published Writings

Chapter 9 offers an assortment of writings for you to read, enjoy, reflect on, and study in relation to your own writing, particularly as you make use of the exercises for revision at the ends of Chapters 6, 7, and 8. As writers read the work of other writers, ideas for their own writing inevitably spring forth. And so we suggest that you keep a pencil in hand for making notes in your journal about ideas, events, memories, or questions that arise as you read: What is *your* idea of the perfect vacation? How do you define *misconception, independence,* or *courage*? What was the most difficult leave-taking in your life? Do you own a VCR? Do you wrestle with it? Do you find yourself staring at people in elevators? Do you look like your father—or your mother? As you read, keep your current "old" writings open to change, as you consider others' beginnings, middles, and endings, and as you take note of the shape of a paragraph or a sentence, or of the aptness of a word.

The selections begin with students' writings in an introductory writing course and end with an excerpt from Russell Baker's autobiography, *Growing Up*. He tells us that at one time, he, like you, was a student sitting in an English course, hating "assignments to turn out 'compositions,'" and then he discovered that what he had written could move others. We hope the same for you. The first ventures in a college writing course, as you will see in this chapter, are often rough. They are anything but polished gems; yet they sit here in company with the more "finished" writings of other students and with published pieces, to give you a range and flavor, to be considered and reconsidered as you write and rewrite.

1. THE ONE-WEEK TOUR IN ONLY THREE DAYS

I've always liked to travel to different places, but rushing about from one spot to another is not my idea of travel. My father, though, has different ideas. One warm summer day when I was twelve, my father said, "Guess what? We are going to Pennsylvania!" I was thrilled! We planned what activities we would do. We would tour all the famous sights and visit the farms for fresh fruits and homemade jellies. It sounded good.

We drove to Pennsylvania and checked into a Holiday Inn. "Oh wow! They've got a color television here!" I screamed.

"Well, you aren't going to be watching it all the time. Hurry and change," said my pop. I frowned. I had forgotten the inevitable: my father's idea of a vacation and mine don't match.

We went to dinner at 5:00, and the next thing I knew, we were racing all around Pennsylvania as if there were no tomorrow. We were going to see all of Pennsylvania in only three days. We visited all of Hershey Park in fifteen minutes, saw a play at the Bucks County Playhouse, visited several local stores and every other possible sight in those three days.

I can't even remember most of the places because we zipped through them like a tornado on the rampage. My mom frequently shouted, "Don't drive so fast; you're scaring me!" to my father, who gunned his Volkswagen as if it were a Ferrari. My sister, brother, and I got restless. "I wanna go home now!" "Don't push me, you dumb baboon!" "I'm hungry." "I gotta go to the bathroom!" "What was that? It looked like a horse!" and "What time is it?" issued from our throats every second we sat in the car. I was mad. I was furious! I wished we could just go home and forget this insane trip.

The third day we left Pennsylvania, and, boy, was I happy. I only regretted not enjoying all the sights thoroughly. A one-week tour in three days was not my cup of tea.

—Jonathan Moy

2. MISCONCEPTIONS

A misconception is a mistaken notion that can result from hearing only a part of a conversation, or from taking another's words literally, or from any number of miscommunications. If you are overly sensitive and tend to take things to heart, you might be susceptible to misconceptions.

Children often expect their parents to know everything, and they tend to take their words as the law. When I was eight years old, I found myself having difficulty with my schoolwork. One night, my father came into my bedroom and found that I was not studying during my study time. He was furious; he shouted at me, "You're not going to fare any better than an uneducated housemaid." I had no idea at the time that he was angry about something else, and he was taking it out on me. I took his words literally. I stopped concentrating on my studies, and I dreamed about my life as a housemaid. My grades fell steeply, and my parents now had a chance to find out what was bothering me.

At a parent–teacher–student meeting, I was forced to let out my story. All this while, I had been fighting the fact that I was capable of more effort than I had been putting into my studies. My parents urged me to try harder and to realize that what a person says is not necessarily what he means. My father explained that he was just trying another approach to get me to study; he had not meant me to take his words to heart. I did understand and, somehow, even at that young age, realized as well that being oversensitive would leave me open to such misunderstandings. My parents, from that time on, were very careful about whatever they said so that I would not misconstrue their remarks.

—Gursimrat Bajwa

3. DEFINING INDEPENDENCE

My life is different from my parents' in terms of independence. Moreover, I feel that there are two types of independence, of which one is characteristic of my parents and the other is characteristic of myself. The first type is mental independence, which can be defined as the mental attitude of wanting to be on your own and believing that you can get along without anyone's help. This is usually attained after one gains a kind of sophistication or a street-wise sense, which in turn comes through social experiences and knowledge. The second type is physical independence, which is simply the ability to get a job and earn money. By doing this, you have stepped into the working field, and that is one step to becoming totally independent.

The latter is characteristic of my parents. When they were young, they had to get jobs to help out with their families. They gained the experience of actually getting a job and learned how it felt to work. They became aware of the financial realities of life, and they became independent in financial terms. By working, they began to go off on their own and to "pay their own way."

I, on the other hand, see myself as independent mentally. Unlike my parents, I haven't *had* to get a job to support myself, and so I have had the time to do other things. I have had time to socialize with friends, and I have had leisure time to watch television, so that I have gained some knowledge of the ways of the world. I have become somewhat sophisticated and street smart and feel that I can take care of myself in any situation. I have come to know how to get along with others, and I am free and liberated. I am mentally independent.

And yet I must say that neither my parents nor I are totally independent. In the case of my parents, I think of the classic story of a hick-town boy who goes to the city on his own. He gets a job to support himself and has no problem in that aspect of his life. But he soon loses all his money to men who swindle him. The boy, like my parents, has no problems in working, but because he is so naive and unsophisticated, he doesn't know when he is being swindled. He has no knowledge of how to get along out there in the "world" because his own world is rather limited.

In my case, I can get along and survive in the "street," but to support myself, I would have to get a job. I, however, do not have the experience of getting a job or of how it feels to work. I have never had to grind away at a menial job, and I know that I would find it very difficult to do so. I would probably be very tired, and I would have a hard time getting used to it. In both cases, my parents' and mine, our "independence" is not full; one needs both the experience of living in the world with others and being able to support oneself.

—Paul Bucaoto

4. OH, LADDIE!

I was four, maybe five years old at the most, old enough to remember, yet too young to care. Oh yes, Mommy's little baby, playful, mischievous, hard-headed, and ready for adventure. It was the heart of summer, hot, exciting, and unrestraining. I sat at the kitchen table, skillfully poking holes in the top of a mayonnaise jar with the point of a pencil. It was almost night, and one could feel the coolness of the moon off in the distance. Once I was finished with the top, I screwed it carefully on the empty glass jar. Surreptitiously, I got out of my seat and headed toward the door. "And where do you think you are going, young man?" with her arms folded, my mother bellowed from across the room.

"Well, stay in the house; it's getting dark out now."

"Mommy, please!"

"No, you heard me, and I don't want to have to tell you again."

I bowed my head in disappointment and left the kitchen without a word. After some time elapsed, the sun went down. My mother was tired, and she went into the back room to relax. There I was, dying of boredom in the living room, when I realized that my mother would not hear me if I quietly went out the door. I slipped out into the night, barely closing the door behind me. Outside, my four older sisters were playing double Dutch under the streetlight. I did not want them to see me, so I ran into the backyard. There I played happily in the excitement of doing something I knew I had no business doing. The lightning bugs glittered in the night like stars broken into a million pieces. I delighted in catching them with delicate hands and placing them gently in the glass jar. There, they were my prized ornaments. Without any regard for their lives, I piled them on one by one until I grew bored. I emptied the jar with frustration; some of them fell lifelessly to the ground and died; others flew to their freedom into the night.

With nothing else to do, I walked into the front yard to look around. I did not want anyone to see me, so I hid in the shadows of some hedges in front of my house. "What else can I do?" I thought. "Maybe I'll go across the street and play with Laddie." Laddie was my neighbor's dog; Laddie didn't bite, at least to my knowledge, so I ran across the street. No one saw me. I crouched down and ran over to Laddie, a big brown and white collie, who sat proudly with his chest swelled before him. "Hi, Laddie," I said as I began to pat him on the head. "How have you been?" I stared at him eye to eye, trying to see how long I could go without blinking. I stood so close to him that the warmth of his breath brushed sharply against my face.

At that moment, I noticed that Laddie was panting with his mouth open and his tongue hanging out. This was something I never understood. Laddie never closed his mouth. I wanted to see him close it. "Close your mouth!" I commanded, "close it or I'll close it for you." The dog simply looked at me and then turned his head as if he were trying to forget that I was there. This made me angry, to the point that I grabbed the dog (who was much larger than myself) by his mouth with both hands and clapped it shut. The dog glared at me as though his tolerance was beginning to fade. We stared at each other straight in the eyes; we began to struggle. Laddie tried to open his mouth, but I was persistent in my grip and held on even tighter. Laddie did not make a sound, no growling, no whining or whimpering. In one savage explosion, he pounced on my body, pinning me to the ground. His mouth opened and unveiled his fangs. Suddenly, I felt the excruciating pain of his fangs ripping into my right cheek just below my right eye. His teeth slid deep into my face until he clamped them into a full bite. Blood squirted from my face and into my mouth, dripping and splashing. I screamed at the top of my lungs, and he loosened his grip for a moment and clamped down again. I continued to scream, to cry, to squirm to escape from his rage.

Then I heard other screams. It was my sisters; they had heard me and ran to see what was happening. Upon their arrival, the dog relinquished his hold and ran into the backyard. Immediately, I jumped up and ran to my older sister, Tatrina. I don't know why, but for some reason I felt that she could help me, more so than any of my other sisters. In my frenzy, I hugged her, burying my face in the warmth of her stomach. She wore a white sweat shirt, which I wrapped my arms around and clutched at the fabric. I sought relief from the pain by feeling her closeness. She sought to comfort me; she hugged me softly and whispered, "What happened?" And then she must have felt the wetness of the blood on her shirt and pulled my face away. She screamed at the sight of me, and I broke away and ran screaming back to the house. The moment I opened the door, I lost my balance and stumbled into the kitchen, feeling very strange. My vision blurred, and I lost all feeling. Everything slowed down. All I could hear was the sound of things falling, echoing, breaking. I fell to the floor and saw blackness.

This incident left four scars on my face; about a year later, plastic surgery would make them less noticeable. I often think about those moments when I look in the mirror. Oh, Laddie, how stupid I was to try to muzzle you. I must have thought I could change the way things are; how little I knew.

—Malverick Hofler

5. THE GRADUATE

Summer was almost over. Whatever warmth the sun still radiated was felt only skin deep. Overhead, the sound of the airplanes' engines zipping across the bluish Salonican sky could be heard and felt. At the airport's departure terminal, people were scampering here and there, saying goodbye to their relatives. Others walked solemnly away with tears in their eyes, after having witnessed their loved ones swept away by some metallic bird. It was to this scene of utter confusion that the taxi bearing my parents and me left us at the terminal's entrance.

'Here, let me take your luggage," my father offered.

"It's all right. I will manage, " I said, thinking to myself that that was what my father was hoping to hear.

"Be careful. Be careful, my child. Careful that you don't hurt yourself," Mother cautioned me. "Tom, go and help him. He is still a child."

"I said I will manage. I can lift them by myself." The authority with which I spoke these words was evident by the surprised looks that registered on my parents' faces.

The three of us made our way inside. I could see the airplanes on the runway now. I wondered which one I would be flying on. A few more minutes, I thought, and I will be on my way.

I looked at my parents. Being that it was Friday, they both looked slightly out of touch with reality, since they were wearing their Sunday clothes. Strange. They appeared rather comical together. I wondered what Dad was thinking. Was he proud of what I had accomplished so far? I knew for a fact that he did not want me to leave and that he had consented to this only because my elder sisters were already living in New York. What was Ma thinking about? Ma was usually rather calm about things. Was she calm now? I didn't really have any trouble convincing her. She knew what was best. Airports. I hate airports. You always have too much time to think there.

Three years. Three years I spent laboring in high school, trying to prove myself to my teachers and fellow classmates, as well as my family. Now after all this hard work, I was leaving for New York, where I was to pick up the pieces and start all over again. It wasn't fair. I felt like an all-star rookie who finds out that he has just been traded to another team for some cash and a player to be named later. Strange, though, how things worked out. It wasn't until these past three years that I really had a chance to know my father better, especially now that he was retired. I tried to imagine what my father was thinking.

. . . Look at him. Doesn't he care about me? He could go to school here, but no, he doesn't care about his father. Nobody cares about me, now that I'm old. Everybody wants to do his own thing. Young kids nowadays don't have any respect for their parents. In my days, we always used to look after our parents when they became old. Still, he has done rather well in school. I can't complain about that. Look at him. He even has a small mustache. Time passes slowly when you're young, and then, suddenly, your own son is taller than you. I guess I have done rather well. Now, let my daughters take care of him. Let's see. What time is it? Why can't we get this over with? Airports. I hate airports; they are always so cramped and noisy. . . .

We were sitting near the metal detector. Father sat staring into space. He was nervously plucking at his shirt sleeve, trying to catch a glimpse of the passing time. Mother sat, lecturing to me about the do's and don'ts of my departure. I was not really paying attention to her words, for, being in my teens, I thought I knew what to expect. I merely pretended to agree by nodding my head affirmatively. I wondered what thoughts were racing through her head.

. . .My child. My only son. I do hope he's careful. He has certainly grown these past few years. I mean, not only physically, but he has developed mentally also. He must eat well to stay healthy. A letter a month would be all right. Our house will feel empty now. No one will play the radio loud, especially during the afternoon siesta hours. No one to wake up for basketball games. Now we will only have the nieces and nephews to add some life to our house. Better check to see if he has everything. Airports. I hate airports. I do hope we don't have to move again. I'm tired of trips and airplanes. . . .

Such must have been my parents' thoughts at the time. We started to talk. The basic small talk of everyday life. Regards to your sisters. Regards to your aunts and uncles, when you see them. Tell us your news. *Write*. Watch what you eat. Watch what you say and to whom. *Write*. Listen to your sisters. Ask them for advice. Don't forget us. *Write*.

My mind started to wander. Some of the conversation was drowned out by the constant hum of the airplane engines. I tried to listen to the voice coming over the loudspeaker:

. . . Mr. Papadopoulos, please report to the baggage-claim area. Mr. George Papadopoulos. . . .

George Papadopoulos? The deposed former dictator of Greece? Ha! What a thought. Of course it wasn't him. Isn't he still in jail? It is obviously some villager with the same name.

. . . Passengers for Flight 068 to Athens please board. . . .

Bored? Not really. Mixed feelings, yes. I do hope that we are served some decent food for a change. The minutes drag on . . .

Suddenly it struck me. The airport was filled with faces without identities: a beautiful stewardess sat behind the information desk, a little boy was crying for some candy. We were all there, thrown together for that one moment and would probably never meet again. Airports. I hate them. One moment you are here, and the next, poof! you are gone.

. . . Gate 4. Passengers for Flight 464 bound for Athens now boarding at Gate 4. . . .

I jumped. I recognized my flight number. Wearily, I lifted myself off the chair. I felt attached to it after sitting on it for so long. My parents stopped talking. They grasped the meaning of the present situation. In a few seconds, I would be gone. Gone somewhere across the ocean. We embrace. Mother pecks me on the cheek. For one brief moment, our minds seem to unite. We are one. Everything else stands still. No teardrop falls.

I proceed through the metal-detecting device. I wonder if my keys will sound the alarm. As I am passing, I am reminded of the opening scene from the movie *The Graduate*. At that moment, I was Benjamin Braddock walking through the airport corridors, with the "Sounds of Silence" playing as a backdrop. The only difference is that instead of entering the airport, I am leaving it, and with it, my parents' life style. I turn to look at my parents. They are together. I wave to them and mutter an inaudible goodbye.

From the airplane window, I tried desperately to locate my parents at the airport window. After some time, I succeeded in doing so. I tried to speak to them right before takeoff to let them know I understand, but I knew that they could not hear me. I knew that they could not see me, but if they had, they would have seen my fingers pressed against the cold glass of the plane's window. From now on, I would be on my own.

—Argyrios Koumas

6. EXHAUSTION AND FULFILLMENT

The quiet landscape lies peaceful and tranquil in the early-morning dew. Five birds swoop by in search of breakfast. A clock chimes in the distance, loud and clear. I stand on the edge of a field, pondering; the fields are soaked from last night's rain. I yawn, then stretch, moving in a wide circle. Quickly, I burst into a series of warm-up exercises. All seems well. I set my timer, look in the distance, take in a deep breath, and then I am off.

What is essential at the beginning is the resolve to reach the saturation point. The progress of the body on the undulating earth, nimble, firm, and consistent, should harmonize with the mind and thus be constantly fueled with drive and determination. Ideally, I should end only when the spirit is making no further progress within me. I should not be fooled, though, by a period of boredom, weariness, or disgust; that is not the end, but the last obstacle before it. Let saturation be serene!

I breathe through my nose, taking in deeply the fresh, cold morning breeze. My ears are nearly frozen. My legs respond quickly to the set surface; though slightly tight, they synchronize perfectly like the beat of a drum. My arms are close to my chest, swinging slightly but still rather stiff. It is very cold. I move on, trying to warm my body as quickly as possible without overworking too soon.

It is the condition of such an activity as cross-country that I entrust myself, stripped of my worldly goods, to nature. Shoes and socks, a shirt, shorts, and a watch: that is the extent of my wealth. To remove all the useless material baggage from myself is, at the same time, to free my mind from petty preoccupations, calculations, and memories. On the other hand, what fabulous and undeveloped mines are to be found in nature, friendship, and oneself! I have no choice but to draw everything from them.

I have come to a heavily wooded hill. There is a path, which I take. I breathe through my mouth now to maximize my air intake. My legs feel like lead. I raise them higher in an effort to maintain my pace. It is painful. I press my head forward and swing my arms vigorously. My blood is warmed, but my muscles are aching. I stumble on a dead branch, but I quickly recover, though it takes even more strength to retain my stride. I focus my eyes to the distance, urging my spirit on. I do not like the color of the sky. The sky is blue, pure blue. Too pure. A hard blue sky that shines over the barren world while the foliated hill chain flashes in the sunlight. Not a cloud. The blue sky glitters like a new-honed knife. I feel in advance the vague distaste that accompanies the prospect of a tedious physical exertion. The purity of the sky upsets me. Give me a good black storm in which I can fight with all the rage and fear I can command. But when I am running very high and alone, the shock of a blue sky is as disturbing as if the impending doom I visualize is playing a game—no, a trick—on me.

I am approaching a long stretch of land as dented as an old boiler. The sole vegetation visible in this threadbare landscape is a series of oil derricks looking like the aftereffects of a forest fire. My feet are burning as the sharp dents and the tiny pebbles press forcefully beneath my soles. I am drenched in sweat. Overall, I am at peace with the body. It is responding smoothly, moving stealthily as a lion tracking its victim. I am thirsty, but that can go unsaid.

I forget the blue sky because right now I have an overwhelming love for all living things. I feel a burning desire to run faster and faster to eternity. I smile at the curious stares of the lizards and birds who I suspect will always consider man their most deadly enemy. I feel overcrowded in my head. The sun makes it even worse. I shouldn't be fooled by these sudden urges; they are a result of a burst of mental activity that is being realized through several channels and so creating this buzz in the head as if I had or was recovering from a rotten hangover.

Now there is a battle going on in my mind. Do I rest or do I continue, regardless of the numbing headache? The Will is being now; it is forcing all thoughts that it finds discouraging out of my system. I have stomach cramps. I slacken my pace reluctantly and bend over slightly to fight the pain. My legs do not approve of the change of pace: a burst of pain is registered by the brain. Blood has flooded my leg arteries; I can feel the heart and pulse behind the kneecaps. Thankfully, the barren land turns to a marsh. Flies hover around me as I shake my head to protect my eyes. My initial thankfulness for the soft surface is wiped out. My feet feel as if I have a clamp of iron jewelry hanging not so gracefully around my ankles. It is hard work as I slog, muttering a wise old saying I learned when I was a child.

My body screams for a reprieve. It announces that it cannot go on. Nonsense! I run six, and I say I'm finished. Rubbish! Here is some blood and air and a change of thought. Run! Runner, run! I draw my will to concentrate on the distance. To consider the joy of self-satisfaction and serenity I will experience after I have accomplished my objective is the ultimate goal in an independent mind. I think not of pain, but of joy, not of reality, but of fantasy; I experience a renewal of body, of spirit, of will. I picture the smug smile of self-approval, the freeing of any guilt of defeat.

I am on my last legs. I feel dehydrated, or am I, maybe, somewhere in between? I virtually drag my feet into simply moving on. I see the farm in the distance all alone standing like a tree growing in the desert, stark naked without protection. I am dying of thirst as I struggle on, keeping eyes on the barn, which seems to be moving farther and farther away from me. I feel like crying with pain, but I know I can't stop now. I begin chanting, "You are nearly there, move on" over and over, my eyes intent on the barn. I am dribbling and sagging under the weight of my chest, which can only stay upright with pain. Bolts of pain arrive from all parts of the body, especially my feet.

O.K. Phew! Puff, puff, puff . . . I fall on the hay in blissful vertigo, my mouth open wide, trying to breathe as quickly as I can. My eyes are watery, my feet sore as hell. I am elated; my timer shows that I beat my personal best by a full minute. I picture the whole race again, the fresh start to the physical and mental exhaustion I now feel. I am at peace with myself, confident, proud, and extremely delighted with me. For a reward, I will go riding today! That is the ascetic way of accomplishment.

—Fillmore Apeadu

7. UNCOVERING THE TRUTHS AND THE MYTHS ABOUT COURAGE

A popular conception of courage is the image of a rugged individual risking life and limb in a fierce struggle, usually for some revered cause such as patriotism, chivalry, or self-honor. I find this definition to be wholly inaccurate on the grounds that it not only excludes subtle but nonetheless legitimate acts of courage, but falsely assumes that violent brawls require bravery on the part of those involved. The latter half of my disagreement, concerning violent disputes, brings to mind Philip, a boy I had known many years ago. Philip was absolutely fearless. He would think nothing of fighting guys twice his size and, on occasion, throw rocks at a passing police car. I wouldn't consider this courage. Bloodletting and danger are as natural and as pleasurable to him as a game of poker is to me. Philip's insanity left no room for courage.

For a deed to be stamped "courageous," it must, I believe, fulfill two requirements: one, it must arouse a feeling of dread within the person involved, and, two, that person must face up to his anxiety and carry out what he believes to be his duty. This definition takes courage out of the barroom full of Hell's Angels and places it into the life of the ordinary citizen. Many of us aren't conscious of the fact that we perform courageous deeds every day. We all have our ''hang-ups'' and must tackle these in the course of daily living. My ''hang-up'' is public speaking. When I'm aware of the inevitability of making a speech, my hands become cold and clammy, and my stomach feels as if I have swallowed a hockey stick. By the time I'm done, it feels as if I have aged five years. Talking among a group may not fit Hollywood's idea of fortitude, but I know the obstacles and pain I had to overcome; I know I was courageous.

One must realize that courage isn't engendered by one's actions, but it's spawned within oneself. One cannot detect courage unless one measures the amount of tension an individual must surmount in order to achieve something.

—Jeffrey Taub

8. THE KARATE CHAMP: A KNOCKOUT!

Last week, a new video game was wheeled into the game room. I felt the anticipation that a child experiences when feverishly unwrapping a new toy. The screen lit up, and behold, here was the game that I had heard such rave reviews about. ''Karate Champ'' was emblazoned in Oriental calligraphy. The image on the screen was then replaced by two figures jousting. The figures seemed to beckon to me to insert a quarter. The screen then flashed that it cost 50 cents. My next deposit was rewarded by the master, a faithful rendition of Fu Manchu, saying, ''Begin!''

When I inserted the quarters, I had a melancholy reminiscence about my karate *dojo*. The figure on the screen reminded me of Master Cho, my master and old family friend; I had had grand dreams when I started at sixteen: black belt and then the 1988 Olympics at Seoul. The realities of life have destroyed some of this dream, but they can't prevent me from dreaming. It will be a while before I get a black belt, but while I play the Karate Champ, I can be in the Olympics.

I decided to forego a practice session, and I eagerly directed my figure, clad in a white *gi,* against the computer's champion, dressed in a red *gi*. (It is interesting that a U.S.A. flag was draped on the scoreboard; I wonder if there was some appeal to Russophobia.)

I was captivated by the complexity of the two joy sticks, which I found to be capable of thirty-six techniques. If, for example, both knobs were directed forward, then a front kick was executed; if the right knob was held at rest while the left knob was pushed up, then a round kick was thrown. I found an additional challenge in combining these techniques in a strategic sequence. If I missed with a round kick, then I could succeed with a sweep or a punch.

The mastery of those damned controls proved both an expensive and a time-consuming process. The game seemed to have an ego booster built into it, which acted to keep my interest as I learned. During each round, as I faced my adversary, there appeared a pretty girl who stared at both of us. Her head would bob back and forth indecisively; the scene would then be disturbed by the master, who signaled for the match to ''begin!'' After a blow was scored, my personification, on the screen, would resume a starting position. This process continued until one side had scored 2 full points (blows being worth $\frac{1}{2}$ or 1 point each).

If I lost, the girl would reappear as my figure turned his back, put his hands to his head, and then cried. The girl would go to his side, and cartoon letters would say: "BETTER LUCK NEXT TIME." If I was victorious, however, the girl would slowly slink to his side, and she would say: "MY HERO!" She then gave a kiss, which caused my hero's head to swell up. This scenario would be repeated after every round, except that she would change her costume to match the round's screen. One screen had her clad in buckskin, and another in a bikini set against a ship's deck.

The master, presiding over the matches, seemed to represent a father figure (or my old master). When I won a bonus round by evading objects, breaking boards, or stopping a bull, he said, "Very good!" The ego boost continued when I finally achieved the high score. After a girl flashed for each round that I won, I was able to put my initials over the screen. I was finally the hotshot, at least until someone topped me or they turned the machine off.

The greatest ego boost, however, came when a group of people came over to watch me play. They saw my success, and they wanted to learn my tricks. I could feel that I had mastered feats that I could never accomplish in real life. I had reached the level of green belt at my karate school and could do the basic kicks and punches; however, I could never do somersaults or throw a good flying kick. Karate Champ, like every video game, provides that curious paradox of instantaneous victory before the inevitable reality of death.

I reflect back to the first video game, Pong, which was hardly something to notice, with simple graphics and a black-and-white screen. Space Invaders, in 1978, and Asteroids, in 1979, started a trend toward increasing sophistication. Pac-Man, in 1980, marked the beginning of the big video craze.

I remember first seeing Pac-Man in a bookstore on Jerome Avenue. I used to walk past the bookstore as I went from the subway to Science High. Basically, Pac-Man involved moving your figure around to eat dots while avoiding the other figures. It was innovative in that it rewarded you a different bonus prize for each round: a cherry, an orange, or a grape. It was a challenge to find out what the bonus would be in the next round. (I lost interest when I found that the highest attainable bonus was a key.) I had companions of a sort in that bookstore. There was always someone standing by the side of the machine, but we were mostly interested in learning the "pattern" that would allow a higher score at Pac-Man.

Video games, like television, filled a void within my life. Here was a set of rules that always applied, unlike so many of the rules that always seemed to change when I faced my peers and the "world." People are often not what they seem, but the machines are always the same. Video games don't deceive, but they can't make you laugh or kiss you when you're down.

When I left high school, the video games were waiting for me in the game room of Queens College. I was greeted there by a multitude of new friends; they were ready to give me the immediate gratification that I needed. I had no strong incentive to make friends, or even to learn how to talk to people (though I was always able to go one on one with my teachers). My playmates were sufficient, and when I tired of one, there was always a replacement waiting in the wings. I have forgotten many of their names, but I remember those that I spent the most on. I immortalize their names for you: Ms. Pac-Man, Pac-Man Junior, Centipedes, Millipede, Pac-Man Plus, Baby

Pac-Man, Super Pac-Man, Zaxxon, Dragon's Lair, Donkey Kong, Jr., Donkey Kong's Revenge, Donkey Kong, Defender, Star Castle, Scramble, Make Trax, Galaxion, Qix, Galaga, Stargate, Star Wars, Major-League Baseball, Tennis, Football, Basketball, Boxing, Space Invaders II, Centipedes II, Secret Agent, and I hope you have grown weary of their names because most of them are now gone or soon will be. Video games are like movies or rock stars: all are constantly challenged by newcomers and the fickle taste of their audience.

A few days after my first encounter with the Karate Champ, I returned to find three guys standing by my machine. Two of them were engaged in a joust, while the third was watching. (The machine has two pairs of joy sticks, which allow two humans to play each other.)

The contrast between my attitude and theirs was striking. It was not their dress that was different; it was their joviality that I lacked. They were not absorbed by the machine; they were relaxed and enjoying each other's company. Each successful score was followed by a joke, rather than by a curse. There was no difference between victory and defeat: it was simply a matter of having a good time.

After they·left, I attacked the machine with a pocketful of quarters. The world vanished as I sweated and smoked at the controls. I was mesmerized and had to continue. Schoolwork, friends, be damned! All that mattered was to defeat the opponent in the red *gi*. I had to survive his attacks until the next round, and then the next. I had to keep playing until I topped the high score and then broke my old high score.

As a game, I give the Karate Champ four stars. It fulfills all that you could ask for in a video game: excellent graphics, a good plot, and a built-in ego enhancer. As a casual pursuit for two people playing each other, four stars. As for me and Karate Champ, I'm not sure; after about an hour of play, I begin to feel nauseated. Strange, though, I continue despite my queasiness. And I find myself, again and again, standing alone at that machine. Karate Champ is not karate; karate prepares one to fight but not to seek a fight. Karate is about Zen, which prepares the mind and soul, as well as the body, for combat with life's problems, which often can be solved without fists.

Karate Champ promotes an anti-karate stance: that through violence, one can obtain fame, travel, sexual conquests, and, most importantly, a way to solve practical problems. The message instilled within these memory chips and all their technological counterparts is sterility and anti-life. Winning is the only thing that matters in this world of circuits, but winning is only momentary before "GAME OVER," death. I can't decide whether this machine appeals to nationalism or to nihilism; what is more obvious is what these machines replace: kisses, chats, hugs, friendship, and all the things we do when we reach out to another person. All that exists is the fumbling for more and more quarters.

—Cliff Staebler

9. A YOUNG SON MAKES A FATHER'S DAY

It was late, I was out the door and racing to make the 7:29 to Grand Central, when my boy called from the front step: "Daddy, do I look like you?"

The question triggered such a rush of thoughts and emotions that I was stopped in my tracks.

I returned to the front door, taking a few extra seconds to compose a reply:

"Edward, you look like me a little, but you're more like a movie star, or a TV star."

He gave me his smile that with a tug of the lips and the drop of his ale-brown eyes conveys embarrassment, shyness and pleasure all in one look.

I thought about his question on and off all day. Had someone in school made fun of him? Had a relative delivered some unthinking remark, made some unfavorable comparison, in his presence? Were they talking about his looks? About mine?

It's amazing, I mused, how one forgets the thousands upon thousands of compliments about looks that one has heard from early childhood until a few hours ago, yet remembers with painful clarity the insults.

One evening long ago when I had exasperated my mother, she turned on me and sputtered, "You ugly duckling!"

It made me miserable, which I'm sure was her intent. Only later could I realize it had probably made her just as miserable. And as much as I had explained the moment to myself, there it remained, tucked in my brain, 25 years later.

My mother has fawned over my looks countless times before and after, and I believe that in her eyes I'm one handsome devil. But now the duck and the devil live side by side.

Edward's question made me think of another terrible moment. I was 12 or 13 and had gone with some chums to a tough neighborhood in Boston where a grocery store had installed a pinball machine.

I was wearing glasses and a knit hat shaped like an aviator's headgear, rendering the wearer not dashing, I soon learned, but possessed of a goofy maroon noggin.

One of the slick older local boys spotted me in the crowd around the pinball machine and said to his pal, "Hey, get a load of this kid." That was it. That was all he said. But I felt homely for a long, long time.

At lunch the day of my son's question I told colleagues about the episode, for it had become more than a passing question.

One told me that his son favored his wife, while his daughter favored him. "She's eight and she's worried," he said. "She asks, 'Dad, when I'm older will I have hair on my chest and under my arms while the hair on top of my head gets thin?'"

It was an easier question to answer than the one lobbed at me. I decided that someone had made a disparaging comment about my looks. When I got home I broached with subject with my 6-year-old son.

"Edward, why did you ask this morning if you looked like me?"

He became uneasy. "Someone said I did."

"Who, Edward?"

"Just someone."

His reluctance to reveal the source or details of the insult aggravated me. I concluded it must have been a mean companion. I was angry that my boy might be hurt. For myself, I was angry and hurt as well.

I began to fume over the slight and the damage it might do to Edward's self-confidence. I wondered if there had been some odious reference to my mustache or perhaps my —well, generous—nose.

Maybe an hour later, in one startling moment, I was struck by a very different thought: What if Edward wants to look exactly like me? I went back to him.

"Edward Salim," I began, adding his middle name in hopes of building the sense of family closeness, "I've thought it over, and you look a lot like me. Almost exactly like me, except as hard as I try, I can't see your mustache. The same nice smart head and special eyes. My hair is short, but it used to be long and terrific like yours is."

Edward Salim beamed. He was happy, and he was proud to learn that he looked so much like his dad. I had spent a day feeding my misgivings about how handsome or plain or homely I was—about what people perceived when they looked at me.

When Edward was asleep later that night, I slipped into his room and approached his bed for another look. He lay with his head to one side, his forehead highlighted in the dimness, his perfect little features serene.

"My son," I said, "how beautiful you are."

—Herbert Hadad,
The New York Times

10. STRANGER'S STARE: BALEFUL OR BECKONING?

They were strangers on a train, two travelers who found themselves sitting across the car from each other. By chance, their eyes met. But instead of quickly looking away, they held each other's gaze. The glance became a fixed mutual stare, as the seconds ticked by. What happened then?

If they were man and woman, it could have been the beginning of a beautiful friendship. If they were two men, though, they might have left the train at the next station platform and started pummeling each another.

"Eye contact means different things to different people," said Dr. Allan Mazur, professor of sociology at Syracuse University. "Two people who make eye contact can be expressing love, hostility, boredom or curiosity. It depends on what's going on in their heads at the time."

Dr. Mazur is one of a small band of social scientists who have been studying eye contact and patterns of social staring. They have identified a remarkable number of well-defined ways in which we use our eyes to communicate, to show submission or to challenge others to establish dominance.

"Most of this behavior takes place below the conscious level," said another eye-contact researcher, Dr. Eugene A. Rosa, assistant professor of sociology at Washington State University. However, the subtle dance of stare and counterstare is a ritual that all engage in, and few are aware of.

In most situations, silent eye contact is inappropriate between two individuals. "To look into someone's eyes nonverbally is impolite, it's often defined as insulting and it's tension-producing," Dr. Mazur said.

There are exceptions: "In a bar, staring silently at a member of the opposite sex would be viewed as nonverbal communication," he said, "and it's common in pickups and sexual encounters."

It is also socially appropriate to look into another person's eyes when at a distance well beyond that for normal conversation. Thus, when two people walk toward each other on the street, they might look at each other until they are 5 to 10 yards apart.

"At this point it's too awkward for them to keep looking at one another, so their eyes disengage," Dr. Mazur said. Even if the two are friends, and they have waved or shouted at one another in recognition, most likely they will not look each other in the eye until they get close enough to talk.

Among conversational partners, eye contact is entirely appropriate. But it appears to be governed by some surprisingly rigid rules. When two people of equal social status converse, the speaker doesn't always have to look at the listener. But it is the listener's task to look at the speaker.

And if that listener holds the speaker in great respect, it may be deemed extremely impolite for the listener to look away—even to glance briefly at his or her watch. However, if the more "respected" person is doing the listening, the unspoken rule is that he or she can look away at will.

"The remarkable thing about these eye-contact situations is that they are so well defined," Dr. Mazur said. One of the most controlled social-staring arenas is in enclosed spaces like elevators, where eye contact with strangers may be taken not only as impolite, but hostile.

To give his sociology students a vivid sense of staring boundaries, Dr. Mazur has suggested that they try staring at other passengers in the university elevators; usually it is appropriate only to gaze at the doors or the floor indicator. "This staring was so anxiety-provoking to both the students and the others in the elevators," he said, "that we had to discontinue asking students to try this. It was *that* stressful."

Dr. Mazur and his colleagues have attempted to assess the relationship of social stress and staring in a variety of published studies. The discomfort of stress is experienced as anxiety, fear or anger. Physiologically, it involves changes in the autonomic nervous system, including the release of adrenaline, noradrenaline and cortisol; changes in the levels of the hormone testosterone, and the shunting of blood from the periphery of the body to skeletal muscles.

Virtually all primate species that have been studied, including humans, show dominance or status hierarchies with respect to power, influence and prerogatives. From their ongoing research, Dr. Mazur and his co-workers have developed theories of face-to-face status interactions involving individuals' attempts to "outstress" each other in fairly well-defined contests. Among apes and monkeys the contest may take the form of aggressive combat, but among humans, it most often involves language and nonverbal behavior.

Such human competitions can take the form of polite conversation, and participants may barely be aware of the test of wills. The contest ends when one individual "surrenders," accepting lower rank and alleviating the stress that both individuals experienced during the competition. Dr. Mazur hypothesizes that dominant members of human societal groups are those most able to withstand stress, and best equipped to impose stress on others.

Some people seem more comfortable with high levels of stress, and when two such individuals look each other in the eye, the result is a staring contest. "Staredowns are common among nonhuman primates, but not so common among humans, especially those in a middle-class American milieu," Dr. Mazur said. "The staredown is a behavior in our repertoire, but not often used. We are primarily language-using animals, and it's much easier to challenge someone by interrupting him than by staring at him.''

Both Dr. Mazur and Dr. Rosa have tested staredown behavior inside and outside the laboratory, doing the latter by staring back at strangers who stare at them. While returning stares, they observe the sequence of events. In some staredowns, blinking is taken as submission, while in others, it is not a factor in determining a victor.

The heady spirit of scientific inquiry is not always observed in such contests. ''I've had a couple of guys want to take me out to the alley to settle things,'' Dr. Rosa said. ''And once, in the San Francisco zoo, I kept staring at a gorilla, and he got so angry that he threw a stick at me.''

Dr. Mazur and his colleagues Caroline Keating and Marshall Segall have also studied the role of eyebrow position in social staring. A study of 1,500 subjects in 11 countries showed that in America, lowered eyebrows are viewed as more dominant, and raised eyebrows are perceived as more submissive. However, in Thailand, the opposite was true: raised eyebrows, rather than lowered ones, were viewed as dominant.

Two people caught in a mutual staring situation may find it easy to misread each other. ''If their eyes meet by chance, usually both people will look away,'' Dr. Mazur said. ''However, this eye contact could be interpreted as curiosity by one person, and as a challenge by the other. Person A may think he has won a staredown if person B looks away. But person B may be saying, in effect: 'Your staring is impolite. I'm turning away now—because you are beneath my notice.' ''

However, a curious feature of staredowns is that the participants don't talk about them. ''You can be in a staredown with a stranger and meet him socially later,'' Dr. Mazur said, ''and you won't *ever* mention the staredown. I've been unsuccessful in getting staredown partners to even admit that we'd just been looking at each other—even after introducing myself as a researcher who's studying staring. It's something people just don't want to admit.''

—Glenn Collins,
The New York Times

11. LIVING WITH MY VCR

When all this started, two Christmases ago, I did not have a video-cassette recorder. What I had was a position on video-cassette recorders. I was against them. It seemed to me that the fundamental idea of the VCR—which is that if you go out and miss what's on television, you can always watch it later—flew in the face of almost the only thing I truly believed—which is that the whole point of going out is to miss what's on television. Let's face it: Part of being a grown-up is that every day you have to choose between going out at night or staying home, and it is one of life's unhappy truths that there is not enough time to do both.

Finally, though, I broke down, but not entirely. I did not buy a video-cassette recorder. I rented one. And I didn't rent one for myself—I myself intended to stand firm and hold to my only principle. I rented one for my children. For $29 a month, I would tape ''The Wizard of Oz'' and ''Mary Poppins'' and ''Born Free,'' and my children would be able to watch them from time to time. In six months, when my rental contract expired, I would re-evaluate.

For quite a while, I taped for my children. Of course I had to subscribe to Home Box Office and Cinemax in addition to my normal cable service, for $19 more a month—but for the children. I taped "Oliver" and "Annie" and "My Fair Lady" for the children. And then I stopped taping for the children—who don't watch much television, in any case—and started to tape for myself.

I now tape for myself all the time. I tape when I am out, I tape when I am at home and doing other things, and I tape when I am asleep. At this very moment, as I am typing, I am taping. The entire length of my bedroom bookshelf has been turned over to video cassettes, mostly of movies; they are numbered and indexed and stacked in order in a household where absolutely nothing else is. Occasionally I find myself browsing through publications like Video Review and worrying whether I shouldn't switch to chrome-based videotape or have my heads cleaned or upgrade to a machine that does six or seven things at once and can be set to tape six or seven months in advance. No doubt I will soon find myself shopping at some Video Village for racks and storage systems especially made for what is known as "the serious collector."

How this happened, how I became a compulsive videotaper, is a mystery to me, because my position on video-cassette recorders is very much the same as the one I started with. I am still against them. Now, though, I am against them for different reasons: Now I hate them out of knowledge rather than ignorance. The other technological breakthroughs that have made their way into my life after my initial pigheaded opposition to them—like the electric typewriter and the Cuisinart—have all settled peacefully into my home. I never think about them except when I'm using them, and when I'm using them I take them for granted. They do exactly what I want them to do. I put the slicing disk into the Cuisinart, and damned if the thing doesn't slice things up just the way it's supposed to. But there's no taking a VCR for granted. It squats there, next to the television, ready to rebuke any fool who expects something of it.

A child can operate a VCR, of course. Only a few maneuvers are required to tape something, and only a few more are required to tape something while you are out. You must set the timer to the correct time you wish the recording to begin and end. You must punch the channel selector. You must insert a videotape. And, on my set, you must switch the "on" button to "time record." Theoretically, you can then go out and have a high old time, knowing that even if you waste the evening, your video-cassette recorder will not.

Sometimes things work out. Sometimes I return home, rewind the tape, and discover that the machine has recorded exactly what I'd hoped it would. But more often than not, what is on the tape is not at all what I'd intended; in fact, the moments leading up to the revelation of what is actually on my video cassettes are without doubt the most suspenseful of my humdrum existence. As I rewind the tape, I have no idea of what, if anything, will be on it; as I press the "play" button, I have not a clue as to what in particular has gone wrong. All I ever know for certain is that something has.

Usually it's my fault. I admit it. I have mis-set the timer or channel selector or misread the newspaper listing. I have knelt at the foot of my machine and methodically, carefully, painstakingly set it—and set it wrong. This is extremely upsetting to me—I am normally quite competent when it comes to machines—but I can live with it. What is far more disturbing are the times when what has gone wrong is not my fault at all but the fault of outside forces over which I have no control whatsoever. The program listing in the newspaper lists the channel incorrectly. The cable guide inaccurately lists the length of the movie, lopping off the last 10 minutes. The evening's schedule of television programming is thrown off by an athletic event. The educational station is having a fund-raiser.

You would be amazed at how often outside forces affect a video-cassette recorder, and I think I am safe in saying that video-cassette recorders are the only household appliances that outside forces are even relevant to. As a result, my video-cassette library is a raggedy collection of near misses: ''The Thin Man'' without the opening; ''King Kong'' without the ending; a football game instead of ''Murder, She Wrote;'' dozens of PBS auctions and fund-raisers instead of dozens of episodes of ''Masterpiece Theater.'' All told, my success rate at videotaping is even lower than my success rate at buying clothes I turn out to like as much as I did in the store; the machine provides more opportunities per week to make mistakes than anything else in my life.

Every summer and at Christmastime, I re-evaluate my six-month rental contract. I have three options: I can buy the video-cassette recorder, which I would never do because I hate it so much; I can cancel the contract and turn in the machine, which I would never do because I am so addicted to videotaping; or I can go on renting. I go on renting. In two years I have spent enough money renting to buy two video-cassette recorders at the discount electronics place in the neighborhood, but I don't care. Renting is my way of deluding myself that I have some power over my VCR; it's my way of believing that I can still some day reject the machine in an ultimate way (by sending it back)—or else forgive it (by buying it)—for all the times it has rejected me.

In the meantime, I have my pathetic but ever-expanding collection of cassettes. ''Why don't you just rent the movies?'' a friend said to me recently, after I finished complaining about the fact that my tape of ''The Maltese Falcon'' now has a segment of ''Little House on the Prairie'' in the middle of it. Rent them? What a bizarre suggestion. Then I would have to watch them. And I don't watch my videotapes. I don't have time. I would virtually have to watch my videotapes for the next two years just to catch up with what my VCR has recorded so far; and in any event, even if I did have time, the VCR would be taping and would therefore be unavailable for use in viewing.

So I merely accumulate video cassettes. I haven't accumulated anything this mindlessly since my days in college, when I was obsessed with filling my bookshelf, it didn't matter with what; what mattered was that I believed that if I had a lot of books, it would say something about my intelligence and taste. On some level, I suppose I believe that if I have a lot of video cassettes, it will say something—not about my intelligence or taste, but about my intentions. I intend to live long enough to have time to watch my videotapes. Any way you look at it, that means forever.

—Nora Ephron,
The New York Times Magazine

12. FROM *GROWING UP*

The only thing that truly interested me was writing, and I knew that sixteen-year-olds did not come out of high school and become writers. I thought of writing as something to be done only by the rich. It was so obviously not real work, not a job at which you could earn a living. Still, I had begun to think of myself as a writer. It was the only thing for which I seemed to have the smallest talent, and, silly though it sounded when I told people I'd like to be a writer, it gave me a way of thinking about myself which satisfied my need to have an identity.

The notion of becoming a writer had flickered off and on in my head since the Belleville days, but it wasn't until my third year in high school that the possibility took hold. Until then I'd been bored by everything associated with English courses. I found English grammar dull and baffling. I hated the assignments to turn out "compositions," and went at them like heavy labor, turning out leaden, lackluster paragraphs that were agonies for teachers to read and for me to write. The classics thrust on me to read seemed as deadening as chloroform.

When our class was assigned to Mr. Fleagle for third-year English I anticipated another grim year in that dreariest of subjects. Mr. Fleagle was notorious among City students for dullness and inability to inspire. He was said to be stuffy, dull, and hopelessly out of date. To me he looked to be sixty or seventy and prim to a fault. He wore primly severe eyeglasses, his wavy hair was primly cut and primly combed. He wore prim vested suits with neckties blocked primly against the collar buttons of his primly starched white shirts. He had a primly pointed jaw, a primly straight nose, and a prim manner of speaking that was so correct, so gentlemanly, that he seemed a comic antique.

I anticipated a listless, unfruitful year with Mr. Fleagle and for a long time was not disappointed. We read *Macbeth*. Mr. Fleagle loved *Macbeth* and wanted us to love it too, but he lacked the gift of infecting others with his own passion. He tried to convey the murderous ferocity of Lady Macbeth one day by reading aloud the passage that concludes:

> . . . I have given suck, and know
> How tender 'tis to love the babe that milks me.
> I would, while it was smiling in my face,
> Have plucked my nipple from his boneless gums. . . .

The idea of prim Mr. Fleagle plucking his nipple from boneless gums was too much for the class. We burst into gasps of irrepressible snickering. Mr. Fleagle stopped.

"There is nothing funny, boys, about giving suck to a babe. It is the—the very essence of motherhood, don't you see."

He constantly sprinkled his sentences with "don't you see." It wasn't a question but an exclamation of mild surprise at our ignorance. "Your pronoun needs an antecedent, don't you see," he would say, very primly. "The purpose of the Porter's scene, boys, is to provide comic relief from the horror, don't you see."

Later in the year we tackled the informal essay. "The essay, don't you see, is the . . ." My mind went numb. Of all forms of writing, none seemed so boring as the essay. Naturally we would have to write informal essays. Mr. Fleagle distributed a homework sheet offering us a choice of topics. None was quite so simpleminded as "What I Did on My Summer Vacation," but most seemed to be almost as dull. I took the list home and dawdled until the night before the essay was due. Sprawled on the sofa, I finally faced up to the grim task, took the list out of my notebook, and scanned it. The topic on which my eye stopped was "The Art of Eating Spaghetti."

This title produced an extraordinary sequence of mental images. Surging up out of the depths of memory came a vivid recollection of a night in Belleville when all of us were seated around the supper table—Uncle Allen, my mother, Uncle Charlie, Doris, Uncle Hal—and Aunt Pat served spaghetti for supper. Spaghetti was an exotic treat in those days. Neither Doris nor I had ever eaten spaghetti, and none of the adults had enough experience to be good at it. All the good humor of Uncle Allen's house reawoke in my mind as I recalled the laughing arguments we had that night about the socially respectable method for moving spaghetti from plate to mouth.

Suddenly I wanted to write about that, about the warmth and good feeling of it, but I wanted to put it down simply for my own joy, not for Mr. Fleagle. It was a moment I wanted to recapture and hold for myself. I wanted to relive the pleasure of an evening at New Street. To write it as I wanted, however, would violate all the rules of formal composition I'd learned in school, and Mr. Fleagle would surely give it a failing grade. Never mind. I would write something esle for Mr. Fleagle after I had written this thing for myself.

When I finished it the night was half gone and there was no time left to compose a proper, respectable essay for Mr. Fleagle. There was no choice next morning but to turn in my private reminiscence of Belleville. Two days passed before Mr. Fleagle returned the graded papers, and he returned everyone's but mine. I was bracing myself for a command to report to Mr. Fleagle immediately after school for discipline when I saw him lift my paper from his desk and rap for the class's attention.

"Now, boys," he said, "I want to read you an essay. This is titled 'The Art of Eating Spaghetti.'"

And he started to read. My words! He was reading *my words* out loud to the entire class. What's more, the entire class was listening. Listening attentively. Then somebody laughed, then the entire class was laughing, and not in contempt and ridicule, but with openhearted enjoyment. Even Mr. Fleagle stopped two or three times to repress a small prim smile.

I did my best to avoid showing pleasure, but what I was feeling was pure ecstasy at this startling demonstration that my words had the power to make people laugh.

—Russell Baker

part 3
A Guide to Usage

chapter

10 | Seeing Sentences

As you now begin Part Three, you may feel that you are taking a step backward. If you have tried your hand at essay writing (and we hope you have), you may wonder why you need to work on sentences.

We recently overheard a teacher announce to his students: ''Now it's time to study grammar. Ugh.'' It is no secret that both students *and* teachers often dread the study of grammar, seeing it as a painful enterprise, unrelated to anything in the real world. Many teachers, in fact, have thrown out the study of grammar, using as their argument several studies suggesting that learning grammar has little to do with improving writing.

The study of grammar alone does not improve writing. *Only writing improves writing.* We have observed, however, that writers who understand the principles of grammar can more easily *control* their writing. Students quietly admit that they are tired of not understanding what fragments and run-ons are; they want to know about sentences because they feel powerless in their writing.

In this book, you can turn to a review of grammar whenever you need to. We know of an *advanced* writing course where students turned to this chapter because they wanted to know, once and for all, what a sentence is. The point is that both inexperienced and advanced writers often do not know what they need to know about sentences. We hope that you will use the chapters in this section as you and your instructor see fit and that you will feel the strength all writers feel as they get grammar under control.

Can you unscramble these sentences?

nut Brazil a *I'm*

SELL WANT CARS TO WE

personal needs he attention

Can you place each of the following words into one blank in the next sentence?

race   racer   racing   raced

That _____ in the silver _____ car _____ in the last _____ .

Why is it that you came up with these results?

I'm a Brazil nut.
We want to sell cars.
    or
We want cars to sell.
He needs personal attention.
That *racer* in the silver *racing* car *raced* in the last *race*.

Why didn't you write this?

That racing in the silver raced car racer in the last race.

10.a YOU HAVE THE GRAMMAR

The answer is that you have a *grammar* that insists you turn up precisely these results. With this grammar, you are able to unscramble sentences because you intuitively know how sentences in your language are put together. The grammar requires one kind of word for each slot, and you have acquired a feel for fitting that kind of word into its place in the sentence.

You've had this grammar for a long time. By the time you reached first grade, you were already an expert in your language. You had absorbed a grammar—that is, a way of producing and understanding English sentences. And now, as you continue to make sentences, many will be brand new, and virtually all of them will also be understandable to other speakers of the language. That's quite amazing, when you stop to think about it.

This chapter will tell you what you need to know about sentences so that you can *see* sentences in your writing. Seeing sentences in your writing involves two things. First, it involves avoiding nonsentences—fragments—as well as avoiding overloaded sentences. Second, it involves actually trying your hand as a writer of sentences. You may be like many students who write short, abrupt sentences most of the time because you don't want to make mistakes. You play it safe, but your sentences are "Dick and Jane" sentences. You're not sure what *run-ons* are, but you think that writing short sentences will help you avoid them. The "labels" of grammar are mysterious to you. *Subject* and *verb, phrase* and *clause* have fuzzy meanings. Sometimes they mean one thing, and sometimes they mean another.

THE GOOD LIFE
Love at first sight
Soviets demand Mideast talks
THE GREATEST BOOKS EVER WRITTEN

The words above were taken from the media—newspaper headlines and magazine advertisements—from the language you see all around you. Which of these illustrations are sentences, and how do you know? Is "Love at first sight" a sentence? Why or why not? Is "Soviets demand Mideast talks" a sentence? Why or why not?

The language you see and hear all around you is filled with bits and pieces of sentences as well as with whole sentences. In college writing, the accepted grammatical unit is the sentence. So, even though you've been speaking sentences for years, you need to *see* them and to understand what makes up sentences in order to write them.

For a moment, let's compare speaking and writing. When you speak, you rely on gestures and pauses, intonations and inflections to get your message across. If someone dashes in front of a car, you might scream, "Hey!" or "Look out!" or you might push the person out of the way of the oncoming car. Your actions are not limited to words on paper. When you speak, you can change your mind in the middle of a sentence; you can smile or wink or cough or emphasize a particular word by raising your voice. You often use very few words to communicate with others:

"Did you see the game last night?"
"Yeah."
"Good, huh?"
"Terrific."

Speech is a kind of shorthand: you don't need to spell things out by saying, "Yes, I did see the game last night." "Yeah" is enough to keep the dialogue going because meanings arise out of the give and take of conversation.

Writing is more like a monologue: the writer writes to an absent reader. In writing, since you can't rely on gestures or screams or shoves to convey your message, you need to spell out your ideas in sentences, which express relationships between ideas. The simplest sentence relates two ideas in a subject–verb unit. For example, an idea of *fish* and an idea of *swimming* produce this sentence:

> Fish swim.

Or the idea of *the Giants* and the idea of *winning* produce this sentence:

> Giants win.

These are sentences because each contains a *subject–verb unit*. Every sentence must contain a subject–verb unit.

Any two words strung together do not produce a sentence:

fish dogs
Giants winning
boys girls
is are
finally faithfully
into on

Only when two words together make up a subject–verb unit is there the possibility of a sentence. In the next section, we will look specifically at how to *find* these subject–verb units.

Throughout the next few chapters, we'll be looking at the grammar of the written sentence—how words are put together to form sentences. We'll be moving toward a *working definition* of a sentence; that is, a definition that will *work* for you when you need to test your own writing for sentence completeness according to standard English grammar.

But *finding* subjects and verbs is not the whole story; you need to *write* sentences and believe in your potential to create sentences in endless combinations, in endless shapes and sizes. You can write very short sentences:

> Bette Midler began.
> Mick Jagger followed.

You also can write sentences that go on and on as you add to the few basic sentence patterns. The *Guinness Book of World Records* tells us:

> A sentence of 958 words appears in *Cities of the Plain* by Marcel Proust and one of 3,143 words with 86 semicolons and 390 commas occurs in the *History of the Church of God* by Sylvester Hassell of Wilson, North Carolina, c. 1884. . . . A report of the President of Columbia University, 1942–43, contained a sentence of 4,284 words.

Here is a fairly "short" sentence, of only ninety words or so, by Herman Melville:

Whenever I find myself growing grim about the mouth; whenever it is a damp, drizzly November in my soul; whenever I find myself involuntarily pausing before coffin warehouses, and bringing up the rear of every funeral I meet; and especially whenever my hypos [old slang for "the blues"] get such an upper hand of me, that it requires a strong moral principle to prevent me from deliberately stepping into the street, and methodically knocking people's hats off—then, I account it high time to get to sea as soon as I can.

—*Moby Dick*

10.b WHAT'S IN A SENTENCE?

If you're not sure how to find the subjects and verbs in sentences, you can look to the following pages for a way to locate them. At the start, remember that every sentence has two grammatical requirements: a subject and a verb. Every sentence can be thought of as having a *subject slot* and a *verb slot*. These slots must be filled. Because the subject and verb act together as a unit, once you find one part of the unit, it's usually not difficult to find the other part. Keep in mind as you begin your search into the sentence that the subject slot can be filled by *one or more words* and that the verb slot can be filled by *one or more words*.

Finding the verb Every verb in a sentence is connected to time—the past, present, or future. Since verbs have this special quality of showing time, you can find the verb by changing the time in a sentence.

Rich Kids Have Problems, Too

Change time: Rich kids *had* problems, too.
Rich kids *will have* problems, too.

The word that changes as you change the time is the verb: *have, had, will have*.

Let's look at this more closely. In a sentence, a one-word verb always shows time:

One-word verb	Sentence	Time
did	Harry *did* it.	past
feel	I *feel* miserable.	present
followed	They *followed* your advice.	past

In a sentence, a verb that is more than one word also shows time:

Verb of more than one word	Sentence	Time
will do	Harry *will do* it.	future
was feeling	I *was feeling* miserable.	past
have followed	They *have followed* your advice.	past

Verbs show different times by changing form. Every verb has several forms. By looking at the following sentences, you can see that all the sentences contain a form of the verb *dance:*

Sentence	Time
Lucy *dances* in the ballet.	present
Lucy *danced* yesterday.	past
Lucy *will dance* tomorrow.	future
Lucy *is dancing* right now.	present
Lucy and Ricky *dance* frequently.	present (denotes a general truth, a habitual action)

Look at the four forms that come from *dance:*

dances

danced

dancing

dance

Like *dance,* most verbs have four forms. (See Chapter 13 for lists of regular and irregular verb forms.)

roar	smile	smirk
roars	smiles	smirks
roaring	smiling	smirking
roared	smiled	smirked

Notice that three of the sentences about dancing contain a one-word verb *(dances, danced, dance)*. In the other two sentences, the verb is two words *(will dance, is dancing)*. In each sentence, the verb is connected to time. Since every sentence contains a verb connected to time, *to find the verb, change the time of the sentence.*

EXAMPLE A 1. Read the sentence:

Families belong together.

2. Change to future time.

If the sentence is not in the future, change it to future time. Add the word *will* to the sentence. Add the word *tomorrow* to signal the time change:

(Tomorrow) Families *will belong* together.

3. Change to past time.

To make certain that you've found the verb, change to a one-word past. Add the word *yesterday* to signal this change:

(Yesterday) Families *belonged* together.

4. Find the verb

The word that changes is the verb:

belong
will belong
belonged

EXAMPLE B 1. Read the sentence:

Everybody came for a last drink.

2. Change to future time.

If the sentence is not in the future, change it to future time. Add the word *will* to the sentence. Add the word *tomorrow* to signal the time change:

(Tomorrow) Everybody *will come* for a last drink.

3. Change to past time.

To make certain that you've found the verb, change to a one-word past. Add the word *yesterday* to signal this change:

(Yesterday) Everybody *came* for a last drink.

The original sentence is in the past.

4. Find the verb.

The word that changes is the verb:

came
will come

EXAMPLE C 1. Read the sentence:

You'll be a better person for it.

2. Change to future time:

You *will be* a better person for it.

The original sentence is already in the future.

3. Change to past time:

(Yesterday) You *were* a better person for it.

4. Find the verb:

'll be (will be)
were

The following narrative, taken from Ernest Hemingway's story "Big Two-Hearted River," is written in past time. The events have already occurred:

Rapidly [Nick] *mixed* some buckwheat flour with water and *stirred* it smooth, one cup of flour, one cup of water. He *put* a handful of coffee in the pot and *dipped* a lump of grease out of a can and *slid* it sputtering across the hot skillet. On the smoking skillet he *poured* smoothly the buckwheat batter. It *spread* like lava, the grease spitting sharply. Around the edges the buckwheat cake *began* to firm, then brown, then crisp. The surface *was bubbling* slowly to porousness. Nick *pushed* under the browned undersurface with a fresh pine chip. He *shook* the skillet sideways and the cake *was* loose on the surface. . . .

By acting as fortuneteller—as one who will predict Nick's actions—you can change the sentences to future time:

(Next summer) Rapidly [Nick] *will mix* some buckwheat flour with water and *will stir* it smooth, one cup of flour, one cup of water. He *will put* a handful of coffee in the pot and *will dip* a lump of grease out of a can and *will slide* it sputtering across the hot skillet. On the smoking skillet he *will pour* smoothly the buckwheat batter. It *will spread* like lava, the grease spitting sharply. . . .

The word that changes in the Hemingway narrative, in each case, is the verb. As you see, in changing a sentence to future time, the spelling of the verb itself may change (*slid* becomes *will slide*), or the spelling of the basic verb may stay the same (*put* becomes *will put; spread* becomes *will spread*). In each case, however, the word *will* has been added. When you change the sentence time by moving from *past time* to *future time*, the verb shows up.

Past time	Future time
stirred	will stir
dipped	will dip
slid	will slide

This contrast between the one-word past and the two-word future (with *will*) should help you find the verb in every sentence.

If a sentence doesn't seem to be in the past time, then shift the sentence to the past. Now you are ready to shift the sentence to the two-word future with *will*. Don't worry about identifying the time of the given sentence, *just make a move*. As long as you change the time, the verb will change also.

Verb signals   Words like *should, can, could, may, might, ought to, must, have to*, and *need to* are important signals for finding the verb. Whenever one of these words appears in a sentence, you can expect another part of the verb to follow:

> I *should have called* him.
> I *must find* her.
> He *needs to talk* to me.

These words, with meanings of their own, are part of the verb. They signal that more of the verb is to follow. Together with the rest of the verb, they make up the whole verb in a sentence. This group of words is called a *verb phrase*.

Other signals for finding the verb may be less reliable. *Do, does*, and *did; am, is, are, was*, and *were; has, have*, and *had* may be part of a verb phrase:

> I *did spend* that money today.
> I *am looking* for work.
> I *have asked* for your help.

But these words can also appear in sentences as verbs alone:

> I *did* it.
> I *am* a friend of hers.
> I *have* green eyes.

Whether the verb is one word or composed of several words, you can always find the verb by changing it to a one-word past or to a two-word future with *will*.

> I *should have called* him.
> I *called* him.
> I *will call* him.

Should have called is the verb in the example.

Exercise 1   Find the verbs in the following sentences.

> Example: Soviets demand Mideast talks.
> (Tomorrow) Soviets will demand Mideast talks.
> (Yesterday) Soviets demanded Mideast talks.

The verb in the example is *demand*.

1. Expos blankety-blank Mets, 7–0, 7–0.
2. The ungreening of America begins with careless fires.
3. Little Maria had been hungry all her life.
4. She will never forget the pain of poverty.
5. Market rises sharply during light trading.
6. My daddy's richer than your daddy.
7. Here comes the bride.
8. I lost 7 pounds and 5½ inches off my waist in nine days.
9. Along came the little people.
10. Sailing in the Arctic is a new challenge in yachting.
11. The essence of a well-attired gentleman lies somewhere between his unmistakable style and his unerring taste.
12. Getting it together also means keeping it together.

Exercise 2 Change each verb in the following sentences to a one-word past and a two-word future with *will*.

>Example: Steel union accepts contract.
>Steel union accepted contract.
>Steel union will accept contract.

1. Storm toll rises to twenty-six.
2. Everybody came for a last drink.
3. Planes nearly collide.
4. Big plane dives to avert crash.
5. Suspect escapes from hospital.
6. Father knows best.
7. They danced till dawn.
8. Life begins at fifty.
9. You're not getting older. You're getting better.
10. Crime rate spurts in nation.
11. Companies report sales and profits.
12. Ohio State defeats Illinois.

Exercise 3 The following paragraph expresses past time with a single word, the verb *got*. *Got* is such a useful word that it is often overused. Practice working with verbs by replacing each *got* in the paragraph with another verb that expresses a more specific action. Keep the time in the past, and try not to repeat any verbs.

>Example: I got up this morning, got dressed, and got my instant breakfast.
>I awoke this morning, dressed, and drank my instant breakfast.

A LOT OF *GOT*

I got up this morning, got dressed, and got my instant breakfast. I got my coat and hat and got the elevator. I got a newspaper at the corner store and got the train. I got to my office and got the morning mail. I got an overdue bill from Con Edison. I got the adjustment manager on the phone and got the matter straightened out. At 10:00, I got a cup of coffee and a doughnut. At 10:15, I got back to work. I got a call from my supervisor. We got together for lunch. I got a tuna sandwich and a cup of coffee. I got back at the office at 1:30 and got caught up on a lot of work. At 5:00, I got my coat and got the elevator and got the train and got home by 6:00. All in all, I got a lot done today.

Exercise 4 After you have rewritten "A Lot of *Got*," change the time of the paragraph to the future. The sentences will require *will* plus the verb ("I *will awake* tomorrow morning, *will dress,* and *will drink* my instant breakfast"). When there are several verbs connected to one subject, it is all right to carry over the *will* from the first to following verbs ("I *will awake* tomorrow morning, *dress,* and *drink* my instant breakfast").

Verbs and Some writers mistake an *-ing* word by itself for the verb in a sentence. An *-ing*
-ing words word alone is never the verb in a sentence. The verb in every sentence must be connected to time—the past, present, or future.

Sentence	**Time**
It *rained.*	past
It *is raining.*	present
It *will rain.*	future

The *-ing* word, however, does not specify the past, present, or future. It is a word that suggests continuation, and it must be combined with a time word (*is, was, will be, are, were,* and the like) if it is to be connected to the past, present, or future.

> It *is raining.*
> It *was raining.*
> It *will be raining.*

When the *-ing* word is connected to the past, present, or future, it is part of the verb phrase of a sentence.

Remember: in standard English, the *-ing* word alone cannot be used as the verb. (See Chapter 12, pp. 278–281, for a discussion of fragments.)

No:	**Yes:**
It *happening* right now.	It *is happening* right now.
She *sailing* in the bay.	She *was sailing* in the bay.
The Yanks *coming.*	The Yanks *are coming.*

An -*ing* word may not be a part of the main verb in a sentence. Try the test for a verb on the following sentence.

1. Read the sentence:

   Toby walked down the street, eating a salami sandwich.

2. Change to future time.

   (Tomorrow) Toby *will walk* down the street, eating a salami sandwich.

3. Find the verb.

   walked
   will walk

But what about *eating? Eating* and the words that follow it (*a salami sandwich*) provide more information about the subject of the basic sentence—Toby. In this sentence, the -*ing* word is not part of the verb. Connected to a time word, *eating* could be part of a verb in another sentence:

   Toby *was eating* a salami sandwich.

Here *eating,* combined with the time word *was,* is the verb in the sentence. Test example sentences A and B, below, for the verb.

EXAMPLE A 1. Read the sentence:

2. Change to future time.

   (Tomorrow) America *will be getting* into training.

3. Find the verb.

   is getting
   will be getting

EXAMPLE B 1. Read the sentence:

   Clutching her shopping bag, the old woman climbed into the bus.

2. Change to future time.

(Tomorrow) Clutching her shopping bag, the old woman *will climb* into the bus.

3. Find the verb.

climbed
will climb

Exercise 5   The following sentences are adapted from Ernest Hemingway's story "Big Two-Hearted River." Determine in which sentences the *-ing* word is part of the verb and in which sentences the *-ing* word is not part of the verb.

1. The tent was starting to get hot.
2. The grasshoppers were already jumping stiffly in the grass.
3. In the bottle, warmed by the sun, they were jumping in a mass.
4. Nick laid the bottle full of jumping grasshoppers against a pine trunk.
5. He slid the grease sputtering across the hot skillet.
6. On the smoking skillet he poured smoothly the buckwheat batter.
7. It spread like lava, the grease spitting sharply.
8. The surface was bubbling slowly to porousness.
9. Nick took it from his hook book, sitting with the rod across his lap.
10. He tested the knot and the spring of the rod by pulling the line taut.
11. It was a good feeling.
12. Rushing, the current sucked against his legs.
13. He floated rapidly, kicking.
14. In a quick circle, breaking the smooth surface of the water, he disappeared.

Verbs and adverbials

WATCH OUT FOR ADVERBIALS

Other words in sentences designate time, but they are *not* verbs. Do not mistake words such as *now, then,* and *tomorrow* for verbs. As you have seen, verbs usually change form to show time. Words or phrases like *tomorrow* or *in a few days* do not have different forms. These elements, called *adverbials,* narrow down the time of the verb. You make the time of your sentence more specific when you use an adverbial. In the following sentences, the verb phrase *will land* designates future time. By adding adverbials, you make the time in the future more specific:

We will land on Mars.
We will land on Mars *tomorrow.*
In a few days, we will land on Mars.
We will land on Mars *by the year 2000.*
We will land on Mars *within the next century.*

Finding the subject

The same word does not necessarily function in the same way in every sentence. A word that works as a verb in one sentence may function as a subject in another. Consider these lines by Elizabeth Barrett Browning, from her poem "How Do I Love Thee?"

	S–V UNIT
How do I love thee? Let me count the ways.	I do love
I love thee to the depth and breadth and height	I love
My soul can reach, when feeling out of sight	
For the ends of Being and ideal Grace.	
I love thee to the level of every day's	I love
Most quiet need, by sun and candle-light.	
I love thee freely, as men strive for Right;	I love
I love thee purely, as they turn from Praise;	I love
I love thee with the passion put to use	I love
In my old griefs, and with my childhood's faith.	
I love thee with a love I seemed to lose	I love
With my lost saints—I love thee with the breath,	I love
Smiles, tears, of all my life!—and, if God choose,	
I shall but love thee better after death.	I shall love

Throughout the poem, the word *love* functions as a verb (except in the line "I love thee with a love . . . ," where the first *love* functions as a verb and the second functions as a noun). In most cases, the subject–verb unit is *I love*. In the following sentences, the word *love* functions as the *subject* of each sentence:

	S–V UNIT
Love is blind.	Love is
Love is love's reward.	Love is
Love is the salt of life.	Love is

The subject–verb unit is a grammatical requirement of every sentence. Every written sentence must contain both a subject and a verb. But what is a subject, and how do you find it in a sentence? In the beginning of this chapter, we state that the subject–verb unit expresses a relationship between two ideas. One idea is expressed as a verb—a time word—and the other is expressed as a subject:

birds	and	flying	=	birds fly
fish	and	swimming	=	fish swim

Connecting ideas means connecting subjects to verbs. Because every subject is connected to a verb, one way to find the subject of a sentence is first to locate the verb, as you did in the preceding section. Once you locate the verb, you can track down the subject by finding the idea that connects to the verb. You do this by setting up a "Who?" or a "What?" question:

EXAMPLE A   1. Read the sentence:

Rich kids have problems, too.

2. Find the verb.

have

3. Ask "Who?" or "What?"

Who or what have?

4. The subject fills the "Who?" or "What?" slot.

Rich kids have

EXAMPLE B 1. Read the sentence:

Nothing slows you down.

2. Find the verb.

slows

3. Ask "Who?" or "What?"

Who or what slows?

4. The subject fills the "Who?" or "What?" slot.

Nothing slows

In most sentences, the subject comes before the verb. This is the usual word order in English. Once you've found the verb, you will generally find the subject before it.

But consider this sentence:

ALONG CAME THE LITTLE PEOPLE

Once you've found the verb, *came,* you then ask, "Who or what came?" *Along* is not the idea that tells who or what came. *Along* cannot come. You must look to the other side of the verb for the answer:

SUBJECT   VERB
The little people   came

In the following sentence, the subject is *man:*

Man Bites Computer

If *computer* were the subject, the sentence would read:

Computer bites man.

Whatever the subject of a sentence is, it can be connected to its verb by asking a "Who?" or a "What?" question. In the sentence "Down fell the rain," the verb is *fell.* To the question "Who or what fell?" the answer is *rain.*

To double-check that the subject you find is correct, you can also:

Look for logical units of meaning in the sentence.

or

Look at the word order in the sentence. The subject *almost always* comes before the verb.

WATCH OUT FOR *THERE* AND *HERE*

The words *there* and *here* are words that often point to the subject:
   There is *my friend.*
   Here comes *the bride.*
   There goes *my dear wife.*
   There are *my brothers.*
   Here *he* comes.
   There *she* is.

Exercise 6 Write sentences in which you use each of the following words as verbs. Use any form of the verb you wish. Then write a second set of sentences, using these *same* words as subjects.

   Example: The Rolling Stones often *play* at the coliseum.
              The *play* attracted huge crowds.

   1. love
   2. hate
   3. scratch
   4. laugh
   5. flower
   6. crash
   7. fly
   8. saw
   9. cut
   10. cheat
   11. burn
   12. run
   13. milk

Exercise 7 Find all the subject–verb units you can in this table-of-contents page from *People* magazine:

Glenn grounded, 38

Fawcett floozied, 64

Lennon listed, 85

UP FRONT □ 38
□ **McGovern, Hollings, Cranston, Anderson** and nine other also-rans recall the fear, the loathing—and the absurdity—of their campaign trails
□ **Princess Margaret's** "tart" retort puts **Boy George** in a snit
□ Denied coverage by Blue Cross and Medicaid for her heart transplant, **Grace Jacques** turned to the public for help—drawing attention to the plight of hundreds of other unprotected patients

OLYMPICS □ 51
For diver **Wendy Wyland,** the L.A. Games may prove a springboard to fame

COUPLES □ 55
The living is breezy for Britishers **Roy** and **Joan Bates,** who gave birth to their own North Sea nation

TOP □ 60
Judith Levy obviously knows what grandmothers want, and her best-selling *Grandmother Remembers* proves it

TUBE □ 64
Farrah Fawcett, Veronica Hamel and even **Debby Boone** have played the latest in evening entertainment: TV doxies

PAGES □ 69
Jean Kent and **Candace Shelton** tell how you, too, can pen passionate prose in *The Romance Writer's Phrase Book*

10.c SENTENCE PATTERNS

Every sentence must contain at least one subject–verb unit. But sentences, as you know, are made up of more than subjects and verbs. Look at the sentence at the top of this advertisement:

Every sentence has room for expansion. The subject can be expanded, the verb can be expanded, and the whole sentence can be expanded. Yet every sentence, regardless of how long or complex it is, falls into one of the basic English sentence patterns. Seeing sentences means knowing the basic patterns so that you can see the structure of a sentence.

Seeing sentences also means understanding that the basic patterns can be developed and that the slots in each sentence can be filled by one word or by a group of words. You saw in this chapter how the verb can be one word or a verb phrase. Now you'll see that the subject can also be one word or a group of words.

The command pattern

As we've mentioned, there are two required slots in every sentence: the subject slot and the verb slot. The words that fill these two slots form the subject–verb unit. In one sentence pattern, the *command,* the verb slot is filled, but no word fills the subject slot. This does not mean that a command has no subject; rather, the subject is said to be *implied,* which means that it is not stated, but is understood. The command orders someone to do something, but the someone is not named:

> Watch out!
>
> Close the door.
>
> Don't do that.

Give your dog
something to smile about.

If you were in a room with a friend and part of the ceiling started to fall, your friend might scream, "Watch out!" You'd know, without question, that your friend was speaking to you. Like "Watch out!" every command speaks to "you"—to one person or to a group of people. That is what is meant by the implied "you." The command qualifies as a sentence because it has the two required sentence elements—a subject and a verb—even though the subject is not stated.

Subject–verb pattern

Grammatically, the subject–verb unit stands as a sentence. Notice how often newspaper headlines use this basic sentence pattern:

SUBJECT	VERB
James Mason	**dies**
Musicians	**return**
Pitt	Wins
Storm Toll	*Rises*

The verbs in this pattern are called *intransitive verbs.*

Subject–linking verb–completer pattern

Linking verbs are forms of the verb *be: am, are, is, were, was, have been, will be, can be, should have been,* and so on.

SUBJECT	LINKING VERB	COMPLETER (COMPLEMENT)
LOVE	**IS**	**A RIVER.**

You're fired!

I *am* hungry.
Bill *was* thirsty.
Mary *has been* sick.
Lunch *will be* ready soon.

Linking verbs are also verbs that express feeling, growing, sensing, tasting, becoming, and the like:

I *am getting* tired.
He *felt* energetic.
Her perfume *smells* terrible.
She *looked* doubtful.
He *seemed* angry.
The milk *tasted* sour.

Every sentence containing a linking verb has a *sentence completer*. A completer is a word or group of words that follows the verb to complete the meaning of the subject–verb unit. The completer of a linking verb always refers to the subject, telling us something about the subject:

S	LV	C
Seymour	is	my brother.

My brother is a noun phrase that tells who Seymour is.

S	LV	C
Seymour	looks	angry.

Angry is an adjective that tells how Seymour looks.

Caroline is a princess.
Money is the root of all evil.
The price is right.

A linking-verb sentence is like an equation in which the verb acts as an equal sign. The linking verb is also called an *intransitive linking verb.*

Caroline is a princess.
Caroline = a princess.

Subject–transitive verb–completer pattern	SUBJECT	TRANSITIVE VERB	COMPLETER (DIRECT OBJECT)
	Blast	**rips**	**oil tank**
	McEnroe	Defeats	Connors
	Ohio State	Defeats	Illinois
	Supersong	**fills**	**the world**

THE DIRECT OBJECT   In the subject–transitive verb–completer pattern, the completer that follows the verb refers to something other than the subject. This completer, which introduces a new element into the sentence, is called a *direct object,* and the verb in this pattern is often called an *action verb,* or a *transitive verb* (*transitive* means "passing across to something else").

Compare these patterns:

Subject–verb:	The Pirates won.
Subject–linking verb–completer:	The Pirates are the winners.
	The Pirates = the winners.
Subject–transitive verb–completer:	The Pirates beat the Orioles.
	The Pirates ≠ the Orioles.

This completer, *the Orioles,* is not equivalent to *the Pirates. The Orioles* adds a new element to the sentence.

THE INDIRECT OBJECT   A second object, called the *indirect object,* can come between the transitive verb and the direct object. The indirect object tells to whom or for whom something is done:

SUBJECT	TRANSITIVE VERB	INDIRECT OBJECT	DIRECT OBJECT
Lucy	offered	Desi	a ride.
Ethel	made	Fred	a pie.

You can tell if a word or phrase is an indirect object by turning it into a *to* or *for* phrase following the direct object:

Lucy offered a ride *to Desi.*
Ethel made a pie *for Fred.*

The passive   The *passive* is a transformation of a sentence with a transitive verb. Watch the shifts in these sentences:

Transitive:	A lion bit the trainer.
Passive:	The trainer was bitten by a lion.

The object of a transitive verb becomes the subject of a passive verb.

Transitive: A lion bit *the trainer*.
Passive: *The trainer* was bitten by a lion.

And the subject of the transitive verb becomes part of a *by* phrase in the passive:

Transitive: *A lion* bit the trainer.
Passive: The trainer was bitten *by a lion*.

See Chapter 13, page 304, for a discussion of the verb in the passive.

10.d FILLING THE SUBJECT AND COMPLETER SLOTS

Look again at the basic sentence patterns:

Subject–verb:	S V The Pirates won.
Subject–linking verb–completer:	S LV C The Pirates are the winners.
Subject–transitive verb–completer:	S V C The Pirates beat the Orioles.

In each of these patterns, the subject and completer slots can be filled by a single word or by a group of words:

S	V
The first baseman	screamed.

S	V
The first baseman, clutching his empty mitt,	screamed.

S	V
The first baseman, clutching his empty mitt and hanging on to the leg of the umpire,	screamed.

S	LV	C
The woman	is	my grandmother.

S	LV	C
The woman serving the sandwiches	is	my grandmother.

S	LV	C
The woman in the yellow bikini serving the sandwiches	is	my grandmother.

S	LV	C
My favorite activity	is	sleeping.

S	LV	C
My favorite activity	is	sleeping in the afternoon.

S	LV	C
My favorite activity	is	sleeping on the job behind the meat refrigerator in the back of the A&P in the afternoon.

S	V	C
The man	entered	the room.

S		C
The man, carrying a box of chocolate-covered cherries,	entered	the hospital room.

S		C
The rain-drenched man, carrying a dripping box of chocolate-covered cherries,	entered	the empty hospital room.

The examples shown here can be used as patterns for your own sentences. In the remainder of this chapter, we will look more closely at the subject and completer slots.

Nouns Single words that fill the subject and completer slots are often *nouns*. All the words below are nouns and can function in sentences as subject or completer. Typically, nouns function as *names*—of persons, places, things, ideas, and qualities. A practical test for a noun is to see how it behaves.

things   authority   Doris Lessing   inspiration

improvement   Eve   mover

people   THOMAS JEFFERSON   JAPAN   SAVINGS

Rabbit   Canadian   RAINBOW   China

power   Lemon   Ideas   Europe   AMERICA

1. Most nouns change their spelling to show a change from one to more than one (from singular to plural):

thing	things
authority	authorities
improvement	improvements
woman	women
Canadian	Canadians

2. Most nouns change their spelling to show possession:

Japan	Japan's
rabbit	rabbit's
woman	woman's

3. Most nouns can be introduced by *a, an,* or *the:*

thing	a thing
authority	the authority
improvement	an improvement

4. *This, that, these,* and *those* often signal a noun:

thing	these things
woman	that woman
rabbit	those rabbits

Pronouns Pronouns are words like *I, you, he, she, it, we, they, him, her,* and *them.* Certain pronouns, called *subject pronouns,* fill the subject slot:

Subject pronouns

I	we
you	you
he, she, it	they

> *He* needs personal attention.
> *I* also need personal attention.
> *We* all do.
> *We*'ve got a secret!

Object pronouns fill the direct-object slot:

Object pronouns

me	us
you	you
him, her, it	them

Roger hit *him* again.
Will you leave *her* alone?
Pauline missed *them* for the second time.

Pronouns enable us to avoid repetition by giving us a shorthand for referring to what has already been named or given. See Chapter 15 for a full discussion of pronouns and the ways in which they are used.

Noun phrases

A *phrase* is a group of related words that does not contain a subject–verb unit. Once you surround a single word (such as a noun) with words that make it more specific, the single word becomes part of a phrase. Watch how that happens:

Noun: woman
Noun phrase: the woman in the yellow bikini serving the sandwiches

Like a noun, a noun phrase can fill the subject or the completer slot:

S	V	C
The woman	is	my grandmother.

S	V	C
The woman in the yellow bikini serving the sandwiches	is	my grandmother.

S	V	C
My grandfather	is	that man.

S	V	C
My grandfather	is	that man in the tan swimsuit serving the beverages.

Watch how the subject slot may be expanded:

		S	V	C
Noun:		Any person	has	one of these.
Noun phrase:		Any well-heeled, self-made, sophisticated, uninflated, pompous, narcissistic, quixotic, average, elegant, down-home person	has	one of these.

Prepositional phrases Prepositions—words such as *up, on, in, at, from, of,* and *with*—connect a single word or a group of words to another part of the sentence. The preposition and the words it connects are called a *prepositional phrase*. Remember, a phrase is a group of words with *no* subject–verb unit. A prepositional phrase often accompanies the noun in the subject or completer slot. In the following sentences, the prepositional phrases are in italics.

	s	v	c
The man		entered	the room.

s	v	c
The man *in the purple striped pajamas*	entered	the room *at the top of the stairs*.

s	v
The woman	fainted.

s	v
The woman *in front of me*	fainted.

The following is a list of familiar prepositions:

about	beside	on
above	between	onto
across	by	over
after	down	since
against	during	through
along	for	till
among	from	to
around	in	toward
as	inside	under
at	into	until
before	like	up
behind	near	upon
below	of	with
beneath	off	

Here is a list of combinations of words used as prepositions:

according to	in place of
ahead of	in spite of
apart from	in view of
because of	on account of
in front of	up to

Sometimes these same words function as part of a compound verb and are called *particles*.

Verbs with particles

drop off	The mailman *dropped off* the package.
call for	We *called for* an appointment.
look over	I *looked over* the checkbook.
think through	You need to *think through* the problem.

See how these words can be used as prepositions in prepositional phrases:

The pencil dropped	*off the table.*
June called	*for hours.*
The guard looked	*over the wall.*
I thought about Bess	*through the night.*

Verbals and verbal phrases A *verbal* may look like a verb (*seeing, covered, to love*), but it does not function as a verb in a sentence because it does not connect to time.

A verbal can work in a sentence by:

1. Filling the subject and completer slots
2. Describing the subject and completer

Verbal

seeing
believing

S	V	C
Seeing	is	*believing*.

to love

S	V	C
To love	is	all.

recycling

S	V
Recycling	**works.**

screaming

The *screaming* woman burst into the room.
(S = screaming, V = burst)

covered

Henry brought a *covered* casserole to the dinner.
(S = Henry, V = brought, C = casserole)

A verbal works along with the words that follow it to form a *verbal phrase*. Like a verbal, a verbal phrase can fill the subject and completer slots:

Verbal phrase

being a kid again

Being a kid again isn't always funny!

to get the facts   # Our job is to get the facts

Verbal phrases can also work as modifiers:

Verbal phrase

covered with mud   The children, *covered with mud,* burst into the kitchen.

seeing the accident   *Seeing the accident,* the woman called the police.

See Chapter 11, pages 260–272, for a discussion of modifiers.

Review of phrases

To summarize, there are two important things to remember about all phrases:

1. A phrase is a group of words that does *not* contain a subject–verb unit:

the lost child
the man in the gray flannel suit
to get the facts
smoking a cigar
Paul Newman's big blue eyes

2. Any phrase can become a part of a sentence:

Phrase	**Sentence**
the lost child	The salesman comforted *the lost child.*
the man in the gray flannel suit	*The man in the gray flannel suit* tripped.
to get the facts	My job is *to get the facts.*
smoking a cigar	*Smoking a cigar* was Groucho's trademark.
Paul Newman's big blue eyes	*Paul Newman's big blue eyes* are color blind.

Exercise 8 Turn these phrases into sentences.

Example: the tall woman in the black suit
The tall woman in the black suit is an investigative reporter for her college newspaper.

1. wishing you were here
2. bumping her head
3. the setting sun
4. in spite of his misery
5. up, up, and away
6. blue suede shoes

7. tumbling out of bed	**14.** running for the bus
8. to go to the store	**15.** eating a nectarine
9. flashing lights	**16.** killed a spider
10. was driving down the street	**17.** painted a room
11. down by the river	**18.** to win the game
12. after the dance	**19.** until the end of my shift
13. star-crossed lovers	**20.** my grandmother's candlesticks

Clauses   A *clause* is a group of related words that contains at least one subject–verb unit.
Each of the following clauses contains a subject–verb unit. These clauses work as sentences:

s   v
Time flies.

s   v
Final exams are scheduled for next week.

s   v
I'll be studying all weekend.

Other clauses, although they contain a subject–verb unit, cannot work as sentences:

when time flies
although final exams are scheduled
because I'll be studying all weekend
whoever passes the test
whatever he pleases

Clauses that begin with such words as *when, although,* and *because* cannot work as written sentences. They will be discussed in Chapter 11. Here we are interested in clauses that begin with such words as *whoever, whatever, who,* and *what,* for these clauses can fill the subject and completer slots:

        s   v   c
Whoever passes this test   passes the course.

The subject of the sentence is:

Whoever passes this test

The subject is itself a clause:

    s   v
whoever passes this test

In the sentence:

  s   v   c
Jeffrey   always   does   whatever he pleases.

the completer is:

> whatever he pleases.

The completer is also a clause:

> s   v
> whatever he pleases

Where you're going is just as important as where you're coming from.

> s   v   c
> Where you're going   is   just as important
>   as where you're
>   coming from.

Exercise 9 The following are bits and pieces of sentences. Taken from newspapers, they reflect much of the language that you see all around you. By adding any words you need, change these pieces of sentences into whole sentences.

Example:

Flu absenteeism on the rise

Flu absenteeism on the rise is a piece of a sentence; it needs a verb, a time word, to qualify as a sentence:

> Flu absenteeism *is* on the rise.

1. **A New Modern Man**

2. Here To Stay.

3. **looking for the good life.**

4. SIGHT UNSEEN

5. **DREAMING OF ITALY**

6. **Better Left Unsaid**

7. **Fooling Mother Nature**

9. **Playing The Game**

10. **A Love Story**

8. Day by Day

11. Taking a Break

12. Smoking in public

13. Around the Nation

chapter 11

Making Connections: Coordinating and Subordinating

As you read through your freewriting and your rough drafts that move toward an essay, you find that some sentences strike you as more important than others. They demand greater attention. You decide that some ideas are general and others, specific; and you distinguish between the big general idea—the controlling idea—that holds the whole piece of writing together and those ideas that provide support for the one big idea. Among the supporting ideas, you also see that some are of greater or lesser importance.

Then, too, among the sentences in your essays, relationships appear that are only hinted at. Ideas may hang next to one another without touching. They call for finer, more precise connections because the exact relationship among them does not show up. In still other sentences, an idea suggests the mine below it; you realize that once you unearth one idea, others emerge.

How, then, to make connections among sentences? How to move beyond the basic sentence patterns so that your reader understands the relationships among your ideas? How to mine your sentences so that you expose the ideas and details within them? How to make the details within your sentences specific and alive? These are the issues of this chapter, as we study two basic processes at work within the sentence: coordination and subordination.

11.a COORDINATION AND SUBORDINATION

> Everybody's got a Helene Tucker.
> Everybody sees her as a symbol.
> Helene Tucker is a symbol of everything you want.
> I loved her for her goodness.
> I loved her for her cleanliness.
> I loved her for her popularity.
> She would walk down the street.
> The street was my street.
> My sisters would yell.
> My brothers would yell.
> They would yell, "Here comes Helene."

What strikes you about these sentences? Do they seem repetitive, monotonous, tiresome perhaps? While they are the original ideas contained in sentences written by the author Dick Gregory, they are not his original sentences, which read like this:

> Everybody's got a Helene Tucker, a symbol of everything you want. I loved her for her goodness, her cleanliness, her popularity. She'd walk down my street, and my brothers and sisters would yell, "Here comes Helene. . . ."

We have unhinged Dick Gregory's sentences to introduce you to the idea of making connections in your own sentences. English offers you a variety of ways to make connections among your ideas so that you aren't limited to delivering your ideas one by one in short, disconnected sentences. Instead, your writing can show how your ideas relate to one another. What you write can reveal the fascinating processes of association that go on, sometimes at breakneck speed, as you think.

But when you speak and when you write, you often depend on different ways to join your ideas. Observe the connectors you use in speech by listening as you and your friends talk. For example, do you hear many *and*'s? Notice how the telephone operator, whose talk about her job is recorded below, links her ideas:

> Say you've got a guy on the line calling from Vietnam, his line is busy *and* you can't interrupt. God knows when he'll be able to get on his line again. You know he's lonesome *and* he wants to talk to somebody, *and* there you are *and* you can't talk to him. There's one person who feels badly *and* you can't do anything. When I first started, I asked the operator *and* she says, "No, he can always call another time."
>
> One man said, "I'm lonesome, will you talk to me?" I said, "Gee I'm sorry, I just can't." *But* you can't. I'm a communications person *but* I can't communicate.
>
> I've worked here for two years *and* how many girls' first names do I know? Just their last name is on their headset. You might see them every day *and* you won't know their names. At Ma Bell they speak of teamwork, *but* you don't even know the names of the people who are on your team.

It's kind of awkward if you meet someone from the company *and* you say "Hi there, Jones," *or* whatever. It's very embarrassing. You sit in the cafeteria *and* you talk to people *and* you don't even know their names. I've gone to a lot of people I've been talking to for a week *and* I've said, "Tell me your name."

—Studs Terkel, *Working*

This is speech, with its abundance of *and*'s. One sentence adds to another, creating a flow of ideas that threatens to keep on going. When you speak, you typically connect your ideas through two important thinking processes —*coordination* and *subordination*. You use these processes unconsciously in your speech. The telephone operator, in describing her job, didn't say to herself, "Now I'm going to use a subordinator in this sentence," or "This sentence calls for a coordinator." In writing, however, where you can't let your sentences drift on and on, where they can't hang next to each other like wash on a line, you need to become conscious of your thinking processes so that you can choose the connectors that get closest to the heart of your meaning.

Let's stop for a moment to define these two words. *Coordination* means putting together ideas or things or people that are of equal rank or importance— police officers, cabinet members, professors, and so forth. *Subordination,* on the contrary, means putting ideas or things or people into positions where one is of greater rank or importance than another. Police officers are subordinate to the chief of police; cabinet members are subordinate to the President; professors are subordinate to the dean.

In speech, we often coordinate ideas by putting one idea right next to another, joining them with *and*. We treat these ideas equally. We also use subordinators, words such as *because, although,* and *if,* to make more deliberate connections. In writing, we are often more conscious of connectors than we are in speaking, and we become more aware of our options for making connections. As you think about making connections among sentences, keep in mind that these processes work similarly in the whole essay.

Consider an essay that you are writing. In your essay, some ideas are more important than others. Your controlling idea is the *primary* one, the one big idea that controls the whole essay. The rest of your ideas are subordinate—or of secondary importance. These subordinate ideas are usually the supporting examples and details that you use to explain your controlling idea.

If you are writing an essay about childhood injustice, you may develop four paragraphs about how young children are treated unjustly. The plan for your essay may look like this:

Controlling idea: Young children are often unjustly treated by adults.
Paragraph 1:   Parents don't listen to children.
Paragraph 2:   Parents don't take children seriously.
Paragraph 3:   Parents make decisions without consulting children.
Paragraph 4:   Parents spank children.

These four examples are *subordinate* to the controlling idea. But, individually, the four examples are *coordinate* to one another because they depend equally on the main idea, that young children are often unjustly treated by adults. They are all of equal rank, and together they all stand in a subordinate way to the controlling idea.

On a smaller scale, a sentence can be similar to an essay because in addition to the one big idea expressed by the subject, verb, and completer, a sentence can add other subordinate ideas. Such a sentence is said to have a main idea and *subordinate* ideas.

But there are also some sentences that differ from essays because they can add another big idea of *equal rank* to the first. Such a sentence expands by a different process. It is said to have two (or more) *coordinate* ideas. As we examine these two processes in the sentence, keep in mind that subordination and coordination make use of different connectors—for example:

Coordinators	Subordinators	
and	as	if
but	before	unless
or	because	since
nor	although	when
for	until	who
yet	so that	which
so	that	while

11.b COORDINATION

Coordination is the linking of similar sentence parts or similar whole sentences of equal rank. Since there are few coordinators in the English language, it's a good idea to memorize them so that you'll become aware of how and when you're making connections in your own sentences. These are the coordinators:

and	for
but	yet
or	so
nor	

Coordinating words and phrases in a series

Petunias, begonias, ferns, cucumbers, and your family will enjoy outdoor living more under a Howmet Domed Skylight patio cover.

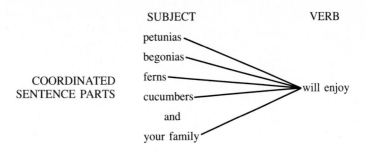

Coordination offers you shortcuts and helps you eliminate unnecessary words. Notice the coordination of sentence parts in this Subaru advertisement: one subject is connected to three verbs:

THE SUBARU 4 WHEEL DRIVE WAGON CLIMBS LIKE A GOAT, WORKS LIKE A HORSE AND EATS LIKE A BIRD.

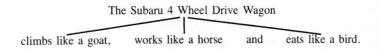

TIPS FOR WRITERS—PARALLELISM

Note the power of this sentence by Antoine de Saint-Exupéry:

A pilot's business is *with the wind, with the stars, with night, with sand, with the sea.*

Saint-Exupéry uses a writing technique called *parallelism*. He selects coordinated sentence parts that are not only close in grammatical structure and meaning, but also close in length. He does this with the repetition of *with*, which slows you down and makes you consider each of the coordinated parts:

with the wind
with the stars
with night
with sand
with the sea

Study the passage; begin to recognize your options for repeating a word like *with*, choosing commas or coordinators, adding or deleting a final *and*. Saint-Exupéry omits the final *and* to guarantee identical emphasis in all. (See Chapter 12, pp. 289-291, for a discussion of parallelism.)

When you coordinate ideas, you make connections among ideas that you think are related as equals. The same subject repeated in several sentences may not advance your writing and often becomes tedious to read:

I loved her.
I loved her for her goodness.
I loved her for her cleanliness.
I loved her for her popularity.

See how Dick Gregory's swift act of coordination brings these ideas together in the same sentence:

I loved her for her goodness, her cleanliness, her popularity.

Exercise 1 **1.** Write a sentence connecting these verbs to one subject:
   a. work, scrimp, worry
   b. investigate, interview, protest

2. Write a sentence connecting these words as subjects to one verb:
   a. the academic senate, the student government, all the deans of the divisions, and the entire faculty
   b. the football team, soccer team, and basketball team

3. Write a sentence in which you connect several subjects to several verbs.

4. Imitate Saint-Exupéry's sentence in the box on page 245 by connecting similar phrases that begin with the word *with*.

5. Write a brief passage in which a series of verbs builds the action, as in the paragraph that follows.

She raced into the house, lay her racket on the kitchen table, opened the refrigerator with one hand, reached for an orange with the other, and flipped on the television to catch herself on the six o'clock news.

6. Write a brief passage in which you build the action through a series of *-ing* phrases, as was done in this selection from the skiing ad that appears on page 284:

You're flying, soaring, feeling your spine tingle, seeing the trees rush by in a blur, laughing inside at the incredible feeling of freedom and beauty and speed . . .

Combining whole sentences by coordination Combine whole sentences into one coordinated sentence when you want to give the sentences equal emphasis. Remember, a sentence is a group of words that contains at least one subject–verb unit. A clause that can stand as a sentence is called an *independent,* or *main, clause.*

1. Join independent clauses with a comma plus a coordinator:

Drivers shout, dogs bark, and the race is on!

He hit a home run, and the crowd went wild.

_____ , and _____ .
_____ , but _____ .
_____ , or _____ .
_____ , nor _____ .
_____ , for _____ .
_____ , yet _____ .
_____ , so _____ .

2. Join independent clauses with a semicolon and omit the coordinator when you want to show a *close* connection between clauses.

_____ ; _____ .

He hit a home run; the crowd went wild.

When you combine whole sentences, you tell your reader that these sentences belong together. The period separates one sentence from another, but the comma and coordinator allow your reader to see how the ideas in the sentences are connected. If you string several sentences together, you give *all* of them equal emphasis:

He hit a home run, and the crowd went wild, and I was at the refreshment stand buying popcorn, and I missed the excitement.

The reader of this sentence might conclude that the batter's hitting the home run, the crowd's cheering, and your buying popcorn and missing the excitement are on the same level in your mind, that they are all of the same importance to you. Don't string your sentences together with *and*'s unless you want to emphasize all of them equally.

You also need to consider *why* you combine sentences. There must be some relation between their ideas. In the following sentence, it would be difficult for your reader to understand why the two clauses are connected:

> I like chocolate-covered raisins, but Albert was reading a book.

What do these two activities have to do with each other? Your reader could make more sense out of the following connections:

> I like chocolate-covered raisins, but Albert prefers coconut patties.
> I tried to speak to Albert, but he was reading a book.

Similarly, when you use semicolons to join sentences, you must be sure that the sentences are *closely* connected. If you use too many semicolons, your reader will have difficulty seeing the relationship among your ideas:

> He hit a home run; the crowd went wild; I was at the refreshment stand buying popcorn; I missed the excitement.

Use the semicolon only when you want to make a brisk, forceful connection between two sentences. The semicolon doesn't slow your reader down, as the period does. Rather, it acts like a weak period, signaling to your reader that two sentences are so closely connected that they should be read together:

> He hit a home run; the crowd went wild.
> The bomb exploded; the bridge collapsed.
> He fell from the ladder; his pants split open.

In each of these sentences, the semicolon indicates the close connection that exists between the two combined sentences.

As a writer, remember that you have options in punctuating sentences. A period stops your reader. A semicolon invites your reader to see a close connection between two sentences. A comma and a coordinator show your reader that you are combining sentences containing related ideas. To make your sentences varied and interesting, use all three options in your writing:

> _____ . _____ .
> _____ ; _____ .
> _____ , and _____ .

Study the effective use of coordination in the following passage:

> I was not a dull or energyless child, or neglected by my parents. Our house was full of books and paints, and sometimes I did choose to draw or ride my bike. But the picture of my childhood that comes to mind is one of a dimly lit room in a small New Hampshire town and a girl listening, leaden-eyed, to some talk-show rendition of "I Left My Heart in San Francisco." It is a picture of myself at age 8, wise to the ways of "Vegas," the timing of stand-up comics, the marriages of Zsa Zsa Gabor, the advertising slogans of Bufferin and Fab.
>
> —Joyce Maynard,
> "I Remember"

WATCH OUT FOR COMMAS WITH COORDINATION

1. Use commas between words, phrases, or short clauses in a series. A series consists of more than two items.

   SERIES
   Words: Michael loves *apples, peaches, pears,* and *plums.*
                                    a, b, c, and *d*
   Phrases: A pilot's business is *with the wind, with the stars, with night, with sand, with the sea.*
                                    a, b, c, d, e
   Short clauses: *Drivers shout, dogs bark,* and *the race is on!*
                                    a, b, and *c*

2. Do not use a comma every time you use an *and.*

3. Do not use a comma between two words or two phrases joined by a coordinator.

NO:	YES:
a, and *b*	*a* and *b*
Michael loves apples, and pears.	Michael loves *apples* and *pears.*
Janet signed, and delivered the letter.	Janet *signed* and *delivered* the letter.
A pilot's business is with the wind, and with the stars.	A pilot's business is *with the wind* and *with the stars.*

4. Use a comma and a coordinator between independent clauses.

   _____ , and _____ .
   His wife was very distressed, and his children were very frightened.
   He couldn't promise to change his behavior, but he promised to try.
   He hit a home run, and the crowd went wild.
   (See Chapter 12, pp. 275–277, for a discussion of run-on sentences.)

5. Do not use a comma when the *and* combines the elements of a compound subject or a compound verb.

   The crowd *went* wild *and rushed* onto the field.

6. Do not begin a new line with a comma.

NO:	YES:
Michael loves apples, peaches , pears, and plums.	Michael loves apples, peaches, pears, and plums.
His wife was very distressed , and his children were very frightened.	His wife was very distressed, and his children were very frightened.

Exercise 2 Expand each of the following sentences by adding a second independent clause.

Example: In winter, we depend on artificial light, but . . .

In winter, we depend on artificial light, but in summer, we invade the parks and beaches, soaking up sun.

1. Darkness causes depression, but . . .
2. Darkness causes depression, and . . .
3. Darkness causes depression, yet . . .
4. Sunlight increases alertness, but . . .
5. Sunlight increases alertness, or . . .
6. Depressed people often move away from northern latitudes, for . . .
7. Depressed people often move away from northern latitudes, and . . .
8. Indoor lighting can affect people's moods, but . . .
9. Indoor lighting can affect people's moods, and . . .
10. In winter, working people see little daylight, and . . .
11. Many Americans have lowered the temperatures in their homes, and . . .
12. Many Americans have lowered the temperatures in their homes, but . . .

TIPS FOR WRITERS—USING *AND* AND *BUT* EFFECTIVELY

1. Coordinators link sentences, even when they're separated by a period. At one point or another, you may have been told that you can't begin a sentence with *but* or *and*. But that isn't so. Begin a sentence with *and* to emphasize the addition of an idea; begin with *but* to emphasize contrariness.

You can make mistakes with any typewriter.
But this one can also erase them.

2. A writer may use *and* between combined sentences for special effects. Combining sentences with *and* creates the effect of conditions coexisting or events happening all at the same time. Consider these coordinated sentences by Ernest Hemingway:

> It was morning and had been morning for some time and he heard the plane. It showed very tiny and then made a wide circle and the boys ran out and lit the fires, using kerosene, and piled on grass so there were two big smudges at each end of the level place and the morning breeze blew them toward the camp and the plane circled twice more, low this time, and then glided down and leveled off and landed smoothly and, coming walking toward him, was old Compton in slacks, a tweed jacket and a brown felt hat.

Use a series of *and*'s deliberately when you want to create these special effects.

11.c SUBORDINATION

Subordination is the making of one sentence part grammatically dependent on another sentence part. A subordinated part never stands alone as a sentence.

You only ride like a Pacer if you're wide like a Pacer.

Knicks Are Ousted in Playoffs As Rockets Post 118-86 Victory

If You Like Fresh Herring, Your Ship Is In

All of the above sentences contain subordinated parts:

if you're wide like a Pacer
as Rockets post 118–86 victory
if you like fresh herring

Words such as *if, because,* and *when* are subordinators when they precede the subject in a subject–verb unit. A subordinator introduces an incomplete expression that is connected in a sentence to an independent clause:

If you smoke menthol cigarettes, you're still subjecting yourself to some of the dangers of tars and nicotine.

No matter how brief or incomplete an expression seems, if it has a subject–verb unit and no subordinator, it qualifies as a sentence:

The sun sets.
It's there.

A sentence takes on meaning from sentences before and after it:

Are you looking for the shoehorn? I just saw it. *It's there.* It's next to the clothes brush.

Out of context, *It's there* has little meaning. But it is a sentence, nonetheless, because it has a subject–verb unit and no subordinator introducing it. But if a subordinator introduces the clause, the clause is *dependent:*

WHEN THE SUN SETS

The subordinator always signals that the dependent clause connects in a specific way to another clause that has no subordinator. In such a sentence, the clause *without* the subordinator is an independent clause:

DEPENDENT   INDEPENDENT
CLAUSE   CLAUSE

When the sun sets, *I feel romantic.*

DEPENDENT   INDEPENDENT
CLAUSE   CLAUSE

Because it's there, *I feel better.*

DEPENDENT CLAUSE   INDEPENDENT CLAUSE

If you want to reach me   you'll find me reading

COSMOPOLITAN®

INDEPENDENT   DEPENDENT
CLAUSE   CLAUSE

It's tough to cut a whisker   when it's down.

INDEPENDENT   DEPENDENT
CLAUSE   CLAUSE

Hobbies Boom   As The Economy Fizzles

The power of subordinators Subordinators, as we've seen, introduce subject–verb units that depend grammatically on independent clauses. Subordinators, as well as coordinators, are the glue of the language because they allow the binding together of ideas so that a sentence shows how one idea relates to another. Some subordinators reflect time connections:

| after | when | since | as soon as | by the time |
| before | until | while | once | whenever |

Notice the changes in meaning that we create when we use different subordinators to relate these two simple sentences:

We ate strawberries and cream. We went home.
We ate strawberries and cream *after* we went home.
We ate strawberries and cream *before* we went home.
We ate strawberries and cream *while* we went home.
We ate strawberries and cream *whenever* we went home.
We ate strawberries and cream *once* we went home.

Other subordinators may show reasons, results, conditions, or, even, place:

unless	because
if	although
so that	where
in case	wherever

Notice the subtle changes in meaning effected by these subordinators:

Subordinator	**Purpose**
Although I was in a wretched mood last night, I went to the movies.	Writer implies that he doesn't enjoy going to the movies if he's in a wretched mood, but he went anyway.
Whenever I'm in a wretched mood, I go to the movies.	Writer asserts that the movies are where she goes when she's in a wretched mood. This mood may be a recurring event.
If I'm in a wretched mood, I go to the movies.	Writer asserts that he goes to the movies on the condition that he's in a wretched mood. The suggestion is that the mood is not habitual.
Because I was in a wretched mood, I went to the movies.	This writer makes her going to the movies a result of her wretched mood.

As a writer, think about your connectors and search for the particular connector that expresses precisely the way one idea relates to another in your sentences. Remember that a *dependent clause* is a grammatical term that means the clause cannot stand as a sentence. For this reason, you might say that a dependent clause is *grammatically* less important than an independent, or main, clause. But this does not necessarily mean the dependent clause is less important in *meaning* than the main clause.

In addition to subordinators that set up relationships of time, reasons, or conditions, the following five words also work as subordinators. They differ from other subordinators, however, in that they stay close to the word or words they describe:

who   whose

whom   that

which

He is a man *who* needs a vacation.
Millie visited Pauline, *whose* house is near the bay.
This is the house *that* I want to rent for the summer.
Allan gave Janet an emerald, *which* is as big as a half dollar.

THE MAGAZINE THAT WINS 52 PRIMARIES A YEAR IS THE ONE THAT REACHES THE PEOPLE WHO LISTEN.

The magazine *that wins 52 primaries a year* is the one *that reaches the people who listen*.

Basic sentence:

        s   v   c

The magazine is the one.

Exercise 3 Expand each of the following sentences by adding an independent clause.

Example: Although our football team has lost every game this season, . . .

Although our football team has lost every game this season, two of our professors have won the Nobel Prize in economics.

1. Whenever cheap mortgage rates are announced by the banks, . . .

2. . . . until the baby is born.

3. As we depend more and more on computers, . . .

4. Since smoking gives some people enjoyment, . . .

5. Although smoking gives some people enjoyment, . . .

6. If I inherited a million dollars, . . .

7. . . . because that is more certain.

8. . . . while she was still at the height of her career.

9. After he lost weight, . . .

10. When Japanese children are very young, . . .

11. Whenever I want to be alone, . . .

12. . . . even though he had a degree in economics.

13. Since she earned her black belt in karate, . . .

14. . . . until he apologizes for both incidents.

15. If I were king of the forest, . . .

Exercise 4 Rewrite the following paragraph so that you use subordinators to show the connections among the ideas.

> Example: John, who is nineteen years old, was speeding down the expressway on his motorcycle.

> John was speeding down the expressway. John is nineteen years old. He was riding his motorcycle. It was a beautiful day. The sun was shining. Suddenly a Dodge Dart was upon him. The car rammed into John. His motorcycle was wrecked. An ambulance arrived within minutes. The driver of the Dodge was concerned. John was rushed to Los Angeles Medical Center. The nurses and doctors were very kind to him. They were competent. He needed forty-three stitches in his left leg. He didn't complain. He didn't press charges.

Exercise 5 Choose an appropriate subordinator to complete each of the following sentences.

Subordinators:	although	whenever	unless
	because	until	in order that
	since	wherever	after
	when	if	
	where	as	

1. _____ it is warm, I am heading for the beach.
2. _____ I love my brother, I argue with him.
3. _____ I wrote a magnificent anthropology paper last night, I did not sleep very well.
4. _____ I wrote a magnificant anthropology paper last night, I stayed up for the midnight movie.
5. _____ we eat at the Servery, we'll run into Professor O'Connor.
6. "Goodnight, Mrs. Calabash, _____ you are."
7. I couldn't read the bottom line _____ I had my glasses on.
8. _____ you like Etruscan art, I'll give you this bronze horse.
9. _____ people seem to like me, I have few friends.
10. _____ people seem to like me, I plan to become a social worker.
11. I don't leave my house _____ my astrologer says my aspects are poor.
12. _____ you like nuts, you won't like this cake.

Exercise 6 Read the following sentences, and determine the relationship between the parts. Fill each empty slot with a semicolon, a coordinator (*and, but, or, nor, for*), or a subordinator (*although, because, since, when, as, after, before, until, wherever, unless, while, in order that*) to show the clearest connection of ideas. Add whatever punctuation is necessary.

1. Research papers demand a lot of time _____ they must be accurate.

2. Many children are still in need of homes _____ foster parents receive a stipend for providing them with a family.

3. Foster parents receive a stipend _____ many children need homes.

4. From his father, William received a sound Methodist upbringing _____ his mother was more concerned with the welfare of the neighborhood poor.

5. From his father, William received a sound Methodist upbringing _____ from his mother he inherited an almost congenital concern for the problems of the poor.

6. They took our seats _____ we left.

7. We left _____ they took our seats.

8. Does your mother still have your baby curls _____ does your father tell you tales of your first howling haircut?

9. Does your mother still have your baby curls _____ your father saves nothing but his memories?

10. _____ Jennifer took an accounting course, she couldn't manage her finances.

11. _____ she took an accounting course, she became a financial whiz.

12. She took an accounting course _____ she could manage her finances.

Exercise 7   Read the following groups of sentences. Rewrite each group in as many sentences as you need to show relationships among ideas. Use coordinators when you want to give equal emphasis to ideas, and use subordinators when you want to show one idea as being more important than another.

> Example: The school budget lost. Programs will be seriously cut again this year. Teachers will lose their jobs. The children will suffer in overcrowded classrooms. More families will move out of the area.
>
> Because the school budget lost, programs will be seriously cut again this year. More teachers will lose their jobs, more children will suffer in overcrowded classrooms, and more families will move out of the area.

1. Fashions change. Hemlines go up. Hairstyles go down. People stay the same.

2. Americans take to their wheels in the summer. The country is a stream of motorcycles. The country is a stream of cars. The country is a stream of campers. The country streams with smoke.

3. The cities are dirty. The suburbs are bursting. Americans are returning to the country.

4. Sally overdresses. Her friends turn up for parties in jeans and T-shirts. Sally glitters in long, sequined dresses.

5. Lindbergh flew across the Atlantic. Seventy-eight others tried before him. He flew the first solo flight. His plane was the *Spirit of St. Louis*. The flight took 33 hours 29½ minutes. He took off on May 20, 1927. He flew from Roosevelt Field. He landed at Le Bourget Airfield in Paris.

6. Babe Ruth hit 714 home runs in his lifetime. Ruth was the champ. He was the champ until 1974. In 1974, Hank Aaron became the champ. Aaron broke Ruth's record. He hit 755 home runs during his career.

7. The best-selling album of all time is *Thriller*. It has sold more than 30 million copies. It has sold copies around the world. It was released in 1982. It was recorded by Michael Jackson.

8. "The Honeymooners" is a situation comedy. It was made in the 1950s. It stars Jackie Gleason. It stars Art Carney. Gleason plays a bus driver named Ralph Cramden. Carney plays a sewer worker named Ed Norton.

9. The computer is an amazing invention. It has many uses. It can perform difficult tasks in an instant. Many people are intimidated by computers.

10. "Hurt Hawks" is a poem. It was written by Robinson Jeffers. It is about a wounded hawk. The speaker feels sorry for the hawk. He tries to heal the hawk. He cannot heal the hawk. He shoots the hawk to put it out of its misery.

11. Elizabeth I was queen of England. She was queen from 1558 to 1603. Her reign was crucial in English history. England defeated the Spanish Armada in 1588. Shakespeare's first plays appeared in the 1590s. Elizabeth died in 1603. She was succeeded by James I.

12. Martin Luther King, Jr., led the March on Washington. The march took place in August 1963. He delivered his most famous speech "I Have a Dream" at the foot of the Lincoln Memorial. He delivered his speech before 200,000 people.

Exercise 8 Read the passages below from an essay, "I Remember," by Joyce Maynard. Fill each empty slot with one of these connectors:

so	and	which
but	if	when

We got our TV set in 1959 _____ I was 5. _____ I can barely remember life without television. I have spent 20,000 hours of my life in front of the set. Not all of my contemporaries watched so much, _____ many did, _____ what's more, we watched the same commercials, were exposed to the same end-of-show lessons. So there is, among this generation of television children, a shared history, a tremendous fund of common experience. These massive doses of TV have not affected all of us in an identical way, _____ it would be risky to draw broad conclusions.

_____ if a sociologist were—rashly—to try to uncover some single most important influence of this generation, _____ has produced Patty Hearst and Alice Cooper and the Jesus movement and the peace movement; _____ he were searching for the roots of 1960's psychedelia _____ 1970's apathy, he would do well to look first at television.

who   and   when   but
because   that   or

My strongest memories are of one series and one character. Not the best, _____ _____ the one that formed me more than any other, _____ haunts me still, _____ left its mark on a goodsized part of a generation: *Leave It to Beaver*. I watched that show every day after school (fresh from my own failures) _____ studied it, like homework _____ the Cleaver family was so steady and normal—_____ my own was not _____ the boys had so many friends; played basketball, drank sodas, *fit in*. Watching that series _____ other family situation comedies was almost like taking a course in how to be an American.

I loved my father _____ I longed secretly for a "Dad" like Ward Cleaver, _____ puttered in a work shed, building bookcases _____ oiling hinges, one _____ spent his Saturday afternoons playing golf _____ mowing the lawn _____ dipping his finger into cake batter whipped by a mother in a frilly apron _____ spent her time going to PTA meetings _____ playing bridge with "the girls." . . .

Occasionally I go to college campuses. Some student in the audience always mentions Beaver Cleaver, _____ _____ the name is spoken, a satisfied murmur can be heard in the crowd.

Exercise 9 Rewrite the following choppy sentences by coordinating and/or subordinating those ideas you want to connect.

I shot out of bed. I grabbed my clothes. I dashed out of the house. At the corner store, I swiped the *Times*. I hijacked a cab. The cab driver looked surprised. I left him standing on the street corner.

At my desk in the office, I opened the morning mail. I glared at a bill from Con Edison. I had already paid it. I screamed at their adjustments manager on the phone. He apologized. He offered to send me $100 for my inconvenience. At 10:00, I drank a cup of coffee. I savored three glazed doughnuts. My superior called at 10:30. We met leisurely for two hours. I finally told him that I disagreed with his office tactics. He was an ineffective administrator. He let the department go to pot. He didn't know how to handle his underlings. He thanked me for my honesty. He gave me a $50-a-week raise.

At 12:30, my day was over. I gathered my swim clothes. I headed for the beach. I lay on the sand the whole afternoon. The day was perfect. The sky was clear. The ocean breeze was cool. Suddenly, I felt a strong tug at my foot. I opened my eyes. My wife was pulling my leg in my own bed. "You're late," she said. "Get up and get going."

Exercise 10 Using the following facts as the beginning of a news story, finish the story by writing several paragraphs. Connect the ideas by means of varying techniques. Add coordinators and subordinators.

> It was 11:00 P.M. It was raining. A woman was walking down Jefferson Street. She was alone. She always walked that street at night. Suddenly out of the darkness appeared a . . .

Exercise 11 Combine each of the following sets of sentences into one sentence. Change any words you wish.

> Example: Jimmy Durante had a raspy voice.
> Jimmy Durante had an oversized nose.
> Jimmy Durante had a talent for bringing down the house.
>
> Jimmy Durante had a raspy voice, an oversized nose, and a talent for bringing down the house.

1. The Beatles played concerts all over the world.
   The Beatles sold more than 100 million record albums.
   The Beatles made several successful movies.
   The Beatles are still popular today.

2. Fleetwood Mac has sold more than 20 million records.
   Fleetwood Mac has played before 2 million people.
   Fleetwood Mac has played in ten countries.

3. The Styx are hard workers.
   The Styx are unfailing enthusiasts.
   The Styx are box-office stars.

4. Foreigner played benefits for blood drives.
   Foreigner did a special show to help rebuild a San Diego museum.
   Foreigner played at Madison Square Garden for four New York charities.

5. Willie Nelson is a country singer.
   Willie Nelson is from Texas.
   Willie Nelson appears on television.
   Willie Nelson was on the "Late Night with David Letterman" show.

6. Michael Jackson has been a star for over ten years.
   Michael Jackson is widely recognized all over the world.
   Michael Jackson wears dark glasses and one white glove.

7. Rock musicians are getting old.
   Some appear on stage in three-piece suits.
   They sing their old songs.

Exercise 12 Rewrite the following passages of sabotaged student writing, drawing the ideas closer by using coordinators and subordinators.

> 1. We all have certain values. Some values are born to us. Other values are acquired through everyday living. Values are like everything else. Values are subject to change. Changes occur for different reasons. Changes occur be-

cause a person's life style changes. Changes occur because the environment changes. Changes occur because attitudes change. Some people have values that do not change. Their values are reaffirmed as they go through life.

2. My friend Smith is a cheap person. He is one of the cheapest people I know. He makes a lot of money. He makes $200 a week. He banks his money. He never has money on him. We go out. He's broke. He refuses to chip in any money. He spends hours shopping. He buys the cheapest clothes. He buys the flimsiest clothes. He tries to save a few bucks everywhere. He is a moocher. He is always the first in line for a handout. He is always ready to be a guest.

3. What are the latest figures on murder rates in cars? The subway might offer a break from gasoline prices. It might offer a break from maintenance expenses. It might offer no insurance. But what about safety? Cars are safe. They are familiar. They are comfortable. Subways are not. They are crowded. They are foul smelling. They are hostile. A policeman is stationed on every train. Cars must stay.

11.d MODIFIERS AS SUBORDINATORS

One way to make connections more explicit is to use *modifiers*—words, phrases, and subordinate clauses that make your ideas more specific, more precise, that bring some ideas into the foreground and push others into the background. That man you see over there is not just any man; he's the tall green-eyed man in purple tennis shoes holding an umbrella. You bring him to life for your reader by using modifiers.

Exercise 13 Rewrite the sentence ''Albert is a worried man'' in as many ways as you can. Although you may change the language, add words, and rearrange words, try to keep to the original meaning as closely as you can. Do not continue reading until you have completed this exercise.

Forms of modifiers What we hope you have discovered is that although you can express approximately the same idea in a variety of ways, you can choose one way over another for reasons of emphasis, compactness, and sentence rhythm. The context of your writing—the surrounding sentences and your intended meaning—determines your choice.

Compare your sentences about Albert with these, and notice that each of the modifiers is a single word, a phrase, or a clause:

Sentence	Kind of Modifier	Example
Albert is a *worried* man.	single word (verbal)	worried
Albert is a man *with worries*.	phrase	with worries

Sentence	Kind of Modifier	Example
Albert is a man *who has worries.*	clause	who has worries
Albert is a man *who is worried.*	clause	who is worried
Albert is a man *worried about his job and his family.*	verbal in a phrase	worried about his job and his family
Something worries Albert.	none	(subject–verb–object)

Single-word modifiers

ADVERBS The most frequent modifiers of verbs are single words called *adverbs*.

DRIVE CHEERFULLY.

Adverbs also modify adjectives:

AND NOW FOR SOMETHING COMPLETELY DIFFERENT

They modify other adverbs:

exceptionally quickly

And they modify whole sentences:

Finally, it's your turn for some applause.

Adverbs have few identifying marks, although many can be formed by adding -*ly* to the adjective:

slow	+	ly	=	slowly
premature	+	ly	=	prematurely

Add -*ly* even when the adjective ends in -*l:*

final	+	ly	=	finally
cheerful	+	ly	=	cheerfully

A few short, common adverbs can be used with or without the *-ly* ending:

Short adverb	Long adverb (with *-ly*)	Both correct
slow	slowly	Drive slow.
		Drive slowly.
tight	tightly	Pull the shoelace tight.
		Pull the shoelace tightly.

Other such short adverb forms are *bright, cheap, close, deep, loose, smooth, quick, wrong.*

ADJECTIVES   That *beautiful* woman is my *maternal* grandmother.

FAST FOODS   good reason

Free Spirit   a clean ashtray

The word that makes the meaning of a noun more specific is an *adjective:*

beautiful	clean
maternal	good
fast	free

Adjectives are descriptive words that usually go before the noun they modify. You can spot certain adjectives by their endings:

-ous	marvelous	-ic	realistic
-al	maternal	-ive	descriptive
-ful	beautiful		

MODIFIERS AS COMPLETERS   In sentences using linking verbs (such as *seem, look, appear, feel,* and forms of *be*), use an *adjective* to show that the completer refers to the subject:

Linking verb: Joanne's dentist is thoughtful.
(*Thoughtful* describes Joanne's dentist.)

Linking verb: Joanne's dentist seems concerned.
(*Concerned* describes Joanne's dentist.)

Linking verb: Joanne's dentist looks eager.
(*Eager* describes Joanne's dentist.)

However, with nonlinking verbs, use an *adverb* to describe the action of the verb:

Joanne's dentist looked *eagerly* into the microscope.

In this sentence, what follows the word *looked* does not describe Joanne's dentist. It describes the action of looking into the microscope, and it takes the form of an adverb.

WATCH OUT FOR *GOOD* AND *WELL*, *BAD* AND *BADLY*, *REAL* AND *SURE*

1. *Good* and *well* can both be used as adjectives.
Linking pattern:

    YES (adjective): She feels *good* when she raises money.
                        (happy, satisfied)
    YES (adjective): She feels *well* when she gets enough sleep.
                        (in good health)

Only *well* can be used as an adverb.
Not a linking pattern:

    NO (adjective): She works *good* with children.
    YES (adverb):   She works *well* with children.

2. Don't use "feel badly about . . ." when you mean "feel bad about . . ."
Linking pattern:

    NO (adverb):   I feel *badly* about Albert and his wife.

                     (To *feel badly* means to do a bad job of perceiving
                     something through your sense of touch—for example,
                     We felt our way badly through the tunnel.)

    YES (adjective): I feel *bad* about Albert and his wife.

3. *Real, sure, good,* and *bad* are inappropriate when used as adverbs in written English:

    NO: We *sure* waited a long time.
    YES: We *surely* waited a long time.
    NO: The chicken with artichokes was *real* special.
    YES: The chicken with artichokes was *really* special.
    NO: Albert doesn't cook *bad.*
    YES: Albert doesn't cook *badly.*
    NO: Albert's wife plays tennis as *good* as Arthur Ashe does.
    YES: Albert's wife plays tennis as *well* as Arthur Ashe does.

Exercise 14 Rewrite the following sentences so that the italicized words can be used in adjective form. Add, delete, or revise when necessary. Use a dictionary if you need help.

    Example: You are a *marvel.*
               You are *marvelous.*

1. Pierre shows a lot of *aggression* when grades are due.
2. His parents take a lot of *pride* in him.
3. Pierre's new car is the color of a blue *metal*.
4. It has many gadgets that are a *wonder*.
5. Pierre has become an *authority* on rear-window defoggers.
6. He showed a lot of *skill* when he installed his tape deck.
7. Pierre has a lot of *curiosity* about the mileage he will get.
8. His ideas about motorcycle motors reveal his *concern* with progress.
9. Once he acquired his own car, his popularity shot upward like a *meteor*.
10. When he talks about his car, he is full of *emotion*.

Exercise 15 Some of the following sentences require an adjective, and some require an adverb. Fill in each blank with the correct form of the word.

1. Mounds chocolate bars are _____ delicious. (indescribable/indescribably)
2. I arrived here yesterday after a _____ rough voyage. (real/really)
3. The sky turned _____ in the afternoon. (dark/darkly)
4. He is unhappy with the _____ buzzing sound in the new piano. (occasional/occasionally)
5. Please speak _____ to Uncle Hugo. (loud/loudly)
6. Walk _____ along the edge of the wall. (steady/steadily)
7. I see everything in a _____ light. (different/differently)
8. Allison went to the Motor Vehicles Bureau _____ after the collision. (immediate/immediately)
9. Ravel _____ felt _____ about reports of a misunderstanding with Toscanini. (sure/surely) (bad/badly)
10. Young Liszt had a _____ precocious imagination. (terrible/terribly)

VERBALS Many modifiers of nouns are formed from verbs.

    1. *-ing* verbals.

Use *-ing* modifiers to add immediacy to your writing. The *-ing* form gives the sense that an action is continuing to happen:

    embarrassing moment
    sagging sofa

a competing airline
flying insects
enchanting places

2. *-ed* verbals.

Use *-ed* modifiers when the action expressed by the modifier has already been completed:

Regular forms
skimmed milk
boiled water

Irregular forms
hidden treasure
ground pepper
cut flowers

for a <u>limited</u> time only

<u>selected theatres</u>

<u>Limited</u> Edition

Broken Pipes

<u>proven</u>   performance

<u>FROZEN</u> YOGURT

<u>Marked</u> improvement

<u>NEEDED</u> IMPROVEMENTS

3. Use verbals to combine sentences:

The sofa sags. It needs repair.	The sagging sofa needs repair.
Hair is unwanted. Hair is removed by electric tweezers.	Unwanted hair is removed by electric tweezers.

Exercise 16 Combine each of the following pairs of sentences into one sentence that contains an *-ing* modifier or an *-ed* modifier.

> Example: I listened to the traffic light for an hour.
> The traffic light was clicking.
> Combined: I listened to the *clicking* traffic light for an hour.

1. I invited the professor to the Spanish Club.
The professor was visiting.

2. Stars warn us of catastrophe.
Stars shoot.

3. The sentence was unnecessary.
The sentence was deleted.

4. Stephanie tiptoed up the steps.
The steps had carpeting on them.

5. The snow will freeze tonight.
The snow is melting.

6. The page had a lot of errors.
The page was typewritten.

7. The dollar bill split in half.
The dollar bill was taped.

8. The students are highly vocal.
The students attend the law school.

9. Amy was the only contestant who wrote the words and the music.
Amy was among the contestants who were winners.

10. The house shone in the sun.
The house was freshly painted.

Exercise 17 Expand the following sentences by adding adjectives, verbals, or other single-word modifiers to the subjects or completers.

Example: The pilot and the stewardess were married.
The *balding TWA* pilot and the *unforgettable Lufthansa* stewardess were married.

1. The elevator crashed.
2. The accountant caught a fish.
3. Citizens bought guns.
4. Monet painted snowstorms.
5. The sign said, "For Sale."
6. Indians hunted game.
7. The child looked for her parents.
8. The oboist played Bach.
9. Soybeans are food.

Modifiers in phrases Whenever a single-word modifier doesn't express your idea with sufficient detail, extend it into a phrase. Then move the longer modifier into position *after* the noun.

Single-word modifiers go before the noun:

Modifiers in phrases go after the noun:

WORLD FAMOUS
HOT DOGS
STEAMED IN BEER

steamed hot dogs

hot dogs *steamed in beer*

machines matched
to your job

matched machines   machines *matched to your job*

CAKES DECORATED
The Way You Want Them

decorated cakes   cakes *decorated the way you want them*

PREPOSITIONAL Prepositional phrases can specify the meanings of nouns and verbs. (See page
PHRASES AS 235 for a list of prepositions.) Their use in English is everywhere—even in this
MODIFIERS sentence. Like other phrases, they always follow the nouns they modify:

Nouns	**Prepositional phrases**
Jazz	at noon
Letters	to the Editor
Winner	of six Academy Awards

CHAMPION   ## OF THE WORLD

Solutions   **to Last Week's Puzzles**

Plane   ## *With 243 Orphans*

Exercise 18 In each of the following sentences, expand the italicized one-word modifier into a phrase and move the phrase to its clearest position in the sentence. Use commas where appropriate.

> Example: No one comforted the *defeated* American skater.
> No one comforted the American skater, *defeated by a seventeen-year-old Japanese girl who had never competed before.*

1. The president appealed to a *divided* Senate.
2. The *redesigned* gardens became an outdoor salon for all the dogs of Bedford Heights.
3. The Napoleonic Wars were a *prolonged* struggle that profoundly taxed Western Europe.
4. Social workers provide juvenile addicts with *needed* strength.

5. "Stompin' at the Savoy" is one of the greatest *recorded* swing numbers of all time.

6. The *stolen* Datsun turned up by the docks.

7. Science has impact because of its *validated* conclusions.

8. The *scattered* homes are for small groups of Georgia youngsters who cannot live in their own homes.

9. Beethoven was suspicious of the *corrected* manuscripts.

10. We tutored three classes of *underprepared* pilots.

Exercise 19 Restrict the meaning of each italicized noun in the following sentences by adding a modifier.

>   Example: *Life* is difficult.
>   Life *during a blizzard in Buffalo* is difficult.

1. *Income* has risen sharply in the past five years.

2. I fear the dangers of *television*.

3. If you study changes in *education*, you will realize how far behind we lag.

4. Robert's *cooking* makes him the envy of all the *men*.

5. *Smoking* can be hazardous to your health.

6. Your *promise* should be appreciated by the neighbors.

7. The *law* requires that the body be disposed of overboard.

8. *Honesty* follows a special code.

9. Her *success* led to a *contract*.

10. *Humiliation* is particularly distressing.

Exercise 20 Rewrite the following sentences so that the prepositional phrases are transformed into one-word adverbs.

>   Example: The middleweight champion drank the Coke *with eagerness*.
>   The middleweight champion drank the Coke *eagerly*.

1. *With vigor* the masseur worked on the boxer.

2. Sid the Kid smiled *in gratitude*.

3. He could now move his left shoulder *without pain*.

4. The reporters remained outside so the Kid could recover *in privacy*.

5. Sometimes they hollered his name *in familiarity*.

6. Sid the Kid answered *without cheer*.

7. *In desperation* he thought that he had fought his last fight.

8. *In misery* he remembered dreams of glory.

9. The masseur patted the Kid *with confidence*.

10. Sid the Kid rose from the table and *with great caution* said farewell to the reporters.

Clauses as modifiers Most of the modifiers we have looked at in this chapter are in reality reductions of longer modifiers:

Reduced modifier	Longer modifier
I like *black* hair.	I like hair *that is black*.
We were passengers on the train during the wreckage *at rush hour*.	We were passengers on the train during the wreckage *that occurred at rush hour*.
Lenore's hair, *black as her heart*, glittered under the moon.	Lenore's hair, *which was as black as her heart*, glittered under the moon.
The *tallest* people in the world are the Watusi.	The people *who are the tallest* in the world are the Watusi.

Streamlining these long clauses produces concise, lean writing. But good writers know that it is neither always possible nor always desirable to reduce all clauses to single words or phrases. Sometimes, to be clear, a clause must be written out fully.

Like all clauses, a clause that modifies a noun has its own subject and verb. It goes after the noun and begins with the word *who, which, that, why, when,* or *where* (and sometimes *whose* or *whom*):

He gave a reason *why his child was late.*
That is the corner *where we met.*

Use *who* for a person:

THE MAN WHO CAME TO DINNER

Use *which* or *that* for something other than a person:

A CAR THAT'S OVERLY LUXURIOUS COULD LITERALLY BORE YOU TO DEATH.

Sometimes modifying clauses appear without *that, who,* or *which.* The object of the clause (*that* or *whom*) is omitted.

We loved the drinking songs the chorus sang.
We loved the drinking songs *that* the chorus sang.
The mugger resembled a man we had seen on Broadway.
The mugger resembled a man *whom* we had seen on Broadway.

Appositives An appositive is a word, phrase, or clause that comes immediately after a noun or noun substitute in order to explain or restate it.

Obituaries make frequent use of the appositive:

Giancana, *Gangster*, *Slain;*

Groucho Marx, Film Comedian and Host of 'You Bet Your Life,' Dies

---

TIPS FOR WRITERS—SAVE WORDS BY COMBINING RELATED SENTENCES

You can move an extra idea into a sentence by adding an appositive to explain or identify a noun:

> My favorite sport is fun all year.
> My favorite sport is swimming.
> My favorite sport,   , is fun all year.
> My favorite sport, swimming, is fun all year.
> Her wish finally came true.
> Her wish was to visit Hawaii.
> Her wish   finally came true.
> Her wish to visit Hawaii finally came true.

WATCH OUT FOR COMMAS WITH APPOSITIVES

1. When an appositive is essential to the meaning of a sentence, do not use commas.

> Her wish *to visit Hawaii* finally came true.
> The racer's fear *that he would die violently* made him give up racing.

2. When an appositive is not essential to the meaning of a sentence, use commas.

> Otto Soglow, *the cartoonist,* died.
> My favorite sport, *swimming,* is fun all year.

Exercise 21 Combine each of the following pairs of sentences into one sentence containing an appositive. Underline the appositive. The sentences are adapted from an article called "Sharks" by Elizabeth Keiffer.

> Example: Sharks are set apart from all other fishes except their relatives.
> Their relatives are the skates and rays.
> Appositive: Sharks are set apart from all other fishes except their relatives, *the skates and rays.*

1. John G. Casey got hooked on sharks some twelve years ago.
John G. Casey is the forty-one-year-old director of the research project.
2. Wesley Pratt is interested in the reproductive cycle of the blue shark.
Wesley Pratt is a thirty-year-old underwater photographer.
3. Charles Stillwell is making a study of what sharks eat.
Charles Stillwell is an experienced diver.
4. Americans never lack for protein.
Americans are notoriously finicky fish eaters.
5. Some species of shark provide juicy white steaks.
These species are notably the mako and the sandbar.

Comparing adjectives and adverbs Adjectives and adverbs can be compared to show greater or lesser degree. They change form according to the following system:

	Positive (Describe *one*)	**Comparative** (Compare *two* and only *two*)	**Superlative** (Compare *three* or *more*)
Most adjectives of one syllable	strong	stronger (than . . .) less strong	the strongest (in the . . .) the least strong
Longer adjectives	suspicious	more suspicious less suspicious	the most suspicious the least suspicious
Adverbs	suspiciously	more suspiciously less suspiciously	the most suspiciously the least suspiciously
Irregular words	good, well bad, badly	better worse	the best the worst

WATCH OUT FOR COMPARISONS

UNNECESSARY REPETITIONS

1. Do not put *more* or *most* before adjectives of one syllable to which you have already added *-er* or *-est*.

NO: *more* better   YES: better
      most greenest   greenest

2. Do not add *-er* or *-est* to adjectives of one syllable when they are preceded by *less* or *least*.

NO: *less* smarter   YES: less smart
      least strongest   least strong

WORSE AND WORST

1. When you compare *two* of anything, use *worse*.
The smog in L.A. is *worse* than it is in Pittsburgh.

2. When you compare *three or more* of anything, use *the worst*.
That city has *the worst* smog in the world.
              (More than two cities in the world have smog.)

3. Do not use *the worse* when you mean *the worst*.

NO: That is *the worse* city in the world.
YES: That is *the worst* city in the world.

chapter

12 Problems with Connections

Students in one of our classes agreed that the grammatical problem that troubled them most in their writing was the *run-on*. Yet when asked to define or give examples of run-ons, they weren't certain what run-ons actually are. Most of them thought run-ons were lengthy sentences, and so they avoided writing long sentences. In this chapter, we will confront run-ons and the other most common sentence problems: fragments, dangling modifiers, and faulty parallelism. To do so, we ask you to keep in mind the following grammatical terms, which are explained more fully in Chapters 10 and 11.

1. *Clause* A clause is a group of words that contains at least one subject–verb unit:

The sun sets.

A clause may be *independent* and therefore a sentence:

The sun sets.

Or it may be *dependent* and not a sentence.

when the sun sets

2. *Phrase* A phrase is a group of words that does not contain a subject–verb unit:

to the store   covered with grease
falling in love   attached to the dog
flying down the street

CHECK LIST FOR A SENTENCE

1. A sentence must contain at least one subject–verb unit:

Willie Stargell whacked a home run.

To find the subject–verb unit, locate the verb by changing the sentence time:

Willie Stargell whacked a home run.
Tomorrow Willie Stargell will whack a home run.

Verbs: *whacked, will whack*
Then connect the subject to the verb:

Who whacked?
   s   v
Stargell whacked

2. The verb cannot be an *-ing* word alone.

Not a sentence: the crowd screaming

Supply a time word in a form of the verb *to be:*

The crowd *was* screaming.

Or connect the phrase containing the *-ing* word to a sentence with a time word:

Screaming, the crowd *watched* the home run.

3. A subject–verb unit introduced by a subordinator (*when, because, if, since,* and the like; pp. 251–254) is not a sentence, but a dependent clause:

DEPENDENT CLAUSE
Not a sentence: when Stargell whacked a home run

Connect the *when* clause to its related independent clause:

INDEPENDENT CLAUSE
When Stargell whacked a home run, the crowd went wild.

4. *Who, which, whose,* or *whom* cannot be the subject of a sentence unless the sentence is a question. A subject–verb unit introduced by these words is not a sentence, but a dependent clause:

which made the crowd go wild

Connect the *who* or *which* clause to its related independent clause:

INDEPENDENT CLAUSE
Willie Stargell whacked a home run, which made the crowd go wild.

12.a RUN-ONS

Although the term seems to suggest it, *run-ons* are not simply sentences that run on and on. There is no limit to the length of a sentence: James Joyce wrote one that traveled on for twenty-eight pages! Seeing where one sentence ends and the next begins is the key to understanding run-ons. Separating one sentence from the next by punctuating allows you to avoid run-ons and to write long, powerful sentences, if you choose. Notice how John McPhee, in his book *A Sense of Where You Are,* builds this sentence about the basketball player Bill Bradley:

> With remarkable speed for six feet five, he can steal the ball and break into the clear with it on his own; as a dribbler, he can control the ball better with his left hand than most can with their right; he can go down court in the middle of a fast break and fire passes to the left and right, closing in on the basket, the timing of his passes too quick for the spectator's eye.

McPhee constructs a larger sentence by coordinating three shorter sentences with semicolons. Another writer might have written these sentences separated by periods:

> With remarkable speed for six feet five, he can steal the ball and break into the clear with it on his own. As a dribbler, he can control the ball better with his left hand than most can with their right. He can go down court in the middle of a fast break and fire passes to the left and right, closing in on the basket, the timing of his passes too quick for the spectator's eye.

But an inexperienced writer carried along by the speed of the basketball game might have produced a single, run-on sentence, with neither semicolons nor periods.

What is a run-on? *Run-on* is a grammatical term for those sentences in which one independent clause is jammed up against another without the accepted mark of punctuation. There are two types of run-on sentences:

1. When two or more sentences are not separated by *any* mark of punctuation, the error is known as a *fused sentence:*

   > Ohio State crushed Michigan on Sunday Art Schlichter triumphed with three touchdowns.
   > Schlichter topped his record of last year he has already scored eighteen touchdowns.

2. When two or more sentences are separated by *only* a comma, the error is known as a *comma splice,* or a *comma fault:*

   > Penn State beat West Virginia 31–6, this is their fourth consecutive victory.

WATCH OUT FOR *AND'S*

Writers sometimes believe that coordinated sentence elements result in run-ons. The following sentence is not a run-on:

> The black cat rolled over on her side and stretched out one paw and then the other and curled her head into her belly and yawned.

Notice that all the verbs relate to the one subject, *cat*. Note, too, that no mark of punctuation is needed within the sentence.

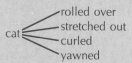

Nor is this sentence a run-on:

> I arose quietly this morning, but the family slept, and not even the early newscast disturbed my feelings of solitude and authority.

Three sentences here are coordinated by commas plus coordinators:

> I arose . . . , *but* the family slept, *and* not even the early newscast disturbed . . .

Eliminating run-ons   First, use the sentence check list on page 274 to determine if you have two sentences. Then, use the options for separating, coordinating, or subordinating sentences.

1. Use a period.

————————. ————————.
The shower went off. Luckily I had another quarter.

2. Use a semicolon.

————————; ————————.
The shower went off; luckily I had another quarter.

3. Use a comma plus a coordinator.

———————— , but ————————
The shower went off, but luckily I had another quarter.

4. Subordinate one clause to another.

When ———————— , ———————— .
———————— when ———————— .
When the shower went off, I luckily had another quarter.
I luckily had another quarter when the shower went off.

Run-ons	Correcting run-ons
We were glad to leave Kansas it was too hot.	We were glad to leave Kansas. It was too hot.
	We were glad to leave Kansas, for it was too hot.
	We were glad to leave Kansas because it was too hot.
	We were glad to leave Kansas; it was too hot.
The shower went off, luckily I had another quarter.	The shower went off. Luckily I had another quarter.
	The shower went off, but luckily I had another quarter.
	When the shower went off, I luckily had another quarter.

He gives the orders, but I'm the boss.

Exercise 1 Read the following passage, which was adapted from Muhammad Ali's book, *The Greatest*. Place punctuation marks wherever they are needed to end or coordinate sentences. Capitalize words as necessary.

> I hit Ernie Terrell until I knew he was out on his feet his eyes were puffed his nose bleeding lips cut and swollen but the referee egged us on I knew that unless I held back he would be injured for life it's against the rules but I began to pull my punches the crowd wanted more blood and those against me hoped he could come up with a miraculous counterattack but he was beaten and there was no point in pounding him any more he had a family sisters brothers and parents just like I had why should I maul him just to satisfy some of the screamers.

Exercise 2 The following selections are taken from a student's journal. If the student were to move beyond this spontaneous writing, he would have to think about sentence structure. Edit his writing—separating, coordinating, or subordinating sentences wherever you choose. Decide which sentences you want to emphasize equally and which you want to subordinate. Omit any word you think unnecessary.

> As I start this journal I hope I am spelling journal right, later on I will look it up in a dictionary. I've been starting this journal for about two or three days. But I finally started it. This notebook has a surplus of twenty pages, I doubt that I will use those extra pages.

> As my alarm clock rang I jumped out of bed and gathered my bags it was five o'clock in the morning and it was still dark, within twenty minutes we were ready to go I quickly said good-bye to my parents who slipped me a twenty dollar bill for food as I kissed my mother good-bye and walked out the door I

knew I would enjoy myself and not miss home Chris met me in his driveway the car was packed the tank was full and we were on our way.

After dinner Chris and I went down to the cliffs of the canyon I saw the most intense sunset I've ever seen, there was a rainbow of colors upon the red and gray shale and the sun sank into the canyon.

The next day we got up at eight o'clock and started walking into the canyon we brought a knapsack with a camera and three cans of beer, as we walked down in the early morning heat we met people coming up who had slept in the canyon over night and were now walking up. All the people we met told us to turn around and go back up, but not us, we said if you could walk down we could so we kept walking down.

On the way down we met a guy and his wife walking up about ten in the morning. The walk down was about eight miles we made time walking down. We reached the bottom about eleven so it took about three hours to walk, there was a river at the bottom everybody was swimming it was so hot I had to go in the water, it was so hot that when my shirt fell in the water it dried in about two minutes.

We swam around for about a half hour and decided to start back up. We started walking at noon by three we were only a third of the way up and had nothing we had drunk all the beer and had nothing to eat, the heat was starting to get to us.

Walking straight up the canyon walls was very tiresome, we had to stop and rest every five minutes. While walking up we met the same people we had met in the morning, we couldn't believe we passed them going up. Each step we took was harder and harder. We reached the top at eight-thirty, when we got to the top we were glad to be at the top, the first thing we did was to run to the snack bar and ate three hamburgers and five beers each.

It took us three hours to walk down and eight and a half to walk up.

12.b FRAGMENTS

Fragments are bits and pieces of sentences that are punctuated as whole sentences. Most often fragments are phrases and dependent clauses that are disconnected from their independent clauses.

Phrases as fragments Remember: A phrase is a group of words without a subject–verb unit. The phrase must be connected to an independent clause, or it will be considered a fragment. The following italicized phrases are fragments:

The man was racing. *Down the street. Tripping on a curb. Running down the street.* He was late. He was a tall man. *Thin, pale, and tired.* He ripped his pants. *And scraped his knee.* He felt like a fool. *A child.* He had been on his way to the co-op. *To buy a dictionary. For his English class.* Now he wasn't sure what he would do. *Go home to change his trousers? Or go to class?* He liked to be punctual. *And meticulous.* He hated to miss class. They were discussing run-ons. *And fragments.*

To eliminate fragments, connect them to nearby independent clauses, or rewrite the fragments as parts of new sentences:

The man was racing down the street. He tripped on a curb. He shouldn't have been running down the street, but he was late. He was a tall man, thin, pale, and tired. He ripped his pants and scraped his knee. He felt like a fool, a child. He had been on his way to the co-op to buy a dictionary for his English class. Now he wasn't sure what he would do. Should he go home to change his trousers? Should he go to class? He liked to be punctual and meticulous. He hated to miss class because they were discussing run-ons and fragments.

Dependent clauses as fragments

Remember: Dependent clauses cannot stand alone as sentences; they must be connected to independent clauses. Memorize the lists of subordinators on pages 252–254 so that each time you use a subordinator, you can anticipate at least *two* parts to the whole sentence, a dependent part and an independent part. Make certain that you are not cutting the whole sentence short, as in the following examples:

The man was racing down the street. *Because he was late.*
He ripped his pants. *Which weren't even paid for.*

To eliminate fragments, connect the dependent clause to the independent clause:

The man was racing down the street because he was late.
He ripped his pants, which weren't even paid for.

A good way to catch run-ons and fragments is to read your writing aloud. Your voice automatically drops at the end of a sentence. Notice the subordinators and coordinators. Catch the places where you have written a period. Does the period cut off a piece of a sentence? When your voice drops, make certain that a sentence either ends or is connected properly to the following or preceding sentence.

If you're having difficulty with run-ons and fragments, there's usually a pattern to your problems. You may be disconnecting *when* or *although* clauses, using *-ing* words as verbs, or running your sentences together with commas and no *and* or *but*. Don't shelve your papers. Look over past papers and study those that are returned to you. If you rewrite nothing else, rewrite sentence errors correctly. Your sentence problems will begin to diminish if you learn to see where your sentences begin and end.

Eliminating fragments

First, use the sentence check list on page 274 to determine if you have a subject–verb unit in every sentence. Then follow these guides:

1. Watch out for *-ing* words.

The *-ing* word cannot stand alone as the verb in a sentence. Make certain that it is fastened to a time word:

Fragment: Henry *eating* a slice of pizza.
Sentence: Henry was eating a slice of pizza.

Do not cut off an *-ing* phrase from its sentence:

Fragment: Henry walked down the street. *Eating a slice of pizza.*
Sentence: Henry walked down the street, eating a slice of pizza.
Fragment: *Being an only child.* Charles was pitifully spoiled.
Sentence: Being an only child, Charles was pitifully spoiled.

2. Watch out for prepositional phrases.

Do not punctuate a prepositional phrase as a sentence:

Fragment: Jean visited her parents in Jamaica. *In the summertime.*
Sentence: Jean visited her parents in Jamaica in the summertime.
Fragment: Ross ate frozen yogurt. *During his break between classes.*
Sentence: Ross ate frozen yogurt during his break between classes.

3. Watch out for *-ed* words.

Do not cut off an *-ed* phrase from its sentence:

Fragment: Bessie baked one of her apple pies. *Considered by her family to be the best in town.*
Sentence: Bessie baked one of her apple pies, considered by her family to be the best in town.

4. Watch out for subordinators:

because	when	after	unless	whose
although	if	until	who	which
since	before	while	whom	that

Do not disconnect a dependent clause from the sentence it belongs to:

Fragment: I admire Henry. *Because he is sensitive.*
Sentence: I admire Henry because he is sensitive.
Fragment: He disliked the man. *Who wanted to marry his daughter.*
Sentence: He disliked the man who wanted to marry his daughter.
Fragment: *Although Lauren never studied the piano.* She plays like a professional.
Sentence: Although Lauren never studied the piano, she plays like a professional.

5. Watch out for these words:

especially	except	such as
instead of	including	for example

Do not disconnect a phrase or clause that begins with one of these words:

Fragment: Jennifer enjoys mint juleps. *Especially when she's relaxing on a hot summer day.*
Sentence: Jennifer enjoys mint juleps, especially when she's relaxing on a hot summer day.
Fragment: Sam bought his stereo at Gimbels. *Instead of at Macy's.*
Sentence: Sam bought his stereo at Gimbels instead of at Macy's.
Fragment: I enjoy traveling to new places. *Such as the Grand Canyon, Yellowstone, and Niagara Falls.*
Sentence: I enjoy traveling to new places, such as the Grand Canyon, Yellowstone, and Niagara Falls.
Fragment: We bought tickets for the whole family. *Except for Edna and Elmer.*
Sentence: We bought tickets for the whole family, except for Edna and Elmer.

Exercise 3   You write fragments when you punctuate phrases and dependent clauses as sentences. Turn the following fragments into sentences.

1. Who was using this towel.
2. Falling off a wild bronco.
3. To love all humankind and to search for the truth.
4. Before she was graduated from college.
5. Drinking a cup of black coffee.
6. The tears streaming down his face.
7. While whistling a tune.
8. Bitten by a mosquito.
9. All through the night.
10. The motorcyclist in her crash helmet.
11. Through the dark alley.
12. Whenever I'm sleepy during my math class.
13. Although I know him well.
14. Strawberries and cream for dessert.
15. Who ripped open the envelope.
16. After payday.
17. If ever I should leave you.
18. Singing in the rain.
19. Raindrops falling on my head.
20. That was on the table.

Exercise 4   Read the following advertisements, which have been adapted for this exercise. Each advertisement contains phrases and dependent clauses that are punctuated as whole sentences. Find all the fragments and either connect them to the sentences they belong to or turn them into new sentences.

1. Advertisement for volunteers

You can help people. In fact, there's a crying need for you. Your talents. Your training. Your concerns. They can make you priceless. As a volunteer in your community.

Take a moment to think of all that can be done. For children. The environment. Sick people. Old people. People who just need someone behind them.

Then take another moment to think of what you can do. Perhaps by applying your job skills. Or personal interests to voluntary action.

There are probably several organizations hard at work in your town. Doing things you'd be proud to be part of. We'll put you in touch with them. Join one. Or, if you see the need, start a new one.

If you can spare even a few hours a week, call your local Voluntary Action Center. It'll do you good. To see how much good you can do.

2. Advertisement for Coca-Cola

If you'll stop and think for just a moment. You'll find more of the good things in this country. Than anywhere else in the world. Think of this land. From the surf at Big Sur. To a Florida sunrise. And all the places in between. The Grand Canyon. The wheat fields of Kansas. Autumn in New Hampshire. You could go on forever. But America is more than a place for good times. It's Saturday night. It's a trip down a dirt road in a beat-up old jalopy. It's your team winning. It's a late-night movie. You could enjoy a thousand times. And, yes, when you're thirsty. It's the taste of ice-cold Coca-Cola. It's the real thing. In fact, all of the good things in this country are real. They're all around you. Plainly visible. We point to many of them in our advertising. But you can discover many, many more. Without ever seeing a single commercial for Coke. So have a bottle of Coke . . . and start looking up.

Exercise 5 Read the following unpunctuated advertisement, which has been adapted for this exercise. Find the sentences, and then separate them, coordinate them, or subordinate them. Capitalize words wherever necessary.

If the Harley-Davidson man seems overly protective there's a good reason for it apparently there's something irresistible about the Harley-Davidson you see it's one of the most ripped-off motorcycles in the country so you can't blame the Harley-Davidson man for taking an extra precaution or two what is it about this machine that attracts such a dedicated following among enthusiasts of every type the answer of course is that the Harley-Davidson occupies a special place among people who know and love motorcycles after seven decades it is still recognized as the ultimate achievement in quality-built precision motorcycles a product of this heritage is the electric start XL-1000 . . . (also available with kick start) the styling and overall beauty of this 1000cc 4-stroke v-twin are timeless the unique ride the spectacular torque and the deep distinctive sound of the powerful engine are pure Harley-Davidson the other members of this family of superbikes include the FX and FXE-1200 and the FLH-1200 all are available for a limited time only with our special "Liberty Edition" option—metal-flaked black finish with full color tank insignia . . . you'll find these superbikes along with our . . . line of classically styled 125cc 175cc and 250cc street and on-off road motorcycles at your AMF Harley-Davidson dealer stop by it's a great way to learn about these superb machines and best of all it's legal.

Exercise 6 Read the following unpunctuated paragraph to determine which sentences belong together. Think about your options for coordinating and subordinating sentences, and then rewrite the paragraph by changing some sentences into dependent clauses or phrases and by coordinating other sentences. You may need to add subordinators and coordinators. Punctuate appropriately.

> I think back on my years growing up in a small Pennsylvania town I feel nostalgic now for those times people cared for each other there they accepted the poor the old and the disabled women in the community baked bread on the weekends they shared it with the poor and sick they invited them to Sunday dinner people grew old they lived with their children no one went to an old-age home or a nursing home many of my friends had their grandparents or an aunt living with them the disabled and even the retarded lived with their families too they were part of the community I can never return to that small town I would like to recapture some of the qualities of small-town life.

Exercise 7 Edit the following piece of student writing for fragments and run-ons.

> Once you've gotten into a habit good or bad it's hard, or close to impossible to break. I have a very good example. I started smoking in junior high school. I'm not sure but I think it was in ninth grade. My brother and I were in the same grade so we bought one pack of cigarettes a week. He smoked ten and I smoked ten. It was always cheaper that way. Because if I were to go out and buy a pack a week. By the end of the week the cigarettes that were left would all be stale.
>
> Four years and a pack a day of cigarettes later. I decided that I had to quit. I wrote away to the American Cancer Society. For tips on quitting. After looking at that book filled with pictures of cancerous lungs. Anybody would stop smoking. I stopped smoking the same day I got the booklet in the mail. I followed their tips of drinking water whenever I had the urge to have a cigarette. Also drinking a lot of V-8 juice. For about a week or so it worked until one Friday night I went out to a bar with my friends. Of course everybody knows that if you're going to drink you're going to smoke.
>
> Well you guessed it on Saturday morning I was smoking again. So much for will power. Another year had passed and I was still smoking but by now I really hated it I kept switching from one brand of cigarettes to another. Finally I figured if I must smoke I might as well smoke a cigarette which wasn't as harmful but after a while I got sick of sucking air. So one day I woke up and said that's it and went cold turkey. It's hard to believe but that was a year and a half ago and I feel I will never smoke again.

You
start
slowly,
gliding easily,
breaking the silence
with the soft "shhh . . . . shhh . . . ." of your skis
as they sweep up sprays of powder
at each turn.
Here and there,
the sun catches snow crystals,
turning them to diamond dust.
Ever so gently
the slope steepens,
drawing you into widening, flowing, sensuous arcs.
And suddenly, magically,
you've found the mountain's rhythm!
You're flying, soaring, feeling your spine tingle, seeing the trees
rush by in a blur, laughing inside at the incredible feeling
of freedom and beauty and speed,
laughing because you just can't believe anything in this world
could be
so
much
fun.

This is skiing—and in less time than you think, you can be doing it!
The Killington Accelerated Ski Method makes it as easy as learning
to fox trot. And this is Killington—52 fantastic trails on 4 separate
peaks, a full 6-month season, heaps of beautiful snow, hosts of lodges,
restaurants, nightspots, a super ski school . . . and the inspiration for
the sentiments expressed above. For more details on the Killington
ski scene, send for our 36-page booklet. Write: Killington Ski Resort,
147A Killington Road, Killington, Vermont 05751.

WATCH OUT FOR FRAGMENTS

REMEMBER: The -ing word is a major cause of sentence fragments.

NO:	YES:
Here and there, the sun catches snow crystals. *Turning them to diamond dust.*	Here and there, the sun catches snow crystals, turning them to diamond dust.
You're flying, soaring, feeling your spine tingle. *Seeing the trees rush by in a blur. Laughing inside at the incredible feeling of freedom. Laughing because you just can't believe anything in this world could be so much fun.*	You're flying, soaring, feeling your spine tingle, seeing the trees rush by in a blur, laughing inside at the incredible feeling of freedom . . . , laughing because you just can't believe anything in this world could be so much fun.

Exercise 8   Locate the verbs in the following sentences, which are from the ski-resort advertisement on page 284.

1. You start slowly, gliding easily, breaking the silence with the soft "shhh . . . shhh . . . " of your skis. . . .
2. Ever so gently the slope steepens, drawing you into widening, flowing, sensuous arcs.
3. You're flying, soaring, feeling your spine tingle, seeing the trees rush by in a blur, laughing inside at the incredible feeling of freedom and beauty and speed, laughing because you just can't believe anything in this world could be so much fun.
4. This is skiing.
5. The Killington Accelerated Ski Method makes it as easy as learning to fox trot.

Exercise 9   The -ing word cannot be used alone as a verb; it must be used with a form of the verb *be* (*is, are, were, was, will be,* and the like), or it must be turned into a one-word form of the verb that is itself a time word (*raced, jumped*). Rewrite each fragment so that it is a sentence.

> Example: Dominick racing for the streetcar.
> Dominick was racing for the streetcar.
> or
> Dominick raced for the streetcar.

1. Jack and Janet kissing passionately on the bus.
2. The playground swarming with children.
3. The police officer dodging a bullet.
4. The old woman chasing a hat.
5. Vivian crying in her bedroom.
6. Walter tickling her toes.
7. Sara staring at the television set.
8. Lauren cracking her knuckles.
9. Nancy hanging the Picasso print.
10. Janis typing her final draft.

Exercise 10   Which of the following clauses are independent and can stand alone as sentences? Which of the clauses are dependent? Punctuate those that are sentences.

1. whenever I feel bored
2. she proposed to me
3. I hate to write
4. although I am her cousin
5. Charles and I love each other
6. if I were king
7. before the semester began
8. while I was sitting on a bench
9. I intend to finish college
10. after Arlene left for Utah

12.c PROBLEMS WITH MODIFIERS

When you use modifiers—words or groups of words that make other words more specific—remember that each modifier must *clearly* refer to the term it describes. Two problems may result when modifiers do *not* clearly refer to the terms they describe.

Misplaced modifiers A *misplaced modifier* is one that is placed near a term the writer does not intend to describe. Faulty placement clouds meaning, causing confusion and, often, unintended humor.

Misplaced modifier	Confused effect	Correctly placed modifier
Stewed in brandy, Uncle Albert served the peaches.	Uncle Albert, not the peaches, appears to be stewed in brandy.	Uncle Albert served the peaches stewed in brandy.
Lenore's hair glittered under the moon, *black as night*.	The moon, not Lenore's hair, appears to be black as night.	Lenore's hair, black as night, glittered under the moon.
Ill-housed, ill-clad, ill-nourished, I see one-third of a nation.	The speaker, not the nation, appears to be ill-housed, ill-clad, and ill-nourished.	I see one-third of a nation ill-housed, ill-clad, ill-nourished.
		—Franklin D. Roosevelt, Second Inaugural Address (January 20, 1937)

Consider Groucho Marx's famous quip:

One morning I shot an elephant in my pajamas. How he got into my pajamas, I don't know. Then we tried to remove the tusks but they were embedded so firmly that we couldn't budge them. Of course, in Alabama the Tuscaloosa. But that's entirely irrelephant . . .

Squinting modifiers A modifier that falls between two terms may require a reader to guess which term the modifier describes. To take the guesswork out of your reader's decision, move the modifier to a position in which your meaning is unmistakable.

Squinting modifier	Confused effect	Correctly placed modifier
The solutions that the students discovered *immediately* impressed their teacher.	Did the students discover them immediately, or was the teacher immediately impressed?	The solutions that the students *immediately* discovered impressed their teacher.
		or
		The solutions that the students discovered impressed their teacher *immediately*.

The teller said *on Friday* the bank would be closed.	Did the teller say this on Friday, or will the bank be closed on Friday?	The teller said on Friday *that* the bank would be closed. or The teller said *that* on Friday the bank would be closed.

Dangling modifiers   A modifier is said to *dangle* when the term being described does not appear in the sentence. When readers see a modifying phrase, they expect it to describe the noun closest to it. But when the intended noun is omitted, the modifier will appear to lean toward the nearest noun in the sentence, creating uncertainty for the reader and, frequently, unintended humor.

Dangling modifier	Confused effect	Improved
Looking out the window, a horse came down the street.	Was the horse looking out the window?	Looking out the window, I saw a horse come down the street. or As I was looking out the window, a horse came down the street. or I looked out the window and saw a horse come down the street.
At the age of seventeen, a car is a challenge.	Is the car seventeen years old? (It is true, of course, that a seventeen-year-old car *would* be a challenge.)	To a seventeen year old, a car is a challenge. or When you are seventeen, a car is a challenge.
Soft and mushy, Albert baked a banana cake.	Was Albert soft and mushy?	Albert used the soft, mushy bananas in a banana cake. or Since the bananas were soft and mushy, Albert baked a banana cake.
Buried under mulch for the winter, Carla settled down to wait for spring.	Was Carla buried under mulch for the winter?	With next spring's lilies buried under mulch for the winter, Carla settled down to wait for spring.

Exercise 11   Ambiguities can result from awkward placement of modifiers. Revise the following sentences by repositioning the modifier or rewriting the sentence completely. In your own writing, make revisions like these as you edit your first draft.

1. The woman with the baby who was complaining about the perfume called the manager.
2. A man rode a horse in swim trunks.
3. After opening the oven door, the chicken cooked more slowly.
4. Pregnant and en route to the hospital, a traffic cop told Mrs. Rogers to pull over.
5. Taking a bath, the water stopped.
6. Members of the Club Español sold tickets for the car wash in their Cervantes class.
7. Blowing through the trees, we pulled on our sweaters.
8. Strolling through the park, a stone lion suddenly appeared.
9. Being a good dancer, Sally entered her brother Curtis in the dance contest.
10. By rewiring the telephone lines on the main road, service was finally restored.

Exercise 12 Rewrite this tragic headline so that the unfortunate and unintended humor is eliminated.

Girl, 13, Found Slain by Road

Exercise 13 Rewrite the following sentences so that the misplaced or dangling modifier clearly refers to its noun.

> Example: Private art collections often are amassed and kept unavailable to scholars *in virtual secrecy*.
> (Which are in virtual secrecy, the scholars or the private art collections?)
> Improved: Private art collections often are amassed *in virtual secrecy* and kept unavailable to scholars.

1. The handsome display was approved by the curators in a separate gallery.
2. One bronze bracelet was guarded by security men in the main showcase.
3. The guide said the unusual pieces of Greek jewelry reflect the taste of the people who owned them on the tour.
4. One of the tourists, herself a jeweler, offered to make Greek-style earrings for my friends with screws in them.
5. The exhibition was sponsored by a local Greek night club on the third floor of the museum.
6. Craftsmen came to study the ancient designs from all over the state.
7. Working in silver, the craftsmen's imitations were excellent.
8. Sketching a second-century anklet, the facing lions' heads met above the ankle bone.

9. Guards passed among the visitors charged especially with the security of a rare bronze head of Hadrian.
10. Viewing those ancient personal treasures, my own necklace felt like a mark of royal identity.

12.d FAULTY PARALLELISM

When you write sentence elements that have similar impact in similar structures, you use a technique called *parallelism*. By matching a noun with a noun, a verb with a verb, a phrase with a phrase, a clause with a clause, the balance and rhythm of parallel forms will move your reader right along.

1. Subject–verb, subject–verb:

Times Change, Traditions Survive

   times change
   traditions survive

2. Verbal, verbal, verbal:
   Mark Fidrych is a loose-limbed, open-mouthed, wide-eyed youth. . . .
   —William Barry Furlong

   loose-limbed
   open-mouthed
   wide-eyed

3. Verb, verb, verb:

There is still a watch
that looks elegant, performs beautifully,
and costs half what you think.

   looks
   performs
   costs

4. Prepositional phrase, prepositional phrase, prepositional phrase:

BY THE CHIMNEY, UNDER THE TREE,
OR IN THE MAILBOX,

   by the chimney
   under the tree
   in the mailbox

**College credit
for knowledge
gained in high
school, on the job,
in life.**

in high school
on the job
in life

5. Clause, clause:

The more you know about life insurance, the more your agent can help you.

the more you know about life insurance
the more your agent can help you

When you line up sentence parts, use similar grammatical structures:

Walt enjoys reading mysteries
and playing his recorder.

Walt enjoys ⟨ reading mysteries
                and
              playing his recorder.

Walt loves to read mysteries
and to play his recorder.

Walt loves ⟨ to read mysteries
               and
             to play his recorder.

If you mix grammatical parts, the structures will not be parallel.

Nonparallel: Walt ⟨ *folded* his handkerchief
                       and
                     straightening his tie.

Parallel: Walt ⟨ *folded* his handkerchief
                     and
                   straightened his tie.

Nonparallel: Sharon needs a *coffee break* and *resting for fifteen minutes*.
Parallel: Sharon needs a *coffee break* and a *fifteen-minute rest*.
Nonparallel: *In the morning, in the afternoon,* and *when evening comes,* Henry races hi German shepherd around the block.
Parallel: *In the morning, in the afternoon,* and *in the evening,* Henry races his Germa shepherd around the block.

When you coordinate sentence parts, your reader expects to see similar grammatical patterns. Once you've used two "in the . . ." phrases, as in the sentence above, you jolt your reader when you use a different grammatical pattern.

Here are some students' sentences that become more effective when the writers line up the elements in parallel forms. The trick to making the elements parallel is to use vocabulary in the form required by the sentence—adjectives to match other adjectives, adverbs to match other adverbs, and so forth:

NO: Reading is very instructive, entertaining, and it can only benefit the reader.

YES: Reading is an *instructive, entertaining,* and *beneficial pastime.*

Vocabulary: Shift from *it can only benefit the reader* to *beneficial pastime.*

NO: The kids from the South Side were poor, tough, and wanted to get ahead.

YES: The kids from the South Side were *poor, tough,* and *ambitious.*

Vocabulary: Shift from *wanted to get ahead* to *ambitious.*

NO: Michael jokes a lot, he is liked by all the kids, and books are among his favorite activities.

YES: Michael is *witty, popular,* and *well read.*

Vocabulary: Shift from *jokes a lot* to *witty,* from *he is liked by all the kids* to *popular,* and from *books are among his favorite activities* to *well read.*

NO: Laughing loudly and I know she will never stop, my sister watches me do my Yoga.

YES: Laughing *loudly* and *incessantly,* my sister watches me do my Yoga.

Vocabulary: Shift from *I know she will never stop* to *incessantly.*

TIPS FOR WRITERS—REPETITION

REPEAT WORDS, PHRASES, AND CLAUSES TO MOVE IDEAS FORWARD

The repetition of words, phrases, or clauses in a sentence is parallel structure carried to its extreme. The reader, gliding forward on the rhythm and words of the repetitions, looks ahead with pleasure to the next unit. Read this paragraph, by James Agee, about movies:

> Charles Brackett and Billy Wilder have a long and honorable record in bucking tradition, breaking rules, and taking risks, according to their lights, and limits. Nobody thought they could get away with *Double Indemnity,* but they did; nobody thought they could get away with *The Lost Weekend,* but they did; apparently nobody thought they could get away with *Sunset Boulevard,* but they did; and now, one gathers, the industry is proud of them.
>
> —*Agee on Film*

Through three examples, Agee impresses us with the daring of Brackett and Wilder; we move on eagerly to read about each exploit as three times Agee repeats "nobody thought they could get away with [it], but they did." The repetition carries us forward.

Exercise 14 The following sentences contain grammatical structures that are not parallel. Rewrite each sentence so that the coordinated parts are parallel.

1. Jogging is inexpensive, relaxing, and can be done alone.

2. You don't need to buy special clothes to jog; in fact, old shorts that are loose fitting, comfortable T-shirts, and a sweatshirt that is baggy will do fine.

3. A hat to block the sun, wearing a T-shirt, and shorts are all you need in the summer.

4. Layers of cotton clothes, sweatpants that are cotton, hands in cotton mittens, and a hat to keep your head warm are essential in the winter.

5. Clothing that is too heavy or bulky clothing will only slow you down.

6. The jogger needs shoes that give you a lot of support and are sturdy and well built.

7. Running shoes come in all shapes, sizes, and there are different colors, too.

8. Some joggers jog to win; others jog for exercise; and some want their bodies to be beautiful.

9. The jogger running down Murray Avenue wore a kelly green down vest, and his shoes were turquoise Adidas runners, and a bright red hat.

chapter
13 | Verbs

As a writer, you must know how to write sentences, each one containing a subject–verb unit. You must also know how verbs work in sentences, and how different forms of the verb express different times and conditions. The choices may baffle you, especially when you confront alternatives like these:

Jeannette's jeans have shrank.

or

Jeannette's jeans have shrunk.

Sam lived in California for ten years.

or

Sam had lived in California for ten years.

You're not facing general questions of *time* in the above sentences because in each situation you're talking about past time. You know that Jeannette's jeans shrank in the past. You know that Sam lived in California in the past. What may confuse you is the exact *forms* you need to express the past. Is it *have shrank* or *have shrunk? lived* or *had lived?* Is there a difference? To answer these questions, you need to understand exactly how verbs work in sentences.

13.a VERB FORMS

Verbs enable you to show differences in time. You can talk about the present, the past, and the future, and you can show activities that continue over a period of time. The verb in a sentence shows a relationship between the time you are speaking (or writing) and the time you are speaking (or writing) about. The "moment of writing" is always the present moment. From this moment, you can comment on the present:

> I am hungry.
> This coffee tastes bitter.
> The soup is too hot.

Or you can refer to the past:

> I was hungry (in the past).
> The coffee tasted bitter (in the past).
> The soup was too hot (in the past).

Or you can refer to the future:

> I'll be hungry (in the future).
> The coffee will taste bitter (in the future).
> The soup will be too hot (in the future).

All verbs have at least four forms. Every verb has a *base:*

eat	love	ring	have
learn	go	cut	do

A CHART OF VERB FORMS

PRESENT	I ask you ask he, she, it asks	we ask you ask they ask
PAST	I asked you asked he, she, it asked	we asked you asked they asked
FUTURE	I will ask you will ask he, she, it will ask	we will ask you will ask they will ask
PRESENT PERFECT	I have asked you have asked he, she, it has asked	we have asked you have asked they have asked
PAST PERFECT	I had asked you had asked he, she, it had asked	we had asked you had asked they had asked

We *add* to the base or change the spelling of the base to produce the different verb forms:

eat, eats, eating, ate, eaten
learn, learns, learning, learned
love, loves, loving, loved
go, goes, going, went, gone
ring, rings, ringing, rang, rung
cut, cuts, cutting, cut
have, has, having, had
do, does, doing, did, done

All verbs have an *-s* form and an *-ing* form:

Base	-s form	-ing form
eat	eats	eating
learn	learns	learning
love	loves	loving
go	goes	going

All verbs have *past forms*. Some verbs have only *one* past form:

Base	Past	Past participle
learn	learned	(have) learned
love	loved	(have) loved

Other verbs have *two* past forms:

Base	Past	Past participle
eat	ate	(have) eaten
go	went	(have) gone
ring	rang	(have) rung

In the next section, you will see how these forms are used to construct different tenses in the English language.

13.b USING VERBS TO EXPRESS PRESENT TIME

The following examples illustrate ways in which we express present time. Remember: The present tense is made up of the base and the *-s* form of the verb:

> **WATCH OUT FOR TENSE AND TIME**
>
> When you're thinking about verbs, it is important to distinguish between two often confusing terms: *tense* and *time*. *Time* refers to actual time, generally understood as past, present, and future. *Tense* is a grammatical term that refers to verb forms as they relate to time. Grammarians say that there are two tenses among the parts of the verb: the present tense and the past tense.
>
> ### PARTS OF THE VERB
>
> | Base | *-s* form | *-ing* form | Past |
> |------|-----------|-------------|------|
> | learn | learns | learning | learned |
>
> **1.** The *present tense* is made up of the base and the *-s* form of the verb:
>
> ### PRESENT TENSE
>
> I *learn*   we *learn*
> you *learn*   you *learn*
> he, she, it *learns*   they *learn*
>
> **2.** The *past tense* is made up of the *-ed* form of regular verbs or the past form of irregular verbs (pp. 300–301).
>
> ### PAST TENSE
>
> I *learned*   we *learned*
> you *learned*   you *learned*
> he, she, it *learned*   they *learned*
>
> **3.** Other *tenses* are expressed by using the base, the *-ing* form, and the past participle with words called *auxiliaries* (pp. 302–303).

I *feel*   we *feel*
you *feel*   you *feel*
he, she, it *feels*   they *feel*

A second tense in the present is formed with *am, is,* or *are* plus an *-ing* word:

I am feeling   we are feeling
you are feeling   you are feeling
he, she, it is feeling   they are feeling

The present tense is used to:

1. Express an activity taking place at the present moment for verbs of being, feeling, knowing, and sensing:

> I *feel* tired.
> I *am* hungry.
> The sun *feels* warm.
> The coffee *tastes* bitter.

'I Am a Doctor'

2. Express habitual activities—actions that occur repeatedly:

> I *exercise* every morning.
> Sam *eats* yogurt every day.
> Every other Sunday I *go* to the country auction.
> In the summer we *visit* my great-aunt in Montana.

3. Express facts and universal truths—things that are always true:

> Susan *lives* in Minneapolis.
> The earth *revolves* around the sun.
> Water *freezes* at thirty-two degrees Fahrenheit.
> She *earns* $23,000 a year.
> Plants *take in* carbon dioxide.

97% of the World's Water *Is* in Oceans

4. Create an immediate effect. Newspaper headlines are usually written in the present tense to draw attention to events as *news:*

Miss Navratilova Routs Mrs. Lloyd To Capture Grand Slam

Farm prices drop

Yanks Win

5. Express continuing activity in the present, using *am, is,* or *are* plus the *-ing* form:

> I *am typing*.
> Harry *is doing* his hard thinking now.
> Rich and Clyde *are waiting* at the corner store.

Our fame is spreading.

13.c USING VERBS TO EXPRESS FUTURE TIME

The future is used to:

1. Express activity that will take place in the future. The future is often expressed with the word *will* (or *shall*) plus the base. Sometimes the *will* is dropped from the future, and the present form of the verb remains.

Will or *shall* + base (future tense):

> In the morning I will fly to Mexico.
> In the morning I   fly to Mexico.

> I *will fly* to Miami tomorrow.
> I *shall finish* this report by tomorrow.
> They *will eat* dinner tonight at nine o'clock.
> He *will attend* a Michael Jackson concert tonight.

Another form is *be going to* + base:

> I *am going to write* my essay later.
> We *are going to start* a food co-op.

2. Express an activity that will be in progress in the future.

Will (or *shall*) *be* + *-ing* form:

> I *will be swimming* in the Pacific this time next week.
> We *will be studying* for exams next week.

13.d USING VERBS TO EXPRESS PAST TIME

Problems most often arise with past time because in the English language, there are several ways to express the past. As you study the following chart, think about each expression of the past in relationship to *time continuing*.

I had lived in California for ten years when I moved to Toronto.

	I lived in California.	I have just moved to California.	I have lived in California for several years.	
			PAST	PRESENT	FUTURE
A past action ended before another past action began.	The action has been completed	The action has recently been completed.	The action continues from the past into the present.	

Now we can return to the question about Sam and decide which of the two sentences to use:

Sam lived in California for ten years.

or

Sam had lived in California for ten years.

The answer depends on the writer's *intention,* on what the writer wants to say. There are several options depending on that intention.

The past tense—*lived*—expresses an action that is completed. If Sam formerly lived in California, you would emphasize this completed action by saying:

Sam *lived* in California.

To tell how long Sam lived there or when he lived there, simply add an adverbial:

Sam *lived* in California *for eighteen years.*
Sam *lived* in California *in 1960.*

Clearly, Sam doesn't live there any longer.

The past perfect tense—*had lived*—expresses a past action that ended before another action in the past occurred. Suppose, for example, that Sam lived in California until 1970, when he moved to Toronto. Then you would say:

Sam *had lived* in California for eighteen years *when he moved to Toronto.*

Notice that *moved* expresses a time *closer to* the present:

DISTANT PAST   MORE RECENT PAST
Sam had lived in California for eighteen years when he moved to Toronto.

Little Maria had been hungry all her life.

Is Maria still hungry? According to the sentence above, she no longer is. *Had + been* presents a completed action that occurred in a time in the past before another past time. If the sentence read "Maria *has been* hungry all her life," we would know that she is still hungry, that her hunger has not yet been satisfied.

13.e REGULAR AND IRREGULAR VERBS

What about Jeannette's jeans? Have they *shrank* or *shrunk?* The question really is which form of the verb *shrink* do we use with the word *have?* And before we can answer that question, we must consider *regular* and *irregular* verbs. There are thousands of verbs in the language. Most of them are *regular,* which means that they have only one past form, an *-ed* form that is used for the past and for the past participle. *The past participle is the form of the verb that is used with* have, has, *or* had.

Base	Past	Past participle
learn	learned	(have) learned
jump	jumped	(have) jumped
laugh	laughed	(has) laughed

Regular verbs are generally not troublesome when you join them with a form of *have* because you use the same form with or without *have.*

The cow *jumped* over the moon.
Sally *has jumped* over her last hurdle.

About 150 verbs in the English language are *irregular,* which means that they do not form the past by adding *-d* or *-ed* to the base. They usually have two past forms, one that is used *alone* and one that is used with a form of *have.*

Base	Past	Past participle
go	went	(have) gone
sing	sang	(have) sung
shrink	shrank	(have) shrunk

Use the past alone:	Use the past participle with *have, has,* or *had:*
Sam *went* to the greenhouse.	Sam already *has gone* to the greenhouse.
He *sang* to his begonias.	He *has sung* to his begonias, but nothing *has happened* yet.
Jeannette's jeans *shrank.*	I see now that Jeannette's jeans *have shrunk.*

To help you determine which verbs are irregular, we provide two charts at the end of this chapter: Chart I shows the patterns that irregular verbs follow. The past participle of some irregular verbs ends in *-n* or *-en.* Other verbs show no change at all (for example, *cut, hit,* and *hurt*). Chart II lists alphabetically the *principal parts*—the base, the past tense, and the past participle—of the most common irregular verbs in the language. Dictionaries also include these parts. If a verb that you are considering is not included in this chart, consult your dictionary. Since all verbs have an *-s* form and an *-ing* form, these forms are not listed in the charts.

Have Jeannette's jeans *shrunk* or *shrank?* To answer this question, we look at the principal parts of the verb *shrink* (p. 319). We find that the past form is *shrank.* This is the form to use alone (without *have*):

Jeannette's jeans *shrank.*

My slacks didn't stretch. I "shrank" 79 pounds.

The past participle is *shrunk.* This is the word to use with *have:*

Jeannette's jeans *have shrunk.*

Exercise 1 Familiarize yourself with the charts on pages 316–320. Find the principal parts of these verbs:

1. bring	**4.** dive	**7.** feel
2. pay	**5.** sleep	**8.** awake
3. swim	**6.** drive	**9.** dream

Exercise 2 Change the verb in each of the following sentences to a single-word past form. Then use the past participle of each verb with *have, has,* or *had.* Check the charts on pages 316–320 or in your dictionary for the principal parts of verbs.

Example: *I Hear the People*

Single-word past: I *heard* the people.

Past participle with *have, has,* or *had:* I *have heard* the people.

1. Viking Robot Sets Down Safely on Mars

2. Yankees Split With Tigers

3. *Pittsburgh takes club to Raiders*

4. Congress overrides job veto

5. *Cubs Sweep Pair With Pirates, 6-1, 2-1*

6. **U.S. women swim to new Olympic high**

7. Summer Schools Undergo a Large Cut

8. *Phillies Beat Pirates, 13-7; Schmidt Hits 26th Homer*

13.f VERBS AND AUXILIARIES

Verb forms can stand alone as verbs:

Base	-s form	Past
They *learn* quickly.	He *learns* even more quickly.	We *learned* quickly.
We *eat* lunch at McDonald's every day.	He *eats* like an elephant.	They *ate* all the cheeseburgers.

Or they can combine with words called *auxiliaries*. These are some auxiliaries:

can	is	must
could	are	ought to
has	was	shall
have	were	should
had	may	will
be	might	would
been		

Combined with one or more auxiliaries, the verb in a sentence is not a single word, but a verb phrase.

Your worn shocks could be wearing you out.

Be and have The most important and frequently used auxiliaries are formed from two verbs: *be* and *have*. *Be* is the most irregular verb in the English language: it has eight forms:

Base	*-ing* form	Present forms	Past forms	Past participle
be	being	am, is, are	was, were	been

The verb *have* has four forms:

Base	*-ing* form	Present forms	Past form	Past participle
have	having	have, has	had	had

Both of these verbs can be used by themselves:

Irving *has* a health-food store.
He *had* a passion for apricot fruit rolls.
Irv *is* a yogurt addict.
He and his wife, Mabel, *are* vitamin freaks.

Or they can be used as auxiliaries:

Irving *has been* working late hours.
He *is working* too hard.
He *has not taken* a vacation.
Instead, he *has increased* his vitamin dosage.

Exercise 3 Fill each empty slot with a form of the verb that suits the time that has already been established in the sentence. State a reason for your choice.

Example: I forgot that there _____are_____ 5,280 feet in a mile. (be)
Reason: Use the present tense for facts.

1. Sam and Harriet were married fifteen years ago; they _____ for fifteen years. (marry)
2. Janice had just taken an aspirin for her headache when the phone _____ . (ring)
3. If you _____ me before, I wouldn't have made such a mistake. (tell)
4. An "R" movie rating recommends that children _____ accompanied by an adult. (be)
5. By the time he arrives, I _____ for several hours. (go)
6. While the child _____ in the surf, the mother was napping on the beach. (play)
7. From 1973 to the present, I _____ in a white house on Locust Avenue. (live)
8. If I had finished this report last night, I _____ this afternoon. (swim)
9. By the time he was four, he _____ to read. (learn)
10. Before I joined Xerox, I _____ for IBM. (work)

13.g ACTIVE AND PASSIVE VERBS

Rangers are beaten by Philadelphia.

A verb is *active* if the subject of the sentence performs the action expressed by the verb. If the subject of the sentence receives the action of the verb, then the verb is *passive*.

```
               s        v      o
Active:    Philadelphia beats Rangers.
               s              v
Passive:   Rangers are beaten by Philadelphia.
```

Action verbs that have objects can be transformed into passive verbs.

```
               s        v         o
Active:    Carew whacked the ball.
               s          v
Passive:   The ball was whacked by Carew.
```

Often the prepositional phrase is dropped:

The ball was whacked by Carew.
The ball was whacked.
Rangers are beaten by Philadelphia.
Rangers are beaten.

To form the passive, use a form of the verb *be* with the *-ed* form of regular verbs (*loved*), or use the past participle of an irregular verb (*cut*):

I *was loved.*
They *were cut.*

Active present	Passive present	Passive past
They love me.	I *am loved* (by them).	I *was loved.*
They love you.	You *are loved* (by them).	You *were loved.*
They love him, her, it.	He, she, it *is loved* (by them).	He, she, it *was loved.*
They love us.	We *are loved* (by them).	We *were loved.*
They love you.	You *are loved* (by them).	You *were loved.*
They love them.	They *are loved* (by them).	They *were loved.*

13.h THE SUBJUNCTIVE

Another verb form, one that is used rarely, is the *subjunctive*. The subjunctive calls for the verb *be* to appear in exceptional circumstances. It also involves using the base form rather than the *-s* form of the verb for subjects *he, she,* or *it.*

Use the subjunctive in the following situations:

1. To express wishes or unlikely situations

YES: I wish I *were* Robert Redford.
                        or
        If I *were* Robert Redford, I would win friends and influence people.
NO: I wish I *was* Robert Redford.

2. To express requirements

YES: The law requires that a working father *support* his children.
NO: The law requires that a working father *supports* his children.

Form the subjunctive according to the following guidelines:

1. Use *be* for all forms of the present subjunctive of the verb *be*.

The law requires that I *be* in court for jury duty.

2. Use the base form for the present subjunctive of other verbs.

The law requires that a working father *support* his children.

3. Use *were* for all forms of the past subjunctive when the verb would otherwise be *was*.

If I *were* a millionaire, I would be generous with my money.
If you *were* a millionaire . . .
If he, she, it *were* a millionaire . . .

13.i CONTROLLING TIME IN YOUR WRITING

In whatever you write, you make decisions about the ways verbs reflect thoughts and events as they relate to time. Your personal narratives most often take form in past tenses. Like history, biography, and news reporting, your narratives record events that have already happened. Writing a statement of your controlling idea—which is a truth or insight about your subject—often takes form in a present tense.

Notice how the three following excerpts from an article on child prodigies reflect different verb choices. The writer, Marie Winn, begins her essay with a general statement about her subject. She is expressing a general truth, and the controlling time is the present:

Child prodigies *have* a bad name these days. Everybody *has* a favorite prodigy horror story—of this little girl, once the toast of kings and queens, gone mad; that little boy, once hailed as a successor to Mozart, now a short-order cook at a diner in Delaware. Hardly anyone now will admit to being a prodigy, to having been one, even to being the parent of one. Euphemisms *prevail*—gifted child, exceptional child, precocious child. Never prodigy.

When Winn cites instances of specific child prodigies, she uses the past:

> For centuries, child prodigies *abounded* on concert stages. With their miniature violins, their fingers too short for octaves, their legs dangling out of reach of the pedals, in their velvet suits and puff-sleeved dresses, they *toured* from city to city, little musical breadwinners. Haydn *was sent* away from a happy home at the age of 5 to earn a living as a church singer. Mozart as a 7-year-old *was dragged* through the royal courts of Europe, *forced* to perform degrading musical tricks at the keyboard and, too often, poorly *rewarded*. Beethoven's father unsuccessfully *tried* to force prodigiousness upon his son. Nicolò Paganini's father *starved* his gifted boy to make him practice 10 hours a day.

And when the writer describes a recent child prodigy, she shifts to the present as the controlling time, but uses the past to reflect the child's past:

> Nine-year-old violinist Charlie Kim, who *was admitted* to the Juilliard Pre-College Division at the age of 6 (the youngest ever), not only *plays* at an annual school recital, but also *performs* with a string quartet he *has formed* with three other Juilliard preteen-agers. . . . Charlie *goes* to a regular school, *takes* weekly tennis lessons, *plays* football (last year, he *broke* a finger) and *practices* two hours a day. . . .
> —"The Pleasures and Perils of Being a Child Prodigy"

If you are writing in one time, you will confuse your reader if you switch to another time *for no apparent reason.* The following draft of a student's essay shows the time wobbling from past to present because the writer has not yet chosen a controlling time (or, as it is sometimes called, a *governing tense*):

> NO: When I *was* a child, my grandmother *drove* me crazy with her neatness. In her house, there *was* always a place for everything, even for little things.The rubber bands *belong* in the Grecian planter. The pens *sat* in a coffee can on the refrigerator. Whenever I *use* a pen, she *yells* at me to put it back before I even *began* to write.

In the final form of the essay, once the writer has chosen to set the time back to her childhood, to speak of events as they occurred, the verbs reflect that choice. The past tense governs her sentences:

> YES: When I *was* a child, my grandmother *drove* me crazy with her neatness. In her house, there *was* always a place for everything, even for little things. The rubber bands *belonged* in the Grecian planter. The pens *sat* in a coffee can on the refrigerator. Whenever I *used* a pen, she *would yell* at me to put it back before I even *began* to write.

But sometimes there are reasons for switching tenses. Perhaps you're *reminiscing:*

> I *remember* how I *walked* down that dirt road to school every day.

The remembering is occurring now in the writer's mind, but the walking occurred in the past.

Perhaps you're *stating a fact:*

I *forgot* that Chicago *is* near Gary, Indiana.

The forgetting has occurred in the past, but the fact that Chicago *is* near Gary, Indiana, remains true now.

WATCH OUT FOR PLOT SUMMARIES

When summarizing the plot of a movie, short story, or novel, the present tense is usually used, as in the following summary:

> One of my favorite movies *is* Bye, Bye, Birdie. The movie *is* a musical comedy about a rock singer who *comes* to a small town to give a concert. The movie *shows* how he *becomes* involved in the lives of the townspeople. When a teen-ager *is* chosen to appear with him on television in a pinning ceremony, her boyfriend *flies* into a jealous rage.

Treat the events of a movie or story as facts that are always true.

Fact: Water *freezes* at thirty-two degrees Fahrenheit.
Movie fact: In *Gone with the Wind,* Scarlett O'Hara *is* a southern belle with an eighteen-inch waist. She *falls* in love with Ashley Wilkes but *marries* Rhett Butler.

Exercise 4 Study the way movie critic Janet Maslin stays with the present tense in her review of the movie *Bronco Billy:*

FILM: EASTWOOD STARS IN AND DIRECTS "BRONCO BILLY"

In a scene midway through "Bronco Billy," the best and funniest Clint Eastwood movie in quite a while, the cowboy of the title strides into a bank. And he starts to cash a check for $3, because in this movie all of the nice people are poor. Suddenly, two bank robbers burst in, and they scare a little boy, one of many innocent customers in the place. The little boy drops his piggy bank and it shatters. This is too much for Bronco Billy. He gives the bandits The Look, an indignant squint that means, roughly translated, "Grrr," and then he hauls off and fires away.

What makes all this unusual for Mr. Eastwood, who directed the disarmingly boyish "Bronco Billy" and stars in the title role, is that the cowboy is more interested in the child than he is in the holdup men, and that he shoots the villains fairly politely, as if he didn't mean to do them any harm. Indeed, Mr. Eastwood is almost playing a very large Peter Pan. The locale may be Idaho instead of never-never land, but the feeling is that of a fairy tale, as Bronco Billy wanders through the West with a troupe of lost boys and girls. This is an emphatically American fable, which is perhaps why it ends with a chorus of "Stars and Stripes Forever."

The beginning of "Bronco Billy," which shows Mr. Eastwood off to his best comic advantage, introduces the cowboy and his traveling Wild West show. Before minuscule audiences composed of children and grannies, Bronco Billy and his fellow performers go through their paces, which involve rattlesnake-rassling, lasso-twirling and the like. Bronco Billy's own act, performed to music supplied by a dusty stereo, involves firing six-guns and hurling daggers at comely assistants, very few of whom last for more than one show.

Bronco Billy believes in his own legend, even as he works overtime to keep it alive. He is full of concern for those small members of his audience to whom he refers, variously, as "little pardners" or "buckaroos," and in his spare time offers them free advice. "I don't take kindly to kids playin' hooky from school," he sternly tells a group of children, handing them free passes and telling them to bring their parents—paying customers—to the show. "I think every kid in America ought to go to school, at least up through the eighth grade." The children, though they are enjoying this lecture, feel obliged to tell Bronco Billy that this is Saturday, and that they aren't playing hooky after all. Bronco Billy is sheepish about this, but it doesn't spoil anybody's good time.

. . .

Mr. Eastwood's direction constantly juxtaposes the old West and the new, as when Billy and the gang try to rob a modern train, and it whizzes right by them with utter indifference. Mr. Eastwood is still sticking to his guns, so to speak; the ideals of the contemporary western, newly fashionable right now, have been as prevalent in his last few films as they are this time. But "Bronco Billy" expresses these sentiments a shade more clearly, and moves along at a quicker, more consistent pace. Mr. Eastwood, who can be as formidable behind the camera as he is in front of it, is an entertainer, too.

Now write a summary of a movie you have seen. Keep to the present tense throughout your summary.

13.j PROBLEMS WITH VERBS

This section offers an index to the most troublesome verb problems.

-ed endings Some writers do not include the -ed ending on verbs because they're not accustomed to pronouncing or hearing the -ed. If you are one of these writers, be especially careful to use the -ed ending. Use the -ed ending for the past of regular verbs:

NO: Yesterday I *return* the book to the library.
YES: Yesterday I *returned* the book to the library.
NO: Last week I *climb* up to the roof.
YES: Last week I *climbed* up to the roof.

When there are several verbs in the past in a sentence, use the -ed ending (or the past form, for irregular verbs) for each verb in the sentence:

NO: He *walked* down the corridor, *stop* at Apartment 3C, *hesitate* a moment, and then *tap* on the door.

YES: He *walked* down the corridor, *stopped* at Apartment 3C, *hesitated* a moment, and then *tapped* on the door.

Give special attention to past forms of *use* and *suppose:*

NO: I *use* to go.
YES: I *used* to go.

NO: I'm *suppose* to come.
YES: I'm *supposed* to come.

If the verb is irregular, don't tack on an *-ed* ending as if it were a regular past (*growed*) or as if the irregular past form required *-ed* (*grewed*). Use the past forms of irregular verbs (pp. 316–320).

NO: The lilies *growed* along the freeway.
          The lilies *grewed* along the freeway.
YES: The lilies *grew* along the freeway.

NO: Jeannette's jeans *shranked* three inches.
          Jeannette's jeans *shrinked* three inches.
YES: Jeannette's jeans *shrank* three inches.

WATCH OUT FOR THE -ED ENDING IN THE PASSIVE

Remember to write the *-ed* ending in the passive:

NO:	YES:
The moon was *walk* on by a man.	The moon was *walked* on by a man.
Lincoln was *assassinate* by John Wilkes Booth.	Lincoln was *assassinated* by John Wilkes Booth.

The best phone system in the world didn't just happen. It was planned a long time ago.

Passive: *was planned*

Past participles Do not use the past participle of an irregular verb (*done*) for a past form (*did*). The past participle cannot be used without an auxiliary.

NO: I *gone* to the movies.
YES: I *went* to the movies.
             or
       I *have gone* to the movies.

NO: They *done* it.
YES: They *did* it.
            or
         They *have done* it.
NO: We *seen* it.
YES: We *saw* it.
            or
         We *have seen* it.

Remember, there's no problem with the past participles of regular verbs, for the past and the past participle are identical.

YES: I *learned* an unforgettable lesson.
YES: I *have learned* an unforgettable lesson.

YES: She *walked* home.
YES: She *has walked* home.

Combine *have, has,* or *had* with the past participle of irregular verbs (*have come, have run*). Do not combine *have, has,* or *had* with the past form of irregular verbs:

NO: I should *have went*.
YES: I should *have gone*.

NO: They *had did* it.
YES: They *had done* it.

Exercise 5 Fill each empty slot with the appropriate *-ed* form of the verb. Then read the sentence aloud emphasizing the endings.

Example: I am on a ____restricted____ diet. (restrict)

1. I am _____ to foods that are high in protein and low in calories. (limit)

2. My milk is _____ rather than _____. (skim, homogenize)

3. I'm told all milk is _____. (pasteurize)

4. I avoid old-_____ desserts with _____ cream. (fashion, whip)

5. _____ and _____ potatoes are on my forbidden list. (mash, fry)

6. For lunch I have a _____ green salad. (toss)

7. Since dressings are out, I add lemon juice and _____ fresh or _____ dill. (chop, dry)

8. I sprinkle a teaspoon of _____ onion over _____ tomatoes and cucumbers and a _____ green pepper. (grate, slice, seed)

9. I prepare _____ bass with soy sauce, _____ ginger, and a tablespoon of vinegar. (steam, mince)

10. When I eat meat, it is carefully _____ of fat and then _____. (trim, broil)

11. _____ butter, _____ brownies, _____ vegetables, _____ lasagne, and _____ ravioli are memories. (melt, frost, cream, bake, stuff)

12. I eat leisurely and take bite-_____ pieces. (size)

13. I have _____ thoughts of thirty-eight _____ pounds so far. (satisfy, drop)

14. Only sixty-two more _____ pounds to go! (damn)

Exercise 6   Choose either the past form or the past participle of the given verb to fill each empty slot. The past form of the verb stands alone, but the past participle must be combined with *have, has,* or *had.* Check the verb charts on pages 316–320.

> Example: After the soprano had _____sung_____ ''America the Beautiful,''
> she _____sang_____ ''The Star-Spangled Banner.'' (sing)

1. The telephone has _____ the entire morning; it even _____ during my lunch break. (ring)

2. Jeannette's new jeans, which have _____ three sizes, _____ beyond an acceptable tight fit. (shrink)

3. After Sharon had _____ from one end of the lake to the other, she _____ back again. (swim)

4. As soon as Charles had _____ the mystery, the phone _____ to ring. (begin)

5. He had _____ a long time to get ready for the party; he _____ much too long. (take)

6. Yesterday, when it was ninety-nine degrees, I _____ more water than I should have _____. At the end of the day, I _____ like a balloon. (drink, feel)

7. He had _____ all the way to the store when he realized that he forgot his wallet, so he _____ all the way home again. (run)

8. I _____ to North Beach every day in the summer although years ago I had _____ to South Beach. (go)

9. You've _____ a long way, Baby, but you _____ too late. (come)

10. How could you have _____ this to me? You _____ the same thing last week. (do)

11. You've _____ all the pretzels, and Clyde _____ the potato chips, ice cream, and peanuts. (eat)

12. Henry has _____ till noon the whole week, but this morning he _____ only until 11:30. (sleep)

Problems with have, has, had The following verbs are often used incorrectly with *have, has,* or *had.* Learn to recognize them as problem verbs.

Present	NO:	YES:
break	have broke	have broken
choose	has chose	has chosen
do	had did	had done
draw	have drew	have drawn
drive	has drove	has driven
eat	had ate	had eaten
begin	have began	have begun
come	has came	has come
sing	had sang	had sung

Although it is natural to slur sounds of words as we talk, do not drop endings of words or merge words in writing. A common writing error is to use *of* instead of *have.* Another is to write *gonna* for *going to.*

NO: I could *of* danced all night.
YES: I could *have* danced all night.

NO: I should *of* bought that dress.
YES: I should *have* bought that dress.

NO: He's *gonna* be president.
YES: He's *going* to be president.

Do not use *would have* in an *if* clause.

NO: If I *would have* studied Chapter 3, I would have passed the exam.
YES: If I *had* studied Chapter 3, I would have passed the exam.

Have and be When using forms of *have* and *be* together, remember that a form of *have* must always precede *been:*

has been   having been
have been   had been

Remember, also, that *-ing* words follow *have, has,* or *had + been:*

has been sleeping
has been working

NO: She *been* sleeping for twelve hours.
YES: She *has been* sleeping for twelve hours.

-ing words   The *-ing* form alone cannot be used as the verb in a sentence. It must be combined with a time word (*is, are, were,* and so forth). See Chapter 10, pages 220–222.

> NO: Samantha *swimming* in the lake.
> YES: Samantha *is swimming* in the lake.

Verbs followed by verbals   Certain verbs must be followed by certain verbals. Familiarize yourself with the following lists.

1. These verbs are followed by an infinitive (*to dance, to kiss, to leave*):

ask	She'll *ask* him *to dance.*
beg	He *begged* her *to marry* him.
care	She doesn't *care to tango.*
decide	She could *decide to sit* this one out.
expect	He *expected* her *to say* that.
forget	She *forgot to apologize.*
hope	He's *hoping to win* her hand.
learn	She's *learning to control* herself.
plan	He *plans to captivate* her.
promise	She *promised to consider* him.
want	He *wants to kiss* her.
wish	She *wished to leave.*

2. These verbs are followed by an *-ing* word (*dancing, kissing, leaving*):

admit	He *admitted dancing* with Janet.
appreciate	I *appreciate* your *coming.*
avoid	They *avoided paying* their bills.
consider	We *considered leaving.*
deny	He *denied seeing* her.
enjoy	She *enjoys swimming.*
escape	He *escaped going* bowling tonight.
finish	She's *finished considering* him.
imagine	He *imagined kissing* her.
keep	She *kept* him *waiting* all night.
mind	Would you *mind eating* out?
miss	He *missed seeing* her.

Three troublesome verb pairs have much in common. Three of the verbs are *transitive;* that is, they take objects. These verbs are *set, lay,* and *raise.* Three of the verbs are *intransitive;* that is, they do not take objects. These verbs are *sit, lie,* and *rise.* The difficulty lies in remembering the principal parts of each verb and in knowing the particular verb's meaning.

1. *set/sit*   *set* (takes an object)   *sit* (never takes an object)

Present	*set*		Present	*sit*
Past	*set*		Past	*sat*
Past Participle	*have set*		Past Participle	*have sat*

Meaning: Meaning:

Set means to put something in a place—to *set* the suitcase down, to *set* the problem aside.   *Sit* means to rest—to *sit* in a chair, to *sit* on a bench.

      s v   o   s   v

I *set* the book on its shelf.   The book *sits* on the shelf.

Yesterday I *set* the book on its shelf.   Yesterday the book *sat* on the shelf.

I *have set* the book on its shelf.   The book *has sat* on the shelf for years.

Note: All three forms of *set* are the same: *set, set, set*.

2. *lay/lie*   lay (takes an object)   *lie* (never takes an object)

Present	*lay*		Present	*lie*
Past	*laid*		Past	*lay*
Past Participle	*have laid*		Past Participle	*have lain*

Meaning: Meaning:

Lay means to place or put something down.   *Lie* means to rest in a reclining position.

      s v   o   s   v

I *lay* the pencil down.   I usually *lie* down after dinner.

Yesterday I *laid* the pencil on the desk.   Yesterday I *lay* in bed all day.

I *have laid* the pencil down.   I *have* often *lain* down after dinner.

Notice where the confusion is: The past of *lie* (recline) is *lay*, which is also the present of *lay* (put).

Present: I usually *lay* (put) my glasses on that table, and now they aren't there.
Past: Yesterday I *lay* (reclined) in bed all day.

3. *raise/rise*   *raise* (takes an object)   *rise* (never takes an object)

Present	*raise*		Present	*rise*
Past	*raised*		Past	*rose*
Past Participle	*have raised*		Past Participle	*have risen*

Meaning: Meaning:

Raise means to lift something up, or to   *Rise* means to stand up after lying or

increase something in size or intensity— sitting down, or to go up—the price of
to *raise* a voice, to *raise* prices. eggs *rose* this week.

S	V	O

She *raises* the window blind at
dawn.

She *raised* the window blind at dawn.

She *has* often *raised* the window blind at
dawn.

S	V

The sun *rises* early in the summer.

Yesterday the sun *rose* at 4:46 A.M.

The sun *has risen* before 5:00 A.M.
every day this week.

Exercise 7 Choose the correct verb form of *rise/raise, sit/set,* or *lie/lay* to fill the empty slots.

Although I had _____ the alarm for six o'clock this morning, I couldn't _____ my weary body when the alarm rang. The sun had already _____ , but I needed to _____ in bed awhile. I remembered the *Time* magazine that I had _____ next to the bed last night and began to read it. The national-news section noted that the price of eggs and dairy products had _____ again. Farmers in the West had _____ the price of wheat so that bread prices would surely _____ in the fall. The news was certainly not promising. After a while, I _____ up in bed, _____ the magazine aside, and _____ the window shade. The day was glorious. I wished that I could _____ in bed the whole morning, but I knew I should _____ out the dog's breakfast and begin the day.

Exercise 8 Fill in the blank with the correct form of the past and past perfect verb.

1. After they had _____ me the house had been robbed, I _____ my sister not to go inside. (tell)

2. They had _____ they would find a gold mine, but after seeing the place, they _____ otherwise. (think)

3. While rummaging through the house, they had _____ the cats, but they never _____ the dog. (awake)

4. They had _____ all the clothing on the floor, but they _____ the jewels into their sacks. (throw)

5. Outside they had _____ only dark glasses, but inside they _____ stockings over their heads. (wear)

6. They took the bronze trophy I had _____ in the bowling league, but left the ant farm I _____ at the state fair. (win)

7. Even though she never _____ anyone's neck before, she would have _____ theirs. (wring)

8. They _____ us letters from prison, but we never got them because they had _____ down the wrong address. (write)

13.k CHART I: PATTERNS OF VERB CHANGES IN IRREGULAR VERBS

Base	Past (used alone)	Past participle (used with *have, has,* or *had*)

1. Verbs such as these show a spelling change before adding *d:*

cry	cried	cried
pay	paid	paid
say	said	said

2. Verbs such as these show a past participle ending in -*n* or -*en:*

break	broke	broken
choose	chose	chosen
drive	drove	driven

3. Verbs such as these show a vowel (*a, e, i, o, u*) change within the base:

begin	began	begun
ring	rang	rung
swim	swam	swum

4. Verbs such as these show no change in the past or past participle:

cut	cut	cut
hit	hit	hit
hurt	hurt	hurt

5. Verbs such as these show the same past and past participle:

bring	brought	brought
catch	caught	caught
stand	stood	stood

6. These three verbs show the same base and past participle:

become	became	become
come	came	come
run	ran	run

7. Verbs such as these have more than one past or past participle. Each is acceptable:

awake	awaked, awoke	awaked, awoke, awoken
forget	forgot	forgotten, forgot

13.I CHART II: PRINCIPAL PARTS OF IRREGULAR VERBS

Base	Past	Past participle
awake	awaked, awoke	awaked, awoke, awoken
be	was, were	been
beat	beat	beaten, beat
become	became	become
begin	began	begun
bend	bent	bent
bite	bit	bit, bitten
bleed	bled	bled
blow	blew	blown
break	broke	broken
bring	brought	brought
build	built	built
burst	burst	burst
buy	bought	bought
catch	caught	caught
choose	chose	chosen
come	came	come
cost	cost	cost
cut	cut	cut
deal	dealt	dealt
dig	dug	dug
dive	dived, dove	dived
do	did	done
draw	drew	drawn
dream	dreamed, dreamt	dreamed, dreamt
drink	drank	drunk
drive	drove	driven

Base	Past	Past participle
eat	ate	eaten
fall	fell	fallen
feed	fed	fed
feel	felt	felt
fight	fought	fought
find	found	found
fit	fitted, fit	fitted, fit
fly	flew	flown
forget	forgot	forgotten, forgot
freeze	froze	frozen
get	got	gotten, got
give	gave	given
go	went	gone
grow	grew	grown
hang (an object)	hung	hung
hang (a person)	hanged	hanged
hear	heard	heard
hide	hid	hidden, hid
hit	hit	hit
hold	held	held
hurt	hurt	hurt
keep	kept	kept
kneel	knelt, kneeled	knelt, kneeled
knit	knit, knitted	knit, knitted
know	knew	known
lay (put)	laid	laid
lead	led	led
lean	leaned, leant	leaned, leant
leave	left	left
lend	lent	lent
let (allow)	let	let
lie (recline)	lay	lain
light	lighted, lit	lighted, lit
lose	lost	lost
make	made	made
mean	meant	meant
meet	met	met
pay	paid	paid

Base	Past	Past participle
prove	proved	proved, proven
put	put	put
quit	quit, quitted	quit, quitted
read	read	read
rid	rid, ridded	rid, ridded
ride	rode	ridden
ring	rang	rung
run	ran	run
say	said	said
see	saw	seen
sell	sold	sold
send	sent	sent
set	set	set
shake	shook	shaken
shine	shone, shined	shone, shined (transitive)
shoot	shot	shot
show	showed	showed, shown
shrink	shrank	shrunk
shut	shut	shut
sing	sang, sung	sung
sink	sank	sunk
sit	sat	sat
sleep	slept	slept
slide	slid	slid, slidden
speak	spoke	spoken
speed	sped, speeded	sped, speeded
spend	spent	spent
spin	spun	spun
spring	sprang, sprung	sprung
stand	stood	stood
steal	stole	stolen
stick	stuck	stuck
sting	stung	stung
strike	struck	struck, stricken
swear	swore	sworn
swim	swam	swum
swing	swung	swung

Base	Past	Past participle
take	took	taken
teach	taught	taught
tear	tore	torn
tell	told	told
think	thought	thought
throw	threw	thrown
wake	waked, woke	waked, woke, woken
wear	wore	worn
win	won	won
wring	wrung	wrung
write	wrote	written

chapter
14 | Subject–Verb Agreement

14.a PERSON AND NUMBER

Look at the following sentences about the President of the United States, noticing how each pronoun refers to the subject differently:

> *I* am the President.
> *You* are the President.
> *He* is the President.

When the subject of a sentence is *speaking about himself*, he uses the singular pronoun *I*, or he uses the plural pronoun *we* if he is part of a group:

> *I* am the President.
> *We* are supporters of the President.
> *We* must win.

When the subject of a sentence is *being spoken to*, the pronoun *you* is used:

> *You* are the President.
> *You* are supporters of the President.
> *You* must win.

When the subject of a sentence is *being spoken about*, we use the pronouns *he*, *she*, *it*, or *they;* or we can use any word or group of words that can be reduced to these pronouns:

James Madison was the President.
or

He was the President.

Dolley Madison was the President's wife.
or

She was the President's wife.

The Steelers must win.
or

They must win.

The subject, as you have seen, can *speak about him-* or *herself, be spoken to,* or *be spoken about.* We call each of these three ways of referring to a subject *person.* The idea of person may have nothing to do with people. All nouns (or noun substitutes) can be changed to *he, she, it,* or *they. It* is called a third-*person* pronoun although it never refers to a human being.

Another quality of the subject is *number,* which means that a subject may be *singular* (one) or *plural* (more than one). We can talk about the *person* and *number* of every subject. Let's look closely at these qualities.

First person   In the first person, the subject speaks about himself or herself. Whenever the pronouns *I* (singular) or *we* (plural) appear in the subject slot, the pronoun is in the first person.

Second person   In the second person, the subject is being spoken to. Whenever the pronoun *you* appears in the subject slot, the pronoun is in the second person. Note that the second-person pronoun has the same form for both singular and plural.

Singular: *You* are the one I adore.
Plural: *You* are the men and women of tomorrow.

Third person In the third person, the subject is being spoken about. Whenever the pronouns *he, she, it* (singular), or *they* (plural) appear in the subject slot, the pronoun is in the third person. Whenever a subject can be reduced to one of these pronouns, the subject is in the third person. *Every subject,* in fact, that does not contain the pronouns *I, we,* or *you* will be in the third person.

He's Swinging in the Rain

She was young

They call us old-hat.

Giants Win Two Ball Games

or
They win.

San Francisco Has Some of the Best

or
It has some of the best.

As you will see in the following chart, every subject in every sentence in the English language can be described by *person*—first, second, or third— and by *number*—singular (one) or plural (more than one).

	Singular	**Plural**
First person	I	we
Second person	you	you
Third person	he, she, it	they
	dog	dogs
	boy	boys
	tree	trees
	one	many

14.b AGREEMENT BETWEEN SUBJECT AND VERB

Whenever you hook up a subject in the *third-person singular* with a verb in the *present tense,* you run into one of the peculiarities of the English language. No other subject presents this problem; no other tense presents this problem.

Let's look now at the verb forms in the present tense:

	Singular	**Plural**
First person	I *walk*	we *walk*
Second person	you *walk*	you *walk*
Third person	he *walks*	they *walk*
	she *walks*	John and Susan *walk*
	it *walks*	
	John *walks*	
	Susan *walks*	

You see that the present tense of a verb is made up of the base *(walk)* and the *-s* form *(walks)*. A *third-person-singular subject always takes the* -s *form of the verb in the present tense.* This correspondence of the subject and verb is called *agreement*.

Watch what happens to the verb *love* in the present tense when you change *cat* to *cats*.

Third-person singular
A cat love*s* Purina.
A cat☐ love⟨s⟩ Purina.

Third-person plural
Cat*s* love Purina.
Cat⟨s⟩ love☐ Purina.

Purina knows
what cats love most

It is a peculiarity of English that when the verb in a sentence has an *-s* ending, there is usually no *-s* on the subject (cat☐ love⟨s⟩). But when the *-s* (for plural) occurs on the subject, no *-s* occurs on the verb (cats love☐). For the one exception to this rule, see the next section, on agreement problems.

There are no problems in agreement between subject and verb in the past or the future tense because all forms of the verb are the same (past: *walked;* future: *will walk*).

WATCH OUT FOR -S ENDINGS

1. Some words end in -s:

LAS VEGAS
SWISS
fuss

This *Actress*
gas Tennis

2. Plural nouns end in -s:

SINGULAR   PLURAL

athlete
problem

Athletes

Problems

Lifestyles

lifestyle
ceremony

Ceremonies

3. Singular nouns form possessives with an 's:

Scott

SCOTT'S LAST VOYAGE

emperor

The Emperor's New Clothes

4. All verbs have an -s form:

BASE   -S FORM

get
say

gets Says

does

do
keep
open

keeps **opens**

14.c AGREEMENT PROBLEMS

Using the -s form   Although you may be able to recognize when your subject is singular *(Vincent, cat, actress),* you may not distinguish between a verb form with *-s* at the end and a verb form without *-s* at the end. You may, in fact, be using the same base form (with or without *-s*) for all your subjects, whether they are singular or plural:

NO: Vincent *walk* to the bus every night.
YES: Vincent *walks* to the bus every night.
                                    or
        He *walks* to the bus every night.

Occasionally, speakers of dialects overcorrect and use the *-s* verb form for every subject:

NO: I *loves* mint chocolate chip.
NO: They *loves* cherry vanilla.

Learn to distinguish the *-s* ending of plural nouns and the *-s* form of verbs. Read the following sentences aloud, pronouncing each *-s* you come upon. Notice that when the subject is singular, the *-s* box for the verb is filled: A *cat*□ *love*⟨S⟩. Notice that when the subject is plural, the *-s* box for the subject is filled: *Cat*⟨S⟩ *love*□.

pain* interferes...

pain□   interfere⟨S⟩

Nouns do not need to end in *-s* to be plural. When a plural noun does not end in *-s,* neither box is filled.

Singular noun	**Plural noun**

The Almond People Invite You To Nibble Your Way Through The Week

2 policemen deliver baby

almond people□   invite□   policemen□   deliver□

Exercise 1   For each subject in the left column, write a sentence using a verb from the right column. Every verb should be in the present tense and end in *-s.*

1. the IRS   to be
2. Boris Becker   to have

3. the queen   to sing
4. an owl   to want
5. "Happy Days"   to buy
6. Barbra Streisand   to sound
7. Bill Cosby   to buzz
8. Ted Kennedy   to seduce
9. my stereo   to screech
                                     to collect
                                     to smash

Exercise 2 Write the following headline in the past tense, the present tense, and the future tense. In which time does the headline appear here?

Your college degree cost over $15,000

Exercise 3 Rewrite the following passage from Judy Syfers's essay "Why I Want a Wife," changing *I* to *she*. Make any other changes necessary because of the shift from *I* to *she*.

> Example: She wants a wife who will take care of her physical needs.

> *I* want a wife who will take care of *my* physical needs. I want a wife who will keep my house clean. A wife who will pick up after me. I want a wife who will keep my clothes clean, ironed, mended, replaced when need be, and who will see to it that my personal things are kept in their proper place so that I can find what I need the minute I need it. I want a wife who cooks the meals, a wife who is a *good* cook. I want a wife who will plan the menus, do the necessary grocery shopping, prepare the meals, serve them pleasantly, and then do the cleaning up while I do my studying. I want a wife who will care for me when I am sick and sympathize with my pain and loss of time from school. I want a wife to go along when our family takes a vacation so that someone can continue to care for me and my children when I need a rest and change of scene.

Exercise 4 The following passage appears in the third-person-plural present tense. Rewrite it, changing *they* to *he*. Make any other changes necessary because of the shift from *they* to *he*.

> They wait, but still there is no sign of her. They look at the clock; they could swear it hasn't moved for hours. They hear footsteps on the porch. They rush to the window, but it's only the neighbor's cat looking for food scraps. "What could be taking so long?" they ask. They stare blankly at the window. It begins to snow. They think that perhaps she has lost her way. They put on gloves, long underwear, overcoats, anything they can find. They haven't been able to pay the

heat bill this month. They jump up and down to keep warm. They wish she'd come. They gave her the last 22 cents they had, and they hope she hasn't run off with it. How far could she get with 22 cents anyway, they ask. They play cards. They throw darts. They clean. They even rearrange whatever furniture they have to pass the time. At last, they spot her a block away, trudging through the snow. They run out to greet her. They are too cold to speak. She hands over the 22 cent stamp. They smile. They feel guilty for ever doubting her. They return to the house and place the stamp on the envelope marked "contest winner." This time they know they're going to win. They have to. The envelope says they're already winners. They don't sleep but stare at the envelope all night. In it rests all their hopes, all their dreams. We have to win, they think. We have to.

Exercise 5 Rewrite the following passage, changing *he* to *they*. Make any other necessary changes.

The way he gets drunk on beer, you'd think he was a human being, rather than an extraterrestrial. He's funny the way he walks into furniture all the time or hides in closets and puts on women's clothing to disguise himself. He is easily frightened. He feels alone. Even though he is cute and funny, he is still a curiosity, a specimen for study, and that's why all the scientists are after him. And when they do get their hands on him, how sad it is to watch him as he wastes away, how he nearly dies until his earthling friends can set him free. Then watch him do all sorts of wonderful magic. How he gets bicycles to fly! How he escapes those people who are after him. He knows how painful it is to be separated from one's loved ones, how dangerous it is to be alone in a strange world when all that people want to do is to study and dissect you. He doesn't know whom to trust; he doesn't know what to do. But he finds a friend. It's important to find a friend when you are so far from home, no matter where you come from.

Recognizing the subject To make certain that your subject and verb agree, you must be able to isolate the subject–verb unit. If you have trouble deciding what the subject of a sentence is, look again at the advice in Chapter 10, pages 223–225. Once you've found the verb in the sentence, ask a "Who?" or a "What?" question to find the subject. What is the subject in the following sentence? *Water? Costs?*

Higher Water Costs Raise Rents

The verb is	*raise*
Who or what	raise?
costs	*raise*

Now reduce the subject to a pronoun *(he, she, it,* or *they)* that fits the subject slot:

What   raise?
They   *raise*

The word that is the subject of the verb is *costs,* not *water.*

    When you're not certain if your subject is third-person singular or plural, reduce the subject to the third-person pronoun, *he, she, it,* or *they.* Practice these steps.

> The *comedians* roar.
>   *They*   roar.
>
> *Lily Tomlin* is a brilliant comedian.
>   *She*   is a brilliant comedian.
>
> Slapstick *comedy* is hilarious.
>   *It*   is hilarious.

    Problems in determining whether a subject is singular or plural arise with *abstract nouns*—that is, nouns that describe ideas or qualities. Abstract nouns are usually singular:

life	improvement	beauty
liberty	necessity	nature
freedom	kindness	solitude
happiness	loveliness	peace

> *Necessity* is the mother of invention.
> *Liberty* creates patriots.
> *Experience* is the best teacher.

    No matter how long and involved the subject is, you can determine whether it is singular or plural by reducing it to a third-person pronoun:

> *An extreme nationalism that drains a country's energy* is destructive.
>   *It*   is destructive.
> *Life, liberty, and the pursuit of happiness* are privileges we expect.
>   *They*   are privileges we expect.
> *Winning the election in November* is his first goal.
>   *It*   is his first goal.

Exercise 6 No matter how long and involved the subject of a sentence is, you can reduce the subject to one of these personal pronouns:

	Singular	Plural
First person	I	we
Second person	you	you
Third person	he, she, it	they

Reduce the following subjects by determining their person and number and then substituting an appropriate pronoun.

	Person and number	Pro- noun
Example: Charles Smith and his sister Mary	third-person plural	They

1. one woman and her dogs
2. one woman
3. her dogs
4. Charles Smith, his sister Mary, and I
5. Charles Smith's sister Mary
6. his sister Mary
7. I
8. the pursuit of happiness
9. the man in the tweed suit and I
10. the man in the tweed suit
11. freedom
12. international companies
13. gross national product
14. electric bills
15. the task force

Exercise 7   Reduce the subject in each of the following sentences to a pronoun.

Example: Musicians' talks hit another snag.   talk⬚S hit☐
                                                                            they☐ hit☐

1. **Losing 37 pounds doesn't sound like much, but look at the difference it made in me.**

2. **Those quaint New England inns do exist**

3. **Fedders heat pump air conditioner cuts winter fuel bills**

4. *Indiana Triumphs Over Mich. State*

Keeping the subject in sight

WORDS THAT COME BETWEEN THE SUBJECT AND THE VERB

Words that come between the subject and the verb may be misleading. Often you'll have to untangle the sentence to find the noun that is the subject. It may help to bracket intervening phrases and clauses.

> The woman in the yellow bikini serving the sandwiches to the girl in dungarees is my grandmother.
> The woman [in the yellow bikini serving the sandwiches to the girl in dungarees] is my grandmother.
>
>   s   v
> woman _____ is

What may confuse you is that the phrase *girl in dungarees* is closer to the verb than the subject is. Don't let it fool you. You're not saying, ''The girl in dungarees is my grandmother.'' You're saying, ''The woman is my grandmother.''

> the *price* of eggs *is* high.
> The *price* [of eggs] *is* high.
> The *price* _____ *is* high.

Don't let the plural form *of eggs* mislead you. What is high is the *price,* and *price* is singular. The phrase, *of eggs,* that comes between the subject and verb should not influence the number of the verb.

> NO: The *price* of eggs *are* high.
> YES: The *price* of eggs *is* high.
> s–v: *price is*
> NO: The *dog* that wants quality biscuits *love* Purina.
> YES: The *dog* that wants quality biscuits *loves* Purina.
> s–v: *dog loves*

JAMBALAYA
**THIS SAVORY CREOLE CONCOCTION FROM THE LOUISIANA BAYOUS
CALLS FOR CHICKEN, HAM, RICE, ONION AND
THE MEAT OF THE TOMATO.**

The verb is	*calls for*
Who or what	calls for?

*This savory Creole concoction [from the Louisiana Bayous]
calls for*

	What	calls for?
Reduce the subject to a personal pronoun (*he, she, it,* or *they*) that fits the subject slot:	*It*	*calls for*
The word that is the subject of the verb is *concoction:*	*concoction*	*calls for*

Do not let the modifiers that come before or after the one word that is your simple subject distract you.

MODIFIER		MODIFIER	
[This savory Creole]	s	[from the Louisiana Bayous]	v
	concoction		*calls for*

Exercise 8 Locate the subject and the verb in the following sentences.

Example: The man wearing a stethoscope and plaid pants is an imposter.
(with s over "man" and v over "is")

1. The day after our visit to my sister's was overcast.

2. Mexico City during the past ten years has experienced a population explosion.

3. People who smoke in bed get burned.

4. Helium, neon, and argon, found in the periodic table, are inert elemental gases.

5. *The Merry Wives of Windsor* by William Shakespeare is a comedy.

6. The two-record set known as *The White Album* is my favorite Beatles' recording.

Exercise 9 Write your own sentences, using each of the following words as the subject. The verbs in the sentences should be in the present tense. Include a phrase or clause between the subject and verb so that your sentence looks like this: subject _____ verb

Example: confusion
            The *confusion* of registering for classes gets me down.

1. United Nations Organization

2. my education and my background

3. the original intent

4. power brokers

5. the most exposed part

6. the glamour and glitter

7. the noise and the confusion

REVERSED WORD ORDER   A preceding noun should never influence a verb whose true subject follows it in the sentence:

> In the early-morning fog *come* the *sounds* of fishing boats off Deer Isle.
> s–v: *sounds come*

> Seated behind her as she campaigned *were her husband and children.*
> s–v: *her husband and children were*

REVERSED WORD ORDER WITH THERE IS, THERE ARE, IT IS   *There is* and *there are* reverse the usual word order: The verb is first and the subject, second. Usually, the number of the delayed subject controls the verb:

> There *were Joe and Bob barbecuing* the chickens in their back yard.
> s–v: *Joe and Bob were barbecuing*

> There *is* no *explanation* for food preferences.
> s–v: *explanation is*

There are still some things Americans know how to do best.

s–v: *things are*

The word *it* always takes the *-s* form of the verb:

> It *was* the O'Connells at the door.
> It'*s* the books I ordered.

SUBJECT, NOT THE COMPLETER, CONTROLS THE VERB   Even when the completer of a linking verb differs in number from the subject, the subject controls the verb:

> The *disturbance* outside the window *was* three men beating on garbage-can lids.

ALTERNATIVE SUBJECTS   When two or more subjects are joined by *or* or *nor,* use the form of the verb that agrees with the *subject nearest the verb:*

> Either Lillian or her *parents are* walking the dog.
> Either Lillian's parents or her *brother is* walking the dog.

Occasions will arise when strict adherence to this rule will produce awkward phrasings:

> Neither the dean nor I am happy with the sleeping arrangements.
> Neither I nor the dean is happy with the sleeping arrangements.

It is often neatest to change the construction altogether:

> I am not happy with the sleeping arrangements, and neither is the dean.

CONSIDER THESE SUBJECTS PLURAL

1. Compound subjects joined by *and:*

   > Max's chipped front *tooth and* his *dimple attract* the girls.
   > s–v: *tooth and dimple attract*

2. "One of those who":

   > Aileen is one of those *poets* who *study* art.
   > Isabel is one of the *lawyers* who *are going* to Washington.
   > Phyllis is one of the *artists* who *like* poetry.

   (Since Aileen is one of many poets who study art, the verb agrees with the plural noun *poets,* and not with *one.*)

   > Aileen is the only *one* of those poets who *studies* art.

   (Since Aileen is the only one who studies art, the verb agrees with *one.*)

CONSIDER THESE SUBJECTS SINGULAR

1. Compound subjects that are considered to be single units or items:

   > Peanut butter and jelly *is* my favorite sandwich filling.
   > A wife and mother *is* an overworked member of the labor force.
   > (*Wife and mother* refers to one person who is both.)

2. *Each, neither, either, anybody, anyone, anything, somebody, someone, something, nobody, no one, nothing, everybody, everyone, everything:*

   > *Either* Sharon or Lauren *walks* the dog in the morning.
   > Each *has* his own stopwatch and *is* ready to begin.
   > Each of them *has* his own stopwatch and *is* ready to begin.
   > (The intervening phrase *of them* does not change the singular subject.)

3. Nouns ending in *-ics* that represent a single field of study:

   > Mathematics *is* a mystery to Harry.
   > American politics *has been* Janet's lifelong passion.
   > Dean Flint's campus politics *are* scandalous.

(Dean Flint's *politics* are not a field of study but are all his maneuvers and strategies to gain power and are therefore considered plural.)

CONSIDER THE TITLE OF A WORK SINGULAR

Ideas and Beliefs of the Victorians is not exactly bedside reading.
Wuthering Heights is about an uncouth fellow named Heathcliff.

CONSIDER THESE SUBJECTS WITH CARE

1. Collective nouns

Though a *collective noun* names a group, it usually refers to the group as a single unit and functions in the sentence as a singular subject. Notice the *-s* form of the verb in the following ads:

SITUATIONS WANTED

Live-in European couple seeks position, handyman, caretaker, auto mechanic, references. 628-2656 after 5 pm.

Couple with 2 children wants live-in, part time caretakers job in exchange for rent. References. 212-CY 8-6259.

Mature couple desires room & bath or small apartment. Away on weekends. 759-0622.

seeks	wants	desires
s–v: *couple seeks*	*couple wants*	*couple desires*

When you focus on the individual members of the group and not on the group as a unit, the subject is plural and requires a plural verb:

WANTED TO RENT

Young married couple, lawyer & school teacher with baby, seek apartment for the summer. Willing to work in turn for rent. Call bet. 9 & 5, 364-2700 ext. 295.

s–v: *couple seek*

Other collective nouns are *jury, orchestra, family, audience, crowd, committee, United States, flock, band, team, faculty,* and so forth.

2. Quantities as subject

A noun of quantity is singular when the quantity is considered as a single unit:

Ten miles is too long to hike in July.
Six dollars is a fair price for that haircut.

But when a noun of quantity refers to the individual items, the subject is plural:

Two-thirds of the nation *are* ill-housed, ill-clad, and ill-nourished.
Three quarts of orange juice *are* barely enough for Steve's breakfast.

3. *The number of* and *a number of*
   The number of is always singular, but *a number of* is plural:

   The number of travel books about Kenya *is* increasing.
   A number of officials in Nairobi *have* expressed concern about relations with Uganda.

4. *A lot . . . are* and *A lot . . . is*
   A lot is plural if the upcoming noun in the *of* phrase is plural, and it's singular if the noun in the *of* phrase is singular:

   A lot *of Coke bottles were* strewn along the highway to Jericho.
   A lot *of Coke is* drunk in East Africa.

5. *None, any, all, more, most,* and *some* can be either singular or plural, depending on the meaning of the sentence:

   Plural: *Some* of the storks *are* standing on two legs.
   Singular: *Some* of the sand *is* in my shoe.

   Plural: *Most* of the lifeguards *were* striking.
   Singular: *Most* of the bathhouse *was* under a foot of water.

   Plural: *None* of us *know* what cholesterol does to our bodies.
   Singular: *None* of our Irish setters *is* expected to win in the state dog show.

Exercise 10 Choose the correct verb form in the following sentences.

1. The racket in the middle of the night _____ three raccoons scratching on the skylight. (was/were)

2. Either Clare or her brothers _____ the key to the apartment. (have/has)

3. Rupert is one of those musicians who _____ the dog howl with distress. (make/makes)

4. Bacon and eggs _____ my usual breakfast. (are/is)

5. George Orwell's "Politics and the English Language" _____ an essay you should read. (is/are)

6. The audience _____ into uncontrollable laughter at the same spots every night. (breaks/break)

7. Every year the high-school basketball team _____ the state championship. (take/takes)

8. Five hundred dollars _____ the going price for a video-cassette recorder. (is/are)

9. Four Big Macs for dinner _____ just about enough to keep Brad going. (are/is)

10. A lot of women these days _____ entering law school. (is/are)

Exercise 11 Supply a verb in present time in the following sentences.

Example: The Bijou or the Valencia _____ *Gone with the Wind* this week.
The Bijou or the Valencia *is showing Gone with the Wind* this week.

1. Clark and Lois _____ each other.
2. Either a cold rain or some snow _____ every afternoon.
3. Some of the musicians _____ to sight-read.
4. Most of the planetarium _____ undergoing a paint job.
5. None of the telephone operators _____ clearly.
6. Some of the mathematics _____ easy to understand.
7. Lucy, together with William, _____ to play Little League ball.
8. Some of the fastest-traveling galaxies _____ no longer visible.
9. Nobody _____ the trouble I've seen.
10. Ten minutes in that ice-cold swimming pool _____ to cardiac arrest.
11. The number of businesses in our neighborhood _____ steadily increasing.
12. A number of supermarkets in our neighborhood _____ open all night.
13. Well, if it _____n't the Waterhouse boys, all dressed to kill and coming up the walk!

chapter
15 | Pronouns

Nobody One ALL **them** **Most**
everything ANOTHER ourselves
its *Whatever* **YOU** She They

There are some words you would hesitate to use at the beginning of a conversation if you wanted your listener to understand your meaning:

"Hello, Alice. Do you remember *him? He's* at Annapolis now."

Or:

"Hi, Jake. *It's* not giving me any more trouble. *It's* been fixed."

What are these speakers talking about? Except for *I* (which always refers to the person speaking) and *you* (which always refers to the person spoken to), the italicized pronouns *(him, he, it)* make little sense. As you can see, when no noun has previously been named, pronouns only hint at meaning. By contrast, you can easily understand the following two statements:

"Hello, Alice. Do you remember *Paul? He's* at Annapolis now."

And:

"Hi, Jake. *Whatever was wrong with my car* isn't giving me any more trouble. *It's* been fixed."

An *antecedent* is the word or words that provide the meaning. An antecedent is a noun *(Paul)* or a phrase or clause functioning as a noun *(whatever was wrong with my car)* that goes before the pronoun and gives it meaning.

In your writing, every pronoun must have a clear antecedent if your reader is to understand your meaning:

My friend Tony gave a *party* last weekend. *It* lasted until four in the morning. Twenty-five *people* attended, and *they* all had a terrific time.

15.a PRONOUNS IN SENTENCES

In a sentence, pronouns can fill the subject slot:

```
 S         V
You       're
```

You're more than a face in the crowd.

Pronouns can be direct objects of verbs:

Our guests love us for our view.

```
   S           V        D OBJ
Our guests    love       us
```

Pronouns can be objects of prepositions:

Come sail with us!

```
         with      us
```

Pronouns also show possession:

Stride Rite fits your baby for each stage of foot development.

your baby

15.b KINDS OF PRONOUNS

I, you, he, she, it, we, and they These words are called *personal pronouns*, not because they refer to people (for example, *it* never refers to a person), but because they refer to the concept of the three persons in grammar (Chapter 14.)

First person: I am the President.
(Subject is the speaker—*I, we*.)

Second person: You are the President.
(Subject is spoken to—*you*.)

Third person: He is the President.
(Subject is spoken about—*he, she, it, they*.)

Nouns usually show plural by adding *-s (pencil/pencils, waiter/waiters, book/books)*. They always add an apostrophe or *'s* to show possession (the pencil*'s* eraser, the waiter*'s* jackets, the book*'s* cover). Unlike nouns, most pronouns change their forms completely to show plural *(I/we, he/they)*. They change to show a subjective form *(I, he, she)*, and objective form *(me, him, her)*, and a possessive form, which never has an apostrophe *(my, his, hers)*.

PERSONAL PRONOUNS

SINGULAR	Subjective pronoun	Objective pronoun	Possessive pronoun	Possessive modifier
First person	I	me	mine	my
Second person	you	you	yours	your
Third person	he	him	his	his
	she	her	hers	her
	it	it	its	its
PLURAL				
First person	we	us	ours	our
Second person	you	you	yours	your
Third person	they	them	theirs	their

Note: *You* is the one personal pronoun that does not change form to show plural. The plural of *you* is *you*. *Youse* and *you all* are not used in standard English.

Problems with personal pronouns Problems with personal pronouns arise when writers are not certain which form to use.

1. *Alice and I/Alice and me*

When the pronoun is part of a compound, writers have trouble deciding whether to use *I* or *me*. Choose the form of the pronoun you would use if the pronoun were alone.

Subject: Alice and *me*/Alice and *I* love Professor Greenberg.
(drop *Alice*) *I* love Professor Greenberg.
YES: Alice and *I* love Professor Greenberg.

Subject: *Her* and the TV repairman/*She* and the TV repairman argued about Mike Wallace.
(drop *the TV repairman*) *She* argued about Mike Wallace.
YES: *She* and the TV repairman argued about Mike Wallace.

Direct object: Professor Greenberg admires Alice and *me*/Alice and *I*.
(drop *Alice*) Professor Greenberg admires *me*.
YES: Professor Greenberg admires Alice and *me*.

Indirect object: Professor Greenberg gave Alice and *I*/Alice and *me* two tickets to *Room Service*.
(drop *Alice*) Professor Greenberg gave *me* two tickets to *Room Service*.
YES: Professor Greenberg gave Alice and *me* two tickets to *Room Service*.

Object of preposition: At the end of the semester, Professor Greenberg took home a bottle of wine from Alice and *I*/Alice and *me*.
(drop *Alice*) At the end of the semester, Professor Greenberg took home a bottle of wine from *me*.
YES: At the end of the semester, Professor Greenberg took home a bottle of wine from Alice and *me*.

As objects of the preposition *between,* both pronouns should be in the objective form: *you* and *me*. Never write *between you and I*.

NO: Between you and *I*, I think Mike Wallace would like to be President.
YES: Between you and *me*, I think Mike Wallace would like to be President.

2. *My mother, she thinks/my mother thinks*

Do not add an unnecessary subject to a sentence in the form of a reinforcing pronoun.

NO: My mother, *she* thinks she's a psychiatrist.
YES: My mother thinks she's a psychiatrist.

3. *We Democrats/us Democrats*

When the pronoun is followed by an appositive, choose the form of the pronoun you would use if the pronoun were alone.

Subject: Every four years, *we* Democrats/*us* Democrats heal our wounds.
(drop *Democrats*) Every four years, *we* heal our wounds.
YES: Every four years, *we* Democrats heal our wounds.

Object: *of we Democrats/of us Democrats*
                   NO: John F. Kennedy embodies the dream not only
                   of we Democrats but of all Americans.
                   YES: . . . the dream not only of *us* Democrats but
                   of all Americans.

4. *It's me/it's I*

It's me is now an accepted form in standard English. Although a linking verb is usually followed by a subjective form, *it's me* is commonly used in informal, and even in formal, speech and writing. To the question "Who is it?" a reply of "It is I" would sound super-correct and unnatural.

It is him (her, them) is commonly used in informal speech and writing, although less often in careful writing. Since language is always in the process of changing, it will be interesting to watch these forms as they make further inroads. Meanwhile, you may want to ask your teacher which form to use. In college writing, your teacher may prefer that you write "it is he," even if you have been saying "it is him" all your life.

Spoken English: I could swear *it was her*.
Careful writing: I could swear *it was she*.

5. *Let he and I/let him and me*

Test which form sounds more comfortable by dropping one of the words after *let*.

Let *him and me/he and I* do the dishes.
Let   do the dishes.   Let   do the dishes.
Let *him* do the dishes.   Let *me* do the dishes.
YES: Let *him and me* do the dishes.

Who, whose, whom, which, and that

These words are *relative pronouns:*

Subjective	Objective	Possessive
who	whom	whose
that	that	
which	which	

Relative pronouns are used to combine sentences:

Jill is the girl. Jill went up the hill.
Jill is the girl __ went up the hill.

Combined sentence:

Jill is the girl *who* went up the hill.

In the combined sentence, the subject–verb unit of the independent clause is *Jill is,* and the subject–verb unit of the dependent clause is *who went.*

Problems with relative pronouns

1. *Who/whom*

Choose *who* or *whom* according to its function in the dependent clause.

NO: Jill is the girl *whom* I think went up the hill.
YES: Jill is the girl *who* I think went up the hill.
(S–V OF DEPENDENT CLAUSE: *who went*)

Who is the subject of *went* and not the object of *I think*. *I think* is an explanatory remark inserted in the sentence.

NO: All night Mark worried about *whom* would win the freestyle.
YES: All night Mark worried about *who* would win the freestyle.
(S–V OF DEPENDENT CLAUSE: *who would win*)

Who is the subject of *would win* and not the object of the preposition *about*. The entire clause *who would win the freestyle* is the object of the preposition *about*.

2. *Whoever/whomever*

Choose *whoever* or *whomever* according to its function in the dependent clause.

NO: The sanitation department will accept *whomever* volunteers.
YES: The sanitation department will accept *whoever* volunteers.
(S–V OF DEPENDENT CLAUSE: *whoever volunteers*)

Whoever is the subject of *volunteers* and not the object of *accept*. The entire clause *whoever volunteers* is the object of *accept*.

Who? Whose? Whom? Which? What?

These pronouns introduce sentences that ask questions:

Who is your agent?
Whose hat are you wearing?
To *whom* is the letter addressed?
What was his name?
Which of these do you like best?

Notice that in questions, the verb precedes the subject, reversing normal statement word order:

      V   S
Who is your agent?

Question pronouns also introduce indirect questions (see p. 362):

I want to know *who* your agent is.
I wonder *whose* hat you are wearing.
She asked to *whom* the letter was addressed.
We never asked *what* his name was.
We want to know *which* of these you like best.

Notice that indirect questions retain subject–verb word order:

            S   V
I want to know who your agent is.

> **WATCH OUT FOR <u>WHAT</u> AND <u>WHICH</u>**
>
> **1.** *What* is a general inquiry.
>
> *What* would you like to eat?
>
> **2.** *Which* asks about one or more of a limited number or group.
>
> *Which* dessert would you prefer, the apple pie or the chocolate mousse?

Problems with question pronouns

1. *Who* is it for?/*Whom* is it for?

Popular usage has been moving toward the elimination of *whom*, especially when it begins a question. Although *whom* used to be required in all positions as object of a verb (*Whom* did you see?) and as object of a preposition (*Whom* is it for?), constructions such as the following, in which *the question word comes first*, are now accepted in standard spoken English and in most forms of written English:

Who is it for?

Nonetheless, in very careful writing (and this may include writing done for your college assignments), the outlook on these constructions is still undergoing change, leaving some readers unsatisfied unless *whom* appears as the object:

Whom is it for?

If you are not sure which form to use in your writing, consult your teacher.

2. For *who?*/For *whom?*

When the question word is not the first word of the question, standard usage has not yet given up using *whom* after a preposition (*To whom* is he married?) and at the end of a question (He saw *whom?*).

Myself, yourself, himself, herself, itself, ourselves, yourselves, and themselves

These words are *reflexive pronouns*. They are used when the subject and object of a sentence (or of a preposition) are identical:

We surgeons pride *ourselves* on our steely nerves.
   (we surgeons = ourselves)
He absented *himself* from the autopsy.
   (he = himself)

'I Did It For Myself'

(I = myself)

The same pronouns are also used for emphasis.

> He *himself* cleaned the house.
> The owners *themselves* couldn't locate the door.

Problems with reflexive pronouns

1. *Hisself/himself*

Never use *hisself, theirself,* or *theirselves.* These forms are not acceptable in standard English.

> NO: They congratulated *theirselves* on the tonsillectomy.
> YES: They congratulated *themselves* on the tonsillectomy.

2. *Louise and me/Louise and I/Louise and myself*

Myself is often mistakenly used instead of *I* or *me* as a polite or super-correct subject or object of a sentence. Do not substitute *myself* for *I* or *me* in an effort to sound grand or polite.

> NO: Louise and *me* won first prize.
> NO: Louise and *myself* won first prize.
> YES: Louise and *I* won first prize.

Although *Louise and myself won* is sometimes heard, *myself* is not fully accepted when it is used as a subject. As the second or later member of a compound object, however, *myself* is accepted in current usage.

> NO: David congratulated Louise and *I.*
> YES: David congratulated Louise and *me.*
> or
>   David congratulated Louise and *myself.*

3. *Than myself/than I* and *as myself/as I*

Standard usage now accepts *myself* after *as* or *than:*

> NO: No one understood the will as clearly as *me.*
> YES: No one understood the will as clearly as *I.*
> or
>   No one understood the will as clearly as *myself.*

This, these, that, and those

This, these, that, and *those* are *demonstrative pronouns.* They point out or show what they refer to. *This* and *these* refer to near objects; *that* and *those,* to distant objects. When the same forms are paired with nouns, they function as modifiers.

Pronouns	**Modifiers**
These are huge.	*These surfboards* are huge.
That sparkles.	*That ring* sparkles.

Problems with demonstrative pronouns

1. *Them workmen/those workmen*

Do not use *them* with a noun to refer to a distant object. *Them* is always a pronoun and stands alone. Use *these* or *those* before a noun.

NO: *Them* workmen will never get finished.
YES: *Those* workmen will never get finished.
NO: He's been watching *them* workmen all day.
YES: He's been watching *those* workmen all day.

2. *This here taxi/this taxi* and *that there woman/that woman*

Do not use *this here* or *that there*. *This* and *that* point out things without assistance.

NO: *This here* taxi is waiting for *that there* woman.
YES: *This* taxi is waiting for *that* woman.

3. *This kind/these kind*

Although modifiers in English do not generally change their form to show plural (*yellow* rose, *yellow* roses), demonstrative modifiers do change form (*this* rose/*these* roses, *that* rose/*those* roses).

We often hear the usage *these kind of shoes* and *those type of earrings* because the emphasis in the speaker's mind is on the plurals, *shoes* and *earrings*, rather than on the singular word *kind* or *type*. Although you are sure to hear these constructions frequently in speech, they are not yet fully accepted in careful writing. Careful constructions match singular *this* with singular *type (this type of earrings)* or plural *these* with plural *types (these types of earrings)*.

Exercise 1

Fill each empty slot in the following sentences with the appropriate form of the pronoun.

Example: Let _____ and me give you the details. (he/him)
Let *him* and me give you the details.

1. Antonio is a tailor _____ I think sews meticulously. (who/whom)
2. They hurried to her house to break the news _____ . (themselves/theirselves)
3. Gordon and _____ jogged to the meeting of Citizens on the Run. (I/myself/me)
4. The commissioner lectured Gordon and _____ about industrial carelessness. (I/myself/me)
5. Benjamin Franklin and _____ adored Paris. (I/me)
6. Between you and _____ , Edward would have made a dandy king. (I/me)

7. Humphrey invited Ida and _____ to tea. (I/myself/me)
8. Watch out for _____ bumps in the road. (those/them)
9. "Who is it?" "It's _____." (me/I)
10. Let Ben and _____ meet her at the Optimistic Café. (I/me)

Exercise 2 Complete the following sentences by inserting the appropriate form of the pronoun into the blank space or by leaving the space blank.

1. Ken and _____ visited our grandmother in the hospital. (I/me)
2. _____ and _____ walked into Room 409 nervously. (He/Him, I/me)
3. Grandma loves Ken and _____ because we always kid around with her. (I/me)
4. She always gives Ken and _____ a big smile. (I/me)
5. Every year, _____ grandchildren fix her breakfast in bed on her birthday. (we/us)
6. Now our grandmother _____ was in bed because she had to be. (/she)
7. Although her illness made _____ grandchildren feel blue, we came in with our usual jokes. (we/us)
8. Between Ken and _____, we soon had her giggling about her stuck bathroom window. (I/me)
9. That tall nurse _____ hated to see us leave. (/she)
10. In spite of being extremely busy, that _____ nurse was always cheerful and kind. (/there)

15.c PRONOUN AGREEMENT

See the confusion that can result when pronouns do not agree with the nouns they refer to:

When a person reads about *an earthquake* in another country, *it* hardly affects them. Of course, they feel bad and upset that people were killed. But because *they* happen in such distant places and because *they* don't affect their own lives, a person is not too traumatized by *it*. If *an earthquake* killed their relatives in California, they would be much more emotionally upset by *them*.

Lack of agreement can create serious problems in writing because whenever the gender, number, and person of the pronoun do not correspond to the gender, number, and person of the antecedent, the reader is suddenly thrown off the trail of the original noun. Although pronouns help you link ideas, they succeed only if you use them consistently. Don't frustrate your reader with chains of pronouns that mysteriously lose their antecedents.

Notice how the chains of reference break down because plural pronouns are used to refer to a singular noun:

a person: them, they, their
an earthquake: they, them, as well as *it*

Here are other sentences in which the pronouns do not agree with their nouns.

NO: When a *student* starts a writing course, *they* may want to keep a journal.
YES: When a *student* starts a writing course, *he* or *she* may want to keep a journal.
Preferred: When *students* start a writing course, *they* may want to keep a journal.

Use the plural wherever possible to avoid the sexist pronoun *he* or the cumbersome *he or she* (pp. 351–353). Pronoun and antecedent agree:

student—he or she
students—they

NO: If *anybody* goes to the admitting office of the hospital, *you* have to fill out *your* Blue Cross forms first.
YES: If *you* go to the admitting office of the hospital, *you* have to fill out *your* Blue Cross forms first.

or

Anybody who goes to the admitting office of the hospital has to fill out *her* Blue Cross forms first.

or

People who go to the admitting office of the hospital have to fill out *their* Blue Cross forms first.

Pronoun and antecedent agree:

You—your
Anybody—her
People—their

As a writer, you can move your ideas forward smoothly and efficiently by using pronouns. Be sure that your pronouns agree with the nouns they refer to, especially in number.

An *indefinite pronoun* does not refer to a specific person or thing. There are many indefinite pronouns:

each	none	one another	something
either	several	another	everybody
neither	all	anybody	everyone
both	any	anyone	everything
some	most	anything	nobody
few	each one	somebody	no one
many	one	someone	nothing
much			

**Problems
with agreement**

1. *One . . . their/one . . . one's*

Never use *their* with *one*. *One* is always singular. Use *one's* or *his* or *her*, or rewrite the sentence:

NO: When a girl's father appears, *one* experiences danger signals going off inside *their* head.

YES: When a girl's father appears, *one* experiences danger signals going off inside *one's* head.

or

When a girl's father appears, danger signals go off inside a guy's head.

2. *Someone . . . their/someone . . . his, her*

Use a singular pronoun when the intent of the antecedent is singular. An indefinite pronoun like *someone* or *everybody* is usually considered to be singular and is referred to by singular pronouns.

NO: *Someone* left *their* umbrella on the chair.

YES: *Someone* left *his* or *her* umbrella on the chair.
       (One person left one umbrella.)

3. *Everybody . . . their/everybody . . . his, her*

NO: *Everybody* drove *their* own car to the field.

YES: *Everybody* drove *his* own car to the field.
       (Each person got into his own car and drove it to the field.)

4. *Some . . . their/everyone . . . they*

Use a plural pronoun when the intent of the antecedent is plural.

Some of the guests left *their* raincoats in the hall.
(Many people left many raincoats.)

Everyone was in the library, but *they* all left to get pizza.
(Although *everyone* looks singular [one] and always uses a singular verb [*was*], this sentence would be illogical if it were carried out in the singular: *Everyone was in the library, but he left to get pizza.*)

WATCH OUT FOR <u>EACH OTHER</u>

Even though these phrases refer to two or more individuals, they are always spelled in the singular:

NO: The students read *each others'* essays.
YES: The students read *each other's* essays.

NO: The sisters rode *one anothers'* bicycles.
YES: The sisters rode *one another's* bicycles.

5. *France and Belgium . . . their/France or Belgium . . . its*

Two nouns joined by *and* require a plural pronoun:

France and Belgium fly *their* flags at the border.

Two singular nouns joined by *or* require a singular pronoun. The intent is alternative—that is, one or the other but not both:

France or Belgium has repainted *its* flagpole at the border.

If one of two nouns joined by *or* is singular and the other is plural, the pronoun usually agrees with the closer noun:

Either the company doctor or the accountants *are* scheduled to receive *their* bonus today.

Either the accountants or the company doctor *is* scheduled to receive *her* bonus today.

15.d CHOOSING A GOVERNING PRONOUN

Point of view is a term writers use to describe the angle of vision they take in their writing. They may use the personal *I* or *we*, address their audience by using *you*, or speak about their subject by using *he, she, it,* or *they*. Choosing a point of view and a personal pronoun to establish that point of view tangles up the best writers at one time or another. There are two main problems in determining which pronoun will govern a piece of writing.

The first problem is the careless shift from one subject to another within a sentence or from one sentence to the next:

When *a person* reads about an earthquake in another country, it hardly affects *you*. Of course, *I* feel bad and upset that people were killed. But because earthquakes happen in such distant places and because they don't affect *your* own life, *people* are not too traumatized by them. If an earthquake killed *my* relatives in California, *you* would be much more emotionally upset by it.

The solution is to rewrite the paragraph using a consistent governing pronoun, or point of view. (See below for alternative ways to rewrite the paragraph.)

Now the second problem arises: Which pronoun should you choose— *I, you, we, he, one, they*—and what will help you decide?

I, of course, is the indispensable pronoun in essay writing. Except in technical writing and in an objective narrative or report, the first-person pronoun is always appropriate. It says you are ready to come forward as the bearer of the news here printed, as the individual who has experienced these events and is willing to be known by name. *We* is also useful, a pronoun that many writing teachers especially recommend as a compromise between the personal, sometimes confessional, *I* and the distanced third-person *he* or *she*.

Can you describe the changes in the effect of the following paragraphs as the governing pronoun changes?

1. When *I* read about an earthquake in another country, it hardly affects *me*. Of course, *I* feel bad and upset that people were killed. But because earthquakes happen in such distant places and because they don't affect *my* own life, *I* am not too traumatized by them. If an earthquake killed *my* relatives in California, *I* would be much more emotionally upset by it.

2. When *we* read about an earthquake in another country, it hardly affects *us*. Of course, *we* feel bad and upset that people were killed. But because earthquakes happen in such distant places and because they don't affect *our* own lives, *we* are not too traumatized by them. If an earthquake killed *our* relatives in California, *we* would be much more emotionally upset by it.

3. When *one* reads about an earthquake in another country, it hardly affects *one*. Of course, *one* feels bad and upset that people were killed. But because earthquakes happen in such distant places and because they don't affect *one's* own life, *one* is not too traumatized by them. If an earthquake killed *one's* relatives in California, *one* would be much more emotionally upset by it.

4. When *a person* reads about an earthquake in another country, it hardly affects *him or her*. Of course, *he* feels bad and upset that people were killed. But because earthquakes happen in such distant places and because they don't affect *his* own life, *he* is not too traumatized by them. If an earthquake killed *his* relatives in California, *he* would be much more emotionally upset by it.

5. When *people* read about an earthquake in another country, it hardly affects *them*. Of course, *they* feel bad and upset that people were killed. But because earthquakes happen in such distant places and because they don't affect *their* own lives, *they* are not too traumatized by them. If an earthquake killed *their* own relatives in California, *they* would be much more emotionally upset by it.

6. When *you* read about an earthquake in another country, it hardly affects *you*. Of course, *you* feel bad and upset that people were killed. But because earthquakes happen in such distant places and because they don't affect *your* own life, *you* are not too traumatized by them. If an earthquake killed *your* own relatives in California, *you* would be much more emotionally upset by it.

15.e SEXIST LANGUAGE

Most writers today are sensitive to the use of sexist language, and few would wish to contribute further to the problem by referring to women in some "second-class" way or by burying women in all-male language. Until recently, people never gave much thought to sentences like these:

A student will enroll in *his* appropriate English course according to *his* placement-test score.

It is the passenger's responsibility to keep *his* ticket visible at all times.

Today, writers pay more attention to the implications of such sentences. To help you avoid sexist language in your own writing as often as possible, we offer these guidelines:

1. Convert from singular to plural whenever your meaning will not be altered by the change in number:

   Students will enroll in *their* appropriate English courses according to *their* placement test scores.

   It is the *passengers'* responsibility to keep *their* tickets visible at all times.

2. Use *he or she* sparingly. You may want to use the whole phrase to show that you are fair, but if used excessively *he or she* becomes cumbersome and tedious to read:

   A student will enroll in *his or her* appropriate English course according to *his or her* placement test score.

   It is the passenger's responsibility to keep *his or her* ticket visible at all times.

3. Omit all unnecessary pronouns:

   Placement-test scores determine which English courses students enroll in.
   Tickets must be kept visible at all times.

4. Use *she* and *her* when the persons referred to are female:

   Everybody in the girls' locker room grabbed *her* sneakers and ran out on the field.

5. Consistently use either *he* and *him* or *she* and *her* when the reference continues over a long passage and none of the above alternatives satisfies you. Although this practice may offend some people, we suggest it in the interest of emphasizing vigorous language, even at the occasional expense of advancing a worthwhile cause.

Exercise 3　All the following sentences employ a sexist term or a sexist form of the pronoun. Rewrite each sentence as gracefully as you can to eliminate the sexist language.

1. The new law firm consists of two real-estate lawyers and a lady lawyer.
2. Invariably, an automated machine displaces a man from his work.
3. Did you ever have a teacher who invited you to her house?
4. A patient in the emergency room—or anybody with him—must supply the triage nurse with his medical-insurance number; she then takes his blood pressure.
5. An architect begins his professional training after he graduates from college.

TIPS FOR WRITERS—AVOIDING SEXIST TERMS

1. *Authoress, poetess,* and *woman doctor* are terms that suggest there is a difference between a real author, a real poet, or a real doctor and a female author, a female poet, or a female doctor. Call an author an author. Similarly, call a Jew a Jew (not a Jewess) and an usher an usher (not an usherette).

2. Avoid using *lady* as the corresponding term for *man.* The female term is *woman.*

3. Some new designations, such as *chairperson,* have caught on. Other sexist terms give way to alternative forms: *workman* becomes *worker; policeman* becomes *police officer.*

4. Be alert to new proposals and combinations:

   S/he has not yet caught on.

   At best, these designations are likely to continue changing and arousing debate.

5. As you think about language, consider your own attitudes, but consider also those of your readers. Until improved strategies arise, our suggestions may help you to offend as few readers as possible and keep your writing free of cumbersome usages.

6. We studied essays by Norman Mailer and Ms. Ellen Goodman; Mailer's work, unlike Ms. Goodman's, was not journalistic, but intense and personal.

7. Any student in need of an adviser should leave his name with the counseling office.

8. A customer must include his phone number on his dry-cleaning ticket.

9. Why don't they post "Men Working" signs on this road?

10. Anyone with Nazi sympathies should think twice about putting down his roots in the United States.

15.f REFERENCE OF PRONOUNS

A pronoun should unmistakably refer to a noun (or a group of words functioning as a noun) stated in the same sentence or in a preceding sentence. Your reader should be able to identify, immediately and with no confusion, the exact antecedent of a pronoun. If there is any chance that your reader will be unsure of the antecedent, replace the doubtful pronoun with an explicitly stated noun or rewrite the sentence.

1. An explicit reference to a noun creates no problems:

   What were the first languages ever spoken? How did *they* sound, and how were *they* structured?
   (*They* clearly refers to *first languages.*)

2. Implied reference to a noun that is not stated in the sentence requires that you rewrite to include the noun:

Confusing: If you are exempted from English 1, *it* won't give you 3 credits. (What won't give you 3 credits? English 1 or exemption from English 1? Add an explicit noun.)

Rewritten: An *exemption* from English 1 won't give you 3 credits.

3. Rewrite if the reference is to a noun in the possessive case:

Confusing: *After Rhoda's analysis of my handwriting, she* respected me more as an artist.

Rewritten: *After Rhoda analyzed my handwriting, she* respected me more as an artist.

4. Replace a vague pronoun with an exact noun:

Confusing: In my old high school, *they* broadcast *Wizard of Oz* records between classes.
(Who are *they?*)

Rewritten: In my old high school, *the media center* broadcast *Wizard of Oz* records between classes.

5. Get rid of unnecessary pronouns:

Wordy: In this comment, *it* says I tend to want to be wordy.

Rewritten: *This comment* says I tend to be wordy.

6. If a pronoun can easily refer to more than one noun, rewrite the sentence to eliminate ambiguity:

Ambiguous: Cliff sat next to an old man and read *his* book.

Cop-out: Cliff sat next to an old man and read *his* (Cliff's) book.

Rewritten: Cliff sat next to an old man and read *a* book.

7. The pronouns *this, that, such,* and *which* can stand for an entire preceding statement as well as for a single, explicit noun:

She wouldn't spend her two-week vacation behind a fishing pole. *That* was the problem, and David knew it.
(The problem was that she wouldn't spend two weeks fishing.)

But don't rely on *this, that, such,* and *which* to link poorly stated ideas and cover incomplete or illogical references:

Confusing: Esther would not admit turning left *which* later became an issue in court.
(What became an issue? Esther's not admitting a left turn or the left turn itself?)

Rewritten: Esther would not admit turning left, and *a left turn* later became an issue in court.

8. To avoid confusion, do not use the pronoun *it* near an *it* used as a structure word. Rewrite to eliminate the structure word:

Confusing: Although your gardenia plant produced flowers last year, *it's* good that *it* has been repotted.

Rewritten: Although your gardenia plant produced flowers last year, *repotting it* was a good idea.

Exercise 4 Rewrite each of the following sentences entirely in the plural. At the conclusion of the exercise, write a sentence explaining why it is preferable to use the plural rather than the singular in these sentences.

Example: Everyone should do as well as they can on the road test.

Rewritten: Candidates for a driver's license should do as well as they can on the road test.

1. If a voter is not properly registered, they may not vote.
2. When a student reads a poem, they often give their own interpretations.
3. Every passenger on this bus has their eyes on the masked gunman with the jar of mayonnaise.
4. Each of them use heavy makeup on their eyes and barbarous language in their conversation.
5. If one tilts one's head to the far left, they can see Orion slipping into view.
6. Johnson and Johnson never cut their knee.
7. The committee worked on its report all weekend, but they still weren't finished by Monday.
8. Everybody in the encounter group stares at their partners for a half hour without touching.
9. Whenever a collection agent calls my dad, they threaten to notify his employer.
10. Everybody waited onstage to do their dance for Mr. Robbins.

Exercise 5 Where necessary, rewrite the following sentences to establish clear reference between pronouns and their antecedents. If a sentence is already clear, mark it *C*.

1. For instance, there are many children living in slum and poor areas with great potentials, but they are not enhanced because they feel they can't get ahead.
2. We've been conditioned to want, to need, to be greedy. We're never satisfied. All this must be changed.
3. I was bombarded with warnings about registration. My friends told me they close down everything by the time freshmen register.
4. Since the French class already had thirty students registered for it, I had to get an overtally slip to enroll, but two other girls wanted them at the same time.

5. Everyone calls me crazy, and that may be true.

6. As people began to think about death, it became ritualized.

7. The governor will allow more water into the rivers which the city says will threaten its water supply.

8. The cottage was situated on a hill which had a splendid view from every window.

9. Walking the dog in the wet grass which I never like is a nuisance in the early mornings.

10. I put the frozen strawberries in the sink because it was leaking.

Exercise 6 Correct any pronoun errors that you find in the following sentences.

1. A college student should be able to buy their lunches at reduced rates.

2. A parent has their eye on you at all times.

3. They brought they tape recorders to the zoo.

4. A person going into business has to decide what kind of business he or she wants to spend their life in.

5. People on airplanes can have the kind of food he or she likes best.

6. Most of us know that if we want to cook nourishing meals you need fresh food.

7. Many people take a holiday to rest yourself.

8. Everyone who parks their car at school is usually late for class.

9. Students can't expect to have a career waiting if you are afraid to speak out and say what's on your mind.

10. Employees have to get to work early if you want a parking place.

Exercise 7 Rewrite the following short paragraphs of sabotaged student writing, using a consistent governing pronoun, or point of view, in each:

1. We are all born into this world as equals, but for various reasons, not all people are treated as equals. This inequality begins when you reach the age of five, for that is when you will enter elementary school. In school, the child is no longer "Mommy's little darling." You now have to prove yourself to the other children and also to your teacher. If one seems different from the other students, they are treated differently, and these differences could be anything: pants, shoes, speech, religion, and so forth. It really doesn't matter. Right from the start, you think that as long as you are different, there is something wrong with you.

2. I know that I will not feel successful if I am not married by the age of twenty-four. Even though with the Women's Lib movement it is now acceptable for you to be thirty years old and unmarried, a person's views can't change. I truly believe that we are all products of our parents' values. And since one's parents have always assumed that they would be married by that age, I have assumed that notion also.

Exercise 8 Rewrite the following paragraphs of sabotaged student writing so that all pronouns agree with their antecedents and the governing pronoun is clear and consistent.

1. Someone once told me that their mother insists on their older brother going along whenever she goes away from home. She knows you can't live that way and develop into an independent person. My friend says that when a person has an older brother, their parents think the brother "watches" the kid sister. She tells me that, on the contrary, they don't care what they do; her brother doesn't even tell anyone they're related.

2. Jerry is a man who knows his blinds—Venetian blinds, I mean. I work for them. They have a blind-cleaning service in Co-op City. If anyone passes Co-op City, you may notice that almost every window of every building has a blind on them. A resident leaves their blinds in the morning, and we do them, or Jerry picks it up. He conducts same-day service for any resident, but they occasionally leave their blinds overnight. Since I am the oldest employee, Jerry gives me a key. They aren't given to anyone else. But one night, he suspected something was going on at night in the shop. They actually thought I wrote the graffiti they found all over the walls.

Exercise 9 Rewrite the following student writing so that each pronoun has a clearly identifiable antecedent with which it agrees. Choose a point of view and keep it consistently. Let one pronoun govern.

When it comes to making a conscious effort to help keep a public place clean, most people just don't make the effort. I'm a maintenance man for a department store. If you did make the effort to help keep the public place where I work clean, we probably wouldn't have a job.

The area that you have to spend the most time cleaning is the employees' lunchroom. They go there during breaks, lunch, and dinner. The maintenance department supplies the waste containers for garbage and the ashtrays for cigarette butts. When they finish their food, they will generally either throw their papers on the floor or leave it on the table. One will on occasion throw their papers in the garbage. An employee who smokes will either flick their ashes on the floor or on their table. Everybody's butts I usually find on the floor and in half-filled soda cups. The cigarettes may be found anywhere other than in the ashtray because you steal the ashtrays or you fill it with gum. Sometimes an employee will remark, "Aren't these people pigs? They don't even clean up after themselves," as they proceed to walk away from their littered table.

Punctuation, Capitalization, and Spelling

chapter
16 | Punctuation and Capitalization

16.a PURPOSES OF PUNCTUATION

> punctuationasweknowittodayisonlyafewhundredyearsoldmanuscriptsofthe
> 1400sdidnthavespacebetweenwordssentencesorparagraphsonewordraninto
> anotherandonesentenceranintoanotherandoneparagraphranintoanother

Did you have trouble reading this? It says: ''Punctuation, as we know it today, is only a few hundred years old. Manuscripts of the 1400s didn't have space between words, sentences, or paragraphs. One word ran into another, and one sentence ran into another, and one paragraph ran into another.'' In those days, no comma, period, capital letter, or paragraph indentation guided readers through a piece of writing. Without punctuation, they had to guess their way through uncharted ground each time they read anything. Many inexperienced writers today don't allow punctuation to work for them. They might as well be back in the 1400s. They're never certain where a comma belongs; they signal full stops where only a pause is needed. Some writers are helpless in the face of a semi-colon or quotation marks and simply never use them. Other writers, to play it safe, over-punctuate and hope for the best:

> Would you believe? that, I, alone (and nobody else!) learned to sail, that sun-fish, out into the bay? I, also, learned to waterski; on ''one'' ski!

Punctuation like this can be as bothersome as none at all. It forces the reader to stop and start and start again to understand the message.

Punctuation shows the relationship between your ideas and emphasizes those ideas that are important. A period at the end of a sentence tells your reader to come to a full stop and *separate* that idea from the next. A semicolon between clauses, on the other hand, tells your reader to *make* connections between your ideas. The same sentence can often be punctuated in several ways, allowing for varied emphases and effects. As a writer, you must punctuate each sentence in the way that best expresses your intent. The key to effective punctuation, therefore, is an understanding of the sentence and its elements as well as an understanding of coordination, subordination, and modification. This subject, built on your understanding of the whole sentence, is divided into four parts:

1. How to see sentences in your writing
2. How to end sentences
3. How to join sentences
4. How to punctuate within sentences

The first part, how to see sentences, is the subject of Chapters 10 through 12. The second, third, and fourth parts, how to end and join sentences and what punctuation is to be used within them, are the subject of this chapter. We will present the currently accepted rules of punctuation and also discuss the options. We encourage you to use punctuation to support your meaning—to join related ideas with a semicolon, to introduce a list with a colon, to show a break in thought with a dash. As you experiment with your writing, you will discover how to call attention to your meaning through effective punctuation.

16.b HOW TO END A SENTENCE

Period Use a period to end a *statement*.

Question mark Use a question mark to end a *direct question*.

Exclamation point Use an exclamation point to end an *emphatic or strongly worded statement:*

Call the police! These hands are a crime!

Use the exclamation point sparingly. You lose emphasis rather than gain it when you overuse exclamation points:

I will not join you for dinner at the Pizza Barn! I hate pizza! I must eat something else, or I'll turn into a cheese-covered pie crust! I've had it!

Your reader says, "Ho-hum. There she goes ranting and raving again," and the exclamation points mean little.

Occasionally, you will use a sentence fragment to emphasize a point. Punctuate the fragment as a complete sentence.

Yes.
Of course!
Really?
That very morning!
Why?

WATCH OUT FOR INDIRECT QUESTIONS

End an indirect question with a period. End a direct question with a question mark.

Do not confuse an indirect question with a direct question.

Direct question: She asked, *"Are you hungry?"*
Indirect question: She asked whether I was hungry.

Learn the differences between a direct question and an indirect question. An indirect question is a statement, not a question, because it includes the idea, but not the exact words, of a question. Since an indirect question is a statement, it ends with a period.

	Direct Question	Indirect Question
VERB	*Are* you hungry?	She asked whether I *was* hungry.
CHANGES	*Will* you *join* us?	She asked if I *would join* them.
PRONOUN	Are *you* hungry?	She asked whether *I* was hungry.
CHANGES	Will *you* join *us?*	She asked if *I* would join *them.*
SUBJECT–	$\overset{v}{Are}$ $\overset{s}{you}$ hungry?	She asked whether $\overset{s}{I}$ $\overset{v}{was}$ hungry.
VERB ORDER	$\overset{v}{Will}$ $\overset{s}{you}$ $\overset{v}{join}$ us?	She asked if $\overset{s}{I}$ $\overset{v}{would}$ $join$ them.

If and *whether* are clues that the sentence is an indirect question and does not end with a question mark.

Exercise 1 Rewrite the following direct questions as indirect questions. Provide a speaker for each indirect question.

Example: Are you hungry?
           Mary Ann asked if I was hungry. (Mary Ann is the speaker.)

1. Do you want to eat lunch now?

2. Do you want to try Burger King or stay with McDonald's?

3. Does Henry like Burger King?

4. Should I go with you or stay with Henry?

5. How are their onion rings?

6. Will you ask for extra pickles?

16.c HOW TO JOIN SENTENCES

There are two ways to join whole sentences when you want to give them equal emphasis.

1. Join sentences with a comma plus a coordinator:
   , and
   , but
   , or
   , nor
   , for
   , yet
   , so

_____ , and _____ .

He hit a home run in the bottom of the ninth, and the crowd went wild.

Their engines may be in the same place, but their prices aren't.

2. Join sentences with a semicolon:

_____ ; _____

He hit a home run in the bottom of the ninth; the crowd went wild.

Knicks Defeat Kings; Haywood Stands Out

When a word such as *however* introduces a second independent clause, use a semicolon before it and a comma after it:

Winfield hit a home run; they lost the game.
Winfield hit a home run; however, they lost the game.

Become familiar with the words and phrases in the following list, and remember that when one of these words or phrases begins a second independent clause, a semicolon goes before the word or phrase and a comma goes after it.

accordingly	however	otherwise
also	indeed	similarly
as a result	in fact	still
at the same time	likewise	that is
besides	meanwhile	then
consequently	moreover	therefore
for example	nevertheless	thus
furthermore	nonetheless	
hence	on the other hand	

Meanwhile, unlike words such as *and* or *when,* can be shifted, with some change in emphasis, to another part of a clause:

> *Meanwhile,* the crowd went wild.
> The crowd, *meanwhile,* went wild.
> The crowd went wild, *meanwhile.*

16.d HOW TO PUNCTUATE WITHIN A SENTENCE

Sentence openers When a word, phrase, or dependent clause precedes the main clause of a sentence, a comma is often used to separate the introductory material from the main clause.

Sentence:	He was an honest man.
Introductory word:	*Yes,* he was an honest man.
Introductory phrase:	*Of course,* he was an honest man.
	Throughout his life, he was an honest man.
Introductory clause:	*When you come to think of it,* he was an honest man.

or

> *Although he was unhappy most of his life,* he was an honest man.

Modern usage is moving away from the comma after introductory material when the introductory words are brief and there is no chance the sentence will be misunderstood if the comma is omitted:

> *In 1492* Columbus sailed the ocean blue.
> *On Elm Street* there is a monument to Columbus.

Sometimes, however, a comma is needed to avoid confusion, even when the sentence opener is brief:

Confusing:	Inside everything smelled of burned wood and smoke.
Clear:	*Inside,* everything smelled of burned wood and smoke.

Note how essential a comma is in the following sentence:

> Before the car had stopped rolling over the officers were out with their hands on their guns.

Without a comma, it sounds as if the car is *rolling over* the officers. The reader must go back to the beginning of the sentence to understand the meaning. A comma following the introductory clause clears up the confusion:

> *Before the car had stopped rolling over,* the officers were out with their hands on their guns.

TIPS FOR WRITERS—USING THE SEMICOLON, THE COLON, AND THE DASH

1. The semicolon (;) doesn't slow your reader down as much as the period does. Both the period and the semicolon separate, but the semicolon suggests a closer union of meaning between two sentences.

> She was in an exuberant mood; her laughter was childlike, bright, brittle.
>
> —Joyce Carol Oates

2. The colon (:) can draw sentences together when the clauses that follow it define or explain the first clause. Consider the following example:

> Life in America has indeed become easier for most people: the car is more efficient than the horse; death in childbirth has sharply fallen; certain diseases have totally disappeared; and even a kind word can be said occasionally for a computer.
>
> —Lillian Hellman

(The four independent clauses that follow the colon explain *how* life in America has become easier.)

3. The dash (—) can also link parts of sentences. Since the material that follows the dash often creates a dramatic interruption, use the dash only when you want this special effect. Observe how the dash is used in this example:

> If you are serious about wanting to improve your writing, the most useful thing you can do is to keep a freewriting diary. Just ten minutes a day. Not a complete account of your day; just a brief mind sample for each day. You don't have to think hard or prepare or be in the mood: without stopping, just write whatever words come out— whether or not you are thinking or in the mood.
>
> —Peter Elbow, *Writing Without Teachers*

Use commas *before* and *after* introductory material that begins a second independent clause.

I usually vacation in Mexico, but, of course, Eddie goes to Hawaii.

Do not let one end of a phrase or clause dangle:

NO: _____, but of course, _____.
NO: _____, but, of course _____.
YES: _____, but, of course, _____.

An alternative way to punctuate this sentence would be to use a semicolon to separate the two clauses:

I usually vacation in Mexico; but, of course, Eddie goes to Hawaii.

> ### TIPS FOR WRITERS—USING COMMAS
>
> Words, phrases, and dependent clauses that follow the main clause of a sentence generally do not require a comma. We pause after a sentence opener, but we sail through the whole sentence when the same material *follows* the main clause. Read these sentences aloud to sense the difference:
>
> | | |
> |---|---|
> | Inside, the cabin was warm. | The cabin was warm inside. |
> | On old Madison Avenue, there is a house of wonders. | There is a house of wonders on old Madison Avenue |
> | If he hadn't lost his wallet, he would have joined us. | He would have joined us if he hadn't lost his wallet. |

Items in a series Words, phrases, and clauses in a series are usually separated by commas:

Wheaties *suits you, courts you, and keeps you hopping.*

He'll use it, enjoy it, and love you for it.

Think of this formula:

a, b, and (or) *c*

Although it is not wrong to drop the comma before the *and* or *or* in a series, it is a good idea to include it; otherwise, you risk running the last two items in the series together. When there are pairs involved, omitting the final comma leads to confusion:

Confusing: The concert featured *Simon and Garfunkel, Elton John, Carly Simon and James Taylor* and *Pete Seeger.*
(It sounds as if Carly Simon and James Taylor and Pete Seeger are a group.)

Clear: The concert featured *Simon and Garfunkel, Elton John, Carly Simon and James Taylor,* and *Pete Seeger.*
(*Pete Seeger* is separated from *Carly Simon* and *James Taylor.*)

Items joined in a series by *and* or *or* do not require commas:

I am taking biology and chemistry and physics next semester.

When the items in a series themselves contain commas, it may be difficult to tell where one item ends and the next begins. To avoid confusion, use semicolons instead of commas to separate the items:

And there were the comings and goings of the other occupants of the house—Morris Fink, muttering malevolently to himself as he swept the front porch;

Yetta Zimmerman herself, clumping down from her quarters on the third floor to give the place her morning onceover; the whalelike Moishe Muskablit, departing in a ponderous rush for his yeshiva, improbably whistling ''The Donkey Serenade'' in harmonious bell-like notes.

—William Styron,
Sophie's Choice

Notice how the dash sets off the series. Two options are available for introducing a long series in a sentence: the colon and the dash. A colon is two periods (:), one on top of the other. A dash, on the typewriter, is two hyphens (--) with no space between them and no space before or after them.

You may use a dash to introduce a series when you do not want the formality of the colon:

There are three sides to every question—*the pro side, the con side, and the inside.*

The colon is most often used to introduce a series. Note how the series is set off from the rest of the sentence.

There are three sides to every question: the pro side, the con side and the inside.

When words like *is, are, like, such as, in,* and *on* introduce a series, they should not be followed by a comma or colon:

NO: The boys in the band are: *John, Jerry, Henry, and Clyde.*
YES: The boys in the band are *John, Jerry, Henry, and Clyde.*

NO: We have traveled in, *Europe, Africa, and Asia.*
YES: We have traveled in *Europe, Africa, and Asia.*

Adjectives in a series

Use a comma between adjectives that independently modify the same noun:

There Is a Rugged, Wild, Exotic, Sprawling, Colorful, and Magnificent America

All the adjectives in the above series describe the noun, *America*. These adjectives are interchangeable and can be separated by the word *and:*

> There is a rugged *and* wild *and* exotic *and* sprawling *and* colorful *and* magnificent America.

Some adjectives, however, fit together to form a phrase and are not separated by a comma:

> We had a *fine old* time.

Here the unit *fine old time* means the same thing as a *good time*. If you separated the two adjectives (*fine* and *old*), you would be saying that you had a fine time and an old time, which doesn't make sense.

Do not separate adverbs from the adjectives that they modify:

> NO: They played a *wildly, competitive* game of poker.
> YES: They played a *wildly competitive* game of poker.
> NO: We saw a *very, funny* movie at the Bijou last night.
> YES: We saw a *very funny* movie at the Bijou last night.

Exercise 2

Punctuate the following passage, which contains items in series. Distinguish between those adjectives in a series that need to be separated by commas and those that belong together and require no commas.

> This summer American families will be holding reunions in the Bronx in Georgia in El Paso and in the Caribbean islands. Toddlers eating hot dogs will be introduced to great-aunts in wheelchairs great-uncles will be cooing to grand-nephews in baby carriages and middle-aged cousins meeting for the first time will be curiously looking each other over for family resemblances. Ever since the publication of Alex Haley's book *Roots* and the television series about it families are calling together their dispersed members in an effort to promote personal worth record family history and—especially among black families—emphasize racial pride. Prizes are offered to the ones who come the farthest bring the largest delegation have the most sets of twins wear the funniest T-shirts or draw the most detailed genealogy charts. High-school gymnasiums backyard patios apartment living rooms and wide-open national parks are some of the scenes for gathering in the clan depending on the size and financial ability of the attending members.

Parenthetical expressions A parenthetical expression is a word, phrase, or clause that interrupts the flow of a sentence to make an additional point. When a parenthetical expression falls within a sentence, it must be sealed off at both ends by *a pair of commas, a pair of dashes,* or *a pair of parentheses:*

Sentence: The local school has been at the heart of the community.

Add a parenthetical expression with:

Commas: The local school has been, *and usually still is,* at the heart of the community.

Parentheses: The local school has been *(and usually still is)* at the heart of the community.

Dashes: The local school has been—*and usually still is*—at the heart of the community.

—Margaret Mead

Remember to seal off the parenthetical expression at *both* ends when it falls within the sentence. Do not let one end hang loose:

NO: The local school has been, *and usually still is* at the heart of the community.

NO: The local school has been *and usually still is,* at the heart of the community.

Use commas to set off parenthetical expressions that interrupt the sentence only slightly:

He was, *after all,* an honorable man.
They were all, *I would say,* honorable men.

Use dashes when you want to emphasize parenthetical material:

The talk of brassieres or no brassieres, who washes the dinner pots, whether you are a sex object—*whatever the hell that is*—has very little meaning unless the woman who slams the door can buy herself dinner and get out of a winter wind.

—Lillian Hellman

Use parentheses when you want to separate parenthetical material from the mainstream of the sentence, thereby subordinating its importance. Parentheses ( ) come in pairs; never use one without the other.

Seymour spent twenty years *(from 1947 to 1967)* in Sausalito.
I often wonder *(don't you?)* if he needs all that underwear.

No punctuation marks are used *before* parentheses, but a comma or end punctuation *follows* parentheses if necessary:

After Sam and Harriet were married (April 24, 1965), they moved to San Francisco and opened a coffeehouse.

When the parenthetical material is set off as a separate sentence, use the necessary end punctuation within the parentheses:

Bill Rodgers won the New York City marathon. *(This is his fourth win in a row.)*

The matter of choosing how to set off a parenthetical expression is up to you, the writer. Practice setting off material in the same sentence in different ways to discover which pair of punctuation marks works most effectively.

Modifiers Use commas to seal off modifiers that follow the word or words they describe when the modifiers *are not essential* to the meaning of the sentence:

The police chief, *with ease,* recommended the promotion.
The police chief   recommended the promotion.

My brother, *who usually spends Sundays reading the paper,* offered
to help me paint the house.
My brother offered
to help me paint the house.

Study the way the commas work to seal off the modifiers in the following sentences:

Grandmother Skinner, *whose sugar cookies never turned out the same twice and whose jars of fruits and vegetables exploded,* used to pinch her son's nose to give it a distinguished look. Grandfather Skinner, *a sometime housepainter,* lacked ambition; the parts of his unsuccessful stove polisher filled the hayloft. Grandmother Burrhus, *who plied the young with apple pie and maple sugar,* was a worrier. Grandfather Burrhus, *who worked for the railroad,* apparently gave her cause to worry.

—Elizabeth Hall

Do not use commas to set off modifiers that *are essential* to the meaning of the sentence:

Hot dogs *steamed in beer* have a gourmet flavor.
(Only hot dogs *steamed in beer* have that flavor.)

Appositives Use commas to set off most appositives from the nouns they describe:

Monty Python, *King of the Goons,* is a nutty guy.
James, *my only brother,* flew in from Brazil yesterday.

For an explanation of appositives, see Chapter 11, page 269.

Exercise 3 Write five sentences in which you use modifying clauses that are essential to the meaning of the sentences.

Example:

THE MAN WHO CONTROLS CORPORATIONS OUGHT TO BE ABLE TO CONTROL HIS OWN CAR.

(The man is not *any* man; he's the one *who controls corporations*. No commas are needed in the sentence.)

Now write five sentences in which you use modifying clauses that are *not* essential to the meaning of the sentences.

> Example: John F. Kennedy, who died in 1963, sparked the imagination of the nation's youth.
> (Here the modifying clause *who died in 1963* is not essential to the meaning of the sentence: *Kennedy sparked the imagination of the nation's youth.*)

Nouns of direct address   Use commas to seal off the name of a person or persons directly spoken to:

All right, *gang,* let's go.
Okay, *Joe,* you're on your way.
Sharon, will you brush your hair?
Please sit up straight in that chair, *Lauren.*

Nice going, Shorty.

Failure to set off nouns of direct address results in confusion:

NO: Please follow Sharon.
YES: Please follow, *Sharon.*

NO: Joe Margaret is already here.
YES: *Joe,* Margaret is already here.

TIPS FOR WRITERS—COMMA SENSE

USE A COMMA (OR COMMAS):

1. To separate independent clauses joined by a coordinator (p. 363):

He hit a home run, and the crowd went wild.

2. To separate items in a series (p. 366):

Words: Steven loves apples, peaches, pears, and plums.

Phrases: A pilot's business is with the wind, with the stars, with night, with sand, with the sea.

Short clauses: Drivers shout, dogs bark, and the race is on!

3. After sentence openers (p. 364):

Of course, he was an honest man.

4. To set off parenthetical expressions (p. 369):

They were all, I would say, honorable men.

5. To set off nonessential modifiers (p. 370):

The police chief, with ease, recommended the promotion.

6. To set off nouns of direct address (p. 371):

Okay, Joe, you're on your way.

7. To set off appositives (p. 370):

Monty Python, King of the Goons, is a nutty guy.

8. To set off dates and addresses (p. 373):

Ross was born on January 13, 1939, in New York, New York.

DO NOT USE COMMAS:

1. Do not use a comma every time you use an *and*.

2. Do not use a comma between two words or two phrases joined by a coordinator:

NO: Michael loves bananas, and yogurt.
YES: Michael loves bananas and yogurt.
NO: Janet signed, and delivered the letter.
YES: Janet signed and delivered the letter.

3. Do not begin a new line with a comma.

4. Do not use a comma to separate the elements of a compound subject or a compound verb:

NO: Janet, and Allan visited their family in New York.
YES: Janet and Allan visited their family in New York.
NO: They often visited the lighthouse, and watched the fishing boats return.
YES: They often visited the lighthouse and watched the fishing boats return.

5. Do not use a comma after a coordinator that joins two clauses:

NO: I've worked very hard this year, but, my bank account is still low.
YES: I've worked very hard this year, but my bank account is still low.

6. Do not use a comma alone to separate independent clauses (see Chapter 12, pp. 275–277, for a discussion of run-ons).

NO: He hit a home run in the bottom of the ninth, the crowd went wild.
YES: He hit a home run in the bottom of the ninth, and the crowd went wild.

7. Do not use a comma to separate the subject from its verb:

NO: The orange-feathered hat with the bullet through the rim, belonged to Jesse James.
YES: The orange-feathered hat with the bullet through the rim belonged to Jesse James.

8. Do not separate a verb from its *that* clause:

NO: He believed, that men should be equal to women.
YES: He believed that men should be equal to women.

Dates, locations, and addresses Use commas to seal off dates, addresses, and locations when they provide additional information in a sentence.

DATES AND LOCATIONS

Ross was born on *January 13, 1939,* in *New York, New York.*
(1939 identifies the year in which the specific January 13 occurred.)

Ross was born in *New York, New York.*
(The second New York identifies the state of New York.)

When the day of the month comes before the month or when the day of the month is not given, commas may be omitted:

Ross was born on *13 January 1939* in *New York.*
Ross was born in *January 1939* in *New York.*

ADDRESSES

Linear: 304 Elm Street, Pittsburgh, Pennsylvania 15213
          504 Weaver Street, New York, New York 10024
Block: 304 Elm Street
          Pittsburgh, Pennsylvania 15213
(Note: There is no comma between the state and the zip code.)

Quotations Quotation marks are always used in pairs to set off the exact words of a speaker or writer. Use a comma or a colon after the remarks that introduce the quotation:

Benjamin Franklin said, ''There never was a good war or a bad peace.''

But he is probably best known for these words: ''Early to bed and early to rise, / Makes a man healthy, wealthy, and wise.''

(When you incorporate lines of verse in your prose, use a slash [/] to show where one line of verse ends and another begins.) Notice that the colon separates the quotation from the opening statement and draws attention to it. The comma allows the quotation to be integrated into the sentence. For further information about quoting sources, see Chapter 18.

Using quotation marks with other marks of punctuation is often tricky. Follow these guidelines:

1. Place introductory commas and colons before the opening quotation marks:

Franklin said, ''There never was a good war or a bad peace.''
Franklin said: ''There never was a good war or a bad peace.''

2. Always place periods and commas inside the closing quotation marks:

Franklin said, ''There never was a good war or a bad peace.''
Franklin said, ''There never was a good war or a bad peace,'' and he also said, ''Little strokes fell great oaks.''

3. Always place semicolons and colons outside the closing quotation marks:

Franklin said, ''There never was a good war or a bad peace''; he also said, ''Little strokes fell great oaks.''

4. Place question marks and exclamation points inside the closing quotation marks when they are part of the quotation:

Juliet called out, "O Romeo, Romeo! wherefore art thou Romeo?"
"O Romeo, Romeo!" Juliet cried, "wherefore art thou Romeo?"

5. Place question marks and exclamation points outside the closing quotation marks when they apply to the whole sentence and are not part of the quotation:

Did Shakespeare say, "Uneasy lies the head that wears a crown"?

6. Do not use two punctuation marks at the end of a sentence. When the quotation ends with a question mark or an exclamation point, the period that would ordinarily end the sentence is omitted:

NO: Juliet called out, "O Romeo, Romeo! wherefore art thou Romeo?"
YES: Juliet called out, "O Romeo, Romeo! wherefore art thou Romeo?"

7. Set off with commas any statements that identify the speaker:

"There never was a good war," said Franklin, "or a bad peace."

Note where the commas are placed:

"_____," said Franklin, "_____."

8. Use single quotation marks to set off a quotation within a quotation:

An admirer of Eleanor Roosevelt said, "We came to know by heart her maxims: 'You can do it,' 'People matter,' 'Try, try again,' 'We must remember those less fortunate than ourselves.'"

—*Remarkable American Women*

DIALOGUE Use quotation marks to set off dialogue—that is, conversation between two or more people. Notice that a *new* paragraph begins each time the speaker changes. Note also that commas and periods set off tag statements that identify the speaker.

"How long will you be gone?" she asked faintly.

"Two weeks," he replied with a wide smile. He went on business trips to Boston like a sailor going on shore leave after months of deprivation on the high seas.

"Business?"

"Mostly. I don't know if I told you—we're thinking of moving to Boston."

Scandalized, Ginny looked at him quickly. "How could you? This is our *home*."

"Not mine it isn't. I've always hated this town. You know that. I intended to stay here just a year, as part of my training for a job in Boston. But then I met your mother, who couldn't bear the thought of leaving Hullsport. Though God only knows why.''

"But how could you just forfeit thirty-five years of memories?'' Ginny wailed, knowing the incredible difficulty she experienced in letting go of anything out of her past, however objectionable.

"Easily. Very easily,'' he said with a laugh.

—Lisa Alther, *Kinflicks*

BRACKETS Use brackets to insert your own words into a quotation. You may draw in a bracket or use the slant key on the typewriter /   / and then add the edges by hand *[   ]*.

"He [Toscanini] used to sing along with the orchestra when he conducted.''

Use brackets to provide a correction:

"The play ran for sixty-four [actually sixty-five] weeks on Broadway.''
(The number *sixty-four*, according to the writer using this quotation, is an error, which he corrects in the brackets.)

To point out that a misspelling or wrong grammatical form was part of an original text, enclose the Latin word *sic*, which means ''thus,'' in brackets:

"His was an unneccesary [*sic*] crime.''

Use brackets to insert an incidental element into an already parenthetical phrase:

(After all the talk [and there was a great amount of talk], she did what she wanted, anyway.)

ELLIPSES Use an ellipsis mark, which is three spaced dots, to show that words have been omitted from a quotation.

Walter said, "I haven't seen her since . . . last summer. How is she?''

If words have been omitted immediately following the end of a quoted sentence, the ellipses follow the period, for a total of four dots.

Ellipses . . .
Period plus ellipses. . . .

Walter said, "I haven't seen her since she had her appendix out last summer. . . .''

If the material omitted from a quotation contains a period, use ellipses with a period.

Walter said, "I haven't seen her. . . . How is she?''

When quoting from a longer passage, use the ellipsis mark to show that you have used only part of the quote:

One of the functions of a society is to make its inhabitants feel safe, and Americans devote more of their collective resources to security than to any other need. Yet Americans do not feel safe, despite (or because of) shotguns in the closet and nuclear bombers patrolling overhead.

—Philip Slater

"One of the functions of a society is to make its inhabitants feel safe. . . . "

or

"One of the functions of a society is to make its inhabitants feel safe. . . . Yet Americans do not feel safe. . . . "

Exercise 4 Provide the necessary quotation marks and other marks of punctuation in the following passage.

Ralph turned over and sat up in bed.
What are you doing Meg mumbled.
Just getting up for awhile I can't sleep Ralph answered.
Where are you going she asked.
I need some air I'll just walk around the block.
What time is it asked Meg as she turned on the light.
Two o'clock.
That late. If you take a walk you'll just wake up more she argued.
Just a few minutes Ralph yawned.
Wait I'll go with you.
But you're tired Ralph rubbed his eyes.
I'll go with you. We can walk down to Sam's and get some ice cream.
But it's two o clock he said.
Suddenly I'm not tired Meg answered throwing off the covers.
I think I'm sleepy said Ralph lying back down.
Terrific said Meg now what am I supposed to do I'm wide awake.

Other uses of quotation marks

TITLES Use quotation marks for the titles of parts of books and of works found in published volumes.

Chapter: "Punctuation and Capitalization"
Article: "The Airline that Shook the Industry"

Use quotation marks for the titles of short stories, poems, and songs:

Short story: "Uncle Wiggily in Connecticut"

Poem:	"Ode on a Grecian Urn"
	"Kubla Khan"
Song:	"Battle Hymm of the Republic"
	"Burning Down the House"
Television program:	"Saturday Night Live"
Radio program:	"All Things Considered"

IRONY Use quotation marks for irony (when you mean the opposite of what you say):

> You certainly are a "big help."

Italics Use italics (which in printed type are slanted letters) for the titles of books, newspapers, magazines, plays, movies, long poems, ships, trains, airplanes, foreign words, or words used as words. Italics can also be used for emphasis. In written or typed papers, words to be italicized are underlined.

Books:	*The Catcher in the Rye*
	Memories, Dreams, Reflections
Newspapers:	*New York Times* or New York *Times* (either is acceptable)
Magazines:	*Playboy*
	Time
Plays:	*Hamlet*
	'Night, Mother
Movies:	*Gone with the Wind*
Long poems:	*Paradise Lost*
Ships:	*Titanic*
	Queen Elizabeth II
Trains:	*Super Chief*
Airplanes:	*Spirit of St. Louis*
Foreign words and phrases:	**It's *amore* at first sip.**
Words used as words:	The word *and* is a powerful coordinator.
	Because often introduces a dependent clause.
Emphasis:	**"Some mornings I hate my skin."**

Exercise 5 Supply the necessary quotation marks and italics in the following passage, which is a brief biography of Elvis Presley, the rock singer, who died in 1977.

Elvis Aron Presley began his rock and roll career touring rural areas of Tennessee under the name The Hillbilly Cat. He had a clever manager, a non-military Colonel Thomas A. Parker, who promoted him locally and then catapulted him onto the national scene. In 1956, Presley's first great hit, Heartbreak Hotel, was released by RCA. Exploding on the musical consciousness of America's youth, this ballad has been described by the New York Times as a blood-stirring dirge about love and loneliness. It pounded on every jukebox and radio station across America, selling finally 2 million copies. In the same year, Heartbreak Hotel was swiftly followed by other songs, Don't Be Cruel, Hound Dog, Blue Suede Shoes, and Love Me Tender. In 1957, Presley began his film career in a movie also entitled Love Me Tender, which, although blasted by the critics, grossed brilliantly at the box office.

But Presley was not a lucky kid who happened to have a style that caught on. In the years before RCA, he worked tirelessly in now historic recording sessions at Sun Records Studios in Memphis, blending into his styles and technique white country music and black blues rhythms. Although his career declined after the Beatles came on the scene, most people's earliest recollections of Elvis Presley will remain those of his first wildly mobbed concerts, and of the gyrating, satin-shirted Elvis the Pelvis who seized the imagination of America's young people in the late 1950s.

16.e PUTTING PUNCTUATION TO WORK

Putting punctuation to work means using punctuation marks to draw attention to your meaning. You make decisions about separating or joining ideas; about emphasizing or deemphasizing material; about clarifying, which is what you're always after. Study the ways the punctuation marks—commas, dashes, and colons—are used in the following biographical sketch of Eleanor Roosevelt from a *Life* magazine Special Report, *Remarkable American Women*.

It wasn't what Eleanor Roosevelt said nor even what she did that people remember best about her. It was what she was—a woman of unfailing ◄——— Dash introduces series.
grace and generosity of spirit, a ◄——————— Commas separate parts of the series.
survivor who outlasted the pain and controversy of her life, and a tireless partisan of the best in herself and in all the rest of us. "She not only ◄——————— Quotation marks set off exact words
believed in but lived all the diffi- of the admirer.
cult, optimistic bluestocking vir- ◄——————— Comma separates adjectives in a
tues," wrote one admirer after her ◄ series.
death in 1962. "We came to know by Comma sets off words that identify
heart her maxims: 'You can do it,' ◄ speaker.
Colon introduces quotations.

'People matter,' 'Try, try again,' 'We must remember those less fortunate than ourselves.'" Shy and awkward as a girl, an orphan at nine, she overcame a painful childhood and gradually emerged as a personality as forceful and vivid as her husband. She brought a new dimension to the role of First Lady: going everywhere in Depression America, inspecting coal mines, visiting ghettos, defending the rights of minorities at a time when it was rash for any public figure to speak up for blacks. Her syndicated column, "My Day," and her radio program brought her presence into every American home. She represented the U.S. at the United Nations, traveled the world incessantly and at home extended herself to meet as many people as she could squeeze into her schedule. "She was as indigenous to America as palms to a Florida coastline," a journalist wrote. In many ways she acted as our conscience, and as such was resented as well as cherished. But she earned the ultimate tribute: our lives were better because they were touched by hers.

Single quotation marks set off quotations within a quotation.

Comma sets off introductory modifier (*shy and awkward*).

Comma sets off a second introductory modifier (*an orphan at nine.*)

Colon introduces series of examples that explain how Mrs. Roosevelt brought a new dimension to the role of First Lady.

Quotes around title of newspaper column. Commas set off name of column, which is an appositive identifying the column.

Comma separates series of verbs (*represented, traveled,* and *extended*).

Colon introduces sentence that defines the *ultimate tribute*.

Exercise 6 The following student writing has been overpunctuated for this exercise. Which punctuation can you remove and why?

In these times of industry, and computer technology, have we lost our pride, in tradition? Christmastime, for example, is supposed to be a time of giving, and sharing. But, big business, has distorted Christmas. How can you get into the Christmas spirit, if thousands of people are shopping; and all they want to do, is beat you, to the cashier's counter? Anyone, who has tried to shop during the three days' before Christmas, knows that it can turn you, into a nervous wreck.

Thanksgiving has also, been distorted. It is supposed to be a time, of thanks. For all, our successes, whether big or small; we should be thankful. It should be a day, when we do remember, how fortunate we are. But, do you know what we do? These days, you'll find most Americans glued to the television, watching the Kansas City Chiefs, and the New England Patriots in a football game!

16.f CAPITALIZATION

Capitalize the following:

1. The first word of every sentence and every sentence within a sentence:

Seeing is believing.
He said, "Seeing is believing."

2. Names of persons, their titles, and their title abbreviations:

	Do not capitalize
Henrietta Smith	woman
Father Wilhelm	father
Saint Augustine	saint
Queen Elizabeth II, or the Queen	queen
President Lincoln, or the President	president

Use capitals when a specific king, president, or the like is referred to or addressed: *The King has arrived to meet the President.* Use capitals when a title is used as a name: *You may leave the convent any time, Sister.*

John Williams, M.D.	doctor
Susan Wilson, Ph.D.	
Margaret Roberts, D.D.S.	dentist
Mr. and Mrs. Berger	
Mother (when used as a name)	my mother
Father (when used as a name)	my father

(Example: *It isn't often that Father visits. It isn't often that John visits.* But: *It isn't often that my father visits.*)

3. Names of specific places and locations:

	Do not capitalize
Willow Street	street
Locust Avenue	avenue
Westchester County	county
Pennyslvania	state
Switzerland	country
Monongahela River	river
Lake Minnewaska	lake
Empire State Building	building
World Trade Center	center

| University of Texas | university |
| Hunter College | college |

4. Specific languages:

English
French

5. Course titles:

	Do not capitalize
Developmental Psychology	psychology
Sociology 101	sociology

6. Religious affiliations:

Catholic
Protestant
Jewish

7. Specific groups, organizations, institutions, and businesses:

Federal Trade Commission
Supreme Court
Alcoholics Anonymous
Xerox Corporation

8. Months, days of the week, and holidays:

	Not usually capitalized
January, September	
Monday, Wednesday	spring
Thanksgiving	summer
Memorial Day	fall
Lincoln's Birthday	winter

9. Titles of works. Capitalize the first and last words in titles and all other words except short words such as *a, an, the, and, of,* and *in.*

"I've Been Working on the Railroad"
Death of a Salesman

10. Names of events or periods in history:

Revolutionary War
Age of Reason

11. Adjectives derived from names:

Shakespearean
English
Lincolnesque

Exercise 7 Supply all the necessary punctuation and capitalization in the following passage by Ben Patrusky, which describes some of the dangers of excessive drinking.

drowning in drink

drinking may help drown your sorrows but excessive drinking before going swimming may literally drown you. according to dr. park elliott dietz and susan p. baker of johns hopkins medical institution alcohol may be involved in as many as half of the 6500 accidental drownings which occur each year in the united states.

dietz and baker based their conclusion on a study of victims who drowned in maryland in 1972 and in baltimore from 1968 to 1972. of the adults who died in baltimore 47 percent had positive blood-alcohol tests. swimming and drinking just don't mix.

chapter 17 | Spelling

17.a PRACTICAL SUGGESTIONS

If you're a writer who has a spelling problem, you may feel as if you have taffy stuck to your fingers. Just as taffy moves from finger to finger, so a spelling error appears to move from word to word. Whatever you do to get rid of it, you're stuck with your problem. And that's not all. Because, unfortunately, if you have trouble spelling, you may also have trouble writing a paper. Rather than encourage yourself to write through a first draft, you stumble over every word because you're worried about spelling. Worse still, you restrict yourself to "safe" words— words you're certain you can spell—often giving up the word you're really after and opting for a weak substitute. *Nice* won't make it if you're after *scrupulous*. *Awful* is a cop-out if you really want *obnoxious*.

Being a shaky speller doesn't mean you're a poor writer. Many effective writers have had spelling problems. Winston Churchill and Franklin Roosevelt, for example, had trouble spelling, and Herman Melville and F. Scott Fitzgerald were such poor spellers that they relied on their editors to correct their misspellings.

Since you don't have an editor handy, learn to become your own editor. Don't let your difficulty in spelling keep you from writing; spelling is one technicality you can confront in the final stages of your writing. This chapter presents some practical suggestions for handling spelling problems.

1. *Write continuously.*   Keep on writing during a freewriting exercise, in a journal entry, or on a first draft of an essay without pausing to worry about spelling. You can check your spelling when you're revising and proofreading.

2. *Use your first-choice word.*   Your uncertainty about spelling shouldn't prevent you from using the word of your choice. Use the word, and spell it the way it sounds. Underline each word you're unsure of so that you won't forget to check the correct spelling when you're revising or proofreading.

3. *Find out how to spell a word.*   If you know the beginning letters of a word, you'll probably be able to find the word in your college dictionary. But the dictionary won't help if you look for *psychology* under the *s*'s. Don't give up. Ask someone—friend, relative, or instructor—for help. Your instructor will respect your initiative and supply you with the beginning *psy-* for *psychology*. Above all, don't be afraid to ask.

4. *Keep a record of your misspellings.*   Once you find out how to spell a word, record it in a notebook or file box. Keep a list of unusual word beginnings. Learn that the sound *n* can be *pn*, as in *pneumonia; gn,* as in *gnaw, gnarl,* and *gnome;* and *kn,* as in *knew, knight,* and *knob.* Remember that *ps* equals the *s* sound in *psychic, psychosis, psychologist,* and *psychiatrist.* Remember that *ch* equals the *sh* sound in *Chicago, chivalry,* and *chateau.*

5. *Write legibly.*   Handwriting can disguise a spelling problem. You may think you're hiding your problem from your readers by blurring letters, hoping they will gloss right over the misspellings. The fact is, you're hiding your problem from *yourself* as long as you avoid it.

6. *Listen to the pronunciation of words.*   Pronunciation may be at the heart of your spelling problem. We tend to spell words as we hear ourselves speak them or hear them spoken by others. Often, letters that are not pronounced when a word is spoken are also omitted when the word is written down. You might ignore the *g* in *recognize,* for example, because you pronounce it *reconize.* The same is true of added letters. If you pronounce *height* with a *th* on the end, you might spell the word *heighth* when you use it in your writing.

    When you hear a word but are uncertain of its spelling, record it. Write it down as it sounds, and then ask someone how to spell it. Pronounce the word to *yourself* the way it is spelled as a memory trick. Pronounce the *s* and *w* in *sword* even though the *w* is silent. Pronounce the *d* in *Wednesday* to help you remember that it's there.

    Try mentally to break a word into syllables. Say the word to yourself, separating and emphasizing each syllable. Say SEP-A-RATE and EM-PHA-SIZ-ING. Check in a dictionary.

7. *Read everything.*   Read signs, advertisements, coupons, labels, ticket stubs, as well as newspapers, magazines, and books. When you see a spelling that puzzles you, write it down.

Many misspellings result from unfamiliarity with the written language. You've undoubtedly been surprised by seeing a word or phrase printed for the first time when you've thought it was written differently. One woman, for example, thought that the phrase ''grain of salt'' was written ''grand assault.'' Although she understood how to use the phrase, she occasionally wondered why it was a military term and concluded that it had something to do with a great battle. When she saw the written words ''grain of salt,'' she realized that what she had seen in her mind didn't correspond with the written words at all. A man who thought the phrase ''up and at 'em'' was written ''up and Adam'' wondered what Adam had to do with the idea—until he saw the phrase in writing. And in an English class, when students were asked to describe their bedrooms, several who had never seen the written phrase ''chest of drawers'' wrote ''chester drawers'' or ''chesto drawers.''

On the other hand, you may know perfectly well how to pronounce a word but may mispronounce it when you see it in writing. When you say the word *colonel,* you may pronounce *kernel,* but when you see the word in print, you may pronounce it *col-o-nel.* Since you never have matched the written and spoken forms of words, you are likely to go on spelling the word as you say it. The more you familiarize yourself with the written language, the better you'll be able to match written and spoken words.

8. *Exercise your spelling power.*   Play word games. Try your hand at crossword puzzles, where an omitted or extra letter will strike you out. Try word-search puzzles, where you must find words by reading forward, backward, up, down, and diagonally.

9. *Devise ways to remember tricky words.*   Remember how to spell a word by your own associations. Remember words within words: record the *dance* in atten*dance,* the *par* in se*par*ate, the *ear* in h*ear* and h*ear*d (the words that have to do with listening.) Remember words that rhyme with each other; *loose* rhymes with *goose,* and *tough* rhymes with *rough* but not with *cough.*

Draw a picture on paper or in your mind, if you will, to remember the *dance* in atten*dance,* the *ear* in h*ear.* Devise whatever associations will work for you.

10. *Find a way to diagnose your spelling problem.*   It may be that you misspell only a few words; it may be that your big problem is using *ie* instead of *ei;* it may be that you're not certain when to drop a final *e* or double a consonant before adding an ending. Make lists of the words you misspell, and see if there are any patterns. Perhaps there is a writing or reading workshop in your college where a tutor will help you diagnose your spelling problem.

Your spelling problem may actually be a reading problem. You may not have learned to read phonetically—that is, to recognize the letters that stand for certain sounds. You may transpose or reverse letters. If you keep track of your spelling errors, you may find that you're making the same kinds of letter-reversal errors in many words. You may need to work with letters made from sandpaper, tracing the letter over and over again with your fingertips until you begin to *sense* the formation of letters in particular words. Above all, find out all you can about your problem. Reading problems inhibit not just your spelling; they obviously inhibit your reading as well, so you have two problems instead of one. If there is no one around who can help you diagnose your problem, gather your own data and try to determine the root of your problem yourself.

When you know what your problem is, check your papers—word by word, page by page—to spot your misspellings. The work may be tedious at the beginning, but as you proceed, you'll be able to spot the spelling errors more quickly and master your problem.

11. ***Proofread every paper.***   Read all your papers aloud. If you type, you're bound to miss a letter or two. Even the strongest spellers make mistakes. Your reading aloud will move you through the paper more slowly than your silent reading, and you will be more likely to catch misspellings. Your voice will also pick up the pauses and hesitations and stops that you may want to punctuate differently. (See Chapter 6, pp. 133–134, for a discussion of proofreading.)

12. ***Don't give up.***   A spelling problem, especially a serious one, demands work and time if it is to be overcome. Changing spelling habits doesn't happen easily or quickly, but if you confront your problem seriously, you will see results. Don't give up.

17.b SPELLING RULES

In the following pages, we present spelling rules that will guide you through some of the most troublesome spots in the English language. Before studying the rules, however, you need a brief spelling vocabulary:

1. A *vowel* is one of these sounds: *a, e, i, o,* or *u.* (The letter *y* often represents a vowel sound; for example, in *lazy* and in *easy.*)

2. A *consonant* is a sound other than the vowels (*a, e, i, o, u*).

Example: *k, m, p, s, t.*

3. A *syllable* is a letter or a group of letters that represents a unit of sound with one vowel sound. *Every* syllable must have one vowel sound.

Example: *Great* is a one-syllable word because the *ea* sounds like one vowel, *a.*

See your dictionary for a full explanation of syllabification.

4. A *root* is the main part of a word to which a prefix or a suffix may be added.

	PREFIX	ROOT	SUFFIX		
Example:	dis	appear	ance	=	DISAPPEARANCE

5. A *prefix* is a group of letters that comes before a root.

PREFIX   ROOT

Example: un   +   wise   =   unwise

6. A *suffix* is a letter or a group of letters that comes after the root.

ROOT   SUFFIX

Example: wise   +   ly   =   wisely

Adding prefixes

Add a prefix to the *whole* root word:

Words like <u>unnecessary</u>

Prefix	+	Root word	=	Word
co	+	operate	=	cooperate
grand	+	daughter	=	granddaughter
il	+	legal	=	illegal
im	+	mature	=	immature
mis	+	spell	=	misspell
un	+	necessary	=	unnecessary

Words like <u>roommate</u>

Retain all the letters of both words when a word is made up of two words:

over	+	rate	=	overrate
room	+	mate	=	roommate
with	+	hold	=	withhold

Adding suffixes

Most spelling problems occur when you add a suffix to the root. You need to know whether to change a *y* to *i* or whether to drop a final *e;* you need to know whether to add *-s* or *-es*. The following is a list of common suffixes:

-able	-ing
-al	-ly
-ed	-ment
-er	-ness
-es	-ous
-est	-s
-ic	-y

ADDING -S OR -ES

Most nouns take an *-s* for the plural:

Words like <u>girls</u>

Singular	Plural
girl	girls
writer	writers

Most verbs take an *-s* for the *-s* form of the verb:

Base	**-s form**
laugh	laughs
seem	seems

Words like buzzes

When a word ends in *ch, s, sh, x,* or *z,* add the suffix *-es:*

box	boxes
buzz	buzzes
dish	dishes
kiss	kisses
speech	speeches
waltz	waltzes

WORDS ENDING IN Y

For words ending in a *y* that is preceded by a consonant, change the *y* to *i* and add *-es:*

Words like stories

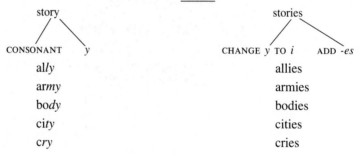

ally	allies
army	armies
body	bodies
city	cities
cry	cries

Words like beautiful

Follow the same pattern when adding other suffixes:

beauty	beautiful
cry	cried
deny	denial
easy	easier
empty	emptiness
gratify	gratification

Words like crying

Do not drop the *y* when adding *-ing* to a word ending in *y:*

cry	crying
deny	denying
study	studying

Words like monkeys

Add an *s* to a word that ends in a *y* preceded by a vowel:

monkey   monkeys

VOWEL   *y*   ADD   *-s*

all*ey*   alleys

attorn*ey*   attorneys

b*oy*   boys

WORDS ENDING IN O   Add an *-s* to most words ending in *o:*

Words like memos

memo   memos

piano   pianos

radio   radios

Words like echoes

Add an *-es* to these common exceptions:

do   does

echo   echoes

go   goes

hero   heroes

potato   potatoes

tomato   tomatoes

veto   vetoes

Words like mottos

Some words take either spelling:

motto   mottos/mottoes

volcano   volcanos/volcanoes

zero   zeros/zeroes

PROPER NAMES   Add an *-s* to proper names to make them plural. (Do not add an apostrophe.)

Names like Smiths

Archie Bunker   Archie Bunkers

McCoy   McCoys

Sally   Sallys (more than one)

Smith   Smiths

Names like <u>Joneses</u>

When a proper name ends in *ch, s, sh, x,* or *z,* add *-es* to make it plural. In these names, the plural ending becomes an extra syllable you have to pronounce:

Jones   Joneses

Spitz   Spitzes

WATCH OUT FOR APOSTROPHES AND PROPER NOUNS

1. Do not add an apostrophe to a proper noun to make it plural.

NO: The *Smith's* bought a house down the block from us.

YES: The *Smiths* bought a house down the block from us.

2. Use the apostrophe for possession.

YES: The *Smiths'* house is near ours.

See the discussion of apostrophes on pages 400–403.

WORDS ENDING IN <u>E</u> When a word ends in an *e* that is preceded by a consonant, drop the *e* before adding *y* or a suffix beginning with a vowel:

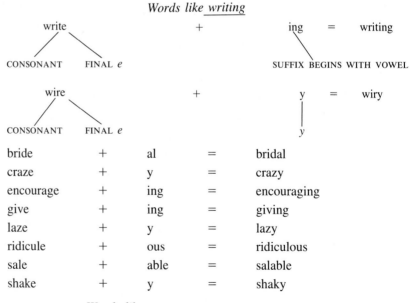

Words like <u>writing</u>

write   +   ing   =   writing

CONSONANT   FINAL *e*   SUFFIX BEGINS WITH VOWEL

wire   +   y   =   wiry

CONSONANT   FINAL *e*   *y*

bride   +   al   =   bridal

craze   +   y   =   crazy

encourage   +   ing   =   encouraging

give   +   ing   =   giving

laze   +   y   =   lazy

ridicule   +   ous   =   ridiculous

sale   +   able   =   salable

shake   +   y   =   shaky

Words like <u>encouragement</u>

Keep the *e* when adding a suffix beginning with a consonant:

encourag*e*   +   *m*ent   =   encouragement

hop*e*   +   *f*ul   =   hopeful

late	+	*n*ess	=	lateness
lif*e*	+	*l*ess	=	lifeless
retir*e*	+	*m*ent	=	retirement
sincer*e*	+	*l*y	=	sincerely

There are some exceptions to this rule:

argue	+	*m*ent	=	argument
awe	+	*f*ul	=	awful
true	+	*l*y	=	truly

Words like *outrageous*

When a word ends in *ce* or *ge,* keep the final *e* when adding a suffix beginning with *a* or *o:*

chang*e*	+	*a*ble	=	changeable
courag*e*	+	*o*us	=	courageous
notic*e*	+	*a*ble	=	noticeable
outrag*e*	+	*o*us	=	outrageous

ONE-SYLLABLE WORDS ENDING IN A CONSONANT When a one-syllable word ends in a consonant that is preceded by a single vowel, double the consonant when adding a suffix beginning with a vowel:

Words like *cutting*

cut	—	one-syllable word
cu*t*	—	ends in a consonant
c*u*t	—	preceded by a single vowel
*i*ng	—	suffix begins with a vowel
cu*tt*ing	—	double the consonant and add the suffix

beg	+	g	+	ar	=	beggar
beg	+	g	+	ed	=	begged
beg	+	g	+	ing	=	begging
plan	+	n	+	ed	=	planned
rob	+	b	+	er	=	robber
run	+	n	+	ing	=	running
sit	+	t	+	ing	=	sitting
snap	+	p	+	ed	=	snapped
swim	+	m	+	er	=	swimmer
win	+	n	+	ing	=	winning

Words like <u>cheered</u>

When all of the above conditions do not exist, do not double the consonant:

cheer	+	ed	=	cheered
great	+	er	=	greater
heat	+	ed	=	heated
knock	+	ing	=	knocking
paint	+	ing	=	painting

MULTISYLLABLE WORDS WITH THE ACCENT ON THE LAST SYLLABLE When a word of more than one syllable is accented on the last syllable and ends in a single consonant, double the consonant when adding a suffix that begins with a vowel:

Words like <u>controlled</u>

admít	+	t	+	ed	=	admítted
begín	+	n	+	ing	=	begínning
contról	+	l	+	able	=	contróllable
occúr	+	r	+	ence	=	occúrrence
omít	+	t	+	ing	=	omítting
permít	+	t	+	ed	=	permítted
prefér	+	r	+	ed	=	preférred

Words like <u>preference</u>

Note these exceptions: When the accent shifts from the last syllable of the root word to the first syllable of the word that is formed by adding a suffix, do not double the consonant:

confér	+	ence	=	cónference
infér	+	ence	=	ínference
prefér	+	ence	=	préference
prefér	+	able	=	préferable
refér	+	ence	=	réference

Words like <u>opened</u>

When the accent is on a syllable other than the last, do not double the consonant:

díffer	+	ence	=	dífference
glímmer	+	ed	=	glímmered
lísten	+	ing	=	lístening
ópen	+	ed	=	ópened
trável	+	ing	=	tráveling

Words like <u>focused</u>

These words have alternative spellings. Both forms are correct:

benefit	benefited/benefitted
counsel	counseled/counselled
focus	focused/focussed
kidnap	kidnaped/kidnapped

Troublesome combinations— <u>ie</u> or <u>ei</u>?

The general rule (although there are a few exceptions) for spelling words in which the letters *i* and *e* appear side by side is as follows:

Use *i* before *e* (*believe, friend*)
Except after *c* (*receive*)
Or when sounded like *a*
As in *neighbor* and *weigh*.

Words like <u>believe</u> and <u>receive</u>

i before e	except after c	or when sounded like ā
achieve	ceiling	chow mein
believe	conceit	eight
brief	conceive	freight
chief	deceit	neighbor
field	perceive	reign
fierce	receipt	reindeer
friend	receive	vein
grieve		weigh

Watch out for exceptions to the rule: *cien*

ancient	efficient
conscience	omniscient
conscientious	proficient
deficient	sufficient

Other exceptions:

caffeine	foreign	protein
codeine	forfeit	science
counterfeit	height	seize
either	leisure	weird
financier	neither	

Troublesome combinations— -ceed, -cede, and -sede

Only one word in the English language ends in *-sede;* three end in *-ceed;* all others end in *-cede.*

Words like proceed, precede, and supersede

-sede	-ceed	-cede
supersede	exceed	accede
	proceed	concede
	succeed	intercede
		precede
		recede
		secede

17.c HOMOPHONES

Words are often misspelled because they are *homophones,* that is, they sound alike but are spelled differently. The following is a list of commonly confused homophones.

aloud—out loud
allowed—permitted

altar—a place for worship
alter—to change

ate—past tense of *eat*
eight—the number 8

bare—naked
bear—to carry; the wild beast

brake—a stopping device on a vehicle
break—to split, mash, or divide into parts

by—a preposition
buy—to purchase
bye—as in *good-bye*

cite—to summon; to quote
site—place; position
sight—the power of seeing; a view

course—a direction or route taken; a path; a series of classes
coarse—rough, not fine

fare—money paid for a trip; food
fair—beautiful; equitable; an exhibition or market

heel—the hind part of the foot
heal—to cure; to grow sound
he'll—contraction of *he will*

here—in this place
hear—to perceive with the ear

isle—a small island
aisle—passage in an auditorium
I'll—contraction of *I will*

it's—contraction of *it is*
its—possessive of *it*

led—past tense and past participle of *lead*
lead—a metal

lone—solitary; alone
loan—a temporary grant

male—opposite of female
mail—letters and other postal matter

meet—to assemble
meat—food; flesh

miner—a worker in mines
minor—one under age

new—not old
knew—past tense of *know*

night—opposite of day
knight—a title of honor

our—a pronoun
hour—sixty minutes

pain—physical or mental suffering
pane—a piece of glass (in a
    window)

pair—two; a couple
pare—to slice thinly
pear—a kind of fruit

passed—gone through; went by
past—having taken place in a time
    before the present

peace—a state of harmony
piece—a part of a whole

peel—skin; outside
peal—sound of bells

plane—a perfectly flat or level
    surface; airplane
plain—level, flat country

principal—invested funds; chief,
    head of a school
principle—a fundamental rule or law

red—a color
read—past tense of *read*

right—just; correct
rite—a ceremony
write—to trace letters or characters

road—a path; a way
rode—past tense of *ride*
rowed—past tense of *row*

root—as of a plant; origin
route—direction; road

sail—to navigate
sale—act of selling

scene—a sight; part of a play
seen—observed

soul—the spirit
sole—only; bottom of the foot; a
    fish

sow—to scatter seed
sew—to fasten, as with a needle
so—in this manner

tale—a story
tail—hindmost part of an animal

their—possessive of *they*
there—in that place
they're—contraction of *they are*

two—a pair; the number 2
too—also; excess, as *too much*
to—a preposition or part of an
    infinitive

wait—to expect; to stay
weight—heaviness; importance

weather—the general condition of
    the atmosphere
whether—if it be the case or fact
    that

whose—a possessive pronoun or an
    interrogative pronoun
who's—contraction of *who is*

your—possessive of *you* (a pronoun)
you're—contraction of *you are*
    (a subject and a verb)

Adapted with permission from "Homonyms,"
The Lincoln Library of Essential Information,
edited by W. J. Redding. Chicago:
The Frontier Press Co., 1976

Fourteen tricky homonyms Devise a way to remember the trickiest homonyms:

1. It's—the contraction of *it is*.

   It's (it is) raining cats and dogs.

2. Its—possessive of *it*. Remember that the possessive *its,* like the possessive *his,* has no apostrophe.

   The cat is chasing *its* tail (the tail of *it*).

3. Here—in this place.

   My great-aunt is *here* for a visit.

4. Hear—to perceive with the ear. Remember *ear* is in *hear*.

   Did you *hear* what I said?

5. There—in that place. Remember that *here*, *there*, and *where* all refer to places. *Here* is in all three words.

   Here is the entrance to the cave.
   There are too many cats in this house.
   Where is my pogo stick?

6. Their—the possessive of *they*. Remember, in *their* is the word *heir*, which means one who will inherit another's possessions. An *heir* will take *possession*.

   They inherited *their* house from a relative.

7. They're—the contraction of *they are*.

   They're (*they are*) coming at last.

8. To—a preposition or part of an infinitive.

   He went *to* market *to* buy a fat hen.

9. Too—an adverb that means "in addition to," "also," or "in excess." Remember that if *very* or *also* can be substituted, use *too*.

   He is *too* old to act that way.
   I want to buy a fat hen, *too*.

10. Two—the number *2*.

    You act like a *two*-year-old child.

11. Whose—a possessive pronoun or an interrogative pronoun.

    Whose handkerchief is this?
    A man, *whose* name is Ivan, stopped by to make an appointment.

12. Who's—the contraction of *who is*.

    Who's (*who is*) going to the theater with me?
    Mary is the one *who's* (*who is*) driving you home.

13. Your—the possessive of *you*.

    Your room is a mess.

14. You're—the contraction of *you are*.

    You're (*you are*) the one.

17.d USES OF THE HYPHEN

Hyphens have several important uses. Leaving out a hyphen from some words can be considered a simple misspelling; but leaving out a hyphen from other words can confuse the meaning of your sentences. Hyphens are most often used to draw two or more words together to act as a single word (*eighty-two, high-school* teacher), to separate some prefixes from the words to which they are attached (*non-European*), and to break a word at the end of a line when there isn't room for the whole word (*impos-sible*). The following guidelines explain in greater detail the uses of the hyphen:

1. *Compound nouns.*
   Use hyphens to form certain compound nouns.

do-gooder	has-been
do-it-yourself	mother-in-law
forget-me-not	stick-in-the-mud
great-grandfather	tenth-grader

   Some compounds were once hyphenated but are now written in one word:

   dropout
   housekeeper
   roommate

   Check your dictionary for the accepted way to write other compounds.

2. *Compound modifiers.*
   Use hyphens between two or more words acting together as a single adjective if (a) the compound comes before the term it modifies and (b) the first word of the compound is itself a modifier:

   > Walter Johnson is a *well-known* lawyer.
   > I hate to perform at *open-air* concerts.
   > This was a *never-to-be-forgotten* day.

   When two or more words acting as a single adjective follow the noun they modify, do not hyphenate them:

   > Walter Johnson is *well known* as a lawyer.
   > I hate to perform at concerts held in the *open air*.
   > The day was *never to be forgotten*.

   Do not use a hyphen between two words when the first word in the pair is an adverb ending in -*ly:*

   > It was a *poorly written* paper.
   > Only a *barely concealed* smile was evident.

Some adjectives are always hyphenated, whether they precede or follow the noun they modify:

even-tempered	long-haired
high-pressure	shirt-sleeved

Check your dictionary for compound modifiers.

3. *Compound numbers.*

Hyphenate compound numbers from twenty-one to ninety-nine:

sixty-three
eighty-two

Do not use hyphens in compound numbers greater than one hundred:

one hundred and one
four hundred and three

Hyphenate fractions used as adjectives:

> He had just *one-half* cup of sugar.
> The car's gas tank was *three-quarters* empty.

Do not hyphenate fractions used as nouns:

> *One half* of a tank of gas is not enough.
> *Three quarters* of the auditorium was empty.

Hyphenate decades written in words:

eighteen-nineties
nineteen-twenties

4. Use a hyphen when prefixes are joined with *proper* nouns or *proper* adjectives:

all-	all-American
anti-	anti-American
mid-	mid-Atlantic
pan-	pan-American
post-	post-Victorian
pro-	pro-Chinese
trans-	trans-Siberian
un-	un-American

When a modifier has two contrasting prefixes, the first one stands by itself with a hyphen:

Pro- and *anti-American* forces clashed.

Check your dictionary for the hyphenation of prefixes joined with common nouns.

5. Hyphenate words with an *ex-* prefix where *ex* means "former":

ex-husband
ex-president

Hyphenate words with a *self-* prefix, but do not hyphenate words in which the root is *self:*

Prefix	**Root**
self-made	selfish
self-respect	selfless
self-satisfaction	

6. Hyphenate words that may be mistaken for other words:

They had a *run-in* about letting boys *run in* the girls' race.
The thieves wanted the upholsterer to *re-cover* the stolen pink sofa in green so that the owner could not identify it and *recover* his property.

7. When you must divide a word at the end of a line because you've run out of room, hyphenate the word between syllables:

The council had considered the pro-
posal; nonetheless, they turned
it down.

Do not break up a syllable:

NO: He dropped out of school becau-
      se he needed to help his family.
YES: He dropped out of school be-
      cause he needed to help his family.

Do not divide contractions:

NO: He hits well, but he can-
      't run.
YES: He hits well, but he
      can't run.

Do not divide numbers written in figures:

NO: The population of the city was 367,-
       463 in 1977.
YES: The population of the city was
       367,463 in 1977.

Do not leave one letter hanging at the end of a line:

NO: He wanted to be a-
       lone.
YES: He wanted to be alone.

Do not break up one-syllable words:

NO: After all was said and do-
       ne, he did what he wanted.
YES: After all was said and done,
       he did what he wanted.

Check your dictionary for the proper syllabification of words.

17.e USES OF THE APOSTROPHE

Incorrect use of the apostrophe is the single most consistent spelling problem in the work of many writers. If you leave out apostrophes or if you put them in where they don't belong, you may need to give your writing a special proofreading in which you examine your work super-closely just for these errors. Taking the time to add omitted apostrophes and remove unnecessary ones will help you avoid a major spelling problem and make your writing easier to read and more publicly acceptable. Chiefly, use apostrophes to show possession or to show that a letter (or number) has been left out. Never use *'s* to show the plural of a noun or to show the *-s* form of a verb. Here are some pointers on where (and where not) to put apostrophes:

1. Use the apostrophe plus *s* to form the possessive of nouns not ending in *s:*

Noun	**Possessive**
Rachel	*Rachel's* boots (boots belonging to Rachel) are in the closet.
children	The *children's* toys (toys of the children) are safe and educational.
men	The *men's* room (room for men) is on the left.

2. Use the apostrophe alone to form the possessive of nouns ending in *s:*

Noun	Possessive
boys	The *boys'* team (team of the boys) was victorious.
ladies	The *ladies'* room (room for ladies) is on the right.
friends	She visited her *friends'* house (house of the friends—meaning more than one friend).

Note the difference:

> My *friend's* house (the house of *one* friend).
> My *friends'* house (the house of *two or more* friends).

You can always determine if a noun is singular or plural by converting the possessive to a prepositional phrase with *of* or *for:*

> The *dog's* tail (the tail of the dog—singular) is mangy.
> The *dogs'* tails (the tails of the dogs—plural) are mangy.
> The *ladies'* room (room for ladies—plural) is on the right.

When a singular noun ends in *s,* form the possessive by adding either the apostrophe alone or *'s.* If adding *'s* would cause difficulty in pronunciation, add the apostrophe alone:

> They were *Moses'* followers (*Moses's* would be difficult to pronounce).
> *Charles's* hats (*Charles'* would also be acceptable) have style.
> *Louis's* hat (*Louis'* would also be acceptable) is on the hat rack.

3. Hyphenated words take the apostrophe after the last part of the word to form the possessive:

He is a *mother-in-law's* delight.
The old barn was a *do-it-yourselfer's* dream.

4. To show joint ownership by a pair or group of individuals, add *'s* to the last word only:

> *Mary and Tom's* house (the house belonging to both Mary and Tom) is in the country.

To show individual ownership, add *'s* to each word in the pair or series:

> *Mary's and Tom's* shoes (the shoes belonging to Mary and the shoes belonging to Tom) are muddy.

5. Use a possessive form before an *-ing* word:

> I was impressed by *Jessica's* learning to drive at fourteen. (This says *learning to drive at fourteen* was what impressed me.)
>
> I was impressed by *Jessica* learning to drive at fourteen. (Jessica herself impressed me because of her accomplishment in learning to drive so young.)

6. Sometimes you need a double possessive (an *of* plus a possessive form) to make your meaning clear:

> A song *of Sally.* (Is it a song *about* Sally or is it *Sally's* song?)
>
> A song *of Sally's.* (Here the meaning is clear; it's Sally's song.)

7. Do not use an apostrophe with possessive pronouns:

Pronoun	Possessive pronoun
he	his
she	hers
it	its
us	ours
you	yours
they	theirs

8. Use an apostrophe to mark omissions in shortened forms. The apostrophe takes the place of the missing letter or letters:

are not	=	aren't (never *are'nt*)	(missing *o*)
cannot	=	can't	(missing *no*)
could not	=	couldn't	(missing *o*)
does not	=	doesn't (never *does'nt*)	(missing *o*)
do not	=	don't	(missing *o*)
he will	=	he'll	(missing *wi*)
is not	=	isn't	(missing *o*)
it is	=	it's	(missing *i*)
must not	=	mustn't	(missing *o*)
she will	=	she'll	(missing *wi*)
should not	=	shouldn't	(missing *o*)
they are	=	they're	(missing *a*)
they will	=	they'll	(missing *wi*)
you are	=	you're	(missing *a*)
we have	=	we've	(missing *ha*)
would not	=	wouldn't	(missing *o*)

9. Use the apostrophe to indicate omitted numerals:

class of 1983	'83
1979	'79

10. Use an apostrophe to indicate the omission of one or more letters in a word:

alligator	'gator
madam	ma'am
rock and roll	rock 'n' roll
sock it to them	sock it to 'em

11. Use *'s* to form the plurals of letters, numbers, words referred to as words, and abbreviations:

p and q	p's and q's
1 and 2	1's and 2's
1920	1920's
and and *but*	*and*'s and *but*'s
GI	GI's

If there is no danger of confusion, an *s* alone may be added:

1920	1920s
GI	GIs

part

5 A Guide to Research

chapter 18 | Writing the Research Essay

Students in a freshman writing class were asked to write down the first words that popped into their minds when they heard the words *research paper*. Their responses included these:

library
stack of books
card catalog
confusion
boring
time consuming
last minute
typing
microfilm
Reader's Guide
why?

Like some of these students, you may think of the research paper as joyless, boring, uninspiring, and meaningless. With its stacks and cards and numbers, books and magazines and microfilm, the library may seem like a maze as you wander from room to room, trying to appear as if you know what you are doing. As you write your paper, you may feel overwhelmed by the amount of expert information around you and be tempted to bury your own good ideas and judgments by simply recording what the ''experts'' say. That is why research papers are often dull, lifeless reports and not essays at all.

But the research papers that you write for your English class and for other classes as well will be essays—essays in which all the writing skills you have practiced come into play. In your writing, you are always making connections—between words, between sentences, between paragraphs—so that all the parts of the essay work together to produce a unified piece of writing. The research essay asks you to make connections in a larger, more complex way by relating your own thinking and writing skills to the ideas and information provided by other writers. This chapter highlights the research paper as another essay by attempting to answer the questions students most often ask and by providing the information and techniques you will need to write this paper.

18.a WHY A RESEARCH PAPER?

No writer knows everything. Beginners or professionals, all writers must eventually go outside their own experiences to find information. You aren't expected to be an expert—on women's fashions of the 1920s, on the life cycle of a snail, on the economic development of China, or on a zillion other specialized subjects—but you are expected to be able to find information when you need it. You've *already* done research in writing personal essays; you've called on your memory and your personal relationships and experiences. Now you must find out how to call on the research of other writers, on the information that they make available to you in their writings, which are based on *their* research—their memories, their personal relationships and experiences, their observations and insights, their scientific experiments and library research.

The research paper you write for your English class is not simply an academic exercise. It has the same goals and involves the same procedures as the research you will undertake on your own, on the job or in upper-class courses, when you need to find information on a particular subject. If you need to find out all you can about teen-age alcoholism because you know of someone who needs help; if an employer asks you to find out what you can about the baby boom of the 1950s; if you need to find out about the effects of marijuana on the human body, you'll have to know how to find the information. You'll need people to talk to and books and articles to read. And you'll have to know what to do with the information you find to get the most out of it.

As a researcher, you learn by finding sources, reading critically, and evaluating and summarizing what you've read. You put all your research together into a paper that you, as a writer, *control*. You credit your sources by providing footnotes and a bibliography. You follow the same procedures professional writers follow when they prepare their manuscripts for publication.

18.b WHAT IS A RESEARCH PAPER?

Students who wrote research papers before college often report that they were not encouraged to include their own ideas and judgments. Their high-school research papers were simply *reports* of their findings on a subject. One student described these high-school reports like this:

> I did the usual high-school "research paper." The research paper that I refer to is the type where you run to the encyclopedia, copy half of the words, maybe change a few by means of a thesaurus, scribble your name at the top, and hand it in.

In your college English class, the research paper that you write is, first of all, an essay. All essays require research. Your personal essays rely on personal research into your observations and memory. Although you may check a book or magazine article to get started on a personal essay, your chief research tool is *you*. (See Chapter 2 for suggestions on getting started.) Now, in the research paper, you turn to information provided by *others*. *Re-search*, in fact, means to *search again* through the same books and magazines and newspapers that others have explored. Your research invites you to see through your own eyes what has gone before and to offer your own ideas about the information that you find.

Because many students feel powerless when confronted with vast amounts of information, they forget the essay part of the research paper. They wind up doing a "patchwork" paper, in which they present the ideas of one writer and then those of another and another. The patches are loosely stitched together, producing a collection of patches, but not a quilt. Think of the research paper as a research *essay*, which you, the writer, must design and write.

18.c WHEN TO BEGIN

One pitfall for many students who are assigned research papers is time; they wait until the assignment is just about due and then dash to the library to find that the books they need for their paper have already been checked out. Time must be on your side when you write a research paper because it is going to take you time to find a subject, settle on a controlling idea, do the research, take notes, write the paper, rewrite it, produce accurate footnotes and bibliography, and, finally, revise. The research essay, because it involves a more intricate balancing of parts than any other kind of essay you have written, needs time for careful revision, for a studied look *after* you have completed what you think is a close-to-final draft. Ideally, you should let this draft sit for a week and then go back to it and revise—checking each sentence and each paragraph for clarity and organization.

18.d HOW TO BEGIN

Chances are your instructor will provide a general subject for your paper— women, politics, the media, education, drugs—and you'll have to narrow the subject to a workable, limited topic. Don't mistake the subject for a topic. In their eagerness to begin, students often adopt a broad subject, such as "women," as their topic and forget all they know about narrowing a subject. If you haven't been provided with a general subject, then you'll need to find one and go through the same process of narrowing.

You can begin narrowing your subject by talking to an expert, by finding an instructor on campus who will talk with you about his or her field—urban politics or mass media or Chinese communes—so that you can begin to think about the range of your subject. You can begin by talking to a reference librarian—by asking where to find materials on housing problems or women in politics or government agencies. Every library provides information on how to use the library, and many provide excellent pamphlets on using the library to do research. Find out.

You may begin by freewriting to find a topic that has *research potential*. The freewriting you've done for personal essays reveals your personal feelings and experiences. Now you can use the same writing at the beginning of a research project to tap your own ideas and *questions* about a general subject. Suppose that you have been assigned a broad subject: technology. You have vast experience with technology: you've seen space walks, played arcade games, even spoken to people over the phone! Where do your experiences take you in your writing? Your focused freewriting may lead you to an interesting idea that has research potential.

Consider the following sample of a student's freewriting on technology:

> Technology, the future, *Star Trek, Star Wars, Starman*—no, that's fantasy, not technology. Technology isn't the future. What is technology? What is technology? Who knows? Computers. Computers know everything. Computers know what technology is. Computers are technology. Computers are everywhere. Big Brother is watching. What is Big Brother watching? Why is he watching? Does Big Brother know about technology? Big Brother is technology. Big Brother goes bowling. Bowling alleys are computerized. What happened to keeping score? The computer always calls a three a three, never a five. Computers have no heart. No emotions. Logical. Computers are logical. Computers are like teachers. Computers are replacing teachers. Computers in education.

The student began with *Star Trek, Star Wars,* and *Starman,* and ended with ideas about computers and education. Along the way, she asked a number of questions, some of which can be answered, some of which cannot: What is technology? What is Big Brother watching? Why is he watching? The first question can be answered by consulting a dictionary and finding that technology is defined as "the science or study of the practical or industrial arts." This might prove to be a dead end, unless the student asks more provocative questions involving the definition. But the student's third question, "Why is Big Brother watching?" raises a major issue involving invasion of privacy or the right of government to investigate individuals for security reasons. With these issues in mind, the student may be on the way to a study of national security versus personal privacy. Or she may follow another lead from her freewriting, researching the subject of computers in education (as she actually did in her research paper, which appears in Chapter 19).

The student next must turn her spontaneous questioning into a *working question* for her research: What are the prices we pay for national security? or What are the effects of computers in the classroom? She can now go to the library armed with a purpose, because she has narrowed a broad subject into a manageable, researchable topic. Along the way, she has discovered a working question, which may be discarded or which may, in fact, be turned into the controlling idea of the paper. Now the research begins. She will have to read and read hard and extensively; she will have to think hard and rethink, write, and rewrite.

18.e HOW TO RESEARCH—THE HUNT

Finding sources for the information you will need is like participating in a hunt. The trail leads to one clue and then to another and finally to the sources you will use in your paper. Another clue may lead to a dead end. In all the research papers you write, the moves are similar: you check through the card catalog, encyclopedias, and periodical indexes.

Check the card catalog   The *card catalog* can be the first step in your research. The card catalog is an alphabetical index to the printed materials within a library. Find out how the card catalog in your library works. Does it catalog books by the Library of Congress system or by the Dewey decimal system? The following tips for researchers show you how to use the cards.

WHAT'S IN THE CARDS?

Author card:

Title card:

Subject card:

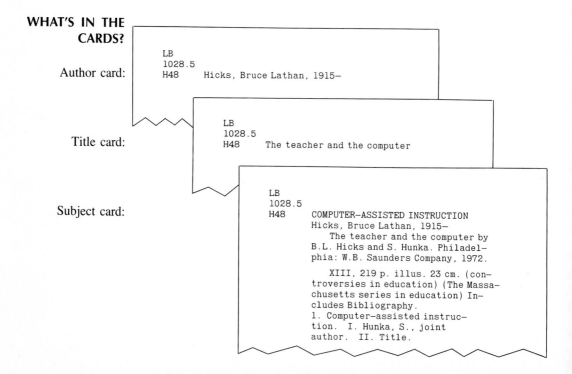

```
LB
1028.5
H48     Hicks, Bruce Lathan, 1915—
```

```
LB
1028.5
H48      The teacher and the computer
```

```
LB
1028.5
H48      COMPUTER-ASSISTED INSTRUCTION
         Hicks, Bruce Lathan, 1915—
              The teacher and the computer by
         B.L. Hicks and S. Hunka. Philadel-
         phia: W.B. Saunders Company, 1972.

              XIII, 219 p. illus. 23 cm. (con-
         troversies in education) (The Massa-
         chusetts series in education) In-
         cludes Bibliography.
         1. Computer-assisted instruc-
         tion.  I. Hunka, S., joint
         author.  II. Title.
```

The card catalog lists every nonfiction book in the library by *author's name*, by *title*, and by one or more *subject headings*. The sample cards reveal the following information:

1. Call number indicating where in the library the book can be found.
2. Subject heading.
3. Author's name and date of birth; the date without a second year (''1915– '') indicates that the author is living.
4. Title of book, place of publication, publisher's name, and year of publication.
5. Format of book: for example, ''XIII'' indicates in Roman numerals the number of pages of the preface; ''219 p.'' indicates the number of pages; ''illus.'' indicates that the book contains illustrations; ''23 cm.'' indicates the size of the book in centimeters.
6. Additional information about the book: this is a cataloger's note indicating that a book includes a bibliography, an index, and the like.
7. Listing of subject headings under which the book is cataloged.

CLUES   The cataloger's note ''Includes Bibliography'' is an important clue, telling you that the book offers a listing of related books that may be useful to you in your research.

The subject heading ''Computer-assisted instruction'' at the bottom of the card offers an additional clue, telling you that the book is cataloged under no other subject heading. So return to the original subject heading, COMPUTER ASSISTED INSTRUCTION, to see what other sources you can find. As you begin your project, you need to follow clues that take you from one possibility to another. If you are looking at cards for a broad subject, for example, you may be tempted to look under only *one* subject heading, even if others are listed on the card. But that may lead you nowhere. The subject heading ''Computer-assisted instruction'' in one library turns up a few cards on COMPUTERS AND EDU-CATION, but at the bottom of the cards under the subject headings, there are other clues—additional reference cards:

See COMPUTERS
See EDUCATION
See TECHNOLOGY—INFORMATION SERVICES

Following the clue ''See EDUCATION,'' you find over 200 cards under such headings as:

EDUCATION—DISCRIMINATION IN EDUCATION
EDUCATION—EDUCATION IN ART
EDUCATION—EDUCATION, ECONOMIC ASPECTS
EDUCATION—EDUCATION AND NATIONALISM
EDUCATION—EDUCATION AND STATE
EDUCATION—EDUCATION, UNITED STATES

Following the clue "See COMPUTERS," you find over 100 cards under these headings:

COMPUTER AIDED INSTRUCTION
COMPUTER CRIMES
COMPUTER ENGINEERING
COMPUTER GRAPHICS
COMPUTER INDUSTRY
COMPUTER INPUT–OUTPUT EQUIPMENT
COMPUTER MUSIC
COMPUTER PROGRAMS
COMPUTER SIMULATION
COMPUTER STORAGE DEVICES
COMPUTER TERMINALS

CHECK THE CALL NUMBERS FOR LIBRARY LOCATIONS As you work through the card catalog, notice the call numbers under which books are listed. Because libraries categorize books by subject, you can find the *general locations* where most of the books on your subject are shelved. In continuing your search for books on computers, you see that many books are stored under:

> 001.64

and

> LB
> 1028

This information takes you to the stacks.

Check the stacks Many libraries store their books in open stacks, where the books are accessible. In that case, once you know where most of the books on your subject are shelved, you can go directly to those stacks to browse. A book that you can hold in your hands will turn up more possibilities (or fewer possibilities) than the card in the catalog can indicate. So take the time to look through the shelves.

If your library has closed stacks, you cannot go directly to the books. From the card catalog, decide on the book titles that look promising. You must then request the books by giving an attendant a slip of paper on which you have written the author, title, and call number of each book. After a short wait, the book is sent to the desk, where you collect it.

Find an overview Find a book that provides an overview of your subject. The overview enables you to see the range of a subject and its research possibilities. You will be able to do some general reading.

How do you find such a book? Again, there are clues for you to follow, contained in the book itself:

1. Consider the title of the book.
2. Read the table of contents.
3. Look at the date of publication.
4. Find out if there is a bibliography within the book.

As you look through the titles of books on computers, for example, you may turn up these titles:

Artist and Computer

Programmed Instruction

The Use and Misuse of Computers in Education

Mindstorms: Children, Computers and Powerful Ideas

Crime by Computer

The Waves of Change: A Techno-Economic Analysis of the Data Processing Industry

Modular Programming

The Information Age

If you know that you want to research the evolving impact of computers on society, two books, *The Waves of Change: A Techno-Economic Analysis of the Data Processing Industry* and *The Information Age* may offer the overview you need. If you want to consider a specific problem of the growing technology, *Crime by Computer* will be a possible source. But neither *Crime by Computer* nor *Artist and Computer* will provide overviews of the whole industry; their titles indicate more specific studies. *Modular Programming* seems more a how-to book, which will probably not be of use in a paper on computer-aided instruction. Of the three titles that directly concern the effects of computers in education, *Programmed Instruction* sounds general enough to provide the overview you need. You pull *Programmed Instruction* from the shelf, glance through the table of contents, and see that the book begins with very broad remarks about humanity and the world:

CHAPTER I: Perspectives and Contexts
1. Dissatisfaction with the Human State
2. Methods for Improving Man
3. The Information Explosion
4. The Urge to Be Objective

The last chapter of the book is called ''Implications for the Future'' and includes sections on the foreseeable shifts in both our concept of education and computer technology.

You note that the date of publication is 1966. This means that the book's study of computer-aided instruction is probably somewhat dated, especially given the advances in the field in the past decade. Naturally, therefore, you cannot expect to find the most recent developments in classroom computers; for that information, you will need to consult other sources. But for a general introduction to the subject, *Programmed Instruction* may still be useful.

In the last pages of *Programmed Instruction,* you find a bibliography. Here is another clue: the author's sources may be your sources as well. You conclude that *Programmed Instruction* is at the very least a good place to start.

CHECK AN ENCYCLOPEDIA The following encyclopedias offer general information on most subjects:

Chambers's Encyclopaedia
Encyclopaedia Britannica
Encyclopedia Americana
The New Columbia Encyclopedia
The Random House Encyclopedia

The *Encyclopaedia Britannica* is one of the best general encyclopedias. The newest edition (1974) is divided into three parts: the *Propaedia* (one volume), the *Micropaedia* (ten volumes), and the *Macropaedia* (nineteen volumes). The *Macropaedia* offers expansive, in-depth articles on many topics. At the end of each entry is a bibliography, which you can scan.

As you read through the encyclopedia, use *note cards* to jot down notes and questions. You can read for general information, but some of the information may lead you to a research topic.

In taking notes, you record what strikes you as interesting or important. The facts may later fit into your paper as evidence of support. The information may lead you to research possibilities. As you read, you weigh the possibilities, think about the evidence, and ask questions. (See pages 420–422 on note taking.)

CHECK A PERIODICAL INDEX Books are not the only sources you bring to your research paper. In fact, if you are researching a contemporary topic or a recent event, you may not find information published in books. Libraries also store periodicals (magazines, journals, and newspapers). Leafing through the 4,000 or so periodicals that many libraries have on hand is an impossibility, but you can use a guide to periodicals, which categorizes articles by subject.

The most useful guide to periodicals is the *Reader's Guide to Periodical Literature,* which is published monthly and is an index to about 160 magazines. Printed below is a sample from the *Reader's Guide:*

The CRT before the horse. il *Time* 122:64 O 10 '83
Education? by computer, naturally [50 year forecast] il *U S News World Rep* 94:A5 My 9 '83
Education in the information society. il *Futurist* 17:65-6 Ap '83
The future of sex education: computerizing the facts of life. P. Rossman. il por *Futurist* 17:69-73 D '83
Get ready for the computer revolution! G. Maeroff. il *Seventeen* 42:147-8+ O '83
How computers are changing the classroom. D. Kaercher. il *Better Homes Gard* 61:17+ Ap '83
Needed: more computers in universities. K. G. Wilson. *Phys Today* 36:128 My '83
New learning games make the grade. il *Bus Week* p81 Ja 24 '83
Newest Apple [Drexel purchases Apple's newest computer to sell to incoming freshmen] *Time* 121:59 My 2 '83
Personal computing in education and research [Carnegie-Mellon Univ.] R. M. Cyert. *Science* 222:569 N 11 '83

Subject: Computers: Educational Use

Title of article: "Personal Computing in Education and Research"

Title of magazine: *Science*

Volume: 222

Page numbers: 569+

Date: November 11, 1983

Another widely used index is the *New York Times Index,* which catalogs articles printed in the *New York Times* from its first issue, September 18, 1851, to the present date. In addition, recent issues of magazines and newspapers are usually available on the shelves or on microfilm in the library. Ask the librarian for guidance in locating the periodicals you need. (On p. 417 is a list of other useful indexes.)

Until you actually examine the periodicals, especially old magazines and newspapers, you will be unaware of the riches stored within them. You will find, very often, the same social concerns in a magazine from the 1920s that you find today: politicians seeking votes, police fighting crime, presidents visiting abroad and toasting foreign dignitaries. Pick up an old magazine—leaf through it; look through the articles and advertisements.

Exercise 1 Find the issue of the *New York Times* from the day of your birth. Record the important news of the day—local, national, and international. What was the weather on the day you were born? What programs were on television? on radio? What was the lead editorial? Describe the concerns of the letters to the editor. Describe the advertisements.

Exercise 2 Find the issue of your local newspaper from the day of your birth. What were the headlines of the day? If there is a "help" columnist like Ann Landers, describe the problems and solutions offered in the columns. Compare the concerns of that day with the concerns you find in a recent newspaper.

Exercise 3 Find an encyclopedia article on your research topic. Check the bibliography entries at the end. Track down one of the sources that looks promising. Describe the source in some detail.

Exercise 4 Find a book that provides an overview of your topic. Check to see if there is a bibliography at the end of the book. If there is, determine whether any of the listed books or periodicals will be of help to you.

Exercise 5 Find five articles on your topic by using the *Reader's Guide to Periodical Literature.* Determine the value of each as a source. Tell why each is or is not valuable to *your* research.

General and special reference materials The following lists supply information about general and special reference materials: encyclopedias, dictionaries, indexes, and other useful sources.

GENERAL ENCYCLOPEDIAS *Chambers's Encyclopaedia,* 15 vols.
Encyclopaedia Britannica: Propaedia, 1 vol.; *Micropaedia,* 10 vols.; *Macropaedia,* 19 vols.

Encyclopedia Americana, 30 vols.
The Random House Encyclopedia, 1 vol.
The New Columbia Encyclopedia, 1 vol.

SPECIAL ENCYCLOPEDIAS Check with the reference librarian to see which specialized encyclopedias your library stores. The following is a brief list of special encyclopedias:

Paul Edwards, ed., *The Encyclopedia of Philosophy* (1973)

Encyclopedia of Banking and Finance (1973)

Encyclopedia of Educational Research (1969)

Encyclopedia of World Art (1959–1968)

H. J. Eysenck et al., eds., *Encyclopedia of Psychology* (1972)

Peter Gray, ed., *The Encyclopedia of the Biological Sciences* (1970)

William L. Langer, ed., *An Encyclopedia of World History* (1972)

Larousse World Mythology (1968)

McGraw-Hill Encyclopedia of World Drama (1983)

McGraw-Hill Encyclopedia of Science and Technology (1982)

Richard B. Morris and Jeffrey B. Morris, eds., *Encyclopedia of American History* (1976)

The New Oxford History of Music (1974)

David L. Sills, ed., *International Encyclopedia of the Social Sciences* (1968)

Robert E. Spiller et al., eds., *Literary History of the United States* (1974)

UNESCO, *World Survey of Education* (1955–date)

Van Nostrand's Scientific Encyclopedia (1968)

Robert C. Zaehner, ed., *The Concise Encyclopedia of Living Faiths* (1959)

ALMANACS, YEARBOOKS, AND ATLASES *Facts on File* (1940–date)
Information Please Almanac (1947–date)
National Geographic Atlas of the World (1975)
The New York Times Encyclopedic Almanac (1970–date)
The New York Times Atlas of the World (1981)
The World Almanac and Book of Facts (1868–date)
Year Book of World Affairs (1947–date)

DICTIONARIES See Chapter 8, page 182.

BIOGRAPHY *Biographical Index* (1947–date)
Chambers's Biographical Dictionary (1976)
Current Biography: Who's News and Why (1940–date)
Dictionary of American Biography (1928–1974)

International Who's Who (1935–date)
Webster's Biographical Dictionary (1976)
Who's Who (1849–date)
Who's Who in America (1899–date)

QUOTATIONS John Bartlett and E. M. Beck, eds., *Familiar Quotations* (1968)
Bergen Evans, ed., *Dictionary of Quotations* (1968)
The Oxford Dictionary of Quotations (1979)
Burton E. Stevenson, ed., *The Home Book of Quotations, Classical and Modern* (1967)

INDEXES Valuable indexes, in addition to the *Reader's Guide to Periodical Literature* and the *New York Times Index,* include the following:

Agricultural Index
Applied Science and Technology Index
Art Index
Biography Index
Business Periodical Index
Education Index
Social Sciences and Humanities Index
United States Government Publications (monthly catalog)
Women's Studies: A Recommended Core Bibliography

SPECIAL GUIDES The following guides will lead you to the title of a book when you have only the author's name or to the author's name when you have only the title. Because these guides are published annually, you can use them to look for recent books on certain topics or to find out if a book is still in print:

Books in Print
Cumulative Book Index
Paperbound Books in Print
Subject Guide to Books in Print

18.f READING HARD AND TAKING NOTES

You must now apply the skills you bring with you as a writer to *reading* the writing of others. As you read, you will be observing and evaluating the support writers provide for their arguments, the development of their ideas, their approaches and attitudes toward their subjects.

To determine the value of a book, consider the title, table of contents, and date of publication—the same things you considered when you were looking for an overview (pp. 412–414). You can also skim the preface or introduction to discover whether the book will be useful for your research.

Everything you read provides you with information, but now you must think critically as you read. If you are after facts, you should not be satisfied with articles in popular newspapers, nor should you accept a writer's opinion as fact. You must read hard to find the substantive information you need to support your own controlling idea. First read headings and topic sentences of paragraphs to get an outline of the author's ideas. Then read for details and facts.

Taking notes does two jobs: it is a way to keep track of what you read, and it is a way to record your own questions and judgments as they occur to you while you are reading. The more accurate your notes, the easier the job of writing your paper will be. In fact, many researchers know that once their note taking is complete, the job of writing the paper itself will go quickly.

Many researchers use 3″ x 5″ index cards to record each note they take and each source they consider. Although experienced researchers may use other means to keep track of their notes, it is a good idea to use index cards for your first papers. The note cards provide an easy way for you to organize your material because they can be arranged and, if necessary, rearranged in any order you choose.

Take your note cards with you on the first trip to the library because the first step in your research is to begin a list of sources.

How to keep a list of sources

Keep track of each source you consider, either on a separate note card or on a list. So that you won't have to relocate the source the night before the paper is due, include all the critical information. For a book, include the call number, author's name, title, edition number (if there is one), place of publication, publisher, and date of publication. For an article, include the author's name, title of the article, title of the periodical, volume number, date, and page numbers. It is a good idea to assign a number to each source.

REFERENCE CARD

④ Hicks, B. L., and S. Hunka. *The Teacher and the Computer*. Philadelphia: W. B. Saunders Company, 1972. (pp. 20 & following.)

If you keep a running list of each source you consider, include documentational information for each book and magazine or newspaper article that sounds promising. As you check each source on the list, cross off those sources that will not be helpful for your paper. Keep those that will provide you with useful information.

The student whose paper is reprinted in Chapter 19 used the following working list of sources to guide her through her research. Notice that she numbered each source.

Working List of Sources

1. Clement, Frank J. "Affective Considerations in Computer-Based Education." _Educational Technology_ 4 April 1981: 28-32.

2. Draper, Thomas. "Praise, Reproof and Persistence..." _Educational Research Quarterly_ 5 May 1981: 31-40.

no good 3. ~~Elmer Dewitt, P. "Slugging It Out in the Schoolyard." Time 12 March 1984: 62.~~

4. Hicks, B. L., and S. Hunka. _The Teacher and the Computer_. Philadelphia: W. B. Saunders Company, 1972.

5. Kendal, S., and E. Benoit. "Hello Mr. Chip." _Forbes_ 23 April 1984: 132-136.

6. Magidson, Errol. "Student Assessment of PLATO..." _Educational Technology_ 18 August 1978: 15-18.

7. Meek, Brian. "Computers and Education." In _Computers and the World 2000_. Ed. Lord Avebury and others. Manchester, England: NCC Publications, 1972: 101-116.

8. Osnin, Luis. "The Survival Principle and the Comparative Evaluation of Instructional Systems." _Educational Technology_ 18 January, 1978: 19-23.

9. Silberman, Charles. "Technology Is Knocking at the Schoolhouse Door." In _The World of Computers_. Ed. John Diebold. New York: Random House, 1973: 205-220.

10. Simon, H. A. "Computers in Education: Realizing the Potential." _American Education_ December 1983: 19-23.

11. Welch, Wayne W. "Computer Learning Inequities." _U.S.A. Today_ 14 April 1984: 13-14.

_no_ ~~12. Williams, D. A. "The Great Computer Frenzy." Newsweek 27 December 1982: 68.~~

How to take notes as you read

Write out essentials in detail: don't rely on your memory. You might think you will remember what you meant by:

Authors provide important research findings on the effects of CAI on students.

But by the time you sit down to read fifty note cards, you probably will have forgotten what the findings were. See the sample note cards on pages 421–422.

1. Devise an identity heading for each note. As you read, you find kinds of information that belong together. If you are researching the effects of computers in education, you may study the effects on children, on teen-agers, and on adults. Some information may strike you as useful for the beginning of the paper; other information may seem slated for the end. Based on the tentative plan for your paper, write a heading for each card ("Effects on Teen-agers," "Good Material for Opening," and so forth). You may change your mind as you shuffle the cards once your research is complete, but you will have a start toward classifying the material.

2. Assign each note card a number. You don't need to copy all information (author's name, title, publisher, date, and so forth) on each note card. Instead, assign each source a number (No. 4–Hicks and Hunka). As you write your note, use the code number and page number:

   4. Hicks and Hunka, p. 20.

3. Write one note per card. Keep track of each piece of information you find on a separate note card. By reserving a note card for each bit of information, you'll be able to shuffle through your cards, placing together those facts and ideas that seem to belong together.

4. Summarize, paraphrase, or quote. You do not always need to copy complete passages on your note cards. Read the following section from the book *The Teacher and the Computer* by B. L. Hicks and S. Hunka. Then study the guidelines for summary, paraphrase, and quote, and consider the sample note cards that follow.

   Within the next decade teachers and computers will become educational partners. Their students will receive both classroom instruction and computer-assisted instruction.

   Today this partnership between teachers and computers is uncommon. Only a few powerful computer systems are dedicated to instruction, and computer-assisted instruction is found in only a few schools. But a large number of the teachers of the future must learn to use and to manage computer-assisted instruction as a new educational resource so that they can find, from day to day, the combination of classroom and computer-assisted instruction that best serves the need of each student.

SUMMARY When you *summarize,* you write *in your own words* the most outstanding points in a passage, a chapter, or an article. A summary is much shorter than the original. It highlights important information or ideas. After you have read the material, it is wise to turn away from it before recording your observations. Write down what you can remember, and then return to the original to make certain that you have not missed an important point. Also, make certain that you have not accidentally taken *actual phrases* from the original.

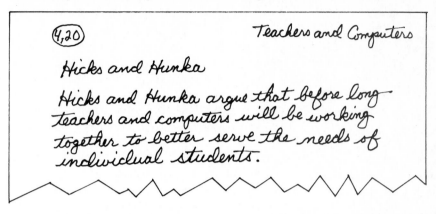

> (4,20)   Teachers and Computers
>
> Hicks and Hunka
>
> Hicks and Hunka argue that before long teachers and computers will be working together to better serve the needs of individual students.

PARAPHRASE In a *paraphrase*, you record an author's ideas *in your own words*. A paraphrase is usually longer than a summary because you record important points and any specifics you think are useful.

> (4,20)   Teachers and Computers
>
> Hicks and Hunka
>
> Hicks and Hunka maintain that over the next ten years, teachers and computers will work side by side, and students will receive instruction from both. At present (1972), this partnership is rare. But soon, teachers in greater numbers will have to learn to use and manage CAI in order to serve each student as effectively as possible.

QUOTATION A *quotation* records an author's *exact words*. Use quotations when you think that the author's words are particularly memorable or convincing. Remember to put quotation marks around the exact words of the author, and be sure that you copy capitalization, spelling, and punctuation exactly.

> Hicks and Hunka (4,20)   Teachers and Computers
>
> According to Hicks and Hunka, "Within the next decade teachers and computers will become educational partners. Their students will receive both classroom instruction and computer-assisted instruction."

YOUR COMMENTS You can also record your own ideas, comments, questions, and judgments. Too often, you forget ideas because you do not record them. Keep track of your own thoughts on note cards.

> (4,20)
>
> *Me:* Question about general remarks by Hicks and Hunka
>
> Since their book was published in 1972, what has happened? Is there a "partnership"? Find out.

WATCH OUT FOR PLAGIARISM

Plagiarism literally means "kidnapping"—stealing another's ideas and passing them off as your own. Some students plagiarize *deliberately*. They know what they are doing, and they risk failing a course or being expelled from school if they are caught.

Other students plagiarize *accidentally*. When they write their papers, they do not credit other writers for the ideas they have borrowed because when they took notes, they stayed close to the original and did not paraphrase. Notice in the passages below how close the "plagiarism" is to the original:

ORIGINAL	PLAGIARISM
Within the next decade teachers and computers will become educational partners. Their students will receive both classroom instruction and computer-assisted instruction.	In the next decade teachers and computers are going to become partners in education. Students will receive instruction both in the classroom from teachers and outside the classroom, assisted by computers.

PARAPHRASE AND QUOTE

Hicks and Hunka predict that soon teachers and computers "will become educational partners," their students receiving both CAI and traditional classroom instruction.

The following guidelines will help you *avoid* plagiarism:

1. Take accurate notes. Distinguish in your notes between your own ideas and the ideas of other writers.
2. Place quotation marks around *all* words or phrases that are not yours, and credit the source.
3. Credit any idea that is not yours even if it is paraphrased or summarized and does not appear in quotation marks.

18.g DESIGNING THE PAPER

By the end of your research, you will have a stack of note cards, a working idea, a working list of sources—and most of the work behind you. Now you will need to design the whole essay, as you have done with other essays. You'll need to examine your controlling idea and the specific points of support to determine how to arrange the essay: cause and effect, comparison or contrast, a generalization with specifics? You'll need to think about the beginning, the supporting paragraphs, and the ending (Chapter 5).

As you shuffle through your notes, you plan the essay by writing an outline. It may be an informal outline like the following:

Introduction: General remarks and questions about computers

Effects: academic (Illinois study)

Effects: psychological (on students and teachers)

Effects: social (computer bias; distribution inequities)

Conclusion: Computers are not the answer

Or you may choose to write a more detailed outline like the one in Chapter 19, page 438.

The final design of the paper is up to you as you weave the research you have done into a paper that is *yours*.

Use your own words   The rule of thumb is to write your research paper in your own words unless you want to capture the exact words of another writer for a special purpose. The following examples show how students have woven research into their own sentences:

■ Theatrical comedy represents a tradition as old as drama itself, and as culturally varied. For example, Japanese actors have staged comedies known as *kyogen* since the fourteenth century (Anderson 15).

The student reports on his research in his own words; he cites the material because the information is *not* general knowledge; it is taken from materials he has researched (pp. 425–429).

■ Strawberry's rookie statistics speak for themselves: 26 home runs, 74 runs batted in, and a .257 average (Salamone 36). What is not apparent is that he accumulated these totals in less than a full season.

Notice how the student controls the material by his own remark: "Strawberry's rookie statistics speak for themselves." He cites the statistics because Strawberry's exact record is not general knowledge.

■ Even as early as 1940, at the peak of Germany's power, Churchill spoke of an Allied invasion of Europe; he advised the conquered populations to remain patient and to gather their strength, to prepare for a time of retribution which was soon to come (Ingersoll 40). Amidst the despair of the defeated and suffering nations of Europe, Churchill remained the lone voice of hope and optimism.

Notice how the student selects from Churchill's advice. He doesn't quote an entire passage, but he chooses the material to fit his own purpose—to demonstrate Churchill's resolve in the face of the general despair of Europe. He says, "Amidst the despair . . . Churchill remained the lone voice. . . . "

Quote for a purpose   Use the exact words of a speaker or writer for a specific purpose:

1. To capture the exact wording because it is memorable
2. To relate the words of a famous quotation to your original ideas
3. To lend authority to your ideas by presenting the exact words of a recognized authority on your subject

When you do use quotations, follow these guidelines:

1. When you want to include only part of a quotation, use ellipses to indicate where material has been left out (pp. 375–376).
2. When you want to emphasize the name of the author or the speaker as well as the quotation, give the name in your text:

   As Benjamin Franklin said, "Little strokes fell great oaks."

3. When you want to use a brief quotation in your own sentence but do not want to emphasize the author's name, cite the name in a parenthetical note.
4. When you use a long quotation, introduce the words with your own remarks:

   As one researcher comments,
   As Benjamin Franklin said,

Read and study the following samples, which are from students' papers.

■ Rommel's diligence and his "ability to adapt his campaigns to the climate and terrain of the desert" (Stevens 86) was not surpassed.

Here the student uses the quotation because he wants to capture the precise phrasing, but he does not want to include the author of the words in his own sentence. He fits the quotation into his sentence, preserving the grammatical integrity of both, and then gives the author's name in a parenthetical note.

■ Promising to return Germany to its former glory, Hitler was jubilantly welcomed as a "true leader . . . a symbol of peace, unity, and social justice" (Frank 69).

Notice how the student tailors the quotation to suit his purpose. Again, he includes the author of the words in the parenthetical citation because his emphasis is on the expression.

■ Off the court, McEnroe is described as charming, witty, even shy. Then why the "Brat" routine? When asked about his controversial style, McEnroe said, "I've always been this way when I compete. Something about the competition brings out a part of me which is not necessarily there all of the time" (Crane 122).

The paper is about tennis player John McEnroe's on-court behavior. Rather than speculate on McEnroe's purposes, the student lets McEnroe speak for himself. Notice how the words of the speaker are introduced: "When asked about his controversial style, McEnroe said, . . . "

■ In her essay "Reunion," Nora Ephron describes the disillusionment she felt when she attended her tenth college reunion:

> I can pretend that I have come back to Wellesley only because I want to write about it, but I am really here because I still care, I still care about this Mickey Mouse institution; I am foolish enough to think that someday it will do something important for women. That I care at all, that I am here at all, makes me one of them. . . . This college is about as meaningful to the educational process in America as a perfume factory is to the national economy. And all of us care, which makes us all idiots for wasting a minute thinking about the place (389).

Notice how the student introduces the long quotation with her own words. She quotes at length because she wants to capture Ephron's phrasing and feeling. Note how she sets off the long quotation by indenting and single spacing it. (The student's typewritten essay will be double spaced.) She does not use quotation marks because indenting and single spacing serve the same purpose: they signal that the words are those of another writer.

Follow these guidelines for using long quotations:

1. Consider why you are using a long quotation: Do you want to capture the style and flavor of a whole passage? Can you just as well restate the information in your own words?
2. Introduce the long quotation with your own words.
3. Use a colon or a comma to set off the long quotation.
4. Set off a quotation of over fifty words by indenting five spaces on both sides and single spacing.
5. Use long quotations sparingly (only one or two to a five-page paper).

For additional pointers on punctuating quotations, see Chapter 16, pages 373–374.

18.h DOCUMENTATION (NEW MLA GUIDELINES: LIST OF WORKS CITED OR WORKS CONSULTED AND PARENTHETICAL CITATIONS)

There are two basic formats for documentation of outside sources. The traditional approach of footnotes and bibliography is explained later in this chapter (pp. 429–435). The newer, simplified approach, used by the student in the sample research essay in Chapter 19, presents brief parenthetical references within the text of the essay, which coordinate with the full entries compiled at the end of the paper; these final entries are called a "List of Works Cited," or a "List of Works Consulted" if you are including works that you have not cited.

What to cite   Citations serve two purposes: they give credit where it is due, and they permit your reader to find your original sources. Generally, *everything* that you have researched should be cited. Cite every quotation, every paraphrase, every summary. Cite all information that is not common knowledge. You know, for example, that Darel Strawberry is a powerful batter, but your research takes you to his record. The facts of his record, which are not general information, should be cited. When in doubt about what to cite and what not to cite, it's better to cite.

How to cite   The newer parenthetical approach to citing sources simplifies what used to be a rather laborious process. First you must determine what your source actually is. If it's a book, was it written by one author or by several authors? Is it an edited book (often a collection of essays that has been compiled by one or more editors)? Is the book a revised edition? If the book was first published in 1921 and revised in 1959, it is important for your reader to know which edition you are using; page numbers in one edition often do not correspond to page numbers in another edition. If you are using an encyclopedia, which one? what volume? In what year was the encyclopedia published?

List of works cited or works consulted   All citations for books have common features. They include the following information:

1. Name of the author or authors (last name first)
2. Title of the book (underlined)
3. Name of the editor or translator
4. Edition number (if other than the first)
5. City where the book was published
6. Name of the publisher
7. Date of publication
8. Page number(s) consulted (if not the whole book)

   A citation for an article published in a periodical, or in a collection of articles found in a book, includes the following information:

1. Name of the author or authors (last name first)
2. Title of the article (in quotation marks)
3. Title of the journal or collection (underlined)
4. Volume number, or edition
5. Date of publication (and if a collection, location and publisher)
6. Page number(s) consulted

Following the new format, all this information, arranged alphabetically by the last name of the author, need appear only once, *at the end of your paper,* in a list of "**Works Cited**" or "**Works Consulted.**" Sample entries are as follows.

BOOKS Book by one author:

> Terkel, Studs. *Working*. New York: Pantheon Books, 1972.

Book by two authors:

> Bernstein, Carl, and Bob Woodward. *All the President's Men*. New York: Simon and Schuster, 1974

(Note that the second author's first name appears first.)

An edition other than the first:

> Stone, L. Joseph, and Joseph Church. *Childhood and Adolescence: A Psychology of the Growing Person*. 5th ed. New York: Random House, 1984.

An edited book:

> James, Henry. *The Ambassadors*. Ed. Leon Edel. Boston: Riverside–Houghton Mifflin, 1960.

(Note that the publisher's special imprint, Riverside, precedes the publisher's name.)

An anthology:

> Cassill, R. V., ed. *The Norton Anthology of Short Fiction*. Shorter ed. New York: Norton, 1978.

A preface or an introduction:

> Edel, Leon. Introduction. *The Ambassadors*. By Henry James. Ed. Leon Edel. Boston: Riverside–Houghton Mifflin, 1960. v–xviii.

A translation:

> Mann, Thomas. *Stories of Three Decades*. Trans. H. T. Lowe-Porter. New York: Modern Library–Random House, 1930.

An encyclopedia entry:

> Haekel, Josef. "Totemism." *Encyclopaedia Britannica: Macropaedia*. 1974 ed.

(If an encyclopedia article is signed, include the author's name first.)

ARTICLES An article in a journal with continuous pagination:

> Berthoff, Ann E. "Is Teaching Still Possible? Writing, Meaning, and Higher Order Reasoning." *College English* 46 (1984): 743–755.

An article in a journal that pages each issue separately:

> Thoreson, Trygve. "Mark Twain's Unsentimental Heroine." *The South Carolina Review* 14.2 (1982): 22–32.

(The reference is to number 2 of volume 14.)

A review:

> Nabokov, Peter. Rev. of *Indian Country*, by Peter Matthiessen. *New York Review of Books* 31 (1984): 44–45.

An unsigned article from a popular magazine or journal:

> "Detroit's Worsening Plight." *Time* 26 May 1980: 42.

(Give the complete date instead of the volume and issue numbers.)

A signed article from a newspaper:

> Hovey, Graham. "Human Rights Group Supports President." *New York Times* 6 March 1977, late ed.: 5.

(If a newspaper article is unsigned, include the title of the article first. Note that if the article were concluded on a later page, the entry would read "late ed.: 5+.")

OTHER SOURCES A film:

> *The Cotton Club*. Dir. Francis Ford Coppola. With Richard Gere and Gregory Hines. Orion, 1984.

A radio or TV program:

> *Inside Russia*. Metromedia News. WNEW-TV, New York. 13 January 1985.

A recording:

> Ragni, Gerome, James Rado, and Galt MacDermot. *Hair*. Original Broadway cast recording. RCA Victor, LSO 1150, 1968.

A theatrical performance:

> *Much Ado About Nothing*. By William Shakespeare. Royal Shakespeare Company. Dir. Terry Hands. With Derek Jacobi and Sinead Cusack. Gershwin Theater, New York. 23 October 1984.

Computer software:

> *Symphony*. For IBM Personal Computers and COMPAQ Portable Computers. Lotus, 1984, disk.

See also the sample list of "Works Consulted" in Chapter 19, page 444.

Parenthetical citations

CITING BY AUTHOR'S NAME AND PAGE Once you have compiled and completed your list of "Works Cited" or "Works Consulted," citations within the text of your paper are greatly simplified under the new format for documentation. All that is required is the author's name and the page number(s), enclosed in a set of parentheses. For example, (Heilbroner 41) refers readers to the list of "Works Cited," where they discover an article by Robert L. Heilbroner entitled "Middle-Class Myths, Middle-Class Realities."

From the information supplied by the list of "Works Cited," readers also know that the article was published in *Atlantic* magazine, volume 238, dated October 1976. They know from the parenthetical citation that the particular note is to be found on page 41.

Keep your parenthetical citations as brief as possible. For example, if the author's name appears in your text, it need not appear for a second time within the parentheses:

CITING BY PAGE ONLY   . . . Heilbroner has alluded to this point previously (39–40).

CITING BY AUTHOR'S NAME, TITLE, AND PAGE   When two or more works by the same author appear in the list of "Works Cited" or "Works Consulted," include the title or a shortened form of the title in the citation: (Wilson, *Sociobiology* 32) and (Wilson, *The Insect Societies* 125).

CITING BY TITLE AND PAGE   The important thing to remember is that the purpose of the reference is to allow your readers to find the work cited; so be sure that you provide them with the author's name, the title if necessary, and the appropriate page numbers. When an article is unsigned, the title will serve in place of the author's name ("Detroit's Worsening Plight" 42).

The key to the simplified format is common sense. Whatever information is necessary for readers to locate the source must be provided by the parenthetical citation in conjunction with the list of "Works Cited." It goes without saying, therefore, that all parenthetical citations must be accounted for in the list of "Works Cited" and that the two notes must agree.

18.i DOCUMENTATION (TRADITIONAL MLA GUIDELINES)

Some teachers may ask you to use the older, more traditional approach to documentation, which involves footnotes and a bibliography. They coordinate in much the same way as the newer format of parenthetical references and list of "Works Cited," except that the footnote is much more complete and autonomous than is the parenthetical note; the footnote allows the reader to locate the source without necessarily referring to the bibliography, which is more or less the same as the list of "Works Cited."

What to footnote   As in the case of the parenthetical citation, the footnote serves two purposes. It gives credit to another writer for an idea of his or hers that you have chosen to use, and it allows the reader to locate the source.

How to footnote   Footnotes look complicated, but they need not be. They include essentially the same information found in the list of "Works Cited" arranged in a slightly different way. Among the differences are the use of commas (instead of periods) between the author's name and the book title, parentheses (containing the place of publication, publisher, and date of publication), and superscripts, which are raised numbers that appear in the text of your paper. Also, the author's name appears with his or her first name first and last name last, indented at the beginning of each footnote; page references are given in the footnotes, not in the text.

BOOKS   Books by one author:

[1] Studs Terkel, *Working* (New York: Pantheon Books, 1974), p. 63.

Book by two authors:

[2] Carl Bernstein and Bob Woodward, *All the President's Men* (New York: Simon and Schuster, 1974), p. 43.

An edition other than the first:

[3] L. Joseph Stone and Joseph Church, *Childhood and Adolescence: A Psychology of the Growing Person,* 5th ed. (New York: Random House, 1984), p. 17.

An edited book:

[4] Henry James, *The Ambassadors,* ed. Leon Edel (Boston: Riverside–Houghton Mifflin, 1960), p. 17.

An anthology:

[5] Michele H. Garskof, ed., *Roles Women Play: Readings Toward Women's Liberation* (Belmont, Calif.: Wadsworth Publishing Company, 1971), p. 116.

An essay in an anthology:

[6] Marlene Dixon, "Why Women's Liberation," in *Roles Women Play: Readings Toward Women's Liberation,* ed. Michele H. Garskof (Belmont, Calif.: Wadsworth Publishing Company, 1971), p. 165.

A preface or an introduction:

[7] Leon Edel, Introd., *The Ambassadors,* by Henry James, ed. Leon Edel (Boston: Riverside–Houghton Mifflin, 1960), pp. v–xviii.

A translation:

[8] Thomas Mann, *Stories of Three Decades,* trans. H. T. Lowe-Porter (New York: Modern Library–Random House, 1930), p. 20.

An encyclopedia entry (because the entries in an encyclopedia appear in alphabetical order, a volume number is unnecessary):

[9] Josef Haekel, "Totemism," *Encyclopaedia Britannica: Macropaedia,* 1974 ed.

[10] "Television," *Collier's Encyclopedia,* 1965 ed.

Footnotes are numbered *consecutively* throughout your paper. They are placed at the bottom (or *foot*) of the page. Footnotes are typed single spaced, and the first line of each footnote should be indented. Leave a triple space above the first footnote; double space between footnotes.

You may be permitted to use endnotes—that is, all your "footnotes" may be placed at the end of your paper. Check with your instructor on college policy.

Once you footnote a source, you do not need to repeat the entire entry if you cite the same source again. Just use the last name of the author and the page number:

[11] Margaret Mead, *Blackberry Winter: My Earlier Years* (New York: Morrow, 1972), p. 73.

[12] Studs Terkel, *Working* (New York: Pantheon Books, 1974), p. 63.

[13] Mead, p. 104.

[14] Terkel, p. 307.

If you immediately repeat the same source, do not use the discarded forms *ibid.* and *op. cit.* Repeat the identifying information of the preceding note.

Footnotes tell a great deal about your paper because they show whether you have integrated your sources. The footnote scheme that follows shows that the writer has used one source, then exclusively another, and then exclusively another ("Terkel, Terkel, Terkel, Mead, Mead, Mead," and so on). The student has probably not integrated the sources and is in danger of producing a patchwork paper:

[22] Terkel, p. 17.

[23] Terkel, p. 17.

[24] Terkel, p. 17.

[25] Mead, p. 43.

[26] Mead, p. 43.

[27] Mead, p. 43.

[28] Bernstein and Woodward, p. 76.

[29] Bernstein and Woodward, p. 76.

[30] Bernstein and Woodward, p. 78.

[31] Carter, p. 11.

[32] Carter, p. 12.

[33] Carter, p. 12.

ARTICLES Footnote 34 is a typical footnote for a signed article from a popular magazine. Notice the differences between it and footnote 35 for an article from a book.

[34] Robert L. Heilbroner, "Middle-Class Myths, Middle-Class Realities," *Atlantic,* October 1976, p. 37.

[35] Perry Miller, "Jonathan Edwards and the Great Awakening," *Colonial America,* ed. Stanley N. Katz (Boston: Little, Brown, 1971), pp. 283–297.

An unsigned article from a popular magazine or journal:

[36]"Detroit's Worsening Plight," *Time,* 26 May 1980, p. 42.

(Note that the title of the article appears first when the article is unsigned.)
A review:

[37]Peter Nabokov, rev. of *Indian Country,* by Peter Matthiessen, *New York Review of Books,* 31 (1984), 44–45.

Scholarly journals often have both issue and volume numbers and often are paged continuously throughout an annual volume.

An article in a journal with continuous pagination:

[38]Ann E. Berthoff, "Is Teaching Still Possible? Writing, Meaning, and Higher Order Reasoning," *College English,* 46 (1984), 743–755.

An article in a journal that pages each issue separately:

[39]Trygve Thoreson, "Mark Twain's Unsentimental Heroine," *The South Carolina Review,* 14, No. 2 (1982), 22–32.

A signed article from a newspaper:

[40]Graham Hovey, "Human Rights Group Supports President." *New York Times,* Late City Ed., 6 March 1977, p. 5, col. 1.

(An unsigned newspaper article, like an unsigned magazine article, would include the name of the article first.)

OTHER SOURCES A film:

[41]Francis Ford Coppola, dir., *The Cotton Club,* with Richard Gere and Gregory Hines, Orion, 1984.

A radio or TV program:

[42]"Inside Russia," Metromedia News, WNEW-TV, New York, 13 January 1985.

Use quotation marks around the title of a one-time TV or radio program or an episode in a series. Italicize the title of the series, e.g., *The Cosby Show*.

A recording:

[43]Gerome Ragni, James Rado, and Galt MacDermot, *Hair,* original Broadway cast recording, RCA Victor, LSO 1150, 1968.

A theatrical performance:

[44]William Shakespeare, *Much Ado About Nothing,* Royal Shakespeare Company, dir. Terry Hands, with Derek Jacobi and Sinead Cusack, Gershwin Theater, New York, 23 October 1984.

If you are writing in a discipline like psychology or biology, your instructor will ask you to follow a footnote form specific to that discipline. If you need footnotes for materials that have not been included here, your school's English department probably provides a manual of style that describes the particular ways papers and research papers are to be written.

18.j THE BIBLIOGRAPHY

The bibliography is a list of the sources that you have consulted for your paper. Notice that there are slight differences between a footnote entry and a bibliography entry:

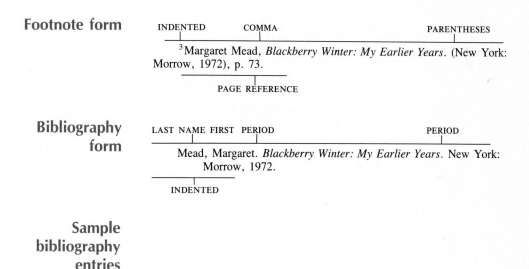

Footnote form

INDENTED   COMMA   PARENTHESES

³Margaret Mead, *Blackberry Winter: My Earlier Years.* (New York: Morrow, 1972), p. 73.

PAGE REFERENCE

Bibliography form

LAST NAME FIRST PERIOD   PERIOD

Mead, Margaret. *Blackberry Winter: My Earlier Years.* New York: Morrow, 1972.

INDENTED

Sample bibliography entries

BOOKS Book by one author:

Terkel, Studs. *Working.* New York: Pantheon Books, 1974.

Book by two authors:

Bernstein, Carl, and Bob Woodward. *All the President's Men.* New York: Simon and Schuster, 1974.

(Note that the second author's first name appears before the last name.)

An edition other than first:

Stone, L. Joseph, and Joseph Church. *Childhood and Adolescence: A Psychology of the Growing Person.* 5th ed. New York: Random House, 1984

An edited book:

James, Henry. *The Ambassadors.* Ed. Leon Edel. Boston: Riverside–Houghton Mifflin, 1960.

An anthology:

> Garskof, Michele H., ed. *Roles Women Play: Readings Toward Women's Liberation*. Belmont, Calif.: Wadsworth Publishing Company, 1971.

An essay in an anthology:

> Dixon, Marlene. "Why Women's Liberation." In *Roles Women Play: Readings Toward Women's Liberation*. Ed. Michele H. Garskof. Belmont, Calif.: Wadsworth Publishing Company, 1971, p. 165.

A preface or an introduction:

> Edel, Leon, introd. *The Ambassadors*. By Henry James. Ed. Leon Edel. Boston: Riverside–Houghton Mifflin, 1960.

A translation:

> Mann, Thomas. *Stories of Three Decades*. Trans. H. T. Lowe-Porter. New York: Modern Library–Random House, 1930.

An encyclopedia entry:

> Haekel, J. "Totemism." *Encyclopaedia Britannica: Macropaedia*. 1974 ed.

> (If an encyclopedia article is unsigned, include the title of the article first.)

ARTICLES A signed article from a popular magazine:

> Heilbroner, Robert L. "Middle-Class Myths, Middle-Class Realities." *Atlantic,* October 1976, pp. 37–42.

> (Include all page numbers of the article.)

An unsigned article from a popular magazine or journal:

> "Detroit's Worsening Plight." *Time,* 26 May 1980, p. 42.

A review:

> Nabokov, Peter. Rev. of *Indian Country,* by Peter Matthiessen. *New York Review of Books,* 31 (1984), 44–45.

An article in a journal with continuous pagination:

> Berthoff, Ann E. "Is Teaching Still Possible? Writing, Meaning, and Higher Order Reasoning." *College English,* 46 (1984), 743–755.

An article in a journal that pages each issue separately:

> Thoreson, Trygve. "Mark Twain's Unsentimental Heroine." *The South Carolina Review,* 14, No. 2 (1982), 22–32.

A signed article from a newspaper:

> Hovey, Graham. "Human Rights Group Supports President." *New York Times,* Late City Ed., 6 March 1977, p. 5, col. 1.

> (If a newspaper article is unsigned, include the title of the article first.)

OTHER SOURCES A film:

> Coppola, Francis Ford, dir. *The Cotton Club*. With Richard Gere and Gregory Hines. Orion, 1984.

A radio or TV program:

> *Inside Russia*. Metromedia News, WNET-TV, New York. 13 January 1985.

A recording:

> Ragni, Gerome, James Rado, and Galt MacDermot. *Hair*. Original Broadway cast recording. RCA Victor, LSO 1150, 1968.

A theatrical performance:

> Shakespeare, William. *Much Ado About Nothing*. Royal Shakespeare Company. Dir. Terry Hands. With Derek Jacobi and Sinead Cusack. Gershwin Theater, New York. 23 October 1984.

chapter
19

Sample Student Research Essay

The following sample research essay was written by a student in a freshman writing course. Allison Sham's personal experience, her own opinions, and her research findings merge in her essay on computers in education. She begins with a personal anecdote (''As I was doing some reading for a computer-science course, . . .'') and leads to her controlling idea (''. . . I feel that a computer-based system will not solve our leading educational problem—the declining motivation of students to learn.'') Allison then weaves her research in among her own ideas to support her developing argument. She ends with a recommendation for caution: ''. . . if we carefully examine the pros and cons, we will see that the teacher remains a necessary part of the learning experience.''

Allison's paper fulfilled the assignment for a 1,200-word research essay. The paper relies on limited research because Allison's instructor encouraged the members of the class to emphasize their own ideas rather than the ideas of others. It incorporates her research as support for her own ideas. Since most students had not written this kind of paper before, the instructor guided them through each step: the class as a group visited the library, the card-catalog room, the reference room, the stacks, and the microfilm area. All students wrote a working question, a working bibliography, and notes that summarized and paraphrased their research findings. They all practiced integrating their research into their texts, and they had the opportunity to read their first drafts to other members of the class.

By the end of this assignment, Allison had not simply seamed together the ideas of several writers; instead, she had designed and written an essay of her own, weaving her research in and out of the text to lend support to her own thinking.

Computers and Education

Allison Sham

English 110

April 15, 1985

Computers and Education

Although your instructor may not require an outline for most of the papers you write, you may be asked to keep track, in outline form, of your ideas for a research paper because your ideas are likely to be complex.

STATEMENT OF CONTROLLING IDEA: A computer-based system will not solve our leading educational problem--the declining motivation of students to learn.

   I.   INTRODUCTION

      A. Teacher-computer partnership

      B. Computer experiments in classrooms (my sister's class)

      C. Failure to solve our leading educational problem

  II.   EFFECTS: ACADEMIC

      A. Introduction to the University of Illinois study

      B. Chart

      C. Analysis of results

         1. No significant academic improvement for CAI students

         2. Higher dropout rate among CAI students

 III.   EFFECTS: PSYCHOLOGICAL

      A. Favorable reactions of students

      B. Motivation increased by "live" feedback

      C. Declining interest of teachers

  IV.   EFFECTS: PERSONAL

      A. Built-in computer biases

      B. Distributional inequities

   V.   CONCLUSION

      A. Understanding, not information, essential

      B. My sister's classroom

      C. Computers not the answer; teachers necessary

2

As I was doing some reading for a computer-science course, I came upon a quotation that stuck in my mind: "Within the next decade teachers and computers will become educational partners. Their students will receive both classroom instruction and computer-assisted instruction" (Hicks and Hunka 20). What interested me about the statement was that it had been made over a decade ago, in 1972. I wondered whether or not the prediction had come true. As I researched the question more and more, I found that during the past ten years we have seen not only the coexistence of teachers and computers in education, but also cases in which the teacher has actually been replaced by the computer. In my own sister's fourth-grade class, "computer time" has now replaced the afternoon story hour, in which the teacher would read to the children such stories as The Wind in the Willows and the Tales of King Arthur. Throughout the country, such experiments in CAI (computer-assisted instruction) are in progress, and the results are being studied and debated. While the powers of the computer cannot be underestimated, I feel that a computer-based system will not solve our leading educational problem--the declining motivation of students to learn.

Advocates of this new teaching method are chiefly concerned with achievement. Can computers really motivate students to learn so that their deficiencies in basic skills are eliminated? Can these "thinking machines" really instill such interest in students that there will be a reduced drop-out rate? Below are the results of a test conducted at the University of Illinois by Professor Richard Montanelli, Jr. (Osnin 21):

LECTURER	TREATMENT	1st hourly exam (Mean Score)	2nd hourly exam (Mean Score)	Final exam (Mean Score)	DROP-OUT RATE (%)
A	non-CAI	91	62	134	4
B	non-CAI	91	62	134	14
A	CAI	92	65	140	15
B	CAI	91	62	135	25

This was a partially computer-based experiment. Students in the CAI program were chosen at random. They attended lectures conducted by their

The essay begins with a personal statement about the way in which the research essay got started: what the student had read aroused her interest in computers and education.

An example drawn from personal experience makes the topic more concrete.

The writer states the controlling idea.

The parenthetical citations are keyed to the "Works Consulted" list on p. 444.

The writer calls on authorities and numerical data to support her point.

respective lecturers for two hours per week and spent an hour or more learning from the computer. Examinations given were standardized. As the chart shows, despite the differences among the four groups, students achieved about the same academic level. Perhaps the most significant numbers are the drop—out rates: a combined average of 9 percent among non—CAI participants, as opposed to a combined average of 20 percent in the CAI courses. The computer—supplemented classes, then, incurred more than twice the drop—out rate of the non—CAI classes. These results are dramatic, and the implications are profound. As for academic achieve- ment, outcomes from various experiments are by and large inconclusive; there is no consistent pattern that indicates that CAI students perform any better than non—CAI students. It seems the computer does not improve the standard of education, as is so often claimed.

Even more uncertainties have been expressed over another issue: Does a computer—based education have a dehumanizing effect on partici- pants? The majority of CAI students do not think so. Instead, they find computers are "exciting to work with" and "friendly" and "not dismayed by . . . mistakes" (Clement 29). But these reactions may be due to the novelty of computer education; surely a student who has been interacting with computers for his entire childhood would find a traditionally con- ducted class refreshing.

But what kind of human beings are going to emerge from computer- based programs? That is the real question that underlies motivation. Professor Robert Hem of Stanford University, who worked with a CAI ex- perimental program involving adolescents, has found evidence of undesir- able personal effects on them. For example, instead of treating the com- puter as a human tool and the human being as its master, the teen—agers seem to be crediting the machine for its own ability (Meek 115). The University of Illinois experiment also included a questionnaire in which participants assessed their instructors; non—CAI students, on the whole,

4

formed much better opinions of their lecturers than did CAI students (Osnin 22). Apparently, one less hour with classroom discussion and one more with computers undermines the personal relationship between lecturers and CAI students.

Advocates of CAI programs point to characteristics of the computer such as patience, indefatigability, an unprejudiced nature, and the individualized attention it supplies. On the surface, then, computers would seem more suitable instructors than people. But the question is not as straightforward as it appears at first. A computer never loses its patience, never complains, and never criticizes; these virtues are true enough. But a recent test shows that perhaps we do need instructors who sometimes are impatient, complaining, and critical. In the test, fifth- and sixth-grade boys were divided into two groups, and they were told to perform a certain task. The first group received appropriate feedback, either positive or negative, and the second group received no feedback whatsoever from the teacher. The students in the latter group tended not to work any longer than necessary, whereas the students in the former group persisted in their tasks for a much longer period of time (Draper 34–40). It seems clear, then, that both praise and reproof are helpful in encouraging students to work more diligently than they would without feedback. And for all the recent advancements, computer feedback remains largely limited to a half-dozen or so stock responses, which tend after a while to become mere signals to proceed. To reduce the monotony, educators have introduced humor into some programmed lessons, but as the pop song goes, "Ain't nothing like the real thing." The best classroom humor is almost without exception spontaneous, and computers will always lack spontaneity. Students also need to voice their own ideas, listen to the opinions of others, and form their own conclusions. A student learning from a CAI system has simply to accept whatever theories, explanations, and data are forced on him. He cannot argue; he simply must

5

accept the given information. Learning theorists believe that "no one can really master a concept unless he is forced to express it in his own words or actions and to construct his own applications and examples" (Silberman 215). The CAI student who never engages in informal discussions and debates and who never expresses his point of view, whether it is right or wrong, will eventually learn less than his non-CAI counterparts.

The danger of monotony, in fact, is really twofold. Not only are students susceptible, but teachers are also. Addressing himself to this issue, Nobel Prize winner Herbert H. Simon comments:

The writer introduces this long quotation and then presents it in indented form, omitting quotation marks.

> As those of you who have experimented with it know, . . . [programming appropriate responses] requires teachers to be able to generate unlimited supplies of interesting problems, and to provide new ones. Faculties simply have neither the time nor the motivation to continue to develop these problems. If they have to be developed by hand, after five years or thereabouts of enthusiasm, the student-paced instruction tends to fade from the scene again and you go back to traditional forms of instruction. (Simon 19)

Another much-stressed advantage of the computer is that it is not biased with respect to students. That much is true. In and of itself, it cannot discriminate against them in any way. But it is quite possible for the contents of the computerized lessons to be prejudiced, as has been pointed out by Brian Meek: "Someone designing or programming an educational computer system could quite easily (and not necessarily consciously) build in his own prejudices" (Meek 102). Moreover, access to computers has become a major issue as well. A recent federal study has revealed "ominous inequities" in computer access due to differences in "social status, gender, and geographic location" (Welch 14). Wayne W. Welch, commenting on the same study, points out: "While access to and use of computers is rapidly increasing in schools, substantial instruc-

6

tion in computer programming remains primarily limited to males attend-
ing computer-rich schools in large cities. . . ." (Welch 14).

The individualized attention a student gets from a computer is
clearly advantageous. Students need not fear embarrassment in wrong answers; nor do they need to fear competition from classmates. However,
this individualized method causes studying to become too mechanical,
and, once again, the problem of monotony arises. Without sufficient motivation, necessary feedback, and peer competition, the student turns
the "studying of history into the learning of dates, or the study of   **The writer uses a striking quotation to launch the ending.**
language into the study of irregular verbs" (Meek 115). In the words of
the philosopher Alfred North Whitehead: "What students need most, therefore, is not more information but greater depth of understanding and
greater ability to apply that understanding to new situations as they
arise. A merely well-informed man is the most useless bore in God's
Earth" (Silberman 209).

CAI in one form or another is, of course, here to stay. We cannot   **The ending returns to the personal experience mentioned at the beginning and reasserts the controlling idea.**
move backward just because technology is not solving all our problems
for us. In my sister's school, though "computer time" is surely a permanent part of the school day, I would hope that an enlightened school
board could restore time for a good reader to read aloud. We must not
become so enamored of technology that we allow it to lead us in circles
and away from the human pleasures of learning together. In the case of
CAI, I feel that if we carefully examine the pros and cons, we will see
that the teacher remains a necessary part of the learning experience.

7

Works Consulted

Clement, Frank J. "Affective Considerations in Computer-Based Educa-
    tion." Educational Technology 4 April 1981: 28–32.

Draper, Thomas. "Praise, Reproof and Persistence in Fifth and Sixth
    Grade Boys." Educational Research Quarterly 5 May 1981: 31–40.

Hicks, B. L., and S. Hunka. The Teacher and the Computer. Philadelphia:
    W. B. Saunders Company, 1972.

Kendal, S., and E. Benoit. "Hello Mr. Chip." Forbes 23 April 1984: 132–36.

Meek, Brian. "Computers and Education." In Computers and the World 2000.
    Ed. Lord Avebury and others. Manchester, England: NCC Publica-
    tions, 1972: 101–116.

Osnin, Luis. "The Survival Principle and the Comparative Evaluation of
    Instructional Systems." Educational Technology 18 January 1978:
    19–23.

Silberman, Charles. "Technology Is Knocking at the Schoolhouse Door." In
    The World of Computers. Ed. John Diebold. New York: Random House,
    1973: 205–220.

Simon, H. A. "Computers in Education: Realizing the Potential." American
    Education December 1983: 19–23.

Welch, Wayne W. "Computer Learning Inequities." USA Today 14 April 1984:
    13–14.

Williams, D. A. "The Great Computer Frenzy." Newsweek 27 December 1982: 68.

Writing That Means Business

chapter

20 | Exams, Précis, Business Letters, and Résumés

In the final chapter of this book, we offer you practical suggestions that may make life a bit easier for you—in and out of college. We have found in our teaching and workshop experiences that most college students have never confronted the challenge of writing the précis. Many students have difficulty taking essay exams, and practically everyone has questions about business writing, especially concerning the job résumé and letter of application.

20.a WRITING A PRÉCIS

Students in an introductory writing class were asked to write a 100-word condensation of a 3,500-word essay. Impossible? No, but difficult and exacting.

A *précis* is a condensation *in your own words* of a short work: an article, an essay, or perhaps a chapter in a book. The technique of précis writing requires that you read closely and write precisely. Writing a précis is excellent practice for taking notes (especially for the research paper—see Chapter 18) and for developing reading and writing skills.

Here are guidelines for précis writing:

1. Highlight the most important ideas, and omit the specifics. Record the bare bones of the article, leaving out all subordinate ideas and modifiers. (See the discussion of generalizations and specifics in Chapter 3 and the discussion of modification in Chapter 11.)

2. Observe accurately. Report exactly what you read *in the order in which it is presented*. Do not inject your own opinion.

3. Make every word count. Eliminate all unnecessary words from your writing. Keep to the bare essentials.

4. Observe the word limit given by your instructor.

A sample article and précis that condenses it follow:

Air Force Tries 'Superglue'

By JOHN NOBLE WILFORD

THE United States Air Force is slowly and cautiously coming around to what model airplane builders have known all along: the importance of glue in assembling aircraft.

Two years of structural tests with a 42-foot-long fuselage section, bonded with epoxy adhesive and almost rivetless, have been completed, and an Air Force engineer last week called the results "more successful than we expected."

Indeed, the Air Force said that manufacturers who bid for the contract to build a new cargo plane, the CX, may be encouraged to employ superglues in the fuselage to reduce the craft's weight and cost.

An adhesively bonded aircraft, Air Force engineers say, would weigh 15 percent less and cost 20 percent less to build and maintain than its riveted counterpart. William Shelton, manager of the adhesives bonding technology project, said that soon airframe manufacturers would be asked to submit ideas on how to incorporate the technology throughout the industry.

The $18.4 million project, called PABST, for primary adhesively bonded structure technology, is managed by the Wright Aeronautical Laboratory at Wright-Patterson Air Force Base in Ohio. The "glued together" test fuselage was constructed by the McDonnell Douglas Corporation at Long Beach, Calif., using an industrial epoxy made by the American Cyanamid Company.

A major advance in the project was learning how to prepare the two surfaces of an aluminum alloy to be joined by an adhesive.

The frequent problems with delamination and corrosion were found to be largely the fault of the bond foundation rather than the glue itself. So an oxidizing technique developed by the Boeing Company, called phosphoric acid anodizing, was employed to create porous surfaces on which both a corrosion-retarding primer and the adhesive would adhere.

Both surfaces to be joined were so treated. After the adhesive was applied, the joined pieces were placed in an ovenlike pressure vessel and cured for an hour at 250 degrees Fahrenheit.

The fuselage survived tests simulating the pressurizing and depressurizing of 120,000 hours of flight, or four aircraft lifetimes. Near the end of the testing, cracks were deliberately cut in the structure, and the adhesive bond lines were found to retard the growth of a crack, according to John Williamson, deputy program manager for advanced metallic studies at the Wright laboratory.

Although the structural fatigue tests have been completed, the fuselage is still undergoing environmental tests in which it is exposed to salty air, high humidity and freezing temperatures.

Various kinds of adhesives are already used in aircraft interiors, on the leading edges of wings and on such control surfaces as rudders and elevators.

Lockheed's L-1011 wide-bodied passenger jet has a laminated aluminum and epoxy exterior, although it is reinforced in places with metal fasteners. Adhesives experts also see a growing application in the construction of automobiles and railroad equipment.

In the first sentence, the précis writer states the controlling idea of the article. The point that model-airplane builders have used epoxy for years is interesting but unessential information.

The details of the research are eliminated in the précis.

Précis

The United States Air Force is hopeful that superglue can be used to assemble aircraft. For two years, the Air Force has been testing fuselage sections held together by epoxy adhesive. Engineers believe that "epoxy-bonded aircraft" will weigh less and cost less than riveted aircraft.

The project, PABST (primary adhesively bonded structure technology), which is directed by Wright Aeronautical Laboratory, cost $18.4 million. The industry found a method of preparing aluminum surfaces so that the epoxy would hold. Fuselage sections have passed structural tests equaling 120,000 hours of flying time and are now undergoing environmental tests.

While glue has been used on the interiors of aircraft, adhesive experts see a future for it in other parts of the aircraft industry and in the automobile and railroad industries as well.

Summary of paragraphs 1–4

Summary of paragraphs 5–10

Summary of paragraphs 11–12

Exercise 1 Write a 100-word précis of the following essay on cannibalism.

Behavior

Do People Really Eat People?

An anthropologist says cannibalism is a myth

Columbus, greeted by the peaceful Arawaks on Hispaniola, was immediately warned about the man-eating Caribs on nearby islands. The conquistadors reported that the Aztecs butchered victims, ate the flesh and fed the entrails to zoo animals. Henry Morton Stanley said he was beset on all sides by savage cannibals dur-

DRAWING BY O. SOGLOW: © 1957 THE NEW YORKER MAGAZINE INC.

ing his famous trek through Africa to find Livingstone. Margaret Mead wrote about the man-eating Mundugumor of New Guinea. There is only one thing wrong with all these reports: they come second or third hand, and are probably false. That is the surprising thesis of a new book called *The Man-Eating Myth* by Anthropologist William Arens, who believes cannibalism may never have existed anywhere as a regular custom.*

Arens, who teaches at the State University of New York at Stony Brook, knows he is taking on the whole profession of anthropology. He feels that the profession is wrong, misled by generations of gullible researchers and inventive travel writers. In fact, he says, cannibalism is a myth used by the West to justify colonialism, slavery and—in the case of the Aztecs—genocide.

The origin of the myth, he thinks, is the tendency of every group to accuse its neighbors of cannibalism. The Arawaks and Caribs are good examples, and Mead was told about the Mundugumor by the Arapesh tribe. But Arens finds no reliable firsthand accounts of cannibalism.

"Like the poor," he says, "cannibals are always with us, but happily just beyond the possibility of direct observation."

Arens' theory arrives at a time when cannibalism is a hot topic in the academic world. Some sociobiologists believe it is evidence of man's inherent aggressiveness. Anthropologists are busy classifying different kinds of cannibalism, or depicting it as a ritualistic denial of death—the victim lives on by being incorporated as food. Columbia Anthropologist Marvin Harris (*Cannibals and Kings*) is a strict materialist who argues that cannibalism was a near universal practice made necessary by a scarcity of protein.

Naturally enough, Harris, like other anthropologists, takes issue with Arens. Says he: "There are all kinds of eyewitness accounts of cannibalism, from castaways, Jesuit missionaries and others. Arens is pushing skepticism to the point of producing nothing but total ignorance about the world."

Arens thinks many of these reports are similar to tales of witches. Often the explorer or traveler simply misinterprets the unfamiliar tribal language. Plagiarism, and the marketability of savage tales from the wilds have also helped establish the existence of cannibalism, says Arens. One example: 16th century accounts of cannibalism among the Tupinamba, a now extinct Brazilian tribe, all use similar wording. Arens thinks it unlikely

*Arens acknowledges occasional acts of cannibalism. Two weeks ago, for example, Emperor Bokassa I, the deposed leader of the Central African Republic, was reportedly accused of practicing cannibalistic rites. Examples of eating human flesh for survival in emergencies (*e.g.*, the siege of Stalingrad, the Andes plane crash in 1972) also abound.

"that a parade of international travelers all passed through a Tupinamba encampment on different days when the Indians were about to slay a war captive while the main characters were repeating similar statements to each other."

Arens says Columbus passed on tales of cannibalism to his Spanish masters to help establish a slave trade. In one report he wrote of the Caribs: "The welfare of said cannibals . . . has raised the thought the more that may be sent over [to Spain] the better." Afterward, on one Caribbean island after another, natives were identified as cannibals, then enslaved. Says Arens: "Thus the operational definition of cannibalism in the 16th century was resistance to foreign invasion followed by being sold into slavery."

Most scholars think Aztec cannibalism is firmly documented. Arens disagrees. He says the Spanish and the Aztecs accused one another of cannibalism —a common result of the collision of two cultures—but the Spanish got to write the history books. According to the author, the Spanish were stunned by the sophistication of Aztec culture and desperately needed justification for destroying it. After the Aztecs were destroyed and the slave trade dried up, both the cannibalism theme and the slave trade turned to Africa. "As one group of cannibals disappeared," Arens writes, "the European mind conveniently invented another."

To Arens, the idea of cannibalism is "a crucial boundary marker" between cultures: those who consider themselves civilized always manage to see cannibalism among those they consider uncivilized. "On this issue, despite other accomplishments," he writes, "anthropologists have emerged as little more than erudite purveyors of a pedestrian myth about other times and places." ∎

TIME, OCTOBER 22, 1979

20.b TAKING AN ESSAY EXAM

Don't stay up the night before.

Stay up the night before.

Don't cram.

Review.

Take a cold shower.

Take a hot bath.

Go to the movies.

Read a good book.

Eat a good breakfast.

Eat nothing.

How-to-study manuals prescribe numerous and often conflicting suggestions about preparing for an essay examination. If you study all the advice, you may feel that you'd be better off eating a bowl of chicken soup than reading another one of these manuals.

When it comes down to it, individuals respond *individually* to taking essay exams. Ask any group of students, and you'll get a number of differing responses. Common ingredients do go into preparing for and writing an exam, but it is up to you, in the end, to rely on your own experience.

In this section of "practical helps," we'll consider three steps in exam taking:

1. Preparing for the exam
2. The night before
3. The exam itself

Preparing for the exam Studying for an exam begins with *reading* your text and your notes. How you attack the chapters, how you establish the points that the author is trying to get across, how you write your notes—all these acts are part of an overall strategy for organizing your thinking.

TIME Give yourself time to study. Opening a 300-page history text for the first time the night before the exam is asking for disaster. Pace yourself. Keep up with the assignments, portion off material to read and study, take notes from your text and from lectures, write outlines, and study as you go along.

FACTS AND IDEAS You need facts *and* ideas. Facts alone are not enough. Many students who memorize dates, names, and places do not piece them together to see or understand ideas. In your reading, search for the general and abstract ideas that hold the facts together (in the same way that your controlling idea holds the details of your essay). Individual details about the War of 1812 may fascinate you, but you need to know what those details mean. Study the facts in relation to causes and effects, comparisons and contrasts, descriptions and definitions. Try to understand.

Your goal as an exam taker is to know the meaning of the facts you learn so that you can present the broad picture of a historical event, a philosophical position, a cultural theory. Facts are an important part of this picture, for general statements alone will not convince your instructor that you know the material. Pay attention to dates, names, places, and the like, and use them as support for your generalizations.

MNEMONICS *Mnemonics* are ways of remembering information that you think is important. Say, for example, that you want to remember four effects of Columbus's discovery of the New World:

1. Discovering a northwest passage to the East
2. Finding gold, silver, and gems
3. Conquering new lands
4. Converting natives to Christianity

You pick a letter from each of the four effects:

E = East
G = gold

L = lands
N = natives

Then you put the letters together to form a word:

GLEN

Memorize the word; associate it with the four effects of Columbus's discovery. When you confront a relevant exam question, call upon the word, peel off the layers, and get to the information you need.

DRESS REHEARSAL Write practice essay questions. The purpose of writing practice exams is not to try to psych out your instructor (although you *may* come up with a practice question that is the same as one on the exam). Rather, the purpose of practice exams is to stimulate your thinking about an issue and to practice writing these thoughts in an essay.

In studying the War of 1812, you learn not only the facts, but also the meaning of the facts. You ask yourself questions like these:

1. Why did the war occur?
2. What were its origins?
3. What were its causes?
4. What were the results (short term, long term)?
5. What were the most important battles?

And you answer them. During this rehearsal, time is less important than the content of your answers. With your goal a complete, well-organized essay, you can work from an outline and use your text and lecture notes to look up answers. Think about the design of the essay: begin with your most interesting point, support it with facts, and conclude.

The night before

REVIEW Ideally, you should spend the night before the exam reviewing your summaries, outlines, notes, and mnemonics. Many students find it helpful to work with other students, asking each other questions and drilling each other on the ideas and facts to be covered on the exam.

TRY NOT TO CRAM If you establish solid study skills, you won't need to cram (that is, learn new material right before the exam). Cramming generally *interferes* with what you already know. By trying to squeeze in the new material, you force out the information that you've already learned.

TRY TO RELAX You sometimes hear people say they work best under pressure, but that may not be the case for you. Pressure can cause anxiety, and anxiety can bring with it fatigue because you've stayed up the whole night worrying. By exam time, you're a wreck, washed out, bleary-eyed, unable to *recall* what you know.

Find your own way to relax if working under pressure doesn't agree with you. Meditation, a TV mystery, a long walk, a banana split—try whatever relaxes you. Don't let anxiety take you over.

The exam The following tale is a typical one: a student who did poorly on a history examination realized afterward that she had not followed the directions. She had been asked to write on *two out of three* questions. She answered *all* three. She had been asked to *compare* the French and American revolutions, but she devoted 90 percent of her answer to the French Revolution and remarked only briefly about the American Revolution. She discussed the *causes* of the American Revolution when she had been asked to describe the *effects*. Although she had studied hard, she fell apart on the exam because she did not pay attention to the instructions.

READ THE INSTRUCTIONS Essay exams usually contain several questions, with a specific amount of time suggested for each. Many exams also indicate the number of points assigned to each question:

Question 1: 30 minutes, 30 points
Question 2: 30 minutes, 30 points
Question 3: 45 minutes, 40 points

By reading these instructions, you know that you have a total of 105 minutes in which to answer all three questions. Because the last question carries more weight, more time is alloted for it. Without reading the instructions, you might take your time with the first question, thereby forcing yourself to answer the most weighted question hurriedly at the end.

READ ALL THE ESSAY QUESTIONS Take in all key words and directives (see "Tips for Exam Takers," p. 455). If you are given a choice of questions to answer (three out of four, for example), make the decision *tentatively*. You can change your mind later on if you begin to feel more confident about another question.

BRAINSTORM ON PAPER Begin thinking by *writing*. If there is one bit of advice most successful exam takers suggest, it is this: they do not begin writing a response to an exam essay until they have brainstormed—begun their thinking—*on paper*. Here is how brainstorming generally works: on a piece of scrap paper (the last page of the exam booklet, perhaps), you write down as fast as you can all the words that come to mind—words related to *one* of the exam questions. As soon as you feel certain about answering this question, begin to jot down a whole outline. (You don't need to answer the questions in the order in which they are presented.)

It's a common experience to read a question, know the answer, but for the moment feel blocked, unable to recall specific concepts and facts. Don't be alarmed. Go on to a question you *can* answer. Although at first reading you can't recall the information you need for the other questions, your careful reading of them has started a process whereby key words and phrases will come to mind *while* you are working on your first or second essay. When these thoughts occur, don't treat them as intrusions upon the question you are answering. Take a moment and *write them down* immediately on the area of the scrap paper set aside for the question or questions they relate to. *You are, in fact, working on more than one question at the same time.* The key to this process is *thinking by writing*. If you sit, staring into space, allowing thoughts to enter and exit, you will not have *concrete evidence* of your thinking. Get that thinking down on paper. Give yourself time to *frame an answer in one sentence*. The first sentence of your essay should respond directly to the question:

> Question: Discuss the causes of the fall of the Roman Empire.
> Answer: (I believe) There were four distinct causes of the fall of the Roman Empire. (What will follow will be a discussion of the four causes.)

WRITE Once you have framed a one-sentence response and have written an outline (from your associative list), you begin to write. As the clock ticks on, you keep writing, referring to your list whenever you need to. You have listed four causes in answer to the question above:

1. _____
2. _____
3. _____
4. _____

In your essay, you explain the first cause, then the second, and so on. Rather than feeling panicky as you work through the exam not knowing what to say next, you use your outline to structure your response and your time. What you are writing is a mini-essay that contains your controlling idea, paragraphs of support, and a conclusion. Your outline allows you to move easily from one part of the essay to another.

If you have time remaining, proofread your responses. Even though you have tried to plan your time carefully, you may run out of time before you've answered a question. If this happens, sketch out a response in outline form. If you write nothing, the instructor has to assume that you know nothing about the topic. But an outline of the essay, as detailed as possible, can go a long way to impress your instructor that you did know a great deal about the question but ran out of time. You may at least receive partial credit for your attempt.

On the following pages, you will find sample exam questions with analyses of their key words and directives. Study these questions. Practice answering any that you can. Set up questions of your own by using these samples as models.

TIPS FOR EXAM TAKERS

Pay attention to all *directives* (words that tell you exactly what to do) and *key words* (words that set down specifics and limits). Familiarize yourself with exam language:

DIRECTIVES:	KEY WORDS:
analyze	after
choose	before
comment	briefly
compare	fully
contrast	only
define	numbers:
describe	250 words
discuss	two out of three
evaluate	all three
explain	three out of five
give an example	
illustrate (give examples)	
list	
outline	
select	
show	
state	
trace	

Consider how these words are used in the sample questions on this page and the next. Notice that some questions are more interesting and inviting than others. Unfortunately, you frequently must answer questions that have no appeal at all.

1. In an *essay* of *250 words, discuss* the following statement made by Enid Haupt, editor of *Seventeen* magazine:

> I've never met anyone who wanted to be a teenager again.

The directive *discuss* often appears in essay exams. As it is used here, *discuss* invites you to react to the statement and to support your point of view with specifics. This question asks you to write an *essay* whose controlling idea might be:

> Enid Haupt is right when she says, "I've never met anyone who wanted to be a teenager again."

2. *Discuss* the *effects* of sleep deprivation on humans.

In this question, *discuss* means to explain what you can about the effects of sleep deprivation. Agreement or disagreement does not enter into your discussion. A controlling idea for your essay might be:

> Sleep deprivation has three major effects on humans.

3. *Compare* and *contrast* the sociological *theories* of Herbert Spencer *and* Karl Marx.

This question asks you to show likenesses (*compare*) and differences (*contrast*) between the two men's thinking on sociology. A controlling idea for your essay might be:

> Although both Herbert Spencer and Karl Marx were responding to similar problems in nineteenth-century European society, their solutions to these problems were quite different.

In one sentence, you will have mentioned similarities (they were both responding to problems) and differences (their solutions were dissimilar).

4. *Describe* living conditions in Russia *before* the Bolshevik Revolution.

Describe asks you to tell how it was. When a question is as broad as this one, it is useful to limit your response to certain groups and then contrast or classify the conditions among these groups. A controlling idea for your essay might be:

> Living conditions in Russia before the Bolshevik Revolution were vastly different for the aristocrats, the common people, and the peasants.

Note the importance of the word *before*. A quick reading may have omitted the word, resulting in a description of Russia *during* or *after* the Bolshevik Revolution.

5. *Trace* and *discuss* the most *important discoveries* of the *nineteenth* century that *influenced* Einstein's theory of relativity.

The most important directive in this complex question is *trace*, which asks you to tell about events in their chronological sequence: this happened and then this and then this. Selection of detail is critical in a question like this one; you will not throw in every detail you remember but will select the ones that were influential to Einstein. A controlling idea for your essay might be:

> Einstein's theory of relativity can be traced to three specific experiments carried out in the late nineteenth century.

20.c WRITING BUSINESS LETTERS

Occasions will arise when you need to communicate with the business world: to request information, register a complaint, place an order, apply for a job. All business letters follow the format of the following sample letter.

1   637 Front Street
Frederick, PA 16339
March 17, 1986

2   Mr. Gene Rollins
Customer Service
General Electric Company
405 Summit Street
Uniontown, PA 15345

3   Dear Mr. Rollins:

4   The General Electric refrigerator I recently bought arrived with two serious defects. First, the freezer compartment does not function properly. I have tried to adjust the freezer dial, but the thermostat is stuck on
low. As a result, nothing freezes. Second, the refrigerator buzzes all the time, creating an annoyance.

I called your office yesterday and was told by your
secretary, Mrs. Smith, that I must register a written
complaint that includes these details: The refrigerator
is Model No. CU-13546. I bought the appliance at Mern's
Department Store in Frederick on March 1, 1986. According
to the guarantee, I am entitled to free service for one
year.

I would appreciate your sending a serviceman to my address as quickly as possible. Please phone my home to set
up an appointment (412 776-3818).

5   Yours truly,

Martin Pearl

6   Martin Pearl

The addressed envelope appears below:

Martin Pearl   STAMP
637 Front Street
Frederick, PA 16339

Mr. Gene Rollins
Customer Service
General Electric Company
405 Summit Street
Uniontown, PA 15345

1. The *heading* includes the writer's full address and the date. If you are using stationery with a printed address, add the date to the right of the center of your paper.

2. The *inside address* includes the name of the person to whom you are writing, the company, and the address. If you know the person's title or position, include it also:

> James McNulty, M.D.
>
> or
>
> Helen M. Witherspoon
> Director of Admissions

3. The *greeting* includes the name and personal title of the person to whom you are writing. Note that the greeting is always followed by a colon:

> Dear Professor Langley:
>
> or
>
> Dear Mrs. Smith:

When you are not writing to a specific person, you may use one of these greetings:

> Dear Sir:
> Dear Madam:
> Gentlemen:
> Ladies:
> Dear Sir or Madam:
> To Whom It May Concern:

Modern usage is beginning to accept "To Whom It May Concern" because it eliminates the risk of offending women by addressing them as men and vice versa.

4. The *body* of the letter includes the specific information you wish to convey. Paragraphs are usually short and single-spaced, but separate the paragraphs by a double space. The opening line of a paragraph may or may not be indented, depending on your preference.

5. The *complimentary close* includes such words as:

> Yours truly,
> Sincerely,
> Sincerely yours,
> Cordially,

Note that only the first word of the complimentary close is capitalized.

6. The *signature* includes your name written in longhand (without a title). Type your name underneath:

> Gertrude Miller
>
> or
>
> Gertrude Miller, Ph.D.
> William Rogers
>
> or

William Rogers
President, Faculty Senate

A married woman uses her own first name in her correspondence, not her husband's. A woman may show the title she prefers to be addressed by if she wishes:

(Mrs.) Sally Johnson
(Miss) Sally Johnson
(Ms.) Sally Johnson

Follow these guidelines when writing business letters:

1. Get to the point right away. If you are writing to complain about a broken freezer compartment, do not waste time talking about how badly you needed a new refrigerator.

2. Use plain English. You do not have to use six-syllable words or hide behind convoluted constructions to state your point. If you write:

   On March 12, the undersigned confronted difficulties with a major appliance.

   your reader will have difficulty unraveling your words. You shouldn't, on the other hand, resort to slang or obscenities, no matter how angry you are. You can say what you must in plain English (Chapter 7).

3. Include all essential information. If the freezer doesn't work *and* the refrigerator makes a buzzing sound, state both problems. Include any other information you think pertinent: model number, date of purchase, guarantees, and the like.

4. If you have enclosed something—a check, money order, copy of a receipt, résumé, or the like—mention it. Your reader will know to look for whatever has been enclosed.

Exercise 2 Write a business letter to a utility company (telephone, gas, water) registering a complaint about an unreasonable bill—for example, long-distance phone calls you know you didn't make.

20.d WRITING A RÉSUMÉ AND A LETTER OF APPLICATION

An advertisement placed in a local paper calling for an experienced summer camp counselor elicited this response, typed on a small piece of blue paper:

```
Dear Sir:

    I saw your ad in the local paper and believe
that I am qualified for your camp job. Please
call me at 452-6178.
                              Yours truly,
```

The prospective employer did not respond.

Writing a résumé and a letter of application are two of the most important writing tasks you will undertake. Here is where your writing counts, for getting to first base with that prospective employer depends on the effectiveness of your application letter and résumé.

The résumé   A *résumé* is a summary of your life that covers four major areas: *personal information, educational background, work experience,* and *references.* It is the accepted way to present yourself on paper when you apply for a job or to graduate school. Because prospective employers and organizations rely on résumés for initial judgments, writing a strong résumé is like passing the first test on your way to landing a job.

Résumés are usually brief—one or two pages. The following sample is a typical résumé of a recent college graduate:

```
Jerome Winters
113 West End Avenue
Douglaston, New York  11356

Home telephone: (718) 123-4567

PERSONAL INFORMATION

Birth date: September 26, 1964
Marital status: single
Health: excellent

EDUCATIONAL BACKGROUND

B.A.  Queens College of the City University of New York, Flushing, New York,
      1986 (Accumulated grade point average: 3.4 on 4.0 scale)

      Major: Psychology

Special abilities: Fluent in Spanish

High-School Diploma: Bronx High School of Science, Bronx, New York, 1982
```

Begin with most recent experience

```
WORK EXPERIENCE
      1985-1986:  Tutor, Math Workshop, Queens College, Flushing, New York

      1985-1986:  Volunteer research assistant, Columbia Hospital, New York,
                  New York

      1984-1985:  Counselor, Crisis Hot Line, Queens College, Flushing,
                  New York

      1984 (Christmas):  Salesclerk, Macy's department store, New York,
                  New York

      1982, 1983: (summers):  Counselor, Camp Sunshine, Wellfleet, Massachusetts
```

Obtain permission of your referents before listing their names on your résumé.

```
REFERENCES

      Professor Joan Clark      Dr. Ross Tauber        Professor Robert Smith, Director
      Department of Psychology  Department of Psychiatry  Math Workshop
      Queens College            Columbia Hospital       Queens College
      Flushing, New York 11367  New York, New York 10025  Flushing, New York 11367
```

TAILORING YOUR RÉSUMÉ Although many people use the same résumé for each application, others tailor their résumés to fit the specific requirements of each job. You can highlight certain information on the résumé itself. For example, under "Work Experience" you can specify your responsibilities or duties:

WORK EXPERIENCE

1985–1986:   Tutor, Math Workshop, Queens College, Flushing, New York

Tutored business math students individually and in groups

1985–1986:   Volunteer research assistant, Columbia Hospital, New York, New York

Interviewed parents and children in studies on hyperactive children; gained experience in analyzing data

1982, 1983
(summers):   Counselor, Camp Sunshine, Wellfleet, Massachusetts

Counselor for emotionally disturbed children

The letter of application

Many applicants use the letter of application to highlight their résumé. Although the résumé is in itself a summary, most applicants go one step further by *summarizing* the summary in a cover letter. The cover letter should emphasize the sections of the résumé that will fit the applicant's qualifications to the job or graduate-school requirements.

The letter of application follows the business-letter format (p. 457) and should include the following:

1. The exact position you are applying for and how you heard of the opening (from a friend, a professor, a newspaper advertisement, an agency)
2. Your qualifications for the job
3. How your experience meets the requirements of the job
4. A mention that your résumé is enclosed
5. An indication of the best way to get in touch with you and an offer to meet for an interview
6. A tone that is sincere and courteous

The following two letters show how you can use your experience in different ways, depending on the position you are applying for. The candidate (whose résumé appears on p. 460) wrote two letters of application: first, for a job as a research assistant in a psychology lab; second, for admission to a graduate school of social work.

In the first letter, the applicant highlights his work as a volunteer research assistant, his advanced psychology courses, and his mathematical skills. In the second letter, he focuses on his work with people. He stresses his work as a volunteer at Crisis Hot Line and at Columbia Hospital, where he learned interviewing techniques and behaviorist approaches. His math skills, in this case, may be less important than his ability to share what he knows with others.

113 West End Avenue
Douglaston, New York   11356
June 30, 1986

Box 786
New York Times
New York, New York   10036

To Whom It May Concern:

Please consider my application for the position of
psychology assistant as advertised in the New York Times,
June 27, 1986. I believe that my background fits the
qualification you require of a college graduate with
research experience. I am enclosing my résumé.

Since June 1985, I have worked as a volunteer research
assistant with Dr. Ross Tauber of Columbia Hospital, New
York, New York. I have assisted him in interviewing parents
and children for his studies on hyperactive children. I have
gained valuable experience participating in every step of
these studies and aiding in the analysis of the data.

I used my experience at Columbia Hospital for a senior paper
on disturbed children. My courses in advanced statistics
and experimental psychology have also given me a firm
grasp of research design. In addition, I have sharpened my
mathematical skills by tutoring undergraduates in the Queens
College Math Workshop.

I would very much appreciate the opportunity for an
interview. You can write to me at my home address or call
me at (718) 123-4567 any weekday after 3:30 P.M.

Sincerely yours,

Jerome Winters

Jerome Winters

113 West End Avenue
Douglaston, New York   11356
June 30, 1986

Dr. James Simpson, Director of Admissions
Bryant School of Social Work
114 Carter Avenue
White Plains, New York   10607

Dear Dr. Simpson:

Please consider my application for graduate study in social work at the Bryant School of Social Work. I understand that a social-work student must display an interest in working with people and have some experience in the field. I believe my qualifications meet both of these requirements.

My experience as a volunteer in two social agencies has given me valuable experience working with both children and adults. As a counselor at Crisis Hot Line, a twenty-four-hour telephone help center, I learned to respond quickly and specifically to people in need. During the past year, I worked as a volunteer research assistant with Dr. Ross Tauber at Columbia Hospital, where I learned interviewing techniques and behaviorist approaches to use with hyperactive children.

In addition, for two summers I worked as a group counselor at a camp for handicapped children. My experience tutoring undergraduates in the Math Workshop at Queens College allowed me to understand a one-to-one teaching situation.

The satisfaction I have received from all these experiences has proved to me that I am interested in working with and helping other people.

As you requested, I have enclosed my résumé and a completed application form. I have arranged for a transcript of my grades to be sent to your office. I would very much appreciate the opportunity for an interview. You can write to me at my home address or call me at (718) 123-4567 any weekday after 3:30.

Yours truly,

Jerome Winters

Jerome Winters

TIPS FOR JOB HUNTERS

Think about what prospective employers (or admissions officers) look for when they read résumés and letters of application. First, they look for credentials: college degree, related experience, and the like. Second, they examine the information you have included and the way you have presented it. Third, they look for *what is missing.*

If there are gaps in your résumé, prospective employers naturally wonder why. Unless they are highly impressed by what you have included, you may not have the chance to explain why you omitted items. For people who have been working for many years, an unexplained gap of a year or more may arouse suspicion: Were you fired from a job? Are you lazy? It is a good idea to account for all your time. Similarly, don't omit needed personal information. Some people, for example, object on principle to stating their birth date. Keep in mind that when you omit information that employers require, you risk not getting fair consideration.

As you write the letter of application, remember that your words reflect you. A letter discourteously written or a letter filled with typographical errors probably won't get you very far.

A successful résumé and letter of application allow you to move to the next step in the job-seeking process—the interview. It may take a little time to write a good résumé and letter of application, but it's a good investment.

Exercise 3 Write a résumé for yourself that includes four parts: personal history, educational background, work experience, and references. Write two letters of application that use the information on the résumé in different ways.

Index

About the Authors

Sandra Schor is assistant professor of English at Queens College (City University of New York), where she teaches writing and has served as director of the writing program. She is the co-author, with Frederick Crews, of *The Borzoi Handbook for Writers* (1985); her essays and reviews on the theory of composition and the teaching of writing appear in many collections and journals. She has been awarded a Mellon Fellowship in composition studies and a grant from the Fund for the Improvement of Postsecondary Education. In recognition of her contributions as a teacher of writing, the City University of New York named her a Master Teacher in the retraining of faculty to teach writing. A poet and fiction writer, Professor Schor regularly publishes poems and short stories in *Centennial Review, Prairie Schooner, Redbook, Commonweal, Ploughshares,* and other national publications.

Judith Summerfield (formerly Fishman) has taught composition and literature since 1963; at Queens College since 1972, she has served as director of the Writing Skills Workshop, co-director of the Queens English Project (a federally funded articulation project), and associate director of the composition program. A former member of the CCC Executive Committee, she has conducted workshops for teachers throughout the country. Co-author, with Sandra Schor, of *The Random House Guide to Writing* and editor of *Responding to Prose: A Reader for Writers* (Macmillan), she is now at work on an interdisciplinary study of narrative as it informs autobiography, fiction, and nonfiction prose. Recent articles have appeared in *WPA, Linguistics and Stylistics, The Journal Book,* (ed. Toby Fulwiler), and the Proceedings of the 1984 New Hampshire Conference on Reading and Writing, where she delivered a keynote address, ''Framing Narratives.''

REVISING THE WHOLE ESSAY
Giving and Getting Reactions

1. What's in this piece of writing? Which parts absolutely have to remain? Why?

2. Do the essential parts get enough attention?

3. Can any part be eliminated? Why?

4. Is there anything you want to hear more about? Why?

5. What do you remember as being outstanding? Why is it outstanding?

6. Is the outstanding feature important to the whole piece of writing? In what way?

7. Can the best part go last?

8. Does any part jar you? Does the paper change course?

9. Do you feel any part can be shortened? Which part, and why?

10. Without looking back at the piece of writing, can you state its controlling idea?

11. What do you remember as the key points in your controlling idea?

12. Do your paragraphs support these points?

13. Do any paragraphs seem unclear to you? Which ones?

14. Can you make your examples more specific?

15. Is the beginning effective? Does it attract you to read what follows?

16. Does the essay satisfy you? Does the ending, in particular, satisfy you? Does it relate sensibly to the beginning?